HELPING STUDENTS WITH READING PROBLEMS

HELPING STUDENTS WITH READING PROBLEMS

ROBERT T. RUDE
Rhode Island College

WILLIAM J. OEHLKERS
Rhode Island College

PRENTICE-HALL, INC.   *Englewood Cliffs, N.J. 07632*

Library of Congress Cataloging in Publication Data

RUDE, ROBERT T.,   (date)
     Helping students with reading problems.

     Bibliography: p.
     Includes index.
     1. Reading—Remedial teaching.   I. Oehlkers, William J.
II. Title.
LB1050.5.R825   1984   428.4′2   83-43132
ISBN 0-13-387498-2

Editorial/production supervision: Marion Osterberg
Cover design: Wanda Lubelska
Photos: Peter P. Tobia
Manufacturing buyer: Ron Chapman

*LB
1050.5
.R825
1984
June/1994*

Printed in the United States of America

10   9   8   7   6   5   4   3   2   1

ISBN 0-13-387498-2

Prentice-Hall International, Inc., *London*
Prentice-Hall of Australia Pty. Limited, *Sydney*
Editora Prentice-Hall do Brasil, Ltda., *Rio de Janeiro*
Prentice-Hall Canada Inc., *Toronto*
Prentice-Hall of India Private Limited, *New Delhi*
Prentice-Hall of Japan, Inc., *Tokyo*
Prentice-Hall of Southeast Asia Pte. Ltd., *Singapore*
Whitehall Books Limited, *Wellington, New Zealand*

To our parents . . .

Arthur and Doris Rude
John and Elsie Oehlkers

CONTENTS

PREFACE

At the turn of the twentieth century, Edmund Burke Huey (1908) wrote ". . . reading is an old curiousity shop of absurd practices."* Almost one hundred years later, we are struck by the fact that much of what occurs in classrooms continues to be "absurd practices." Perhaps nowhere is this more evident than when teachers confront disabled readers. Maybe it is frustration, naiveté, or lack of adequate knowledge that accounts for the strange methodological practices we witness in some schools today. Whatever the reasons, however, all students, and especially those with reading problems, deserve the best instruction teachers can give.

When working with teachers and disabled readers, one quickly realizes that many of the problem readers in our schools need not exist. They are victims of a system that in many cases has failed them. This is not to say that our educational system is responsible for all of today's reading problems. Indeed, parents and society as a whole must share the blame. But the fact remains that we, as educators, could do more to reduce the incidence of reading failure in the nation.

We do not believe that teachers willfully provide inappropriate instruction. To the contrary, we believe that given a sufficient understanding of the reading process and a handful of tests and teaching suggestions, teachers are

*Edmund Burke Huey, *The Psychology and Pedagogy of Reading* (Boston: The MIT Press, 1968), p. 9. (First published in 1908 by the Macmillan Company.)

capable of teaching well. Yet as we reviewed many of the popular texts covering diagnosis and remediation, we were overwhelmed by the fact that many reading difficulties were depicted as having esoteric, complex causes. Randomly select any of the popular books in this area and you are immediately confronted with terms such as *learning modality, perceptual deficits, dyslexia, alexia, cerebral dominance, cross-modal transfer, ego functioning,* and many others. Is it any wonder that teachers are perplexed?

Helping Students with Reading Problems, as we hope its title connotes, is a straightforward, matter-of-fact presentation of what teachers need to know about reading and how they can help disabled learners become better readers. The text is an outgrowth of our combined forty years of working with teachers, administrators, and most important, problem readers. Moreover, it reflects our belief that much of what is presented in methodology texts is either not helpful or not important. We have attempted to lace effective teaching practices with an explicit belief about the reading process. In our estimation, this is where many texts, and hence, instruction fall short; they are in essence, atheoretical, either by design or by omission. Without a theory of instruction, teaching may become erratic. Throughout each chapter, we have tried to offer suggestions in line with the theory presented in Chapter 3.

In order to provide the comprehensive coverage necessary to understand the field of reading disabilities, we have chosen to present our ideas in twelve distinct chapters. Each chapter, although unique in itself, is linked by the theory of reading, which we offer early in the text.

Chapter 1, "Introduction," is a short description of eight themes that we believe are the hallmarks of exemplary remedial reading programs.

Chapter 2, "Students with Reading Problems," describes how to identify these students. The use of reading expectancy formulas is discussed and their limitations noted. We also offer some personal suggestions for determining who should receive special help.

"Understanding the Reading Process," Chapter 3, is simultaneously the most theoretical and practical chapter in the text, because in order to be a good teacher, you must have a theory of reading. As a sage once said, "There is nothing so practical as good theory." Reading instruction is based on teachers making decisions. We offer numerous explanations on how decisions can be made and then suggest what we feel is the most logical. The current interest in reading theory is also reviewed. Finally, we present three popular ways of looking at reading and offer what we feel is the most usable model. Chapter 3 forms the backbone for much of what is discussed in later chapters.

To better understand reading disabilities, it is important to explore the correlates that may be associated with a student's difficulty. Chapter 4, "Correlates of Reading Disability," does just that. An in-depth examination of physical, psychological, sociological, and educational factors and their influence on reading ability is provided. An extensive bibliography supports the positions in the chapter.

Chapter 5, "Diagnosis and Word Identification," gets to the heart of most reading problems, for unless students can "unlock" unknown words, comprehension cannot occur. In this chapter we explain how assumptions that teach-

Meet the authors, Bob Rude and Bill Oehlkers.

ers hold about reading can influence the diagnostic process. Furthermore, a rationale for assessing word identification is offered.

"Teaching Word Identification," Chapter 6, complements the preceding chapter, for here the intricacies of showing students how to unlock unfamiliar words are presented. Unlike some texts which list seemingly endless exercises to teach every conceivable skill, this chapter presents four levels of word identification skills: sight vocabulary and context clues, consonants, vowels, and multisyllabic words. Within each level, an array of tried-and-tested techniques for developing each skill is developed. Rather than simply list "cookbook ideas," the chapter illustrates how these skills must be fused when the student is reading connected text, for it is only then that reading truly takes place.

In Chapter 7, "Diagnosing Comprehension," a wide variety of techniques that can be used to assess comprehension ability is presented. At one end of the spectrum, formal instruments might be used. At the other end, informal observation should also play an important role. Both positions are covered here.

The functions of norm-referenced and criterion-referenced tests are presented to demonstrate the two broad divisions of thought in comprehension assessment.

Nowhere is the integration of reading theory and pedagogy more important than in the teaching of reading comprehension. Accordingly, the reader will find a close relationship between Chapter 3 and Chapter 8, "Teaching Comprehension." Four major concerns are addressed in this chapter: (1) whether students have sufficient word identification skills for comprehension to occur, (2) the importance of skill development such as predicting and main idea, (3) how deficiencies in background knowledge limit comprehension, and (4) the necessity for creating motivation. Don't look for a long list of suggested materials to help you teach comprehension; you won't find one. What you will find, however, is an explanation of how reading comprehension can be taught, keeping in mind the reader, the material, and the skill of the teacher.

An important facet of teaching that is sometimes overlooked is motivating students to read independently. Instruction that provides only for cognitive development will fall short—especially with disabled readers. So teachers won't overlook this aspect of teaching, we explain why students sometimes dislike reading and then show what to do about it. Activities to excite students about text and "nonbook" reading materials are all presented in Chapter 9, "Motivating Students to Read."

One of the reading teacher's major jobs is to write reports. Chapter 10, "Individualized Educational Plans and Case Studies," explains, step-by-step, how to do this. Practical suggestions are offered on how to improve report writing, and actual examples of reports are offered for examination. Once teachers have read this chapter and spent some time practicing their skills, report writing should no longer be so difficult.

In "Evaluation of Reading Tests and Programs," Chapter 11, we have tried to put testing and evaluation in its proper perspective. First, we describe how evaluation is an integral part of our educational system, whether we are discussing the "state of the nation" or an individual teacher's classroom. Next, we acquaint the reader with some of the important terms used to describe tests. Then we discuss the overriding differences and uses of norm-referenced and criterion-referenced reading tests. Included in this chapter is a description of how to go about selecting a reading test (complete with a review form). Finally, an explanation of how summative and formative evaluation can be used by teachers and administrators is offered.

The final chapter, "Getting It All Together," is just that: a discussion about organizing programs and the roles and responsibilities of reading teachers. Included are the specialist's role in working with students, teachers, school administrators, parents, and other professionals. We also describe how to select and schedule students in the program. Last, guidelines for organizing reading centers are explained. After finishing this last chapter, you should be ready to assume the duties of a reading teacher.

ACKNOWLEDGMENTS

This book, although solely our responsibility, was influenced by the thoughts and writing of our mentors. In particular, we are deeply grateful to Russell G. Stauffer and Wayne Otto. Both these scholars raised our level of understanding beyond conventional wisdom. Whatever strengths this book may possess is due in part to their scholarship and practical insights.

Thanks are also due to the many students and friends, particularly Carol Hauser, who carefully read and reacted to an earlier draft; to our editor Susan B. Katz, who patiently guided the manuscript through to production; and to our typists, Ann Szlashta and Camille Allen.

We also need to express our appreciation to our wives, Pat and Lois, for their encouragement and willingness to let us retreat for long periods of time to our writing. Our thanks go out to our children, Tracy, Laura, Ruth, Peter, and Beth, who over the years have frequently been the first to experience our ideas.

Finally, for their helpful suggestions and enduring patience, we would like to thank our reviewers: Roger De Santi, University of New Orleans; Patricia H. Duncan, Virginia Commonwealth University; Lawrence Erickson, West Virginia University; Ruth Garner, University of Maryland; Carol J. Hopkins, Purdue University; Lana Smith, Memphis State University; and Dixie Lee Spiegel, University of North Carolina at Chapel Hill. Their sharp pencils and eagle eyes have helped us as we have put our thoughts to paper. Thank you.

HELPING STUDENTS WITH READING PROBLEMS

1

INTRODUCTION

Becoming a first-rate reading teacher requires hard work and perseverance. There are several directions, which we have called *themes,* toward which teachers should focus their effort. As you read this book, eight important themes will continually reappear:

Teachers hold specific beliefs about the reading process. Anyone who has spent time with educators, either in a school or social setting, quickly realizes that most teachers love to "talk shop." After listening to their discussions, even a non-educator can generalize about the beliefs some of them hold about students. This same phenomenon occurs with reading teachers but in a slightly different context. Both the words and actions of reading teachers reveal explicit and implicit beliefs about the reading process. The materials, the grouping plan, the skills covered, and the interactions with students all reveal the teachers' assumptions about the reading process. Although there will always be professional disagreement, the ideas we espouse in this text clearly reveal our feelings about reading. Naturally, we feel these beliefs are appropriate for all reading teachers to adopt since they are based on what researchers tell us about the reading act. As you read these chapters, see if you agree or disagree with our position. If you disagree, try to understand why you feel as you do. Or see if we support our stands with adequate documentation. By thinking about reading, you will probably become a better teacher of reading.

Understanding the reading process is more important than accumulating instructional materials. Most teachers, from preschool instructor to advanced graduate school professor, are envious of peers who have more teaching materials than they. Perhaps this is only natural since instructional aids can help us be more effective teachers. But unless we understand what we are doing, materials are of limited use. What good is a filmstrip on decoding short vowels if the dialect of your pupils is vastly different from that of the film? The same is true of workbooks, worksheets, games, audiotapes, and any of the other supplementary materials publishers contend we need. Obviously, we need some materials, but they should be selected with our teaching objectives firmly in mind. And unless we have objectives, our materials will simply be a potpourri of odds and ends. Before we use instructional materials, we must know what we are doing.

Effective teachers are made, not born. Throughout this book we discuss the importance of the reading teacher. Understanding the reading process, knowing how to diagnose a student's reading levels, pacing instruction, understanding principles of learning, using appropriate teaching behaviors and materials, writing coherent reports, selecting appropriate tests, and organizing an instructional program are not inborn gifts. To be an exemplary reading teacher requires considerable thought and experience. Although some desirable traits, such as patience and compassion, may be learned outside of an educational setting, they alone will not make an effective teacher. A certain amount of native talent can help anyone in one's chosen profession, but most individuals become successful primarily because they have a drive to be the best in their field. It's no different for reading teachers.

Experience is necessary to become a great teacher. Because students with reading problems possess such unique needs, formal education can take teachers only so far. In the previous paragraph we identified some abilities that good reading teachers have in common. But education being what it is, there are times when even the most sage advice offered in a text will be inappropriate for a teacher's particular situation. Throughout this book we have tried to be as specific as possible without being prescriptive. Like a physician trying to make a diagnosis over the telephone, we may have unintentionally overlooked some data. So although we may appear to offer explicit advice for what to do in a specific situation, keep in mind that your experience, coupled with our message, may be a better guide than our words alone. So use your experience to refine the thoughts you encounter as you read each chapter. In this way, your learning should be more meaningful, and you will be well on your way to becoming a great teacher.

Testing should supplement teachers' judgment. As educators, we occasionally need to step back in order to look more objectively at what we are doing. In no place is this more true than in our testing practices. In the last two or three decades, teachers, it seems, have become less confident in their judgment about students' reading achievement. The most questionable practice we have witnessed by teachers is putting total faith in test scores and doubting their own professional judgment. What troubles us most is that many of the instruments teachers use are of questionable quality. To put things in proper perspective, we have tried to point out in most chapters that testing should be used to verify teachers' judgments and not to supplant the role of professional decision making. Our intention is to show that test scores are only one of many types of data that should be considered when rendering judgments about students' reading competence. Test scores should seldom be allotted more prestige than the judgment of a professional teacher.

Students' attitudes are as important as instruction. How often do teachers plan for the cognitive aspects of lessons but fail to consider how students feel about reading? Instruction always takes place in an affective context. As you read through this text we hope you will consider the feelings of students as they are being tested and instructed. The old adage about leading a horse to water but not being able to make him drink has special meaning for disabled readers since many of them have built up negative attitudes about reading tasks. A teacher's job is to make the student "thirsty" for reading. Although we devote an entire chapter to affective concerns, much of the text tries to illustrate how important it is to enlist the cooperation of disabled readers before trying to teach them to read.

Students must be actively involved in their reading if learning is to take place. We believe there are two basic types of disabled readers: those who know how to read but dislike reading and those who are unable to read and hence are discouraged about learning. The first type frequently views reading as a passive experience requiring little if any personal involvement; the second type usually ends up in special reading programs. Teachers need special techniques and strategies to assist both types of individuals to become better readers. As these chapters unfold, we hope you will begin to see how the home and school can play vital roles in promoting reading as an active, meaningful undertaking requiring a high degree of personal involvement.

Students learn to read by reading. Throughout these pages we will urge you to teach reading, whenever possible, through the use of connected text. Reading is most meaningful when a message is to be had, and seldom are messages

The only way to become a good reader is through practice.   (Peter P. Tobia)

contained in skill worksheets or drill exercises. But we have found that teachers are almost apologetic for permitting silent reading of library books in their classrooms. If disabled readers are to become fluent and confident readers, they must have ample opportunities to read interesting, connected text. Reading takes practice. We believe that the suggestions we offer show how reading should be taught. It is up to teachers, however, to translate these ideas into practice.

2

STUDENTS WITH READING PROBLEMS

Upon completion of this chapter, you should be able to

1. Describe what is meant by the term *remedial learner*.
2. Identify those students who could most benefit from special instruction in reading.
3. Use one or more reading expectancy formulas to determine a student's reading expectancy.
4. Explain the limitations of expectancy formulas in identifying problem readers.
5. Discuss additional techniques that can be used to determine reading expectancy.

IDENTIFICATION OF PROBLEM READERS

Three teachers were recently overheard in a teacher's lounge discussing a student whom all had known. "I really think Bobby has a serious reading problem," one of the teachers remarked. "Yes, his older brother had dyslexia, you know!" the second one chimed in. "Why is it that so many students today have learning disabilities?" the third inquired.

This situation and similar ones are replayed thousands of times daily in our nation's schools. What initially began as a seemingly innocent statement (". . . Bobby has a serious reading problem.") was quickly transformed into a session where labels were attached to an individual without adequate documentation to support the allegation. Such labeling frequently promotes misunderstanding of a student's reading problem.

There are a number of reasons why these labels are potentially damaging. First, labels often connote a degree of finality. A physician who informs you that you will be an "invalid" because your ankle is broken, for example, implies that you will be partially immobilized for several weeks. An auto mechanic who says your car is a "lemon" and shows you a recall notice implies that you will be without transportation for a period of time. In each case, a label connotes a negative feeling.

Allington (1975) has provided a number of other good reasons for not labeling students: (1) labeling is professionally unsound; (2) labels fail to communicate useful information; (3) etiologies (origins) of reading problems are sometimes unknown; (4) the etiology may not help overcome the problem; (5) the labels may be outside our area of expertise, and perhaps most important, (6) the use of labels puts the onus of responsibility for the problem on the child, when in fact others may be to blame for the disability.

Although it may be impossible to eliminate totally the use of labels, we caution teachers to be wary of their potential danger. Since we know so little about esoteric learning problems, confusion and misunderstanding are apt to occur if teachers persist in labeling students who have difficulty in learning to read. Terms such as *dyslexia* and *learning disabled* frequently connote a degree of understanding that presently doesn't exist. For this reason, we generally prefer not to use them.

Many terms have been used to identify students who could benefit from special reading instruction. And since these terms repeatedly appear in the literature on reading disabilities and are used to differentiate among students with reading problems, it is important to define them. But before we do, recognize that more important than the terms used to identify these students are the procedures used to determine who receives special help.

Basically, two techniques have been used to identify problem readers: predictive studies and ongoing diagnosis. To provide the reader with a better perspective, we need to examine each in more detail.

Predictive Studies

Predictive studies are those investigations that attempt to identify problem readers before their disability actually occurs. Such studies usually require a variety of tests to be administered to young children—usually prereaders—and

6

another battery of tests to be administered to these same students at a later time. By correlating the scores on the predictor variables (the pretests) with scores received on the dependent variable (the posttest), it is sometimes possible to identify those pretests that best predict which students will have difficulty in reading as they progress through the elementary grades.

Satz and Friel (1974) tried to identify the precursors of reading disability several years before the disorders were clinically diagnosed in their sample of students. They considered whether any of twenty-two variables could be reliable predictors of later reading failure. Some of the more common variables examined were (1) age, (2) handedness, (3) ability to tap out codes with fingers, (4) intelligence, (5) ability to identify figures in an embedded figures test, (6) verbal fluency, (7) ability to recite the alphabet, (8) auditory discrimination, (9) listening ability, (10) behavior, and (11) parents' socioeconomic status. They found that a finger localization test and a recognition-discrimination test were the most predictive measures. The exact nature of these two tests were not described, however. Nevertheless, the investigators concluded that ". . . the reading achievement levels of children at the end of grade 1 can be validly predicted . . .a year and a half earlier" (p. 442).

A slightly different strategy to predict reading failure was used by Feshbach and his associates (1974). They designed a forty-one item teacher-rating scale to assess kindergarten students' learning potential. Five general categories of behavior were assessed:

1. Impulse control.
2. Verbal ability and language development.
3. Perceptual discrimination.
4. Recall of necessary classroom information.
5. Perceptual-motor skills.

Kindergarten teachers were asked to rate students on these five variables to determine if a significant relationship existed between them and later reading success. The investigators concluded that ". . . first grade is too early a period in which to define reading failure in a clinical sense . . ." (p. 643).

Thus, depending on the study, predictor variables may or may not prove to be an effective way of identifying problem readers, and therefore, predicting reading failure is a risky business. At the present, relatively little is being done to identify reliable predictors of reading ability, although perhaps this will be an important movement in the next decade.

From our vantage point, we believe predictive studies serve a valuable purpose. Primarily, they allow teachers to identify subjects who may be "at risk" when it comes to reading failure. At the present time, however, predicting reading failure is uncertain.

Ongoing Diagnosis

If it is difficult to predict who will have trouble learning to read, what other means are available to identify students with reading problems? And perhaps equally important, who will benefit most from additional reading instruction? These two questions continually face educators who are attempting to organize programs for disabled readers.

The most common way to find students who need additional help is to administer norm-referenced reading tests. Such tests compare the relative performance of individuals with others in their grade level across the nation. Students can then be ranked on their overall reading performance. Those who score poorly on the test are often considered likely candidates for remedial instruction. (In fact, some federal programs require that only students who rank in the lower percentiles of their class can receive special reading instruction.) These reading test scores are generally supplemented by teachers' recommendations, and herein lies the dilemma. Frequently teachers will recommend students for instruction because the students' observed reading performance is low even though they scored in the high ranges on the test. Or a student who may have done poorly on the test may in the teacher's opinion be a much better reader than the test indicated. To overcome the problem of relying on one test score to determine eligibility for instruction, many reading teachers rely on the ongoing collection of test data and subjective judgment to help them identify the students most in need. Frequently, it helps to think of students as slow learners, developmental learners, corrective learners, or remedial learners. (We don't consider these to be labels but merely broad, flexible categories that can help us think about students who may be eligible for and benefit from supplementary instruction.) To understand each of these categories better we need to examine them more closely.

SLOW LEARNERS   Slow learners are students who are considered to be working up to their ability, but because of limited intellectual capabilities, they seldom, if ever, are able to read at grade level. In fact, as they continue their schooling, they fall further and further behind their more capable peers. It is

Teaching itself provides valuable insights into students' ability to learn.   (Peter P. Tobia)

interesting to note that today, because of federal legislation, more and more slow learners are being mainstreamed into regular school classrooms. As a result, some classroom teachers feel that these students are likely candidates for additional reading help. Generally, however, slow learners should not be included in special supplementary reading programs, because they are already working up to their potential under the guidance of the regular classroom teacher. These students need adapted rather than supplemental instruction.

DEVELOPMENTAL LEARNERS   Developmental learners are those individuals who comprise the bulk of classroom readers. Specifically, they are students who are able to learn to read without any special adjustments in the classroom reading program. Perhaps 75 percent of the students in an "average" classroom could be considered developmental learners. They suffer from no serious inhibiting factors and, hence, make good progress in most basal reader programs.

CORRECTIVE LEARNERS   Occasionally students of average or above-average intellectual ability develop "gaps" in their reading skills. These may be caused by missed instruction due to extended school absences or by failure to learn a skill in the allotted time. Even though these pupils may have reading difficulties, their problems are usually not so severe that extensive out-of-classroom instruction is required. Their weaknesses are of a limited nature, and large skill deficiencies are usually not evident. Competent teachers who are capable of providing focused instruction are usually able to help these students in the classroom.

REMEDIAL LEARNERS   Students with severe reading difficulties and yet of average or above-average intelligence are typically referred to as remedial learners. These individuals suffer from such a lack of decoding and/or comprehension skills that they are unable to read almost anything satisfactorily. In a real sense, they are truly "reading disabled."

Since remedial learners have such limited reading ability it is difficult for classroom teachers to find sufficient time to work with them. For this reason, these students are usually referred to a teacher with specialized training in reading, who instructs these students either in the classroom or in a special room.

Regardless of where instruction occurs, the ultimate goal of the reading teacher is to provide appropriate instruction so that these students may eventually be dropped from the specialist's case load and picked up once again by the classroom teacher. Hence, reading teachers often work with remedial learners only until they are able to perform satisfactorily in the regular classroom program.

ADDITIONAL INSIGHTS   Frequently it is difficult to select accurately those students who could most benefit from additional help in reading. Information from the student's parents, other classroom teachers, the school principal, or other specialists in the school may help teachers decide who should be included in their case load.

Frequently, however, teachers will be asked to put in writing their policy for selecting students who have reading problems. Funding agencies such as the state and federal governments usually require such statements. Sometimes the selection criteria are mandated by the funding agency. In other instances teachers are free to establish their own selection procedures. Herein lies a dilemma facing many reading teachers.

Some state and federal agencies require that only students who score below a specified percentile score on a specific reading test can be included in a funded program. Typically, a statement such as "Students who score below the twenty-fifth percentile on the XYZ test shall be considered for inclusion in the Chapter I reading program." Students of limited intellectual ability—those earlier identified as slow learners—often fall into this category. This kind of selection process, then, may result in filling remedial programs with students who are working up to their potential and who will not benefit to any degree from additional instruction.

When reading teachers are given more flexibility in establishing entrance criteria for the remedial program, they may decide to exclude some students who have limited intellectual ability in favor of those with a greater potential for improvement. A poor reader with an intelligence test score falling within the "above-average" range, for example, stands a greater chance of improving than does someone with a "below-average" score, all other things considered equal. The selection of students on the basis of potential has sometimes been referred to as the "most to benefit" plan.

In reality, reading teachers will probably use a combination of selection criteria. Obviously, much will depend on the specific requirements established by the district or government agency.

In an effort to select students who will most profit from remedial instruction, educators have turned to reading expectancy formulas, two of which are discussed in the next section.

POPULAR READING EXPECTANCY FORMULAS

Reading expectancy formulas attempt to quantify objectively the degree to which a reading problem exists. Most formulas require an intelligence test, thereby providing some measure of intellectual capability. These formulas, when used in conjunction with a student's mental age score, help determine whether the student is a slow learner or someone with the capacity for improved performance. To better understand how these formulas work, two different methods of computing reading expectancy will be presented, followed by some safeguards that need to be exercised.

The Bond–Tinker Formula

Perhaps the most widely used reading expectancy formula is that developed by Guy Bond and Miles Tinker (1979). Bond and Tinker believed that a student's reading expectancy could be determined by dividing the intelligence quotient (IQ) by 100, multiplying this figure by the completed number of years in school (not counting kindergarten or grades repeated), and then adding 1.0 (the potential reading ability upon entering first grade). The written formula appears like this:

$$\text{reading expectancy} = \frac{IQ}{100} \times \text{years in school} + 1.0$$

For example, let's examine a third-grader with an IQ of 120. By using the formula, we could quickly determine this student to have a reading grade level expectancy of 4.6. Here's how we computed the score:

1. Divide the IQ by 100 (120/100 = 1.2).
2. Multiply the answer by the number of years in school—omit kindergarten (1.2 × 3 = 3.6).
3. Add 1.0 to the answer to determine expectancy (3.6 + 1.0 = 4.6).

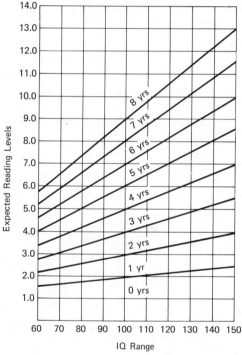

Figure 2-1 Bond–Tinker Formula of Expected Reading Levels [(IQ × years in school) + 1.0] From "Determining, Using Expectancy Formulas" by Leo V. Rodenborn, *The Reading Teacher*, December 1974, p. 290. Reproduced with permission of the author and the International Reading Association.

Directions: Find 100 IQ vertical line. Move pencil up to approximate number of years in school, estimate to nearest tenth. Do not count preschool, kindergarten, or years repeated. (At the beginning of second grade a child has been in school one full year.) Move pencil left or right along an imaginary line between the years in school bars. This point estimates expectancy which can be read off at the left or right.

If this student were reading at a second-grade level, we would infer that there was a 2.6 year discrepancy between his actual reading level and his expectancy level.

Suppose, however, we knew a third-grader who had the same reading level but had an IQ of 80. Using the formula once again we could determine this individual's reading expectancy:

1. Divide the IQ by 100 (80/100 = .8).
2. Multiply the answer by the number of years in school—don't forget to omit kindergarten (.8 × 3 = 2.4).
3. Add 1.0 to the answer to determine expectancy (2.4 + 1.0 = 3.4).

Thus, at the conclusion of third grade we would expect the second student to be reading at the 3.4 reading grade level. Since the child has a slightly below-average intelligence quotient, he would not be expected to read up to grade level, according to Bond and Tinker.

Rodenborn (1974) has devised the chart in Figure 2-1 to give a gross approximation of reading expectancy when using the Bond–Tinker formula. Try using this chart with the two examples just discussed.

The Mental Age Formula

Perhaps the easiest to use of all the popular reading expectancy formulas is the mental age formula. Expectancy is computed simply by subtracting 5.0, the number of years spent learning before attending school, from the mental age. The most common expression of the formula is

reading expectancy = mental age − 5.0

Using the mental age formula, we can figure that a twelve-year-old with a mental age of 16.11 would have an expectancy level of 11.11. The following two steps illustrate how we computed the expectancy score:

1. Reading expectancy = 16.11 − 5.0.
2. Reading expectancy = 11.11 (reading grade level).

An eight-year-old third-grader who had an intelligence quotient of 80 and a mental age of 5.5 would have an expectancy level score of .5, or would be expected to be reading slightly below first-grade level:

1. Reading expectancy = 5.5 − 5.0.
2. Reading expectancy = .5.

The mental age formula can also be expressed in graphic form:

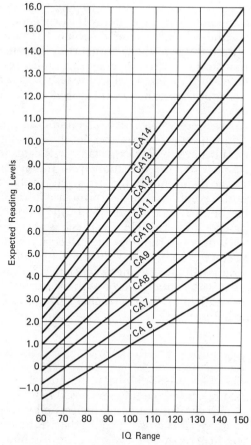

IQ Range

Directions: Find 100 IQ vertical line. Move pencil up to approximate Chronological Age (CA), estimate to nearest month. Move pencil left or right on an imaginary line between the CA bars to correct IQ. This point estimates expectancy which can be read off at the left or right.

Figure 2-2 Mental Age Formula of Expected Reading Levels (MA-5.0)   From "Determining, Using Expectancy Formulas" by Leo V. Rodenborn, *The Reading Teacher*, December 1974, p. 289. Reprinted with permission of the author and the International Reading Association.

We should point out that there are a number of other reading expectancy formulas, but the two we have discussed are the most popular. Regardless of which formula is used, however, teachers should be aware of some safeguards that need to be exercised when trying to determine reading expectancy.

LIMITATIONS OF EXPECTANCY FORMULAS

First, reading expectancy scores are only *estimates* of an individual's potential. Most expectancy formulas require the prior computation of a student's intellectual capability. When you consider that many of the tests that attempt to measure intelligence have questionable validity it becomes evident why expectancy scores are open to question. Moreover, the inherent error in any test score means that there may be a substantial range within which the true score may be found. This variance may account for a significant range in the eventual reading expectancy score. Finally, there is the fact that students from diverse cultural backgrounds may be intelligent but simply fail to score well on intelligence tests because their life experiences are so different from those abilities measured by the instruments.

Second, a student's expectancy score may vary depending on the intelligence test score and the reading expectancy formula chosen. Although students of normal intelligence generally have similar expectancy estimates regardless of which formula is used, the greater the deviation from the average IQ (between 90 and 110) the greater the difference in the various formulas' expectancies. Thus, by simply using a different expectancy formula you can alter a student's expectancy score. According to Rodenborn (1979), the Bond-Tinker Formula identifies a higher proportion of lower IQ individuals as needing reading assistance. The Mental Age Formula has the opposite effect; more high IQ subjects will appear to need assistance.

Since there is apt to be a range of any student's expectancy, our advice is to use reading expectancy formulas with caution. Perhaps their greatest benefit can be derived if they are used to confirm or reject a teacher's hypotheses about who may profit most from remedial instruction.

OTHER TECHNIQUES
FOR ASSESSING READING EXPECTANCY

In addition to expectancy formulas, there are additional techniques that teachers might want to use when selecting subjects for reading services. The first is to use the students' listening level as an indicator of potential; the second is to rely on day-to-day observations of students' performance. Yet another technique is to observe students' ability to respond correctly to questions after listening to the reading of a passage.

The listening test is based on the idea that students may be able to understand better when listening to a passage being read to them than when having to decode and comprehend simultaneously. Listening frees students of the burden of decoding, and therefore they may devote 100 percent of their attention to comprehension. The ability to understand reading materials is often considered to be a sign of a student's potential level, also referred to as the auding level. For instructional purposes, consider this level reached when approximately 75 percent of the material can be comprehended through listening. (The specifics of determining this level when using an informal reading inventory are discussed in detail in chapters covering the diagnoses of word identification and comprehension.)

SOME PERSONAL RECOMMENDATIONS

Now that we have presented some of the popular procedures that have been used to select candidates for remedial instruction, we feel obligated to present our own views (and biases). Like so many other things in life, it would be great if we could suggest a simple, fail-safe procedure. Unfortunately, reading problems are usually complex and, hence, defy simple solutions. Regardless of plans, there will usually be exceptions to consider. If teachers keep this in mind, they can develop selection procedures that are systematic, yet flexible. These steps should be considered as *one way* to determine who might profit from help.

    1. First, solicit recommendations from classroom teachers. It is important, however, to have these recommendations backed up by some form of empirical data. Standardized test scores, informal reading inventory scores, or performance on criterion-referenced (skill) tests will require teachers to support their recommendations with objective information. Reading specialists want to avoid having classroom teachers recommend only students who are behavioral problems or slow learners. This is not to say that some legitimate remedial learners will not have behavioral difficulties. But conversely, many students with behavioral problems do not have reading problems. Asking teachers to give objective evidence about reading achievement will help screen out students who are not legitimate candidates for remedial reading. You should also make sure not to accept only slow learners. Slow learners might be performing to the best of their ability. They do not need additional instruction; they simply need the pace of instruction slowed down. They are not remedial cases in the true sense of the word, and for this reason they should receive adjusted instruction from their classroom teacher.

    2. Attempt to gather evidence regarding students' intellectual capabilities. Occasionally, recommended students have taken intelligence tests before being recommended. If no test has been given you can usually administer an easy-to-give test such as the Slosson Intelligence Test or the Peabody Picture Vocabulary Test. Either instrument will provide a general estimate of intellectual ability that can later be used with an expectancy formula. If teachers are fortunate enough to have the services of a school psychologist, they might enlist that person's support by having him or her administer tests such as the Wechsler Intelligence Scale for Children—Revised or the Stanford-Binet to candidates suspected of being reading disabled.

    3. If teachers decide to use a reading expectancy formula, they should consult two or more to give them independent predictors of potential. We have already mentioned that various expectancy formulas may yield different results. For this reason, we suggest that teachers use more than one formula when attempting to predict reading expectancy. The scores can then be compared and professional judgment exercised. The graphs provided earlier should make this job relatively painless.

    Regardless of how reading expectancy scores are generated, it is important to remember that they are only gross indicators of potential. They should be interpreted cautiously and combined with teachers' observation when deciding who should be eligible for special help.

    4. Remain flexible. Occasionally teachers may select students who do not need extensive supplementary reading instruction. Or they may overlook a likely candidate or two. Teachers shouldn't be afraid to revise their case loads should the need arise. Selecting students is largely a subjective matter and mis-

takes are apt to be made. Having some flexibility will allow teachers to pick up or drop students as the needs arise.

WHAT TO EXPECT

Now that we've offered some guidelines on how to select subjects for the reading program, teachers might be interested in learning what a "typical" supplementary reading program resembles. Reading teachers may want to compare their programs with these data.

Bruininks and his associates (1973) claim that teachers should expect between 8 and 15 percent of the average school population to have reading problems, and up to 28 percent of the students may be reading below grade level. Hecherl and Sansbury (1968) contend that the majority of these students have average or above-average intelligence.

In an extensive review of the characteristics of students in compensatory reading programs, Sawyer (1979) found that 57 percent of the enrollees were boys. The incidence of referrals due to physical problems was low and not significantly different from the general population. A considerable number of students had adjustment problems and came from troubled families. The usual reason for inclusion in a compensatory program was below-grade-level reading performance.

Occasionally, federal or state criteria are specified to determine who qualifies for compensatory reading assistance, for example, the requirement that a student be reading one or more years below grade level. Sometimes reading teachers are able to select students who do not meet these criteria providing they can legitimately defend these exceptions. Sawyer's review revealed that disadvantaged students comprised a substantial portion of the typical compensatory program, but were by no means a majority. She also learned that students were likely to have been in the program for more than one year.

Thus, the characteristics of special reading programs may, in part, be determined by the degree the program is funded by state or federal sources. Typically, such funding is accompanied by specified entrance criteria. The type of students may also be influenced by how schools become eligible for compensatory funds in the first place (for example, low-income areas). Nevertheless, it appears that most remedial readers have average or above-average intelligence and do not suffer from serious physical handicaps. All do suffer from the same malady, however: poor reading.

SUMMARY

One of the reading teacher's most important responsibilities is to select those students who can benefit from instruction. Identifying problem readers is not as easy as it may seem. Some scholars have tried to predict who will have difficulty in reading by administering tests to students before the disability appears. These predictive studies suffer from a major drawback, however. Usually an extensive battery of tests must be administered to find those instruments that yield accurate predictive scores. Hence, most classroom teachers are unwilling to commit the time and resources needed to administer all the tests until more valid and reliable predictors have been identified.

Another procedure for identifying disabled readers is to use teachers' observations, coupled with test scores. The intuitive feelings of teachers supported by reading scores often are enough to indicate who needs special help. Early in this chapter we described the types of students who could profit most from supplementary instruction.

Since teachers and administrators frequently need objective information to identify legitimate remedial learners, two popular reading expectancy formulas were introduced: the Bond-Tinker Formula and the Mental Age Formula. Several examples were provided to illustrate how the various formulas work, as well as a series of cautionary notes.

Finally, some personal suggestions were offered for selecting students for additional reading instruction.

RELATED ACTIVITIES

1. Define in your own words gifted and slow learners. How are these students similar and different from remedial learners?
2. Review three or more different texts on reading disabilities. See what each says about the concept of reading expectancy. Make a list of the different formulas that are discussed as well as their advantages and limitations. Using fictitious data, see how the formulas affect the scores of several hypothetical students.
3. If possible, interview the directors of programs for the disabled readers and for the gifted. Ask how each group is identified. Try to determine if any provisions are made for errors in the selection process. Ask each to specify the role of teachers' judgment in the selection process.

RELATED READINGS

BOND, GUY, MILES A. TINKER, AND BARBARA B. WASSON. *Reading Difficulties: Their Diagnosis and Correction.* Englewood Cliffs, NJ: Prentice-Hall, 1979.

HARRIS, ALBERT J. "An Overview of Reading Disabilities and Learning Disabilities in the U.S." *The Reading Teacher*, 33, no. 4 (1980), 420–25.

KOENKE, KARL. "Testing the Minimal Competencies." *The Reading Teacher*, 33, no. 1 (1979), 118–22.

MONEY, JOHN, ed. *Reading Disability.* Baltimore, Md.: The Johns Hopkins Press, 1962.

———, ed. *The Disabled Reader.* Baltimore, Md.: The Johns Hopkins Press, 1966.

SAWYER, DIANE. "A Profile of Children in Compensatory Reading Programs." In *Teaching Reading in Compensatory Classes.* Robert C. Calfee and Priscilla A. Drum, eds. Newark, Del: International Reading Association, 1979.

REFERENCES

ALLINGTON, RICHARD L. "Sticks and Stones . . . But, Will Names Never Hurt Them?" *The Reading Teacher*, 28, no. 4 (Jan. 1975), 364–69.

BOND, GUY, MILES A. TINKER, AND BARBARA B. WASSON. *Reading Difficulties: Their Diagnosis and Correction.* Englewood Cliffs, N.J.: Prentice-Hall, 1979.

BRUININKS, ROBERT H., GERTRUDE M. GLAM-
AN, AND CHARLOTTE R. CLARK. "Issues in
Determining Prevalence of Reading Retardation." *The Reading Teacher,* 27, no. 2 (Nov.
1973), 177–84.

FESHBACH, SEYMOUR, HOWARD ADELMAN, AND
WILLIAM W. FULLER. "Early Identification
of Children with High Risk of Reading
Failure." *Journal of Learning Disabilities,* 7, no.
10 (December 1974) 639–44.

HECHERL, JOHN R., AND RUSSELL J. SANS-
BURY. "A Study of Severe Reading Retardation." *The Reading Teacher,* 21, no. 8 (May
1968), 724–29.

RODENBORN, LEO V. "Determining, Using
Expectancy Formulas." *The Reading Teacher,*
28, no. 3 (Dec. 1974), 286–91.

SATZ, PAUL, AND JANETTE FRIEL. "Some Predictive Antecedents of Specific Reading Disability: A Preliminary Two-Year Followup."
Journal of Learning Disabilities, 7, no. 7
(Aug./Sept. 1974), 437–44.

SAWYER, DIANE. "A Profile of Children in
Compensatory Reading Programs." In
Teaching Reading in Compensatory Classes.
Robert C. Calfee and Priscilla Drum, eds.
Newark, Del.: International Reading Asso-
ciation, 1979.

3

UNDERSTANDING THE READING PROCESS

Upon completion of this chapter you will be able to

1. List, describe, and evaluate several strategies for making decisions in reading instruction.
2. Compare a bottom-up and a top-down view of reading and explain the difficulties that arise when either position is overemphasized.
3. Describe an interactive model of reading and its implications for instruction.

MAKING DECISIONS IN READING

Teachers of reading are faced with countless decisions every day. Many of them, of course, are quite ordinary—assigning students to reading groups, selecting workbook pages, and choosing skills to teach. These decisions are similar to driving to work along a frequently traveled route. The trip is routine, and we arrive at our destination without consciously remembering being on a particular street or highway. Teaching reading is sometimes like that; instruction becomes routine.

This routinization is particularly true if students are reading at or near grade level. In these situations the teacher can usually rely on a basal reader series with a copious teacher's edition and a plethora of teaching aids. Each lesson in the manual offers suggestions, not only in *how* to teach reading, but also of *what* skills and strategies to teach, when they should be introduced, and when they should be reviewed and overlearned. The teacher's guide provides the questions to ask and frequently supplies the appropriate answers as well. As long as students are making satisfactory progress, teachers can follow conventional instructional procedures.

The decision-making process becomes more complex, however, when students are having trouble learning to read. What do teachers do with students who cannot read at all? How can they teach students who are struggling unsuc-

The search for understanding reading is never ending. (Peter P. Tobia)

cessfully or help those who have ceased to struggle altogether? In these cases, no prepackaged manuals, teaching aids, or activities are likely to solve all the problems they may face. Now decisions come more slowly; teachers may become reluctant decision-makers.

Teachers may attempt to help a disabled student by resorting to recipe-type manuals, and this step-by-step approach works as long as the problem is relatively simple. However, when problems are more complex, recipe book solutions prove woefully inadequate. The more serious the problem, the less helpful will be the manuals, guidebooks, teacher's editions, and activity books. These materials may supply answers which appear quick and easy, but they may also be simpleminded . . . and even wrong.

Several alternative decision-making processes are at hand when teachers are confronted with students' reading problems:

1. If faced with just two alternatives, they could flip a coin to determine what approach to follow.
2. They could resort to tradition by trying to recall their own teacher's strategy for solving a similar problem many years ago.
3. Expert opinion is another source of decision making. They could call on the expert teacher down the hall, the principal, the school reading specialist, or even a nearby college or university professor.
4. Common sense may also help. Teachers make many decisions on the basis of common sense, often with satisfying results.
5. Finally, they can search their own personal experience. How is this problem like others they have had? What has worked for them before?

Unfortunately, all these decision-making strategies have their limitations. We ordinarily resist making decisions by random selection—the coin-flipping approach—and consider it as a last resort. We usually prefer more rational alternatives. Tradition is of little value if the problem is novel and lies outside our particular tradition. Expert opinion frequently falls short of its promise because the experts often disagree. In diagnosing the same reading case, for example, trained reading specialists may propose a variety of interpretations. Even common sense is often disappointing. As one wag put it, common sense is not all that common. Furthermore, the more complex the problem, the more disagreement there may be concerning what constitutes a commonsense solution. Finally, even our past experience may prove inadequate. We may lack the experience to solve a particular reading problem, or even if we possess the required experience, we may interpret our experiences in light of faulty assumptions and simply confirm our original belief. Years of teaching may harden our assumptions; observers can frequently predict our diagnosis of a reading problem—largely because they recognize these assumptions. To put it another way, we tend to interpret new situations or events in light of what we already know.

In summary, decisions are made in four ways: (1) Tradition, or what the past has taught; (2) authority, or what the experts advocate; (3) common sense, or the appeal to pragmatic reason; and (4) personal experience. Each of these methods can be helpful, but every one contains inherent limitations which inhibit their effectiveness.

THEORY IN READING

How and Why in Reading

In reading instruction, these four decision-making strategies have led to a heavy emphasis on teaching methods in which *how* to teach has been preeminent. Unfortunately, this emphasis has come at the expense of understanding—the *why* of the reading process. A methods orientation, of course, may not appreciably harm the many students who learn a good deal about reading on their own initiative. On the other hand, high-risk students or those who have already failed may need considerably more than a new method or approach to help them become proficient readers.

Responsive Teaching

Making appropriate decisions about reading instruction requires a basic understanding of the reading process. This understanding also encourages teachers to focus on the students' behavior rather than on teaching techniques. Listening carefully to students' oral reading, for example, reveals that they add, delete, and substitute words often without affecting the meaning of the text. The understanding that reading is a form of language and that this language exerts considerable influence on the reading of written text can enable teachers not only to discern the reasons for these substitutions but also to help them feel comfortable in accepting rather than correcting these apparent errors. It is this kind of understanding that can reduce reading from a collection of numerous, unrelated behaviors to a few key ideas from which instructional decisions can flow. Understanding theory is thus one of the most practical tools available, and the teacher of disabled readers cannot afford to be without it.

An understanding of reading, of course, is only a potential force for good. Understanding doesn't teach reading; people do. Unless understanding of the intellectual process is accompanied by both commitment and sensitivity on the part of teachers, it will do little to improve instruction.

Finally, understanding does not apply directly to practice. William James (1958) said it well when he stated,

> I say moreover that you make a great, a very great mistake if you think that psychology being the science of mind's laws, is something from which you can deduce definite programmes and schemes and methods of instruction for immediate school room use. Psychology is a science and teaching is an art, and sciences never generate arts directly out of themselves. An intermediary inventive mind must make the applications, by using its originality. (pp. 23–24)

In other words, a one-to-one correspondence does not exist between a theory of reading and a specific practice. A particular theory may generate several teaching practices. Teaching requires teachers to take these broad general ideas about reading and creatively apply them to specific situations. In this text these large ideas are presented along with the implications for instruction.

THREE MODELS OF READING

To help you understand what happens in reading, three models or interpretations of the reading process are presented. They are not necessarily of equal value, but they serve as vehicles to communicate a central theoretical concern: to read well requires appropriate attention to print as well as meaning in the mind of the reader. Some of this discussion will contrast opposing views and facilitate understanding. To understand the concept of a goat, for example, it is helpful to know what is *not* a goat. It is by contrasting ideas that we frequently develop a clearer picture of a concept and are better able to abstract from concrete examples those attributes that define the concept. The first model has often been described as a "bottom-up" view of reading.

Reading from the Bottom Up

The bottom-up view of reading was described by Philip Gough (1972) when he speculated what it would be like to explore a single second of reading behavior. A diagram of the process as Gough understood it is seen in Figure 3-1. Several details of Gough's model have been eliminated, and emphasis has been placed on those aspects of the process indicated in the rectangular, numbered boxes. The direction of processing is well defined in Gough's model and represents clearly one view of reading.

According to Gough, reading starts with the fixation of the eye upon print during which a visual pattern is projected onto the retina of the reader's eye. Reading, in this view, begins with print. In the icon, step 1, a brief image of the letters, up to twenty letter spaces, is created. This fades rapidly, lasting less than half a second. During this brief time, however, the image or icon is transformed, serially, from left to right into letters as it is acted on by a pattern recognition device. This is the letter identification phase.

In the character register, step 2, a further conversion occurs. Here the reader maps the letters onto their corresponding phonemes or sound representations. At the phonemic tape stage, step 3, the phonemic representation is matched with words held in a kind of mental dictionary, the lexicon. The lexicon processes meanings; the meaning of each word is recovered, one word at a time, in left-to-right sequence. These meanings are held in primary memory, step 4, while waiting to be organized into a sentence. Primary or short-term memory holds information for several seconds but has a limited storage capacity.

At this point, Merlin, a colorful term for a process which operates on the string of words, attempts to determine the meaning, or deep structure, of the sentence. This process is more complicated than dealing with individual words, however, for the reader must now take into account the grammar of the text whereby the sentences can be understood. (The complexity of this task and our limited understanding of this phase probably led Gough to give it a magical connotation.)

If Merlin does decipher the meaning of the sentence, the sentence enters TPWSGWTAU, *The Place Where Sentences Go When They Are Understood*, step 5. Again, Gough has resorted to imaginative language when relatively little is known about the processing of the text. In the final step, script, step 6, the phonological rules which convert meaning into speech are applied, and the reader proceeds to read the selection orally.

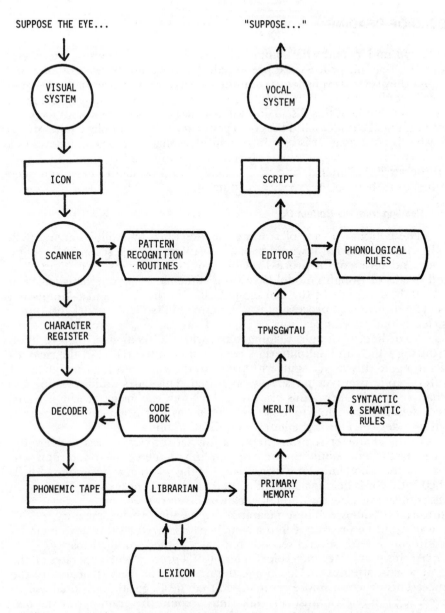

Figure 3-1 Gough's One Second of Reading   Reprinted from *Language by Ear and by Eye,*
ed. James F. Kavanagh and Ignatius G. Mattingly by permission of The MIT Press,
Cambridge, Massachusetts, 1972. Copyright © 1972 by The Massachusetts Institute of
Technology.

Of chief concern in this process is the direction it takes. Note the upward
movement, up from print. The model begins with the marks on a page, the
letters, and then moves into units of higher order, the words and sentences, and
finally ends in meaning.

Because the process starts with sensory input and proceeds upward to more abstract levels, it has been called a *bottom-up model* of reading (Kamil, 1978). Other names used by authorities are *plodder* (Rozin and Gleitman, 1977), *outside-inside* (Smith, 1979) (since the process starts with print, which is outside the reader's head), and *data-driven* (Bobrow and Norman, 1975). Data-driven refers to the fact that the emphasis is placed on the data before the eyes of the reader rather than the nonvisual information already in the cognitive structure.

Implications of Bottom-Up Model

A model such as Gough's suggests that reading instruction should concentrate on the letters and their corresponding sound values (that is, a decoding approach). Reading would thus stress the translation of print to speech. The application of meaning would occur later in the process; in this model meaning can be considered a separate phase. It is frequently argued, according to this view, that the meaning of the text is self-evident to the reader once the material is turned into speech, assuming that the reader is a native speaker of the language.

A student's language ability and cognitive background would be acknowledged, but these would come into play after print had been converted to speech. Thus, reading would be viewed as a process distinct from general language and cognitive functioning with stress placed on those aspects of reading, namely decoding to sound, which are unique to reading as opposed to those processes it holds in common with other intellectual activities.

In this view, reading instruction would probably emphasize skill development. Skills, in word identification and comprehension, would be identified and arranged in a hierarchy. Systematic teaching would be provided to insure their mastery. The task of diagnosis would be to determine which skills had not been learned.

A Psycholinguistic Model

A bottom-up view of reading represents only one position. An opposing theory, the top-down model, can be illustrated with a few examples. Suppose a particular text read, "The family lived in a large three-story house," but one student read *home* for house. Later the text read, "The auto raced down the street," but the student read, "The *car* raced down the street." In a third account, the text read, "The man runs every day to prepare for the marathon," but the student rendered it, "The man, he run every day to prepare for the marathon." How can these deviations from the text be explained? In the first example the student may have simply substituted a word that looked like the correct word. *Home* is obviously similar to *house*. The student, however, did not substitute just any similar word. That is, he did not insert *horse*, which is even closer in appearance. Instead, a word with a semantically similar meaning was substituted.

In the second example, the substituted word, *car*, shares only one common letter with the correct word, *auto*, although configuration and length are similar. But again, it is a synonym for *car*. The deviation from the text in the third example is more extreme. Here the reader inserts a word which is not in the text, *he*, and deletes the *s* on *run*. Some authorities (Goodman, 1967) have theorized that all three mistakes or miscues have perfectly reasonable explanations if we understand how the text was processed.

An explanation for these miscues does more than satisfy idle curiosity. It has direct implications for instruction. It may tell us whether we should correct the student's miscues or not. It may suggest whether we should interrupt at all. Finally, it may provide some guidance about what promptings we should give to students in order to have them read the text correctly.

One explanation for each of these students' miscues is that reading involves more than meets the eye. Reading, in this view, deals not only with print, which is visible and seen, but also with a good deal of information that is invisible and unseen. The nonvisual data consist of the individual's life experiences and conceptual background as well as his or her understanding of the rules of language. The influence of this invisible information is often so potent that it overrides the data on the page. In the previous three examples, the reader's invisible information led to particular miscues. (The word *miscue* is used instead of *error* since it conveys the idea that a deviation from the text is based on a rational decision on the part of the reader rather than random guessing.)

In the first two examples, the student's knowledge of word meaning permitted a substitution of a synonym. In the first case, in which *home* was substituted for *house,* the student may have also been influenced by the graphic or sound similarity between the words. In the *car* for *auto* miscue, however, the meaning of the sentence probably exerted more influence than the visual aspects of the word. In the third example, in which the student changed *runs* to *run* and added a word to the sentence, the influence of dialect is seen.

According to a psycholinguistic interpretation of the reading process, reading does not necessarily begin with print at all but originates with the language of the reader and all this language represents. Students begin reading with specific purposes as well as expectations. As they proceed, they compare these purposes and expectations with the text and seek confirmation of their hypotheses. This is essentially a process of prediction in which readers draw upon information which is stored in their cognitive structure, a kind of sophisticated, cross-indexed mental file. In contrast to print, which is visible, this information is invisible or nonvisual in nature. Though unseen, it plays a vital role in reading.

The invisible information, which is also called world knowledge, can be divided into four categories:

1. Semantic (meaning).
2. Syntactic (relationship of words in a sentence based on the reader's grammar).
3. Orthographic (relationship of letters in a word to one another).
4. Phonological (rules by which spoken words are pronounced).

Semantic information, in turn, can be organized in three ways:

1. Concepts (dogs, humans, trust).
2. Generalizations ("humans can be aggressive"; "tigers are carnivorous").
3. Relationships ("How is my uncle related to my father?" "How is a sheep related to a goat?").

Semantic information also includes the labels or vocabulary for these ideas. Speakers may understand the idea of transporting objects from one place to another, but some will use the word *carry* whereas others prefer *tote*. The foreign-language-speaking adult who is trying to read English may possess a rich conceptual background but lacks the English names for many of these ideas.

Syntax or word order also plays an important part in the reading process. In English, the sequence of words in a sentence is designed to communicate meaning. In the sentence "The teacher helped the student," *teacher* is considered to be the subject and *student* the object because of their positions in the sentence. The meaning is changed considerably if one word is substituted for another and the sentence reads "The student helps the teacher." The fact that the syntax of sentences is governed by rules allows the reader to anticipate the words in the oncoming text. In the phrase, "in the forest," we expect the first two words *in* and *the*, a preposition and an adjective, to be followed by a noun or another adjective because that is the only possible pattern that can occur in English. By anticipating either a noun or adjective, readers are able to reduce their uncertainty concerning the next word. This syntactic patterning allows us to make decisions about words more readily and thus makes reading easier.

In addition, the reader has invisible knowledge about the orthography of print and knows that letters within words occur in patterns and are predictable. For example, in a three-letter word, beginning with *th, th* is more likely to be followed by an *e* than an *o* and cannot in English be followed by an *a*. This ability to detect sequential patterns in words and use them as cues in word identification can assist the reader. Beginning readers, of course, have a limited understanding of orthography. As they read, however, they become sensitive to patterns in print, and even then these are likely to be below the conscious level.

The reader possesses considerable phonological information about how words are to be pronounced. This information helps in pronouncing words in which the visual information alone is incomplete. Rules of phonology state, for example, that the letter *s* at the end of *hats* should be pronounced with the /s/ sound, whereas the /z/ sound should be used at the end of *logs*.

According to psycholinguistic theory, readers need not perceive every letter or word but can reconstruct the author's meaning by sampling the text. In the sampling process, they read just enough of the print to compare it with what they are anticipating. If their expectations are continually confirmed, the reading will flow almost effortlessly. If new information or information which conflicts with their expectations is presented, more attention to print may be necessary.

Readers use the invisible information available to them along with information contained in print to reconstruct the author's message. Frank Smith (1982) has suggested that a partial trade-off takes place in this process. The more nonvisual information available to readers, the less attention they need to give to print. On the other hand, when the readers can bring less nonvisual information to the page, they must attend more carefully to the printed text itself. This view, in which Goodman (1967) describes reading as a psycholinguistic guessing game, emphasizes the importance of the meaning that the reader brings to the page. Print serves to confirm or reject the reader's expectations and plays a relatively minor role compared to the influence of language. Paul Kolers (1968) has helped to popularize this view with his statement that "Reading is only incidentally visual."

A psycholinguistic view of reading has received these labels: *top-down* (Kamil, 1978), *explorer* (Rozin and Gleitman, 1977), *conceptually driven* (Bobrow and Norman, 1975), and *inside-outside* (Smith, 1979). (The process starts inside the reader rather than with print, which is outside the reader.)

Implications for Instruction

Several implications for instruction flow from this model. First, students are encouraged to make maximum use of nonvisual information, such as sentence context, in identifying words. Reading activities would involve connected text rather than words in isolation. Care would be taken not to correct the reader's miscues, particularly if they made sense or did not change the meaning of the sentence. The miscues should be analyzed carefully, however, to determine how students utilize their language as a cue to decoding words.

Instruction would emphasize the need to change students' cognitive structure in order for them to understand a written account. The challenge of reading a social studies text, for example, would not consist of the previous mastery of skills but the possession of sufficient nonvisual information assumed by the textbook author. Care would also be taken with the development of textual material so that sentence structure and semantic organization did not interfere unduly with students' reading.

A psycholinguistic model emphasizes that students learn to read largely by reading and that direct instruction in such activities as phonics is unnecessary and even detracts from an emphasis on meaning. (Not every proponent of a psycholinguistic view, however, constricts the role of phonics.) Every attempt would be made to deal with reading as an indivisible whole, rather than dividing it into discrete skills. Thus, this model of reading would focus on reading as an intellectual activity that has much in common with other thought processes.

Limitations of Speech and Language Models

A bottom-up and top-down approach represent two alternative views of reading. A bottom-up approach begins with print, whereas a top-down view places much more emphasis on the anticipation of text and the reader's use of language. Much reading instruction is guided by either one of these two views, though in practice, it is difficult to find a pure form of either. Both have become incorporated into so-called "eclectic" reading programs which attempt to combine the best practices of both points of view. Students today, for example, are usually asked to use both context and phonics to identify unknown words. A bottom-up view would probably have a student "sound out" the word, whereas a top-down approach would urge the use of context as a first strategy.

Both points of view, if held to rigidly, have shortcomings. The bottom-up view may be mystifying to students, for the alphabetic principle is abstract; we can point to letters, but how do we point to a sound? And how do we convey the idea that these visible letters are related in some fashion to an unseen sound?

Henderson's study (1980) of young children's metalinguistic knowledge about words and phonics shows that children in the early stages of reading have difficulty conceptualizing a sound-symbol system. Critics claim, furthermore, that the bottom-up view overemphasizes the alphabetic system at the expense of other aspects of language (that is, meaning) which students can more readily grasp. The result is that students may either become frustrated over their inability to unlock the code or overattend to letters, sounds, and words and thereby fail to comprehend. If the readers learn at all, they become barkers at print, word-callers, those who parrot words with little understanding of the text.

The bottom-up model has been criticized too on theoretical grounds. Rumelhart (1977) and Wildman and Kling (1978–79) point out that a bottom-up position assumes that reading, like a one-way staircase, moves from lower levels (letters and sounds) to higher ones (meaning). They contend, however, that higher levels of thought influence lower thought processes very early in the reading of the text. The most obvious example are students' miscues in which their language background shapes their responses.

An overemphasis on top-down processing also has disadvantages. An example is those students who have considerable difficulty accepting the fact that reading should be influenced by the text at all. They may "read" words or even whole sentences which aren't on the page. These deviations may bear little relationship to the rest of the text. Individuals who perform this way may possess a limited concept of reading and may even feel that a paraphrase or a highly imaginative interpretation of textual material is acceptable. A few may believe that attending to print is too demanding, and hence, they create a meaning for themselves, regardless of what the author was trying to communicate.

A psycholinguistic orientation to instruction cannot be blamed for a student's cavalier attitude toward print, but some students are not helped either by asking them "to use the context." This advice may encourage them to invent their own interpretation of the text. These students must pay more attention to print, not less. In addition, critics maintain that using context may seem to make reading easier for the beginner, but it delays the student's need to deal with the complexities of print. Since students must eventually deal with the alphabetic system, they argue, to withhold it in favor of meaning approaches is to do them a disservice.

In summary, both models can suffer from limitations. A bottom-up model does not allow higher levels of linguistic processing to influence lower levels and is frequently too abstract for the beginning reader. A top-down approach is subject to abuse by those readers who would invent or create their own meaning rather than reconstruct the author's.

These two positions can also be seen in our orthographic system as well. The view that reading is primarily a process of translating print to speech is emphasized by the alphabetic principle in which letters are related to sounds. The second view, emphasizing the importance of language with print playing a secondary role, is seen in words like "nation" and "national" in which the alphabetic principle is sacrificed to meaning. The persistence of both positions suggests two things: first, that both views have merit; second, that neither provides an adequate description of reading.

An Interactive Model

A third alternative, which goes beyond a simple eclectism in which divergent views are combined, is Rumelhart's model. It involves both the concepts of bottom-up and top-down processing but stresses the interaction of one with the other. Interactive theory is like a two-way staircase in which one can begin at either the top or bottom.

Perhaps an analogy will make the interactive model more understandable. (The reader is referred to Rumelhart's discussion, 1977, for a more detailed explanation.) Imagine that students have gone to a zoo and confront a sign which says "The Alligator." A top-down approach might attempt to identify the words by means of context. Given a pond filled with particular flora and fauna, the reader's nonvisual information would be brought into play. A bottom-up approach, on the other hand, would begin with the letters in "The Alligator" and attempt to relate them to their corresponding oral code. The difference is not that each approach ignores meaning or letters but that they start the reading process from different perspectives. An interactive model would deal with "The Alligator" in a different manner. Suppose that a group of students was attempting to decode the word. These "word attackers" would divide into a number of committees, each with a different task. The first committee would deal with letter-sound associations; the second committee would explore sentence or phrase syntax. Committee number three would work with semantics, and committee number four with the larger context of the situation, the setting of the zoo.

Each committee would attempt to gather data about the sign at its particular linguistic level. In time, they would generate hypotheses about the identification of the word. It might be possible for one level of analysis to reduce uncertainty about the word to the point where a decision could be made, but information would ordinarily be drawn from all four levels before closure was reached.

Coordination of this effort would be obtained by sending the hypotheses to someone stationed at a "message center." Hypotheses regarding letter-sound associations would interact in the "message center" with those concerning syntax, semantics, and general context. The probability of accepting or rejecting a hypothesis would be determined by how much support it received from the various levels. For example, the word *crocodile* might be suggested if general context, semantics, and syntax were considered. It would not be upheld at the letter-sound level, however, and therefore the chance of *crocodile* being selected would decline. Until a final decision was made, however, *crocodile* might still be considered. At the same time, a hypothesis suggesting *albatross* might be advanced by the letter-sound associations. Syntactic hypotheses generating a noun would also be compatible. *Albatross* might be a reasonable guess. Unfortunately, the general context would not support such a word, since an *albatross* is unlikely to be found in a zoo. As hypotheses continued to be forwarded, the "message center" itself would generate new hypotheses, which would be sent "up" and "down" for checking against the information available at each level.

If *alligator* were hypothesized, this would be checked against its probability at the letter-sound, syntactic, semantic, and general context level. A decision would be made when the "message center" felt that it had received sufficient confirmation. Precisely how much data would be needed would depend on the "message center" itself. Some centers would tend to make decisions before sufficient data were collected and analyzed. Others might insist on far too much information before deciding. A committee might lack knowledge of a particular letter-sound association or know little about animals or zoos. In this case it would take longer to reduce uncertainty sufficiently. In the interactive model, the precise nature of the "message center" is not fully understood. It does suggest, however, that the reader takes information from various sources, generates hypotheses at all these levels, and seeks out additional information at other levels to confirm or reject predictions.

In this theory, the relationship between levels of processing is not linear but interactive. That is, we do not begin with letters and work up to meaning, nor do we start with meaning and work down to print. Rather, information at each level flows to a "message center," which allows predictions from various sources to be analyzed simultaneously.

Advantages of Interactive Model

Flexibility is the key feature of the interactive model. Processing can begin at either the letter or meaning level, but more important, information from these two basic sources simultaneously influences each other. Thus, our processing of information at one level is influenced by our handling of information at another level, either higher or lower on the perceptual-cognitive continuum. The model strongly suggests that reading instruction must take seriously both visual and nonvisual aspects of reading. In addition, the model helps us appreciate the relationship between both sources. Thus to adopt the interactive position means paying sufficient attention to word detail, and also recognizing the limitations of word identification in isolation.

The interactive model also suggests implications for instruction. First, any method of instruction must deal with all levels of processing: semantic, syntactic, orthographic, phonic, and general context. Bottom-up processing has not encouraged the use of nonvisual information to reduce uncertainty and make reading easier. Students subsequently may have difficulty integrating these cueing systems, a problem exacerbated by a skill-by-skill approach to reading. The process could be facilitated if students were encouraged to make use of higher levels of linguistic functioning while their understanding of the orthography and letter-sound associations was being developed.

At the same time, the proponents of a top-down view may have been far too idealistic in their description of the reader as a seeker of someone else's meaning. Some students habitually pay too little attention to the information in print and overrely on what they already know. These students ignore the text and substitute their meaning for the author's.

An interactive model can serve as a curb to both extremes. It forces the reader to deal with both visible and invisible data, not in isolation or in serial fashion, but in a coordinated, simultaneous manner. It encourages teachers to correct the poor habits of those who overuse phonics as well as those who depend too much on their own interpretation and tend to ignore letters and words. Since many students have one of these problems, an interactive model helps us understand them.

The precise use of the model depends on the students' reading behavior. If they are plodders, more attention to higher-level processing is called for. If, on the other hand, they invent the author's message, it will be necessary to have them attend more carefully to print without fragmenting the reading process by the overuse of skills and words in isolation. Explicit instruction in phonics and other word attack skills may be needed.

Many questions about reading theory still remain. A key issue is how models which were based on the reading behavior of the proficient reader can be applied to the novice. In orthography, for example, our present system—with its concern for both the alphabet and meaning—may be the best available once an individual has mastered certain fundamentals, but how should students be taught in order to reach that level? What implication does the model have for the student who is learning to read words for the first time? We will address these and related questions throughout this text. The practical instructional sequences which follow will grow out of the discussion presented here.

SUMMARY

In this chapter we have tried to make two points:

1. The person who tries to teach the problem reader needs more than a storeroom of material or a repertoire of teaching tricks. An understanding of the reading process facilitates sound decision making and is especially helpful when common sense, tradition, expert opinion, and authority fall short.
2. Reading theory has traditionally followed two lines of thought. One view suggests that reading is the translation of print to speech. A second position contends that reading involves language and meaning from the start. The tenacity of both views suggests that each may contain some truth although neither is a completely accurate description of the reading process.

Finally, we suggested that an interactive model in which information is processed simultaneously at both letter-sound and meaning levels can serve as a welcome alternative in teaching students who overrely on letters, sounds, or meaning. The challenge is to make reading easy through the use of nonvisual information while reconstructing with reasonable accuracy the message of the author. This quest for a more perfect balance between the visible and invisible is the goal of this text.

RELATED ACTIVITIES

1. Observe a class of beginning readers. What instructional activities reflect a top-down or bottom-up view of reading?
2. Examine a set of basal readers. What procedures flow from a data-driven approach to reading? From a conceptually driven orientation?

3. Interview teachers to determine the basis for their instructional decisions, particularly for disabled readers.
4. It would seem logical to expect that teachers' instructional practices would be based on a particular understanding of the reading process. Examine the professional literature to determine the relationship between teachers' theories of reading and their teaching practices. Determine the pragmatic considerations that influence their decision making.

RELATED READINGS

BAWDEN, ROBERT, SANDRA BUIKE, AND GERALD G. DUFFY. *Teacher Conceptions of Reading and Their Influence on Instruction*. East Lansing: Institute for Research on Teaching, Michigan State University, Research Series No. 47. ERIC/RIE No. 174-952.

HUEY, EDMUND B. *The Psychology and Pedagogy of Reading*. New York: Macmillan, 1908. Reprinted Cambridge, Mass.: MIT Press, 1968.

PFLAUM-CONNOR, SUSANNA, ED. *Aspects of Reading Education*. Chapters by Carroll, Samuels, and Schachter, Kamil. Berkeley, Calif.: McCutchan Publishing, 1978.

REBER, ARTHUR S., AND DON L. SCARBOROUGH, EDS. *Toward a Psychology of Reading*. Hillsdale, N.J.: Lawrence Erlbaum, 1977.

RUMELHART, DAVID. "Toward an Interactive Model of Reading." In *Attention and Performance*, VI. Stanislav Dornic, ed. Hillsdale, N.J.: Lawrence Erlbaum, 1977.

SMITH, FRANK. *Reading Without Nonsense*. New York: Teachers College Press, 1979.

REFERENCES

BOBROW, D. G., AND DONALD A. NORMAN. "Some Principles of Memory Schematic." In *Representation and Understanding: Studies in Cognitive Science*. D. G. Bobrow and A. M. Collins, eds. New York: Academic Press, 1975.

GOODMAN, KENNETH S. "Reading: A Psycholinguistic Guessing Game." *Journal of the Reading Specialist*, 6 (May 1967), 126–35.

GOUGH, PHILIP B. "One Second of Reading." In *Language by Ear and by Eye*. Cambridge, Mass.: MIT Press, 1972.

HENDERSON, EDMUND H. "Developmental Concepts of Word." In *Developmental and Cognitive Aspects of Learning to Spell*. Newark, Del.: International Reading Association, 1980.

JAMES, WILLIAM. *Talks to Teachers*. New York: W. W. Norton and Co., Inc., 1958.

KAMIL, MICHAEL L. "Models of Reading: What Are the Implications for Instruction in Comprehension?" In *Aspects of Reading Education*. Susanna Pflaum-Connor, ed. Berkeley, Calif.: McCutchan Publishing, 1978.

KOLERS, PAUL A. "Reading Is Only Incidentally Visual." In *Psycholinguistics and the Teaching of Reading*. Kenneth Goodman, ed. Newark, Del.: International Reading Association, 1968.

ROZIN, PAUL, AND LILA R. GLEITMAN. "The Structure and Acquisition of Reading II: The Reading Process and the Acquisition of the Alphabetic Principle." In *Toward a Psychology of Reading*. Arthur S. Reber and Don L. Scarborough, eds. Hillsdale, N.J.: Lawrence Erlbaum, 1977.

RUMELHART, DAVID E. "Toward an Interactive Model of Reading." In *Attention and Performance*. Stanislav Dornic, ed. Hillsdale, N.J.: Lawrence Erlbaum, 1977.

SMITH, FRANK. "Conflicting Approaches to Reading Research and Instruction." In *Theory and Practice of Early Reading*, Vol. 2. Lauren B. Resnick and Phyllis A. Weaver, eds. Hillsdale, N.J.: Lawrence Erlbaum, 1979.

———. *Understanding Reading*, 3rd ed. New York: Holt, Rinehart & Winston, 1982.

WILDMAN, DAVID, AND MARTIN KLING. "Anticipation in Reading." *Reading Research Quarterly*, 14, no. 2 (1978–79), 129–64.

4

CORRELATES OF READING DISABILITY

After reading this chapter you should be able to

1. Summarize the major findings regarding correlates of reading disability.
2. Explain the relationship between acuity and discrimination as they pertain to vision and hearing.
3. State how health and neurological functioning can affect reading performance.
4. Suggest how intelligence, self-concept, and emotional well-being are related to reading.
5. Discuss how sociological factors may influence a child's reading ability.
6. Indicate how the educational setting can foster or inhibit reading performance.

Reading teachers soon discover that greater progress can be made in treating problems if they understand what caused the problems in the first place. Many reading problems are the result of multiple causes or the result of causes not fully understood (for example, neurological disfunction). Individuals who work with disabled readers should realize that even when causes are determined, only appropriate, focused instruction can provide the impetus for overcoming the disability.

This chapter explores some of the frequent correlates of reading disability. Correlates, simply stated, are factors that are related to reading disability. They may not have caused the disability, however. Thus, a cause is always a correlate but a correlate need not be a cause. For expository purposes we have separated these correlates into four major categories: physical, psychological, sociological, and educational. In the real world of the schools, however, causes of poor reading are complex and, more often than not, intertwined. Nevertheless, being aware of possible causes should allow you to become more sensitive to your students and more judicious in your instructional planning. Both of these qualities mark important steps in becoming an effective reading teacher.

PHYSICAL FACTORS

Before children can make satisfactory progress in reading, they should be physically healthy. Specifically, their visual and auditory mechanisms must be intact and operating correctly. Furthermore, they must be free of any major health problems which may interfere with their ability to learn. Finally, their neurological systems must be functioning appropriately so that stimuli can be processed and comprehended. The first section of this chapter will illustrate how physical problems in any of these areas can interfere with learning to read.

Vision

You no doubt remember your earlier school days when students were given a vision screening in the health room or a vacated classroom. A large chart hung on the wall while the students stood twenty feet away and attempted to discern the letters on the chart. What you probably didn't comprehend at the time was the rationale for this screening. Most children knew it was "to see if we need glasses" but few, if any, understood the nature of good vision and its relationship to reading.

ACUITY   The human eye has frequently been compared to a camera. (We should point out, however, that the similarities are strictly anatomical in nature. The processing of print in the human is much more complex than simply perceiving an image. This process has been described in depth in Chapter 3.) Both the eye and the camera have lenses and both must be focused if a clear image is to result. If either the eye or the camera is unable to be focused, a blurred image results. In the eye, focusing is accomplished by expanding or contracting muscles which are connected to the crystalline lens (see Figure 4-1). This expansion-contraction capability permits the shape of the lens to change. In the camera, the physical properties of the lens remain unchanged and, instead,

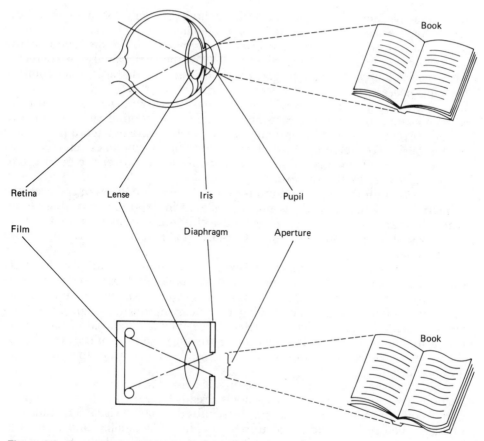

Figure 4-1 Cross Sections of an Eye and a Camera

the lens is moved toward or away from the film, thus resulting in the same phenomenon—a change in focus.

In the eye, images are projected onto the nerve cells of the retina; in the camera, images are projected onto film. The amount of light permitted to pass through the lens is controlled by the iris in the eye and the diaphragm in the camera. The resultant diameter of each is known respectively as the pupil and the aperture. For simple illustrative purposes then, the eye and the camera perform essentially similar functions. The clarity of the visual image received is what we commonly refer to as visual acuity.

Visual acuity can be impaired in various degrees. At best, restricted acuity may result in only mildly blurred images. At worst, it may mean double vision or vision impaired so badly that images cannot be recognized. Obviously, the severity of the problem may have varying consequences on the student's ability to read. In one case, only moderate discomfort or headaches may result. In other instances, vision may be so restricted that print cannot be perceived.

In many cases, problems in vision can be eliminated through prescriptive corrective lenses. Farsightedness (the ability to see only distant objects clearly), or hyperopia, and nearsightedness (the ability to see objects in close proximity), or myopia, are easily corrected. Astigmatism, or a distortion of the surface of the cornea (the outermost portion of the eye), can also be corrected with special lenses. Corrective glasses, then, assist in the accommodation or focusing process.

Occasionally, the eyes will fail to work efficiently together. A musculature imbalance of the eyes (strabismus) or the suppression of vision in one eye (amblyopia) may occur. The resultant effect may be restricted depth perception or stereopsis. To overcome the amblyopic condition (sometimes referred to as "lazy eye"), the doctor may prescribe a patch to be worn over the good eye to restore acuity to the unused eye.

Although there are numerous other physical anomalies of the eyes, the primary task of the educator is not to make an in-depth analysis of students' visual deficiencies but simply to spot those children who may suffer from reduced visual acuity and refer them to more qualified individuals for a more professional diagnosis.

Some symptoms of possible visual difficulties are relatively easy to detect whereas others are more covert and less discernable. Redness, excessive watering, imbalance, and squinting of the eye; poor posture while seated; and cocking or turning of the head while reading may be symptomatic of an underlying visual problem. More difficult to detect since they are internal in nature are headaches, blurred vision, dizziness, and a burning sensation of the eyes. Unless the student explicitly mentions these problems, there is a chance that they might go undetected.

One way to avoid overlooking possible visual inadequacies is to establish a school screening program. Many schools already have such programs in operation. In other instances, children may be required to have a visual screening by a physician before being admitted to school. The most familiar and frequently used instrument to measure far-point acuity is the Snellen Test. According to Jobe (1976), this instrument is the best single test to detect those students who suffer from myopia, astigmatism, and hyperopia. The "E Chart" is preferred over the "Alphabet Chart" since knowledge of the alphabet is not then a prerequisite for measuring acuity (an important consideration when testing bilingual children or illiterate adults).

The Snellen Test measures only monocular acuity, and the pass/fail score is an arbitrary one. Scores are computed by using the "Snellen fraction." The term *20/30 vision*, for example, means that the test was administered at 20 feet (the numerator), whereas most people are able to read the symbols at 30 feet (the denominator). The fraction does not imply a percentage of vision, however. Thus, if you were told you had 20/100 vision, you would see at 20 feet what most people would see at 100 feet. In other words, you would be a prime candidate for corrective lenses. Generally, to "pass" the examination, an individual needs to identify correctly four of six symbols on the line designed to assess 20/20 vision.

Although the Snellen Test performs an important function in identifying students with vision problems, its major drawback is that it assesses acuity only at the far-point range. To assess vision at near-point (approximately sixteen inches or forty centimeters), the distance at which most books are read, other tests must be used. The most popular way to measure near-point vision is with a stereoscope especially designed to measure near-point and far-point vision. Stereoscopes are essentially side-by-side lenses through which a series of cards or plates are viewed. The plates consist of two scenes that when viewed together, represent a single scene. (Remember the stereoscope in grandmother's attic? Or the vision test you took for your driver's license?) The stereoscope permits the examiner to measure near-point and far-point acuity as well as monocular and binocular vision. If desired, color-perception can be assessed, too, with pseudoisochromatic plates consisting of colored dots embedded in a background of contrasting dots.

Two popular stereoscopes used in many schools are

Keystone Visual Survey Telebinocular
Keystone View Company
2212 East 12th Street
Davenport, Iowa 52803

Bausch and Lomb School Vision Tester
Bausch and Lomb
Rochester, New York 14802

Tests for each instrument can be administered in less than ten minutes by an experienced examiner.

As we mentioned earlier, the criteria for referring students to a qualified vision specialist once a school vision screening has been conducted are somewhat subjective. And since only vision specialists can determine whether corrective lenses are indeed necessary, school and clinic personnel continually face the problems of underreferring students (those who pass the screening test but who

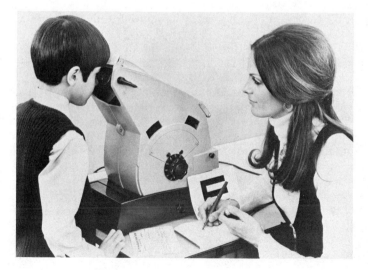

Figure 4-2 Bausch and Lomb School Vision Tester

need glasses) or overreferring students (those who fail the screening test but who pass a professional eye examination).

If there is any doubt whether a student should receive a professional examination, teachers should recommend that the parent or guardian make an appointment with a vision specialist. Many charitable organizations will finance an examination and glasses for parents who could not otherwise afford them. Given these conditions, there is no reason why correctable visual handicaps should stand in the way of learning to read.

Although clarity of vision is indeed an important prerequisite to effortless reading, in actuality few reading problems are caused solely by poor vision. Some highly motivated students learn to read even though they possess less than perfect vision. The muscular strain caused by having continually to adjust to reading print, however, can quickly lead many students to dislike reading itself. And that is the real danger of inadequate near-point vision.

We should point out that care needs to be exercised when referring subjects for professional eye examinations. It is a good policy simply to state that a child needs to schedule an examination with a vision specialist rather than suggest a specific individual or type of specialist. Since there are a number of specialists who deal in eye care, it's important that you understand the function of each.

Opthalmologists are medical doctors who have been trained to diagnose and treat diseases of the eye and to perform surgical procedures if necessary. They interpret vision to mean the functioning of the eye in a physical or mechanical sense. To most ophthalmologists, good vision means seeing in a clear, singular fashion.

Optometrists, on the other hand, do not treat diseases of the eye even though they can identify most visual problems. Optometrists are graduates of schools of optometry. They have been trained to test visual skills and prescribe corrective lenses or, if necessary, visual training. Visual training usually consists of activities which purport to develop binocular vision. Optometrists are more concerned with the functioning of the eyes, whereas ophthalmologists focus on the physical aspects. This sometimes leads to conflicting philosophies about eye care.

The optician is responsible for filling prescriptions for patients. Opticians grind lenses and help patients select lenses and frames. They do not become involved in the diagnosis of visual deficiencies.

As a teacher of reading, you should have a keen interest in your district's visual screening policies. If no screening program exists in your system, you might be instrumental in establishing or serving on a committee designed to draw up program guidelines. Parents, eye care specialists, and educators, by working together, could develop plans to identify those children who might have inadequate vision. Such a committee can make a major contribution to eliminating an important correlate of reading difficulty—poor vision.

DISCRIMINATION   Unlike visual acuity, visual discrimination is primarily a mental act which takes place in the brain and not in the eye. The terms *visual discrimination* and *visual perception* are sometimes used synonymously. Hammill and his associates (1974) said it well when they spoke of visual perception as ". . . those brain operations which involve interpreting and organizing the physical elements of the stimulus rather than the symbolic aspects of the stimulus . . ." (p. 470). The commonly confused lower-case *b* and *d* are perceived as possessing the same physical attributes but are sometimes misperceived as being the same letters.

Since visual discrimination (perception) is a mental operation, it is perhaps only natural that attempts have been made to improve perception through specialized training programs. One such program is the Frostig-Horne Perceptual Development Program (Frostig, 1966). A series of diagnostic tests is given to students, after which a series of up to 359 worksheets can be prescribed in an effort to improve their visual perception. Although such efforts to overcome a student's reading or learning disability are well intended, in reality such programs have usually not been found to improve reading ability. Instead, improvements in performance have been found only on the perception tests. In other words, transfer from visual discrimination and perceptual training to reading has not occurred.

Parents and teachers of students with severe learning problems, eager to help, have frequently turned to visual training programs. These efforts have generally been so unrewarding that the American Academy of Pediatrics, the American Academy of Ophthalmology and Otolaryngology, and the American Association of Ophthalmology have issued a joint statement contending that visual training is ineffective in treating learning disabilities and may even cause a delay in proper treatment (Dreby, 1979).

Our advice to teachers who work with severely disabled readers is to be critical of programs that offer simplistic solutions to complex visual perception problems. The validity of most programs remains questionable.

Hearing

A second important physical factor which can contribute to reading ability is hearing. Hearing, like vision, is comprised of two distinct subcategories: acuity and discrimination. To understand fully how hearing acuity and discrimination are related to reading, we need to examine each more closely.

Acuity   Although the ability to hear clearly is not essential to learning to read (after all, deaf students learn to read), unless spoken sounds are received and transmitted without significant distortion, progress may not occur at a normal pace. And since learning to read is so closely related to language development, it is imperative that obstacles to faulty hearing are overcome as soon as possible.

To better understand how we hear, allow us to present a simplified explanation. The ear consists of three major parts: outer ear, middle ear, and inner ear. We normally see only the outer ear, or auricle, which collects the sounds we eventually hear.

The middle ear consists of the eardrum and three bones: the malleus (hammer), the incus (anvil), and the stapes (stirrup) (see Figure 4-3). Sound waves generally strike the eardrum, which sets up a series of vibrations that move from the eardrum to the hammer and on to the anvil and then to the stirrup.

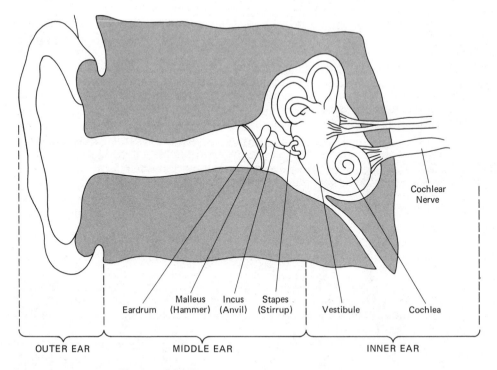

Cochlear
Nerve

| Eardrum | Malleus (Hammer) | Incus (Anvil) | Stapes (Stirrup) | Vestibule | Cochlea |

OUTER EAR   MIDDLE EAR   INNER EAR

Figure 4-3 Simplified Diagram of the Ear

The inner ear consists of the vestibule, which is connected to part of the middle ear, the cochlea, and the cochlear nerve. Vibrations are turned into nerve impulses inside the coiled cochlea and then are transmitted to the brain by the cochlear nerve.

Although the actual process is more complex than we have described, the idea we wish to communicate is that sound is transmitted by vibrations through a series of connected bones until nerve endings are stimulated. This, in turn, is translated into sounds. Obviously, should any part of this intricate mechanism fail to operate properly, a hearing loss may result.

Teachers are frequently quick to observe that a student may suffer from some hearing abnormality. A discharge or drainage of the ears, a cupping of the hand behind the ear, complaints of buzzing in the ears, strained or unnatural speech, and the need to tilt the head or body while listening are all signs of a potential hearing loss. Students with suspected problems should be referred immediately to the school nurse or the speech and hearing specialist.

Hearing acuity is usually measured with an instrument such as the Western Electric Model 4C Audiometer or the Beltone Audiometer. Audiometers are designed to measure two facets of sound: intensity (loudness) and frequency (pitch). Intensity is measured in decibels, and frequency is measured in cycles per second. To give you some referents, a whisper usually registers 15 decibels; a

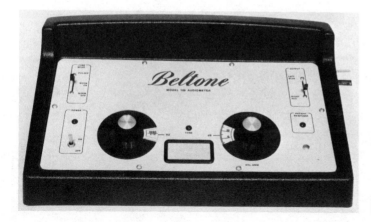

Figure 4-4 Beltone Audiometer

jet airplane flying 100 feet away produces a sound of approximately 140 decibels. Frequency, the other facet of hearing ability, is probably more important as far as reading instruction is concerned. The human ear can usually discern frequencies between 20 and 20,000 cycles per second. The lowest note on a piano occurs at 27 cycles per second whereas the highest piano note is at about 4,000 cycles per second. A person with a hearing range of 50 to 10,000 cycles per second has adequate auditory acuity to enjoy a full symphony orchestra.

The Beltone Audiometer measures a person's hearing at ten selected frequencies (cps):

125 cycles per second
250 cycles per second
500 cycles per second
750 cycles per second
1,000 cycles per second
2,000 cycles per second
3,000 cycles per second
4,000 cycles per second
6,000 cycles per second
8,000 cycles per second

In addition, the intensity at which each of these frequencies can be heard can be adjusted over a wide range of settings. Thus, a profile of a student's hearing threshold (minimum level at which sound can be detected) can be mapped for both left and right ear. Students who receive abnormal profiles can be referred to a certified otologist for more extensive testing and/or treatment.

Figure 4-5 is a profile of an actual child's hearing. You will notice that the left ear's hearing thresholds are recorded with an "X"; the right ear with an "O". (Remember, thresholds are described as the lowest setting, dB, at which a particular frequency can be heard.) The hearing threshold in the left ear was

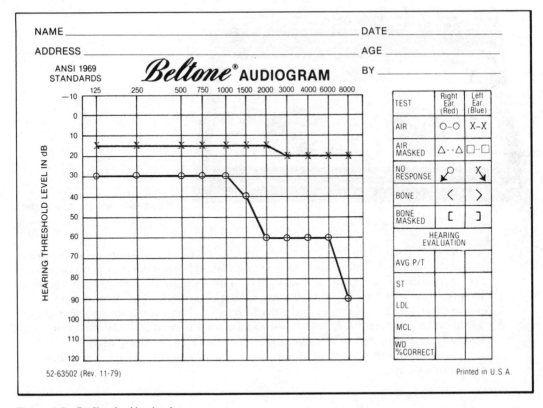

Figure 4-5 Profile of a Hearing Loss

relatively constant at 15dB until the 3,000 cps frequency was encountered. At that level, a 20dB setting was needed before the student could discern a tone. The 20dB setting was the threshold level for the 4,000, 6,000, and 8,000 cps frequencies as well. In summary, the profile of acuity for the left ear is relatively stable and no significant hearing loss is apparent.

The profile of right ear acuity, however, reveals a strikingly different picture. From the 125 to 1,000 cps range, the threshold of hearing was at 30dB. At 1,500 cps, it increased to 40dB; at 2,000 to 6,000 cps, the threshold was recorded at 60dB; and at the 8,000 cps level, the lowest level at which the sound could be heard was at 90dB. This profile reveals a student with a severe right ear hearing loss at the higher frequencies. This child could have difficulty learning to read if a highly phonic reading system was used for instruction, since many of the consonant sounds are relatively high-pitched and hence might not be heard.

DISCRIMINATION Although the evidence supporting the necessity of good auditory acuity as a prerequisite for progress in reading is clear, the role of auditory discrimination is open to question. A review of the literature in this area reveals that the relationship between auditory discrimination and reading ability is tenuous at best.

If we accept the common definition of auditory discrimination to mean the ability to hear likenesses and differences between minimally contrasting word pairs (for example, *pat* and *pot*), we may begin to appreciate the problems of trying to assess or teach auditory discrimination. Suppose, for example, you gave a test of twenty word pairs. The student was to respond "same" or "different" to each pair. In order to insure that you were, indeed, actually measuring the student's ability to hear these differences, the following testing conditions must exist:

1.   Both examiner and student must speak the same dialect.
2.   If the second word of the pair is the same as the first, it must be reproduced in an acoustically identical fashion.
3.   The child must completely understand the task, including the concepts of "same" and "different."
4.   No visual or extraneous clues can be made available to the student.
5.   No extraneous sounds or distractions can be present while testing takes place.

From our experience, these five conditions seldom, if ever, occur simultaneously in testing.

Regardless of this fact, auditory discrimination tests and materials continue to be used uncritically in the teaching of reading. For example, educators continue to accept auditory discrimination test scores as unquestionable evidence of whether or not a student is an "auditory learner." In our opinion, such practices lack empirical support and may actually inhibit progress in reading by misdirecting instructional efforts.

For those who are interested in examining tests that purport to measure auditory discrimination, though, the following might be reviewed:

Wepman Auditory Discrimination Test (1973)

Goldman-Fristoe-Woodcock Test of Auditory Discrimination (1970)

Roswell-Chall Auditory Blending Test (1963)

Again, however, we caution you that such instruments should be scored and interpreted with caution. We do not recommend their use for students who speak black dialect or for whom English may be a second language. The lack of match between the phonemes of standard English and a foreign language will invalidate any test scores.

Health

If students are to make progress in reading, they need to be free of health problems that may impede learning. It is difficult for individuals to attend to instruction if they are hungry, tired, chronically ill, or suffer from allergies.

One area of health that is sometimes neglected is eating habits. Occasionally children are left to make their own breakfasts. In many instances, they come to school without any type of early-morning nourishment. Learning how to read when the primary concern is hunger is difficult at best.

Many communities require a yearly physical examination before a child can be enrolled in school. This practice permits health problems to be identified before they interfere with learning. Nevertheless, teachers need to be continually on the lookout for signs that may point to a student's ill health. Complaints of nausea and headaches, runny noses, persistent coughing, and fatigue are just a few of the signs that may indicate poor health.

Having children with allergies, we feel especially compelled to alert teachers to the discomforts allergic students must face. Pollen, house dust, animal dander, grass, and certain foods are some of the items that can trigger an allergic reaction. Shortness of breath, coughing, and a persistently runny nose accompanied by sneezing are usually the symptoms of an allergy. Frequently, allergic children have problems sleeping at night. Asthma, which often accompanies the allergies, compounds the problem. These students sometimes miss several consecutive days of school. Although desensitization shots are available to help these individuals, treatment is a long-term process. In the meantime, frequent absenteeism may persist, and gaps in reading skill development may occur as a consequence.

Park and Schneider (1975) tried to connect abnormal health and reading disabled students. By analyzing blood samples, they were able to correctly identify those students who were classified as dyslexics. They concluded that functional dyslexia is associated with a systematic change in metabolism related to thyroid functioning.

At present, though, teachers of the reading disabled are better off being suspicious of efforts to identify reading disabled students through extensive pediatric workups. Such efforts are only in the embryonic stages, and for the most part, the findings are inconclusive. Besides, most school districts don't enjoy the luxury of having a pediatric neurologist available to assist in day-to-day diagnosis.

Neurology

During the past decade, there has been a resurgence in the interest in neurological functioning and its relationship to reading disorders. This is in part attributable to the field of learning disabilities (LD) and the political support it has received. According to Myklebust, students with a learning disability suffer from a poor organization of the intellect, and hence, the cognitive process is modified (Wallbrown et al., 1975).

Recent studies have attempted to discern the role of the two hemispheres of the brain and how they respectively affect reading acquisition. For the most part, the left hemisphere is believed to handle the comprehension of written material, language, and other higher-order mental functions (Benson, 1976; Giordano, 1978). The right hemisphere, on the other hand, is responsible for lower-level functions (for example, form discrimination). Researchers and educators have speculated that in order for fluent reading to take place, both hemispheres must be fully developed, lateralized, and integrated. Poor readers, it was hypothesized, could be identified from fluent readers by abnormal hemispherical development (Vernon, 1977).

Although there are documented cases where lesions (an injury or wound) or infarctions (an area of dying or dead tissue caused by a deprived blood supply) have resulted in an inability to read (alexia), these cases are relatively uncommon and hence are rarely encountered by most school personnel.

Nevertheless, there is still the belief that some students do suffer from a neurological deficit which impairs their reading. Sometimes called minimal brain dysfunction (MBD), or brain damage, these labels have been used to classify students who for various reasons have failed to learn to read. Basically, our belief is that MBD becomes a catchall label for the school's failure to educate.

Black (1976) states that

> . . . the results of the perceptual and achievement comparisons . . . do not demonstrate the educational utility of the "brain damage" syndrome or syndromes. Children with both suspected and documented neurological dysfunction . . . appear to be similar in nature and should respond to remedial efforts without an undue emphasis upon labeling or differential diagnosing. (p. 187)

Bateman (1974) claims that labels such as MBD are irrelevant to educational practice and have provided nothing more than a sophisticated, supposedly respectable excuse for poor teaching. According to her, "Any one or even all of the characteristics said to accompany MBD can also be found in children labelled normal, gifted, emotionally disturbed, disadvantaged, mentally retarded, and so on" (p. 663). She contends that the term "learning disabled" should be replaced by "teaching disabled," thereby reflecting the shift in emphasis from a pathological disorder to a teaching disorder.

Eaves and his associates (1974) were led to offer similar advice to educators. Speaking of neurological labels assigned to students, they said such descriptors have little practical significance for the teacher since they do not imply a specific prescription, a standardized form of therapy, or remediation.

The brain behavior of reading and learning disabled subjects was also studied by Rourke (1975). Using electroencephalogram (EEG) profiles, he was unable to discern significant relationships between them and performance on psychological tests by learning disabled students.

Our advice to teachers is not to become enamored by medical terminology and unfounded theory when working with reading and learning disabled students. To date, efforts to identify either group through the use of neurological examinations have failed. Moreover, unique instructional techniques do not exist which can guarantee a simple solution to students with severe reading problems.

PSYCHOLOGICAL FACTORS

The relationships among intelligence, self-concept, emotional well-being, and reading have long been recognized and studied. At the turn of the century Huey (1908) wrote,

> And so to completely analyze what we do when we read would be the acme of a psychologist's achievements, for it would be to describe very many of the most intricate workings of the human mind, as well as to

unravel the tangled story of the most remarkable specific performance that civilization has learned in all history. (p. 6)

Now, nearly a century later, psychologists and educators continue to examine how the mind and body interact during the reading process. In this section, we will explore how intelligence, self-concept, and emotional stability are related to learning to read.

Intelligence

A complex relationship exists between intelligence and reading. Morphett and Washburne (1931) claimed that children must have a mental age of at least 6.5 years before they have a reasonable chance of learning to read. Gates (1937) in a critique of Morphett and Washburne's investigation demonstrated that mental age, per se, was not nearly as important a factor in learning to read as was the degree of individualized instruction the students received.

Although there is a moderate correlation between intelligence and reading ability, most authorities agree that this is primarily caused by the fact that highly intelligent students read very well whereas less capable students often do not. If we were to examine the majority of students, however, say those with intelligence quotient scores between 85 and 115, we would probably find a low correlation between intelligence and reading ability. Our experiences as classroom teachers, reading teachers, professors of reading, and directors of reading clinics has repeatedly demonstrated to us the fact that many highly intelligent students fail to learn how to read and yet their less gifted peers sometimes have no difficulty whatsoever.

If the correlation between intelligence and reading is suspect, you are probably wondering why intelligence tests continue to be used in schools and reading clinics. In our judgment, there are two reasons for this. First, the measurement of intelligence has historical significance in psychology and education. These tests have been given to students for so many years that it is difficult to concede that their use should be terminated. A second and more defensible purpose is that intelligence tests frequently help to identify those problem readers who have the potential or capacity to do better. These are the students on whom reading teachers should concentrate most of their efforts and whom we described in Chapter 2 when discussing expectancy formulas.

Since intelligence tests will no doubt continue to be used in our nation's schools, teachers should be aware of the different kinds available. The best type of intelligence tests to use with nonreaders or disabled readers (or any students for that matter) are those that are individually administered. Group-administered intelligence tests frequently require students to be able to read. Obviously, a student who has limited reading ability will be penalized by receiving a depressed test score. Scores from group-administered intelligence tests or those that require reading should be considered suspect. Perhaps an even greater problem with IQ tests centers on the very concept of measuring intelligence. It is difficult to agree on what factors describe this nebulous thing called "intelligence." Does it comprise a language component, a performance component, both, or neither of these factors? Implicitly, these issues are all related to test validity; that is, "does the test measure what is sets out to measure?" If these issues can be resolved, there is still the question of how and on whom the test was normed. Unfortunately, many questions of test validity defy simple answers.

Since intelligence testing receives so much emphasis in education, teachers should be familiar with some of the commonly administered instruments. We have chosen to describe briefly four tests since they have often been used in schools and reading clinics around the country: (1) the Wechsler Intelligence Scale for Children–Revised, (2) the Stanford-Binet Intelligence Scale, (3) the Peabody Picture Vocabulary Test, and (4) the Slossen Intelligence Test.

Wechsler Intelligence Scale for Children–Revised

The Wechsler Intelligence Scale for Children (WISC) was originally published in the late 1940s but was revised in 1974 and is now called the Wechsler Intelligence Scale for Children–Revised (WISC-R) (1974). The basic difference between the two instruments is that the latter covers a slightly older age range (six years, zero months, to sixteen years, eleven months). The WISC-R contains a total of twelve subtests entitled the same as the subtests found on the original WISC. The subtests and a brief description of each follow.

Information. Like its predecesor in the WISC, this subtest includes thirty items. Precise responses are required that measure an individual's available information obtained through native endowment and cultural experience.

Similarities. This is a seventeen-item subtest which measures verbal concept formation. This subtest might be thought of as measuring a student's verbal comprehension.

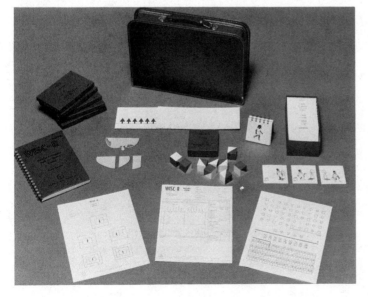

Figure 4-6 Wechsler Intelligence Scale for Children—Revised

Arithmetic. This subtest is a series of eighteen timed items which require the direct counting of concrete quantities, simple addition, subtraction, division, and multiplication. A few items require more advanced performance.

Vocabulary. This subtest measures word knowledge. These thirty-two items are generally considered to be an excellent measure of a student's intelligence. Since it is a vocabulary test, experiential and educational background probably have some bearing on the student's performance.

Comprehension. This subtest attempts to assess an individual's "common sense" through seventeen questions asked by the examiner. The examiner must exercise subjective judgment in scoring this subtest.

Digit Span. In this subtest subjects are asked to repeat a series of between two and nine digits spoken by the tester. Some of the digit sequences are required to be reproduced in reverse order. Attention and short-term memory play an important part in this test.

Picture Completion. This subtest has twenty-six items that require subjects to recognize pictures and identify the missing parts. Concentration, reasoning, perception, and judgment are just a few of the abilities which are tapped. Unless students can discern essential from nonessential items, this test may prove difficult.

Picture Arrangement. This twelve-item subtest requires arranging complete frames in a correct sequence. Basically, this is a nonverbal test of reasoning ability. Anticipation, judgment, and antecedent-consequence abilities are measured.

Block Design. On this subtest eleven items, all timed, assess the subject's ability to organize perceptual information. Patterns on a series of blocks are broken down and then reassembled to match a given pattern. Motor ability and color vision may have some bearing on test scores.

Object Assembly. This is one of the shorter of the WISC-R subtests. Only four items are included, each a jigsaw puzzle. The puzzles include a car, a manikin, a horse, and a face. The test requires visual perception and visual-motor coordination.

Coding. This is a two-part subtest in which subjects are asked to print a coded sequence of shapes or symbols from a given sequence. This is a test of psychomotor speed which measures visual-motor coordination, short-term memory, and speed of thinking.

Mazes. This subtest includes nine mazes which require a subject to possess good planning ability as well as visual-motor control. All items are timed by the examiner.

After all the subtests have been completed, the WISC-R scores are combined and reported as verbal, performance, or full scale scores. Each of these major subsections has an extremely high reliability estimate. The WISC-R test

Figure 4-7   Stanford-Binet
Intelligence Scale

should be given only by a qualified individual who has been trained in its administration and interpretation.

Stanford-Binet Intelligence Scale

The 1960 Form L-M of the Stanford-Binet Intelligence Scale (1973) represents the latest in a series of revisions which the instrument has undergone since the early 1900s. The test is appropriate for subjects ranging from two years to adult. It includes over 100 subtests, many of which assess a verbal component. Unfortunately, like many intelligence tests, it fails to measure a student's originality or creativity. Nevertheless, it has undergone extensive validity and reliability reviews and continues to be one of the frequently used instruments to measure children's intelligence.

Peabody Picture Vocabulary Test

Unlike the two previously described instruments, the Peabody Picture Vocabulary Test (PPVT) (1970) can be administered with only minimal training. It consists of 150 numbered plates, each one illustrating four clearly drawn line drawings. The examiner asks the subjects to identify one of four pictures on a plate in response to the examiner's directions. The subjects need only point to the correct response. Plates are arranged from easy to difficult throughout the booklet. Administration time is approximately fifteen minutes, although the test is untimed. The test is appropriate for most school-age children, and alternate forms are available.

Since the test is a measure of familiarity with vocabulary, some subjects may receive inaccurate scores (Neal, 1976). In our experience, minority students frequently tend to receive depressed scores compared to their middle-class peers simply because they may be unfamiliar with some of the "middle-class" pictures. Interpreting scores for these culturally different subjects must be done cautiously. Generally, the WISC-R and the Stanford-Binet are considered to be more accurate measures of academic ability than is the PPVT.

Figure 4-8   Peabody Picture Vocabulary Test

Slosson Intelligence Test

The Slosson Intelligence Test (SIT) (1974) is similar to the PPVT in that a relatively untrained examiner can administer it in less than thirty minutes. Some of the items are adaptations from the Stanford-Binet.

Essentially, the test consists of a series of questions asked by the examiner (for example, "Milk is white. Butter is ————."). The questions or tasks become increasingly more difficult. Since the test is primarily a measure of vocabulary, language-deficient subjects will tend to score lower than expected.

Since many of the items on the SIT are similar to those on the Stanford-Binet, the overall scores of the two tests correlate highly. Like the PPVT, the SIT can be used by reading specialists who wish to gain a general measure of a student's intelligence. And like the PPVT, the SIT is not a substitute for the WISC-R or the Stanford-Binet.

Self-Concept

Anyone who has taught can testify how one's self-concept can quickly be affected by failure to learn to read. Nonreaders and poor readers may become emotionally unstable, antagonistic, and inattentive and may lack the social confidence of their better-reading peers. At the lower elementary grades, these symptoms may be less pronounced; instead, students with reading problems may act immature, be indecisive, seem insecure, or lack motivation.

Students with reading difficulties are often unsure of themselves. They may perform well above average in mathematics, science, and physical education, but for some reason, they haven't been able to learn to read. Given enough time, students with even the best self-concept will soon begin to question their worth if they do not learn to read. Once this happens, negative behavior can rapidly develop and learning becomes even more difficult.

Parents play an important role in a child's development of a self-concept. Their overt and covert behaviors toward their children are quickly perceived as the child continues to grow and develop. One not so humorous incident occurred not long ago with a child in our reading clinic. During a conference with a parent of one of our disabled readers, the mother remarked, "Oh, John is retarded just like all his other brothers!" This is hardly the kind of comment that encourages a positive self-concept.

Teachers, too, can affect their students' self-concept. We have known individuals who continually belittle and yell at their students for no apparent reason. The introverted student is especially susceptible to suffering under these conditions. Obviously, such behavior on the part of teachers cannot be tolerated.

Because self-concept and reading disability are so interrelated, it is usually difficult to determine whether the disability caused the poor self-concept or vice versa. The important consideration, however, is not so much how the two are interrelated but what can be done to improve the self-concept. That is the subject we'll explore in detail in Chapter 9, "Motivating Students to Read."

Emotional Factors

Emotional difficulties, self-concept, and reading disabilities are often closely related. Emotional difficulties, unlike self-concept, however, are related to adjustment difficulties students with reading problems may encounter. One fourth-grade student exemplifies how emotional problems may interfere with learning. The child's mother was blind and her older brother was using illegal drugs. Several years earlier, she had seen her father commit suicide. Now, she was trying to learn to read while continually having to deal with an unsettled home environment. To seek attention, she resorted to blurting out profanities during reading instruction. Her acting out behavior and the need for recognition severely inhibited her learning to read.

There are other types of emotional disorders which can also inhibit learning. The child coming to school for the first time may become tense and unable to attend to instruction. Occasionally, highly successful parents will inadvertently pressure their child to the point where the student refuses to learn in an attempt "to get even." Some students will simply avoid learning to read since there is a chance to fail. Rather than risk failure, they refuse to become intellectually involved in any type of instruction.

Reading teachers who encounter students with emotional problems should not hesitate to seek the assistance of other professionals. Guidance counselors, social workers, psychologists, and psychiatrists are trained to help individuals whose learning is impaired. A team approach is usually more fruitful than trying to tackle the problem by yourself.

SOCIOLOGICAL FACTORS

There is growing evidence that sociological factors are influencing students more than we once thought. The home environment, cultural expectations, socioeconomic level of the family, and the language patterns learned before entering school have been found to contribute to the learning-to-read process. In this section we will explore the impact each of these areas has on the students' learning and see how our pluralistic society affects reading behavior.

Home Environment

It is a well-established axiom that a child's first teacher is his or her parents. By the time most children reach kindergarten, they have already begun to establish beliefs and attitudes toward education. For the most part, these feelings are learned behaviors reflecting the perceptions of their parents toward learning in general and about schools in particular.

Many professionals believe that the most important part of parenting involves the first five years of a child's life. During this preschool period, in some families, many activities revolve around short trips to parks, zoos, museums, aquariums, and the like. These outings are designed to expose young children to a myriad of experiences, all of which will, their parents hope, contribute to success in school. To reinforce these adventures, parents may read to the children about each activity once a trip is concluded.

Napoli (1968) reported that substantial differences occur in the homes of good versus poor readers. Books and reading materials, for example, are seldom discussed in the homes of poorer readers. Better readers also read more often as a leisure-time activity.

The dynamics of the family unit also can vary between families with good or poor readers. Peck and Stackhouse (1973) contend that "Reading problem families apparently have taught the child how not to learn and the child has reciprocated by developing the art of being stupid" (p. 510). They also point out that parents in families with poor readers are notoriously poor decision-makers, apparently caused by poor communication among family members.

Finally, Flood (1977) reports that parent-child interaction during reading episodes varies widely among homes. Parents who encourage questioning by their children during reading are apt to witness positive gains. Reinforcing the child's questioning and providing poststory evaluative questioning also contributes to reading growth. Obviously, families that don't foster reading in the home cannot benefit from these episodes.

Cultural Expectations

The role that societal pressures play in producing reading failures has been a topic of interest throughout the years. Some researchers would have us believe that reading problems are so intimately linked to our cultural expectations there is little if anything that can be done to change the matter.

There is one fact that is indisputable when examining the literature on reading failures: boys with reading disabilities far outnumber girls. The exact ratio is difficult to pin down, but estimates range from as low as 2:1 to as high as 10:1. Naiden (1976), found that males outnumbered females by approximately four to one in the learning disability classes in the Seattle public schools. Wanat (1971) states that 90 percent of the referrals to reading clinics in the United States are boys.

The reasons for this occurrence are unclear. Some authorities contend that boys exhibit more undesirable classroom behavior and hence may not pay attention during instruction. Others point out that most primary-grade teachers are females, which might have some bearing on male students' performance. A few believe that society conditions children to behave in predetermined patterns, which in turn influence school behavior. Each of these positions appears to have some merit.

Anyone who has taught in the primary grades has noticed the behavioral differences between boys and girls. This was made especially clear to one of the authors after viewing a videotape of a lesson he had done with a group of kindergarten students. The girls in the group sat patiently and attentively throughout the lesson. The boys, on the other hand, were less attentive and more active. We have observed this phenomenon in many classrooms throughout the country.

To gain a greater understanding of the role culture plays in determining reading achievement, Johnson (1976) examined the reading ability of second- fourth-, and sixth-graders in four English-speaking countries: England, Nigeria, Canada, and the United States. Interestingly, he found that boys scored better than girls in England and Nigeria, whereas the opposite was true in the two North American countries. He conjectured that this difference was due in part to cultural expectations. In the United States and Canada, for example, young boys are encouraged to participate in nonacademic endeavors such as sports. As they reach late adolescence and adulthood, however, they are expected to turn to academics as a preparation for college or employment.

Preston (1979) tried to determine if the sex of the teacher might account for the performance difference between males and females. Klein (1979) had pointed out that in Germany, for example, reading retardation is more pronounced in females. Since most primary-grade teachers in Germany are male, it might be possible that female children fail to identify with male instructors. Preston did not find this to be the case, however. In his study, female teachers were more successful with both sexes than were the male teachers (pp. 524–25). Thus, sex role identification between youngsters and their teachers does not seem to be a critical factor in learning to read.

Socioeconomic Levels

Implicitly, the socioeconomic level of a student's parents is related to the home environment and to some degree the language that the child uses. It is difficult to determine where the influence of one factor ends and the other begins. Generally speaking, students who come from high socioeconomic backgrounds have higher reading scores than those from low socioeconomic backgrounds. Within all levels, however, there are cases of reading disability as well as a share of outstanding readers.

Perhaps your state department of education tests the reading ability of students from various communities within your state. If they do, and if you could compare the average income and test scores of the many communities, you would probably notice a positive relationship between median family income and a district's average reading performance. Over the years, this positive correlation has continued to exist. According to Entwisle (1977) speech and child-rearing practices—both closely related to socioeconomic levels—may explain in large part why this difference exists. This theory was also supported by both Allington (1979) and Sawyer (1979) who report that the students who end up in compensatory reading classes typically come from lower socioeconomic classes.

Language

A rich verbal background is necessary for both comprehension and effective use of the three decoding strategies students commonly use: phonological, semantic, and syntactic (Vellutino, 1977). Exactly how language assists in these functions was discussed in detail in Chapter 3, "Understanding The Reading Process."

Although the importance of language in learning to read has been documented, there are still several misconceptions regarding language that teachers should be aware of. One of the most serious relates to the relationship between black dialect and reading. Some teachers mistakenly believe that black English is a deficient system when compared to standard English. This is simply not true. In appropriate social contexts, black children are as verbal as most white middle-class children. Furthermore, the interaction between mothers and their children is as great as it is in nonblack families. What does appear to hinder many black children from becoming better readers is that many come from lower socioeconomic classes and hence do not have the same experiential backgrounds as other students. Also, too few teachers recognize the problems that arise when a highly phonic approach is used with speakers of black dialect. In essence, a communications breakdown occurs because of the mismatch between systems of standard English and black dialect. Phonic interference (the inability to hear all the phonemic sounds of a language) results, and students are unable to comprehend and complete some of the assignments. This is no place more evident than when teachers try to get speakers of black dialect to discriminate among short vowels—especially the short *e* and *i*. In black dialect, these two sounds are homophones and hence are indistinguishable.

A second misconception is that some popular tests can diagnose students' linguistic capacities and thereby permit appropriate remedial effort to be planned and implemented. One such test is the Illinois Test of Psycholinguistic Ability (ITPA) (Kirk *et al.* 1968). According to Newcomer and Hammill (1975) this test is used extensively to measure the abilities which supposedly underlie language development. However, studies have clearly shown that the specific subtests within the ITPA lack this ability. Newcomer and Hammill go on to state,

> One may conclude therefore that the existing research indicates that diagnosed psycholinguistic strengths and weaknesses based on the ITPA performance of school-aged children cannot be viewed as having any relationship to a child's observed difficulties in at least one basic skill— reading. (p. 738)

Hammill *et al.* (1975) and Newcomer *et al.* (1975) also found this statement to be true.

Thus, we can safely say that (1) language is an important correlate of learning to read, (2) socioeconomic considerations are more intimately related to reading ability than are ethnic characteristics of the student, and (3) some tests designed to diagnose underlying linguistic processes appear to lack any practical use.

EDUCATIONAL FACTORS

It is ironic that schools, the institutions designed to educate our youth, are responsible for creating a substantial number of reading failures. Although it is impossible to estimate the exact percentage of reading disability cases caused by inappropriate teaching, we are led to believe that between a third and a half of all problems children encounter when learning to read are caused by educational factors.

There are a variety of reasons why schools, and specifically teachers, contribute to reading failures. In this section we will explore how instructional level, pace, and materials affect a student's progress. We will also see how teaching methods can influence reading progress. In conclusion, we shall examine how teachers directly affect the ways students learn.

Instructional Level

If students are to learn to read, they must use material that is challenging but not so difficult that it becomes frustrating. In other words, students should never be asked to read at their frustrational level. Yet as we visit classrooms and talk to children, it becomes abundantly clear that many students are asked to read materials that are much too difficult. Not only are their reading textbooks too challenging but also their social studies and science texts are written at even more advanced levels. It is an unfortunate truism that many students are required to read materials daily that are too advanced for them. Such requests soon lead to frustration, anger, and frequently, inappropriate behavior.

On the other hand, there are some students whose reading abilities are so advanced that they soon become bored unless challenged. We have seen this phenomenon occur more often in affluent communities. Many of these "average" students are making satisfactory progress but their teachers force them to demonstrate mastery of unnecessary skills in order to progress to the next reading level. Before long these students lose interest in assignments and fail to pay attention.

It is important to understand the necessity of placing students at their correct reading level. Being able to recognize the majority of words and to comprehend meanings frees students to use additional energies to decode occasional unfamiliar words. But being forced to apply continually a host of word identification skills in every sentence will soon lead to a rejection of reading. Without sufficient practice, it is unrealistic to expect reading growth.

Instructional Pace

Complementing instructional levels is the idea of determining a student's correct instructional pace. It is difficult to accept the idea that all individuals should learn the same material at the same rate. As one educational sage so aptly stated, "Good instruction should increase the differences among children." Unfortunately some teachers gear their instructional pace to only the average learner.

If reading problems are to be averted, teachers must be sensitive to the fact that many students need additional skills. Teachers who have a wealth of educational materials are probably more able to cope with this problem than are those who either by choice or necessity stick to only one text or pace. To a degree, criterion-referenced tests (mastery tests) have enabled more teachers to determine whether students indeed have learned specific units of content. Used judiciously, these instruments should help educators determine the correct instructional pace for each student.

Instructional Materials

Most educators, regardless of the level at which they teach, are continually searching for additional instructional materials. Yet it is not the materials that ultimately help problem readers overcome their disability. It is the teacher who makes the real difference. Nevertheless, teachers can be more effective if they have appropriate materials.

One of the most serious problems teachers face in working with poor readers is finding suitable and sufficient materials written at low reading levels yet possessing a high interest level. The majority of books found in school libraries are too difficult for poor readers. But unless easy-to-read materials are available, these students will do little if any recreational reading, something they desperately need if they are to overcome their reading problems.

Teaching Method

By and large, no one method of reading instruction has been found to be superior over any other method. But regardless of what method is used, there are two important areas which contribute to reading problems.

Within the past few years, we have increasingly noticed an erroneous conception of reading on the part of problem readers. Many of these nonreaders have received such an extensive and intensive drilling on phonic principles that they perceive the phonic cueing system as being the only technique that can unlock unfamiliar words. They tell us they have continually been admonished to "sound it out." Unfortunately, their teachers have neglected to acquaint them with how the semantic and syntactic cueing systems can also be used—usually more efficiently—to decode unfamiliar words. Since these students use only the most laborious decoding technique, it is no wonder that many have negative attitudes about reading.

A second problem is the lack of consistency among teachers. We are not implying that all teachers should use the same method. But it seems to us that a coordinated, systematic, schoolwide attempt should be made to see that some general principles of reading instruction are followed. The use of testing materials, a policy of independent reading, the use of the library, and the role of phonics are just a few of the areas related to instructional method. If one teacher uses an intensive phonic program, another uses only the language-experience approach, and a third uses an individualized library reading program, it is only natural that students become bewildered. Consistency of purpose must be part of the school reading program.

Teachers

It has long been said that the teacher is the most important educational variable affecting instruction. Until recently, however, not much was known about which characteristics were the important variables. Educators and researchers are now beginning to identify these characteristics, and we hope that training programs will be designed and implemented to improve the quality of teachers of reading. Some factors that have been demonstrated to be related to good teaching include (1) the quality of attention students receive (Emans and Fox, 1973), (2) diagnostic ability of the teacher (Powell, 1969), (3) organizational ability (Powell, 1969), (4) the teacher's knowledge (Powell, 1969), and (5) the amount of time students spend reading (Artley, 1975).

Another factor is the amount of effort expended in teaching. According to Blair (1976), there are three types of teachers: those who perform less than the minimum requirements of teaching; those who perform the minimum requirements satisfactorily but seldom go beyond what is expected (these two groups, according to Blair, comprise the largest percentage); and those who go beyond the minimal requirements of the job. Unfortunately, according to Blair, this last group is small in number. In studying pupils' performances and teachers' efforts, he found that teachers who made the effort to (1) teach diagnostically, (2) use a variety of materials to meet individual needs, (3) differentiate instruction according to ability, (4) keep records on students' work, and (5) maintain close contact with interested persons concerning a student's progress produced significantly better achievement from their pupils than someone who didn't put forth an equal effort. In other words, good teachers are conscientious; mediocre teachers aren't.

Others have found similar results. Lambert and Hartsough (1976), using a different measurement than Blair, found that good teachers used a greater variety of teaching activities, worked more closely with their students, and interacted with children more frequently than did their less effective peers. Good teachers of reading spend time planning, assigning, and supervising reading lessons. Instructional time and pace are carefully adjusted for the students. Furthermore the classroom has a good learning atmosphere. All in all, the conditions for learning are carefully controlled by the teacher (Harris, 1979).

We need to make one last point about how reading teachers might have a positive effect on their students. Presumably, teachers serve as models for their students. It seems hypocritical, then, to expect students to become avid readers when most teachers read very little themselves. Data presently available show that teachers read few professional journals and seldom read books (Mour, 1977). Should we be surprised that our own students are reluctant readers?

SUMMARY

By now you can see that learning to read successfully depends on a number of important factors. Physical, psychological, sociological, and educational abnormalities can contribute to the incidence of reading problems.

Good vision and hearing are important if learning is to take place, especially in reading. Not only must students be able to see and hear clearly but also they must be able to discern fine differences in visual and auditory stimuli. In addition, they must be free of any major health problems as well as have an adequately operating neurological system.

In order to progress satisfactorily in school, students must receive instruction that is appropriate to their intellectual abilities. Their intellectual and academic growth will to some degree affect their self-concept as well as their emotional health. If students have poor self concepts or if they suffer from emotional difficulties, there is a high probability that their reading performance will suffer.

Four areas that are intimately linked and over which teachers have only limited control are home environment, cultural expectations, socioeconomic level, and the child's language. These factors are so intertwined that it is difficult to determine the exact bearing each contributes to learning problems. Together, however, they are a major influence on the degree to which students succeed or fail once they enroll in school.

Although it is difficult to manipulate the sociological factors related to reading disabilities, educational factors are under the direct control of teachers, administrators, and publishers of curricular materials. If the number of reading problems is to be reduced, students need to use appropriate materials and progress at a rate commensurate with their ability. Teachers, too, need to know about various methods of teaching so that they will be able to use the approach that offers the best chance of reducing the incidence of failure. As we have already stated, and will continue to emphasize throughout this text, teachers, to a large degree, are ultimately responsible for the success or failure of their students.

RELATED ACTIVITIES

1. Arrange to have a physician or a vision specialist speak to your class. Ask the specialist to address the issue of reading disabilities from his or her perspective. Compare how your ideas about reading problems are similar or different from those of the guest speaker.
2. Arrange to examine the WISC–R intelligence test. Review several sources to see what they say about using specific subtests for differential diagnoses.
3. Record the language of children from a variety of socioeconomic classes. Compare their language patterns and describe how these patterns might affect their reading ability.
4. Visit a school and examine the different ways reading is taught. Might any of these practices have a bearing on the reading ability of students? Make a list of the "exemplary" practices as well as those that might be changed.
5. Interview five teachers in one building. Ask them to describe what they believe to be the major causes of reading disability. Compare your findings with someone else who did a similar "study" in another building or district.

RELATED READINGS

CALFEE, ROBERT C., AND PRISCILLA A. DRUM, EDS. *Teaching Reading in Compensatory Classes.* Newark, Del.: International Reading Association, 1979.

GUTHRIE, JOHN T., ED. *Aspects of Reading Acquisition.* Baltimore, Md.: The Johns Hopkins University Press, 1976.

JOBE, FRED, W. *Screening Vision in Schools.*

Newark, Del.: International Reading Association, 1976.

LAFFEY, JAMES L., AND ROGER SHUY, EDS. *Language Differences: Do They Interfere?* Newark, Del.: International Reading Association, 1973.

OTTO, WAYNE, NATHANIEL A. PETERS, AND CHARLES W. PETERS. *Reading Problems: A Multidisciplinary Perspective.* Reading, Mass.: Addison-Wesley, 1977.

REFERENCES

ALLINGTON, RICHARD L. "Communities and Schools." In *Teaching Reading in Compensatory Classes,* pp. 19–39. Robert Calfee and Priscilla Drum, eds. Newark, Del.: International Reading Association, 1979.

ARTLEY, A. STERL. "Good Teachers of Reading—Who Are They?" *The Reading Teacher,* 29, no. 1 (Oct. 1975), 26–31.

BATEMAN, BARBARA, D. "Educational Implications of Minimal Brain Dysfunction." *The Reading Teacher,* 27, no. 7 (Apr. 1974), 662–68.

BENSON, D. FRANK. "Alexia." In *Aspects of Reading Acquisition,* pp. 7–36. John T. Guthrie, ed. Baltimore and London: The Johns Hopkins University Press, 1976.

BLACK, F. WILLIAM. "Cognitive, Academic, and Behavioral Findings in Children with Suspected and Documented Neurological Dysfunction." *Journal of Learning Disabilities,* 9, no. 3 (Mar. 1976), 182–87.

BLAIR, TIMOTHY. "Where to Expend Your Teaching Effort (It Does Count!)." *The Reading Teacher,* 30, no. 3 (Dec. 1976), 293–96.

DREBY, CATHERINE. "'Vision' Problems and Reading Disability: A Dilemma for the Reading Specialist." *The Reading Teacher,* 32, no. 7 (Apr. 1979), 787–95.

EAVES, L. C., D. C. KENDALL, AND J. U. CHRICHTON. "The Early Identification of Learning Disabilities: A Follow-up Study." *Journal of Learning Disabilities,* 7, no. 10 (Dec. 1974), 632–38.

EMANS, ROBERT, AND SHARON FOX. "Teaching Behaviors in Reading Instruction." *The Reading Teacher,* 27, no. 2 (Nov. 1973), 142–48.

ENTWISLE, DORIS R. "A Sociologist Looks at Reading." In *Reading Problems: A Multidisciplinary Perspective,* pp. 74–88. Wayne Otto, Charles W. Peters, and Nathaniel Peters, eds. Reading, Mass.: Addison-Wesley, 1977.

FLOOD, JAMES E. "Parental Styles in Reading Episodes with Young Children." *The Reading Teacher,* 30, no. 8 (May 1977), 864–67.

FROSTIG, MARIANNE. *Developmental Tests of Visual Perception.* Palo Alto, Calif.: Consulting Psychologists Press, 1966.

GATES, ARTHUR I. "The Necessary Mental Age for Beginning Reading." *Elementary School Journal,* 37 (1937), 497–508.

GIORDANO, GERALD. "Convergent Research on Language and Teaching Reading." *Exceptional Children,* 44 (May 1978), 604–11.

Goldman-Fristoe-Woodcock Test of Auditory Discrimination. Circle Pines, Minn.: American Guidance Service, 1970.

HAMMILL, DONALD, LIBBY GOODMAN, AND J. LEE WIEDERHOLT. "Visual-Motor Processes: Can We Train Them?" *The Reading Teacher,* 27, no. 5 (May 1974), 469–78.

HAMMILL, DONALD, RANDALL PARKER, AND PHYLLIS NEWCOMER. "Psycho-Linguistic Correlates of Academic Achievement." *Journal of School Psychology,* 13, no. 3 (July 1975), 248–54.

HARRIS, ALBERT J. "The Effective Teacher of Reading, Revisited." *The Reading Teacher,* 33, no. 2 (Nov. 1979), 135–40.

HUEY, EDMUND BURKE. *The Psychology and Pedagogy of Reading.* Cambridge, Mass.: The MIT Press, 1908.

JOBE, FRED W. *Screening Vision in Schools.* Newark, Del.: International Reading Association, 1976.

JOHNSON, DALE D. "Cross-Cultural Perspectives on Sex Differences in Reading." *The Reading Teacher,* 29, no. 8 (May 1976), 747–52.

KIRK, S. A., J. J. MCCARTHY, AND W. D. KIRK. *Illinois Test of Psycholinguistic Abilities.* Urbana, Ill.: University of Chicago Press, 1968.

KLEIN, HOWARD A. "A Closer Look at Cross-Cultural Sex Differences in Reading." *The Reading Teacher,* 32, no. 6 (Mar. 1979), 660–64.

LAMBERT, NADINE M., AND CAROLYN S. HARTSOUGH. "APPLE Observation Variables as Measures of Teacher Performance." *Journal of Teacher Education,* 27 (Winter 1976), 320–23.

MORPHETT, MABEL, AND CARLTON WASHBURNE. "When Should Children Begin to Read." *Elementary School Journal,* 31 (Mar. 1931), 496–503.

MOUR, STANLEY, I. "Do Teachers Read?" *The Reading Teacher,* 30, no. 4 (Jan. 1977), 397–401.

NAIDEN, NORMA. "Ratio of Boys to Girls Among Disabled Readers." *The Reading Teacher,* 29, no. 5 (Feb. 1976), 439–42.

NAPOLI, JOSEPH. "Environmental Factors and Reading Ability." *The Reading Teacher,* 21, no. 6 (Mar. 1968), 552–57, 607.

NEAL, ANNIE W. "Analysis of Responses to Items on the Peabody Picture Vocabulary Test According to Race and Sex." *The Journal of Educational Research,* 69, no. 7 (Mar. 1976), 265–67.

NEWCOMER, PHYLLIS, AND DONALD D. HAMMILL. "ITPA and Academic Achievement: A Survey." *The Reading Teacher,* 28, no. 8 (May 1975), 731–41.

NEWCOMER, PHYLLIS, BETTY HARE, DONALD HAMMILL, AND JAMES MCGETTIGAN. "Construct Validity of the Illinois Test of Psycholinguistic Ability." *Journal of Learning Disabilities,* 8, no. 4 (Apr. 1975), 220–31.

PARK, GEORGE, AND KENNETH A. SCHNEIDER. "Thyroid Function in Relation to Dyslexia (Reading Failures)." *Journal of Reading Behavior,* 7, no. 2 (Summer 1975), 197–99.

Peabody Picture Vocabulary Test. Circle Pines, Minn.: American Guidance Service, 1970.

PECK, BRUCE B., AND THOMAS W. STACKHOUSE. "Reading Problems and Family Dynamics." *Journal of Learning Disabilities,* 6, no. 7 (July 1973), 506–11.

POWELL, WILLIAM R. "The Effective Reading Teacher." *The Reading Teacher,* 25, no. 7 (Apr. 1969), 603–607.

PRESTON, RALPH C. "Reading Achievement of German Boys and Girls Related to Sex of Teacher." *The Reading Teacher,* 32, no. 5 (Feb. 1979), 521–26.

Roswell-Chall Auditory Blending Test. New York: Essay Press, 1963.

ROURKE, BYRON P. "Brain-Behavior Relationships in Children with Learning Disabilities." *American Psychologist,* 30 (Sept. 1975), 911–20.

SAWYER, DIANE. "A Profile of Children in Compensatory Reading Programs." In *Teaching Reading in Compensatory Classes,* pp. 40–53. Robert Calfee and Priscilla Drum, eds. Newark, Del.: International Reading Association, 1979.

Slosson Intelligence Test. New York: Slosson Educational Publications, 1974.

Stanford-Binet Intelligence Scales. Boston: Houghton-Mifflin, 1973.

VELLUTINO, FRANK. "Alternative Conceptualizations of Dyslexia: Evidence in Support of a Verbal Deficit Hypothesis." *Harvard Educational Review,* 47 (Aug. 1977), 334–54.

VERNON, MAGDALEN, D. "Varieties of Deficiency in the Reading Process." *Harvard Educational Review,* 47, no. 3 (Aug. 1977), 396–410.

WALLBROWN, JANE, FRED H. WALLBROWN, ANN W. ENGIN, AND JOHN BLAHA. "The Prediction of First Grade Reading Achievement with Selected Perceptual-Cognitive Tests." *Psychology in the Schools,* 12 (Apr. 1975), 140–49.

WANAT, STANLEY F. "Language Acquisition: Basic Issues." *The Reading Teacher,* 25, no. 2 (Nov. 1971), 142–47.

Wechsler Intelligence Scale for Children–Revised. New York: The Psychological Corporation, 1974.

Wepman Auditory Discrimination Test. Chicago: Language Research Associates, 1973.

5

DIAGNOSIS AND WORD IDENTIFICATION

Upon completion of this chapter, you will be able to

1. Discuss the following assumptions and principles of diagnosis:
   a. Testing is influenced by a teacher's understanding of both reading and diagnosis.
   b. Diagnosis should assist in decision making.
   c. Diagnosis includes a study of the reader as a person.
2. List decisions which may be made on the basis of word identification tests.
3. Describe the administration and interpretation of the following kinds of tests:
   a. Informal word identification.
   b. Connected text.
   c. Language-experience assessment.
4. Discuss skills management systems and explain their advantages and disadvantages.

INTRODUCTION TO DIAGNOSIS

Diagnosis, the assessment of students' strengths and weaknesses in reading, is always the first step in instruction. This "getting to know you" process entails the use of a variety of informal and formal measures. You may, for example, check students' cumulative folders for information about past performance, administer a battery of tests, or listen to students read from familiar and unfamiliar material. You will also try to learn about your students' interests, personalities, and goals because you realize that success in reading depends not only on the transmission of skills but also on an understanding of the total person.

You would be particularly interested in collecting diagnostic information if you were assigned several underachieving readers. Kevin, who is typical of the group, has had a long history of reading failure. You suspect that he knows only a handful of words and has acquired few skills. You have heard that his usual litany is, "Do I have to read today?" In view of both his extreme difficulty and his negative attitude, you will want to conduct a thorough diagnosis of his reading ability before attempting to correct his problems.

Identifying students' word identification abilities is just one step in a thorough reading evaluation.   (Peter P. Tobia)

Tests, Diagnosis, and Observation

Frequently, when confronted with disabled readers, a first reaction might be to search for a test that is easy to administer, can be scored in minutes, and provides an in-depth diagnosis of the students' problems. We believe that such a test does not exist. Furthermore, the role of tests is often overemphasized in diagnosis. In reality, two other factors, observation and an understanding of reading play a much more critical role.

Observation is important because it focuses on a variety of student behavior on a day-by-day basis. Application of learned skills, for example, is difficult to test in a formal manner. Students may have been taught to identify main ideas but their use of this skill in everyday reading can best be evaluated by observing their performance.

Understanding the reading process is also essential. Scoring the tests is usually straightforward, but an interpretation of the scores requires an informed teacher. Unless a teacher is knowledgeable about the process of diagnosis and reading, a file cabinet of test scores will provide little help in decision making.

Diagnostic Assumptions

All discussions about diagnosis are based on certain assumptions about the diagnostic process. It is important to become aware of these assumptions since they invariably influence our decisions.

NATURE OF DIAGNOSIS   First, the selection and interpretation of tests are influenced by the teacher's understanding of diagnosis. Generally, two perspectives—or models—of diagnosis are commonly employed: the disease model and the developmental model (Ozer, 1977). The disease model, the art of recognizing a disease from its symptoms, is borrowed from the medical profession. This model implicitly asks where the deficiency is located and what caused it. Unlike its use in the field of medicine, the disease model of reading diagnosis does not locate the deficiency in an organ of the body or a specific area of the brain. Instead it speaks of "pinpointing" the difficulty in terms of weaknesses in a process or a skill (for example, auditory discrimination, drawing conclusions).

One problem with pinpointing is the presumption that a tested deficiency is the source of a student's difficulty in reading (Sawyer, 1974). If a student doesn't know vowel sounds, it may be concluded that the source of the deficiency has been located. However, two equally valid alternative interpretations exist. First, the student may not be ready to learn vowels. In this case, teaching vowel sounds would be an inappropriate solution. Second, McNeil (1974) has shown that both good and poor readers can possess the same skills and yet differ in reading ability. Thus, a direct correspondence may not necessarily exist between a specific skill deficiency and reading behavior. Specific deficiencies may simply be symptoms of inability to read.

The disease model emphasizes locating the cause of the difficulty. In reading diagnosis this presents another dilemma. First, a number of causes (poor teaching, parental neglect, nutritional deficiencies) rather than a single factor may have combined to depress students' reading ability. Furthermore, school records are often sketchy and memories of teachers and parents fade quickly, so determining the cause(s) of the disability is difficult. More important, knowledge of the cause is most helpful if a true medical condition exists and can be remedied. If, for example, the students' difficulties are due to poor visual acuity, and the problem can be corrected with eyeglasses, a knowledge of the cause can aid remediation. If, on the other hand, the causes are nonmedical in nature and occurred in the past, they cannot be undone. It is preferable, therefore, to deal with current, overt behavior rather than search for underlying causes of the difficulty.

This does not mean that background information is of little value in the diagnostic process. We see three possible uses for the study of causality. In some instances, understanding the cause can influence the manner in which teachers set expectations for the student. If, for example, a child was often absent in first grade because of illness and was also exposed to several substitute teachers that year, the student's problem may be due to lack of continuous, systematic instruction, and barring other difficulties, the problem should be easily remedied when more adequate teaching is provided. Pinpointing the cause of the disability may also make teachers more sympathetic to the student's plight. When we learn of a student's wretched past, we may be more willing to accept the student's low achievement. Finally, in some cases, knowledge of possible causes may relieve the anxiety of both parents and teachers. If the student, for example, has a bona fide physical problem, parents and teachers may be more accepting of the present behavior and be less tormented by guilt—"We must have done something wrong with this child"—or less likely to blame the victim—"He's just lazy. He could read if he tried." In none of these instances, however, does a knowledge of the cause tell us how to develop the student's basic reading abilities.

The study of observable behavior leads to a discussion of the developmental model, a model we believe is more satisfactory in diagnosing reading difficulties. The developmental model asks, "What can the student do? What does the student need? What will help the student?" (Ozer, 1977). The first question suggests that diagnosis should emphasize students' assets. All positive behavior, both personal and reading related, should be accentuated. Although the identification of deficiencies is a part of the diagnostic process, testing that does no more than catalog shortcomings is not only discouraging to the student but also suggests a pessimistic prognosis to those who review the diagnostic report or must work with the student. A young Asian refugee, for example, lacked many reading abilities, including sight vocabulary, phonics, and structural analysis. In this case, emphasis was rightfully placed on the student's curiosity about the world, strong desire to learn to read, and ready acquisition of English. Another use of the developmental model is the interpretation of oral reading errors (miscues) as evidence of students' language and meaning competencies rather than weaknesses in word identification. If instruction should begin where the student is, it would seem appropriate that diagnosis should begin there also and stress the student's assets.

The second question in the developmental model is "What does the student need?" Need is determined by the gap between performance and expectation and may include needs in sight vocabulary, word attack and comprehension strategies, rate of reading, and study skills. It is not essential to list all needs, simply those that require immediate attention.

The third question, "What will help the student?" implies that diagnosis interacts with teaching. Diagnosis is not merely a prelude to instruction but should be embedded in the teaching-learning process. Thus, diagnosis is a continual process in which teachers observe students' reading and reading-related behavior (tests, formal and informal, and daily observation) and plan flexible instructional programs in response to their changing performance.

Continual diagnosis implies that the assessment of pupils' behavior occur in virtually every teacher-pupil contact and that it consists chiefly of teacher observation rather than formal tests. Too often a student is sent off to be diagnosed and then returned to the original instructional setting with a sheaf of recommendations. Initial diagnosis, which is the focus of this chapter, is simply the beginning of the diagnostic process. After several instructional sessions teachers can learn more about the student from careful observation than from any amount of formal testing. Initial testing, for example, rarely provides time to collect sufficient data on oral reading errors, but opportunities for collection and analysis are available on a day-to-day basis every time a student reads aloud.

NATURE OF READING   A second assumption of diagnosis is that the teacher's view of the reading process affects the diagnostic procedures which are employed. If teachers believe that reading is essentially a bottom-up decoding process they will be more likely to select tests which emphasize word identification skills, particularly phonics. On the other hand, if they feel that reading is a top-down meaning-gathering process which relies heavily on the reader's language background, they are more likely to test words in context and select instruments that assess comprehension abilities.

Our own view is that reading is an interactive process and relies on both bottom-up and top-down processing. We believe that the question is not "Should decoding or meaning be emphasized (particularly in beginning reading)?" but "How can we best balance the need of the reader to employ both decoding and meaning?" A result of this view is that although we sometimes test words and assess phonic skills in isolation, we also evaluate word identification abilities through miscue analysis, a system for judging the quality of students' errors in word identification. In miscue analysis, stress is placed on the reader's use of semantic and syntactic cueing systems as well as the graphophonic.

Principles of Diagnosis

A thorough diagnosis involves the collection of considerable information and can be a very complex process. Before describing the technical procedures in diagnosis, we present two guiding principles. They focus on decision making and the need to know the reader as a person.

DECISION MAKING   The purpose of diagnosis is to help make instructional decisions. Test scores and related data are useful only when they can be translated into reading programs for students. One way to check on the usefulness of test results is to see if the data assist in decision making. If they don't, the use of these particular instruments should be seriously questioned.

A focus on decision making can help to determine the amount and type of testing required in a specific situation. If, for example, new students are assigned to a class and the teacher needs to place them quickly (and temporarily) in a basal text, it may be sufficient to administer a very informal word identification test. If, on the other hand, the teacher is diagnosing students who have failed to develop a sight vocabulary, despite average intelligence and several years of school, a more in-depth analysis may be required. In both instances, the kind of decision helps to determine the extent of the evaluation.

Another advantage of a decision-making emphasis is that it encourages parsimonious testing. By this we mean that once the teacher has determined the questions to be asked, the collection of overlapping data can be avoided and the time saved can be used for direct instruction. Equally as important is the fact that poor readers are often unable to attend to tasks for lengthy periods of time. If testing is overlong, students' responses may reflect their distractability rather than their optimal reading behavior. Furthermore, overtesting can contribute to an aversion to future evaluation.

A decision-making emphasis is particularly helpful if the teacher must test an entire classroom of students. For those students whose records indicate they are reading at grade level, the teacher need only confirm this judgment by asking them to read orally and recall information from a basal or trade book at that grade level. Additional diagnosis would be needed only if the teacher were still uncertain of their reading ability. Students who score low on word identification or comprehension tests and those already classified as corrective or remedial readers would also require a more thorough evaluation.

A plea for a decision-making approach may seem to belabor the obvious. We have frequently observed two situations, however, in which this principle is disregarded and testing appears to serve no useful purpose other than to accumulate test scores. In the first instance, numerous norm-referenced tests are administered and the results are reported as raw scores, percentiles, grade equivalents, and stanines. Unfortunately, the implications these scores have for instruction is frequently not forthcoming. That is, the tests serve to describe students but are not used to prescribe an instructional program.

Another example takes place when students reading at a primer level are given extensive batteries of tests when in many instances the necessary information for decision making could be obtained from an informal word identification test and a quick language-experience assessment. There is no need in this instance to administer test after test which contain duplicate information, unnecessary information (for example, blending of phonic elements), or information we could have safely predicted without further testing.

DIAGNOSIS OF THE INDIVIDUAL   The original meaning of the word *diagnosis* provides the basis for the second principle. The word first meant "to know thoroughly" and is composed of two parts, *dia* meaning "through" or "thoroughly," "to distinguish" or "discern," and *gnosis* meaning "to learn to know" (Klein, 1966; Murray, 1897). Further study of *dia* implies a knowing acquired by taking apart or looking through an object, perhaps dividing it in the middle, much as we would slice open an orange to see it "through the middle" (Liddell and Scott, 1940).

The etymology of *diagnosis* suggests to us that it consists not only of a knowledge of students' assets and liabilities in reading but also an assessment of the student as a person. The most challenging task confronting reading teachers

1. Name
2. Address
3. Telephone
4. Age   Birthday
5. Family members (including ages of siblings)
6. Present school and teacher(s)
7. Present grade
8. Previous schools and grades
9. Friends and ages
10. Activities with friends
11. Radio interests (Do you listen to the radio? What do you listen to? What is your favorite station?)
12. Television interests
13. Hobbies
14. Clubs or organizations
15. Sports
16. Travel/Vacations
17. Reading (Do you read? What do you read? How often? When?)
18. Reading class (What do you do in the reading class?)
19. What kind of reader do you think you are? (With elementary students you may wish to draw a vertical line on the paper and say, "Suppose the best reader in your class is at the top and the worst reader is at the bottom. Mark the line to show where you are.")
20. Favorite and worst subjects in school
21. Sentence completion (Read the statements to the student and ask the student to finish the sentence orally.)
    1. My favorite color is
    2. My best friend is
    3. I wish I could
    4. I think that school
    5. The thing that bothers me most
    6. Boys
    7. My brother (sister)
    8. I am afraid when
    9. Girls
    10. I wish I could be like _____ because
    11. I like
    12. I don't like
    13. My mother
    14. I get mad when
    15. It is easy for me to
    16. I never want to
    17. My father
    18. Inside
    19. Outside
    20. At night
22. Three wishes
23. Career aspirations

Figure 5-1 Individual Interview Schedule

is often not instruction in reading skills but overcoming student discouragement and reluctance to participate in learning activities. An understanding of students' lifestyles, and their views of themselves both as readers and persons, is the first step in obtaining this cooperation.

The Interview

There are many informal ways to become acquainted with disabled readers. One method is to be a good listener. Students are usually willing to talk, particularly if they detect a sympathetic ear. If we listen, we can learn how they view themselves. You'll want to listen with the so-called "third ear" in which you tune in to the feelings being expressed as well as the actual information the student is transmitting.

A more systematic approach for getting acquainted with the student is by using an Individual Interview Schedule. A sample schedule (Figure 5-1 on page 69) provides several questions to help accomplish this objective.

Frequently, responses gathered during the interview will give you insights into why a word identification or comprehension problem exists in the first place. Thus, interviewing and word identification testing should not be thought of as mutually exclusive components of a reading diagnosis but instead should be considered as complementary steps to determine the underlying difficulties.

An interview schedule is used most effectively if teachers follow a few simple rules. First, do not feel obliged to complete the entire schedule. Not all questions apply to every student, nor does every question lead to significant information. Omit much of the biographical data when interviewing high school students and adults and concentrate on a discussion of their reading ability, past schooling, and future goals. Second, ask additional questions to follow up on atypical responses. Students, for instance, can be expected to say that recess is their best subject in school, but if they say it is their worst, be sure to ask why. Third, maintain a neutral attitude toward responses. Indicate acceptance by repeating the response (for example, "You play hockey every morning before school.") or responding to the feelings expressed ("You feel that reading is hard for you.") and reacting nonverbally through an occasional nod of the head. Avoid outright approval ("Isn't it wonderful that you do the laundry for the entire family?") or rejection ("Can't you think of a better way to spend your time than watching television or pitching pennies?").

Interview students even if you think you already know them well. An individual interview can often reveal a dimension of the student not apparent in the typical classroom. Even if you interviewed the student last year, repeat the process. The student may have matured and developed new interests and outlooks. The annual interview can help you keep abreast of these changes.

DIAGNOSING WORD IDENTIFICATION ABILITIES

The remainder of this chapter will be devoted to the diagnosis of students' abilities in word identification. Tests of word identification provide a quick though tentative assessment of instructional level, the level at which students can function comfortably under teacher direction. They can also be used to tap students' word identification skills and strategies. This information will help teachers make three instructional decisions: (1) temporary placement of the student in a book or reading group, (2) selection of skills the student should be immediately taught, and (3) strategies the student needs to employ while reading connected text.

There are a number of reasons for conducting an evaluation of word identification abilities before assessing comprehension. Although the evaluation of words and word attack abilities is specific, an assessment of comprehension is considerably broader and diffuse. Furthermore, testing students' word identification ability can usually be accomplished quickly. This assessment can also readily determine the level at which students should be evaluated in comprehension. Of course, no diagnosis is complete until students' comprehension has been measured.

Although word identification and comprehension are intimately related, our decision to discuss word identification and comprehension in separate chapters is made deliberately. The temporary separation of these topics will allow us to focus on that aspect of reading which distinguishes it from other mental activities—the printed word. Since many poor readers have serious word identification problems but can understand oral material at much higher levels, this is another reason for temporarily dealing with this area apart from comprehension. We believe that it is better to diagnose word identification ability before becoming involved in the more complex area of comprehension.

Word identification, as we've noted, cannot be completely divorced from meaning and comprehension. Words are a means toward understanding the author's message, not an end in themselves. Not even the most ardent proponent of a decoding emphasis believes that word identification is the ultimate goal of instruction. Furthermore, facility in recognizing words is influenced by context, and this requires an understanding of the selection. In some cases, individual words cannot be identified until the reader comprehends the message the writer is trying to communicate (Smith, 1978). The pronunciation of the word *lead* in the sentence "We have no lead," for example, is ambiguous. It is only when the sentence is presented in a fuller context, such as a sign in a gasoline station window, that we are able to identify it correctly. Thus, word identification is closely linked to comprehension and cannot be entirely separated from the understanding of the text.

Word identification tests which we will examine in this chapter are divided into two types: informal screening tests and tests of words in connected text (context).

INFORMAL WORD IDENTIFICATION TESTS

The informal tests of word identification have been described as "quick and dirty." Constructed by arranging words from basal readers and word lists such as Thorndike and Lorge's *The Teachers' Word Book of 30,000 Words* (1944), they are simple to administer, can be completed in minutes, and provide a tentative instructional level. They are "dirty" in that they test words in isolation and do not measure comprehension or the use of context. This lack reduces the applicability of their results to normal reading. Despite these limitations, the fact that a high correlation exists between the identification of isolated words and reading words in connected text (Spache, 1976) justifies their use for initial screening and placement.

The administration of these tests is straightforward. Students are shown individual words and are given a few seconds to identify each one. The use of isolated words requires students to identify a word by sight or through phonics and/or structural analysis, not through context.

Several informal word identification tests have been developed and are frequently used by reading specialists. Some of the most popular instruments are

San Diego Quick Assessment (LaPray and Ross, 1969).
Harris-Jacobson Core Lists (Harris and Sipay, 1980).
Wide Range Achievement Test (Jastak *et al.*, 1981).
Slosson Oral Reading Test (Slosson, 1963).
Peabody Individual Achievement Test (Dunn and Markwardt, 1970).
Queens College Tests (Harris, 1970).

We have found the San Diego Quick Assessment to be an especially suitable device for quickly and tentatively determining students' instructional reading level. The test (Figure 5-2) is administered as follows:

1. Type out each list on a separate index card. For primary-age children, use a primary typewriter.
2. Identify the level of each list in code. One method is to write a series of digits and letters at the top of the card with the second and third symbols identifying the level; for example 6PPA is the preprimer list, and 804T is the fourth-grade list.
3. Begin one level below a student's suspected reading level, if you have information about reading performance. It is generally a good practice to begin testing on a level on which students are likely to succeed. This will encourage them to attempt the more difficult lists.
4. If no information about the student's reading performance is on hand, begin with the first list. Ask the student to read down the list until he or she makes two or more mistakes on two successive lists. Terminate testing when scores drop below eight, as in Student A's case:

STUDENT A

LEVEL	PERCENT CORRECT
PP	100
P	80
1	40

As the student reads, keep a mental note of the number of words read correctly and record this number and the reading level in a convenient location

Reader _____			Tested by _____	
Age _____ Grade _____			Date of Test _____	

PP	P	1	2	3
see	you	road	our	city
play	come	live	please	middle
me	not	thank	myself	moment
at	with	when	town	frightened
run	jump	bigger	early	exclaimed
go	help	how	send	several
and	is	always	wide	lonely
look	work	night	believe	drew
can	are	spring	quietly	since
here	this	today	carefully	straight

4	5	6	7
decided	scanty	bridge	amber
served	certainly	commercial	dominion
amazed	develop	abolish	sundry
silent	considered	trucker	capillary
wrecked	discussed	apparatus	impetuous
improved	behaved	elementary	blight
certainly	splendid	comment	wrest
entered	acquainted	necessity	enumerate
realized	escaped	gallery	daunted
interrupted	grim	relativity	condescend

8	9	10	11
capacious	conscientious	zany	galore
limitation	isolation	jerkin	rotunda
pretext	molecule	nausea	capitalism
intrigue	ritual	gratuitous	prevaricate
delusion	momentous	linear	risible
immaculate	vulnerable	inept	exonerate
ascent	kinship	legality	superannuate
acrid	conservatism	aspen	luxuriate
binocular	jaunty	amnesty	piebald
embankment	inventive	barometer	crunch

Figure 5-2 San Diego Quick Assessment of Reading Ability Score Sheet   From Margaret LaPray and Ramon Ross, "The Graded Word List: Quick Gauge of Reading Ability," *Journal of Reading*, 12, no. 4 (Jan. 1969), 305–307. Reprinted with permission of Margaret LaPray, Ramon Ross, and the International Reading Association.

(for example, on the back of the interview sheet). Do not record the errors themselves, as this slows down the testing. The highest level at which the student scores 80 percent is considered the tentative instructional level.

Scores on the San Diego Quick Assessment can be used to place the student tentatively in an appropriate basal reader and/or reading group. Some adjustments for comprehension will undoubtedly be necessary, but the initial placement has taken only a few minutes. The speedy administration of this test is an important advantage if you work with many students. Another advantage is that testing can be easily terminated if the student performs poorly on the initial lists, sparing the student unnecessary embarrassment.

LaPray and Ross (1969) found that scores on the test agreed with classroom teachers' judgments in 96 of 100 cases. Remember, however, the test does not measure comprehension, so it can be considered only a preliminary judgment of reading ability. Furthermore, placement may be less accurate beyond the primary grades and even speculative past sixth grade since comprehension plays an increasingly larger role as grade levels progress.

Other informal tests differ in that each word can be presented twice to the student. The reader's first exposure to a word on the list is on a timed or "flash" basis in which a word is shown very quickly—less than a second—and then covered. This is intended to assess the reader's sight vocabulary. If the student cannot identify the word from a timed exposure, the word is presented again, and the student is given additional time to analyze it. The second exposure measures the student's ability to analyze words more thoroughly on the basis of phonic, structural, and orthographic cues. These tests also consist of randomly selected words from basal reader lists or lists of high frequency words. They tend to be longer and thus more reliable. Their length, though, also increases the administration time of the test.

The word lists begin at the preprimer level and generally terminate at grade six. It is reasoned that if students can successfully read words at the sixth-grade level they have mastered the essential word identification skills and can read most words in their listening vocabulary. Students who perform well at the sixth-grade level and still exhibit reading difficulties usually have problems in comprehension, rate, or attitude.

Some informal reading inventories, both the commercial and teacher-made varieties, present words in both timed and untimed formats. If you use a commercial version, directions for their administration and interpretation may vary somewhat from these instructions. Some current commercial informal reading inventories are listed here:

Analytical Reading Inventory (Woods and Moe, 1981).

Diagnostic Reading Scales (Spache, 1972).

Durrell Analysis of Reading Difficulty (Durrell, 1980).

Standard Reading Inventory (McCracken, 1966).

Diagnostic Reading Inventory (Jacobs and Searfoss, 1979).

The Contemporary Classroom Reading Inventory (Rinsky and de Fossard, 1980).

Informal Reading Assessment (Burns and Roe, 1980).

Classroom Reading Inventory (Silvaroli, 1976).

Construction

If you do not wish to use a commercial instrument, you can always construct your own informal word identification test by following these steps:

1. Randomly select twenty words each from the basal reader preprimer and primer levels and twenty-five words each from grades one to six. Formerly it was possible to select these words from the new vocabulary lists at the end of each basal reader. The use of these lists for this purpose has become increasingly difficult as publishers have liberalized their concept of vocabulary control. Many words are introduced in primary texts for purposes of interest and may not be repeated in subsequent stories. Furthermore, publishers are relying less on specific vocabulary to control the readability of the selections. As a result, vocabulary lists are often not available beyond the primary grades. In some series they are not supplied at any level.

As an alternative, a number of high frequency word lists have been developed from which words may be randomly chosen: the Johnson Basic Vocabulary for Beginning Readers (1971), the Harris-Jacobson Basic Elementary Reading Vocabularies (1972), and the Dolch Word List (1955).

2. Prepare a teacher's booklet by typing the words at each grade designation vertically on $4\frac{1}{4}$-by-11-inch sheets. It is preferable to use primer type, particularly if you are testing young children. Number each word and double-space the typing. The booklet will be more durable if it is covered with a file folder which extends just beyond the edges of the pages. Figure 5-3 shows a page from the teacher's booklet.

3. Prepare copies of a student response sheet on which to record students' reactions to the words. Type each list vertically with the words double-spaced on a separate $8\frac{1}{2}$-by-11-inch sheet. At the top of the page, list the grade designation and number each word to correspond with the teacher's booklet. Two response columns, "Flash" and "Untimed," are provided. Prepare multiple copies of the response booklet as each student requires a separate copy. Figure 5-4 illustrates a page from the response booklet.

Administration

To administer the test you will need the following:

1. Teacher booklet containing all the vocabulary lists.
2. Student response booklet (one booklet for each student to be tested).
3. Pencil or pen.
4. Two 3-by-5 index cards.

Sit next to the student. If you are right-handed, sit to the student's right; if left-handed, to the student's left. This position allows you to present the words without obstructing the student's view. Ordinarily, begin with the first list unless you believe that the student can read at a higher level.

Say to the student, "I am going to show you some words. First, I will show you each word quickly. If you need another look at a word, I will show it to you again." Open the teacher's booklet to the first list and immediately cover the first words with the index cards. Place the cards so that if you were to lower the

1. around
2. bike
3. book
4. car
5. father
6. goat
7. him
8. house
9. know
10. man
11. now
12. one
13. pet
14. saw
15. show
16. some
17. thank
18. too
19. train
20. yellow

Figure 5-3 Informal Word Identification Test—
Teacher's Booklet

bottom card, the first word would be exposed. Be sure you have the reader's attention before "flashing" the word. Lower the bottom card to expose the word and then cover it instantly with the second card. The exposure time will ordinarily be less than a second, but should be conducted smoothly so that the reader is not distracted by any awkward movements. If the flash exposure creates undue anxiety or resistance on the part of the student, allow a longer flash exposure, but note this on the response sheet. The student's response to the word is also recorded on the student response sheet.

PREPRIMER READER LEVEL

| | Response | |
Stimulus	Flash	Untimed
1. and	_____	_____
2. at	_____	_____
3. big	_____	_____
4. call	_____	_____
5. come	_____	_____
6. did	_____	_____
7. dog	_____	_____
8. for	_____	_____
9. funny	_____	_____
10. go	_____	_____
11. have	_____	_____
12. help	_____	_____
13. I	_____	_____
14. is	_____	_____
15. little	_____	_____
16. make	_____	_____
17. mother	_____	_____
18. no	_____	_____
19. play	_____	_____
20. red	_____	_____
Percent Correct	_____	_____

Figure 5-4 Informal Word Identification Test—Response Booklet

PRIMER READER LEVEL

Stimulus	Response	
	Flash	Untimed
1. around	_____	_____
2. bike	_____	_____
3. book	_____	_____
4. car	_____	_____
5. father	_____	_____
6. goat	_____	_____
7. him	_____	_____
8. house	_____	_____
9. know	_____	_____
10. man	_____	_____
11. now	_____	_____
12. one	_____	_____
13. pet	_____	_____
14. saw	_____	_____
15. show	_____	_____
16. some	_____	_____
17. thank	_____	_____
18. too	_____	_____
19. train	_____	_____
20. yellow	_____	_____
Percent Correct	_____	_____

Figure 5-4 (*Continued*)

To save time, move to the next higher list if the student reads the first ten words correctly (see Figure 5-5, PrePrimer List). The score on this list is pro-rated; that is, the score is based only on the words actually presented. Discontinue testing when the student misses about every other word on a flash basis. Testing on this last list may also be terminated after the first ten words and scored on a prorated basis. If, for example, the student (Figure 5-5, Third Reader List) incorrectly identifies six of the first ten words, stop testing and compute the score (40 percent) on the basis of responses to these ten words.

Recording Procedures

The second-grade list of Figure 5-5 illustrates the recording procedures:

1. If the student knows the word correctly on either a flash or untimed response, make no marks on the scoring sheet. This saves administration time, particularly when the student must read many lists (see word 1).
2. If the student substitutes a word (for example, word 5), write it in the appropriate column. Record all words the student calls out (word 16). If the response is a pseudoword (word 12), write it as best as possible, using diacritical marks, accents, and syllabication.
3. If the student does not respond to a word, draw a line (word 15) through the flash or untimed column.
4. If a student self-corrects a word (words 17 and 22) on the flash response (that is, the student reads the word incorrectly and then immediately says the word correctly), record the initial incorrect response and then place a check alongside the word. This check will affect the final word identification score.

In addition to the formal scoring, record the students' verbal reactions. Some students, for example, rationalize their inability to read the words with statements like "I really knew that one. . . . That was a stupid mistake. . . . I didn't get a good look at that word." Other students express discouragement: "I never knew how to read those words. . . . I'm really dumb in reading."

Note any apparent strategies. Some students will seek out "little words" in big words, spell the words letter by letter, or try to sound out every word.

Scoring and Interpreting

Each list is scored by comparing the correct words with the number of words in the list. In the first-grade list (Figure 5-5) the student knew fifteen of the twenty words on a flash presentation and therefore received a score of 75 percent. Since all words known on flash would also be known on the untimed presentation, these words are automatically counted as correct, and the student is given credit for eighteen of the twenty correct, or 90 percent. When a word in the flash column has been checked, indicating that the student self-corrected an error, points are added to the basic flash score. In the second-grade list (Figure 5-5) the student received no credit for the initial response but is given four points (the number of points for each word is determined by the total number of words in the list) for each of these words on a "plus" basis. In this case the

PREPRIMER READER LEVEL

	Response	
Stimulus	Flash	Untimed
1. around	_____	_____
2. bike	_____	_____
3. book	_____	_____
4. car	_____	_____
5. father	_____	_____
6. goat	_____	_____
7. him	_____	_____
8. house	_____ P.R.*	_____
9. know	_____	_____
10. man	_____	_____
11. now	_____	_____
12. one	_____	_____
13. pet	_____	_____
14. saw	_____	_____
15. show	_____	_____
16. some	_____	_____
17. thank	_____	_____
18. too	_____	_____
19. train	_____	_____
20. yellow	_____	_____
Percent Correct	_____	_____

*Prorated.

Figure 5-5 Recorded and Scored Informal Word Identification Test

FIRST-READER LEVEL

	Response	
Stimulus	Flash	Untimed
1. as		
2. bee		
3. brown		
4. coat		
5. does		
6. fight		
7. friend	freed	—
8. had		
9. her		
10. it's		
11. long	—	
12. morning	mor —	
13. or		
14. picture	pick	
15. ready		
16. sing		
17. street	string	string
18. thing		
19. truck		
20. way		
Percent Correct	75	90

Figure 5-5 (*Continued*)

Stimulus	Response Flash	Untimed
1. aunt		
2. bone	done	
3. button		
4. clear		
5. dad	bad	
6. each		
7. face		
8. float	flat	
9. grandfather		
10. honey		
11. keep		
12. library	lī b-ray	libby
13. mind	mid	mid
14. number		
15. people	—	—
16. queer	creed, queen	queen
17. rope	rap ✓	
18. shape	shop	
19. slide	slice	slid
20. star		
21. swish	wish	
22. tiny	tinny ✓	
23. ugly		
24. wide		
25. you'll		
Percent Correct	52 + 8	80

Figure 5-5 (*Continued*)

Stimulus	Response	
	Flash	Untimed
1. aboard	a—	—
2. balcony	ball—	
3. blizzard	blister	blister
4. cape		
5. club		
6. curtain	curt —	—
7. distance	distant	distant
8. enter		
9. flour	floor	
10. given		
11. hidden		
12. invention		
13. lesson		
14. medicine		
15. nod		
16. present		
17. refrigerator		
18. scatter		
19. shy		
20. sparkle		
21. storm		
22. team		
23. touch		
24. valley		
25. worn		
Percent Correct	40	40

Figure 5-5 (Continued)

student received a 52 plus 8. The plus score indicates the student's lack of certainty about words.

The flash score suggests a tentative instructional level. This is the highest grade level at which the student scores approximately 75 percent. In Figure 5-5 we would place the student's instructional level at grade one.

A comparison of scores in the flash and untimed columns provides some information about the student's word identification skills or word attack ability. If a 20 percent or more difference exists between flash and untimed scores, you can conclude that the student may be able to decode words which he or she is unable to read by sight (Stauffer *et al.,* 1978). This is particularly true if the student's flash score is relatively low (in the 40 to 50 percent range, as in Figure 5-5, the second-grade list). In this case it can be concluded that the student possesses relatively good identification skills despite a deficient sight vocabulary.

Traditionally, students' responses to untimed words have been compared with the actual words in an attempt to determine precise strengths and weaknesses with specific phonic elements. There are a number of reasons why such a diagnosis is of dubious value. First, too few errors are committed by a student to detect a conclusive pattern of misreadings—though it might allow us to generate hypotheses which could be confirmed by further testing. Second, a misreading does not necessarily mean that the student does not know a particular phonic element. Support from this view comes from an investigation by Cohn and D'Alessandro (1978) who asked students to read words they had originally missed on the word analysis subtest of the Durrell Analysis of Reading Difficulty. The students were able to correct 78.6 percent of the initial errors if they were told to try again. This research suggests that misreading on the untimed presentation does not always indicate a specific skill deficiency. The value of the test is that it can suggest whether the reader has some word identification skills even though the test cannot pinpoint the deficiencies.

Allington and Franzen (1980) have also shown that errors in isolation are very different from errors in context. They compared the mistakes of elementary students who read a selection in connected text with their errors when reading these same words arranged horizontally in random order. They found that although the correlation between the students' overall responses in isolation and connected text was high (r = .94), the specific errors common to both formats for poor readers was low—18 percent. In other words, students' errors in isolation are quite different from their errors in connected text. Thus, we cannot draw definite conclusions about the strengths or disabilities of students in word identification skills from tests of isolated words. Even if we were confident that an analysis of words in isolation had diagnostic value, the only available data show that students are most likely to identify the initial sound of a word correctly, followed in relative order by the final and medial sound of the word (Weber, 1968). If this is true of most students, the pattern could be predicted even before the test was administered and provides no new information.

It is possible, however, to use informal word identification tests to determine students' peculiar strategies. Some students may attempt to sound out virtually every word. Others may be unwilling to read words they cannot identify at sight. Other students may respond impulsively to words, suggesting that they either wish to avoid reading entirely or fail to attend to sufficient graphophonic information before making a decision.

Although it may not be possible to determine precise word identification skills on the basis of students' responses, the tentative instructional level can suggest their general skill development.

Skill Assessment

PRIMARY   Since word identification tests do not provide specific information about skill development, other techniques must be employed to obtain this information. The precise technique depends on the students' tentative instructional level. If students are reading at grades one to three, a step-by-step evaluation of word identification skills can be undertaken. If, on the other hand, students are reading at intermediate levels, it is preferable to assess word identification ability by re-presenting the multisyllabic words they were unable to identify in an untimed presentation. Both procedures are described here.

If students, for example, were reading at the second-grade level, it could be hypothesized that they probably know all consonant elements, may know some vowels, but are unlikely to possess many skills relating to multisyllabic words. For screening purposes, their knowledge of vowels could be assessed, and it could be assumed that they have not learned more advanced word identification skills.

A more complete evaluation could be conducted to confirm these hypotheses. Consonant substitution exercises, in which initial consonant elements are substituted in a word (for example, the *f* in *fat* is replaced by *b*), could be given. We have found it helpful to refer to a list of phonic elements (see page 138) such as Smith and Robinson's (1980). You could also create your own list by consulting the teacher's edition of a basal reading series. This list would have the added advantage of indicating at which level specific skills are usually taught. Figure 5-6 shows the skills which should be mastered by the end of second grade.

To test knowledge of consonants, we might begin with the word *sing*, which the student knew on the flash list (Figure 5-5), and substitute several initial consonants, for example, *wing; ring;* and a blend, *fling*. If other familiar words were used as the base word, knowledge of additional consonants, blends, and digraphs could be tested in this manner. Here are some words from the word identification list (Figure 5-5) which you could use for this purpose, together with words beginning with appropriate consonants, blends, and digraphs:

CALL	MAKE	HOUSE	CAR	WIDE	TRUCK
tall	bake	louse	tar	tide	chuck
wall	rake	mouse	bar	slide	stuck
small	drake	blouse	far	bride	cluck
	stake		jar		pluck
	brake		star		

As indicated earlier, a precise listing of all known and unknown phonic elements is not usually necessary. It is often sufficient to assess categories of phonic skills.

The substituted words should include words in the students' listening vocabularies that are unlikely to be in their sight vocabularies such as *blouse, bride,*

Single consonants	b	g	l	q	v	z
	c	h	m	r	w	
	d	j	n	s	x	
	f	k	p	t	y	

Consonant blends	bl	pl	sm	br	tr
	cl	sl	sn	fr	tw
	fl	sc	sp	gr	qu
		sk	st	pr	

Consonant digraphs	ch	sh	th	wh

	Short	Long
Single vowels	a	a
	e	e
	i	i
	o	o
	u	u

r-influenced vowels	ar
	er
	ir
	or
	ur

Figure 5-6   Phonic Skills to Be Mastered at Second-Grade Reading Level

and so on. Students should not be able to respond correctly simply because they already know the word at sight. Unfortunately, we cannot always be sure if a particular word is already part of a student's sight vocabulary. For this reason some examiners suggest the use of nonsense words (Johnson, 1973). Nonsense words look and sound like real words but have no meaning, for example, *lup, nid, domp.* In view of recent research (Cunningham, 1976) which suggests that nonsense words may be more difficult for the student than real words, and thus mask the fact that students have acquired the skill, an inability to respond correctly to nonsense words should be interpreted with caution.

Students' knowledge of inflectional endings such as *s, ed,* and *ing* could also be tested at this point. This testing is quickly accomplished by writing known words like *play, float* and *clear,* adding the appropriate endings, and asking the student to read the word.

Students' knowledge of vowels would also be systematically evaluated. Since many students can identify the names of the vowel letters but have difficulty dealing with the sound-symbol correspondences, determine knowledge of short and long vowels by selecting known words from the word identification list and substituting the short vowel sounds. The following is a list of base words from the word identification test along with the substitutions which may be used for this purpose. If additional base words are needed, use any word which the student already knows by sight.

BIG	HIM	SING	TRUCK
bag	hum	sung	trick
beg	hem	song	track
bog			
bug			

In developing these lists, note whether your students in their ordinary speech actually pronounce the new words with the short vowel sound, especially when you are testing students with divergent dialects. Words such as *ham* follow the short vowel pattern, but in some parts of the country they are not pronounced with the short *a* sound because of regional, social, or ethnic dialects. Also, be sure not to overlook this fact when choosing commercial tests and workbook exercises, as they may ask questions or use exercises which assume a different pronunciation of the vowels.

To test the long vowels, you can use three-letter words like *cap, rip,* and *hop* and add a final *e*. See if the student can identify the new word. If several examples are provided, you can usually determine if they know this skill. Here are some words which you might use for this purpose: *mad(e), fin(e), can(e), fat(e), dim(e), hid(e), pin(e), kit(e), not(e), plan(e),* and *slid(e)*. In all substitution exercises, students should be able to identify the base word without difficulty. If the initial word cannot be readily identified, the validity of the evaluation is reduced.

INTERMEDIATE   At the intermediate-grade level, word identification skills become increasingly complex, and it is frequently time consuming to test all the skills a student should have acquired. In addition, knowledge of skills may have little relevance to the skills or strategies the student actually applies in identifying words. For example, a student may know the vowel sounds but fail to apply them in identifying a word. In fact many readers frequently possess more skills than they automatically apply. Teaching, then, might focus initially on the application of existing skills rather than on the teaching of new, unknown phonic elements.

To assess intermediate-grade students' decoding skills, use words which students miss on the informal word identification test. One student missed these words: *balcony, refrigerator, ability,* and *persuade*. From this list we selected all but *persuade,* since the sound-symbol relationship in this word is not easily predicted.

Because diagnosis seeks to determine how the student attempts to identify unknown words, a good procedure is to ask, "What will you do now to figure out this word?" This question is designed to compare the skills the student believes should be used with the skills actually possessed. If the student responds, "I try to break it up into syllables," say, "Then try to break this word into syllables." When this has been done, ask the student to read the word. If necessary, provide help with syllabication or the pronunciation of phonically irregular syllables. In providing this guidance, which is not ordinarily available to students, a teacher can determine how much assistance a student requires in order to identify a word.

If the student has trouble with regular, predictable syllables, supply a word in the student's sight vocabulary which contains that syllable and see if the student can transfer that knowledge to the unknown syllable.

When a student responds incorrectly, write down the word which was said, point to it, and say, "This is what you said" (Stauffer, 1969). This allows the reader to compare the actual word with the response and focus on alternative

Figure 5-7 Summary of Informal Word Identification Tests—Isolation

	TESTS WITH UNTIMED PRESENTATIONS ONLY	TESTS WITH BOTH TIMED (FLASH) AND UNTIMED PRESENTATIONS
Purpose	Quick but crude identification of student's reading level.	
		Tentative assessment of students' skill development in phonics and structural analysis. Assessment of strategies in dealing with unknown words.
When to Use	To quickly place students in a specific text or reading group—temporarily.	
		To obtain a tentative assessment of students' overall word identification ability.
Example	Helen was just transferred into your class from another school. You have neither her past school records nor time for extensive testing but would like her to join a reading group immediately.	Tom needs to be placed in a reading group but you also wish to make a tentative diagnosis of his word identification skills in order to begin developing an instructional program.
Construction	Words randomly selected from specific vocabulary lists such as Thorndike, Dolch, Harris-Jacobson, and Johnson.	
Exposure	Students are allowed to look at each word for several seconds.	Students are shown a word in a timed exposure; unknown words are re-presented on an untimed basis.

renderings of the difficult grapheme or syllable. If necessary, this procedure can be repeated. The technique reveals the amount of assistance the student needs as well as resourcefulness in dealing with a particular phonic element or syllable.

In the word *refrigerator,* the student had difficulty with only one element, the soft *g.* Once the student was told this sound, the word was identified correctly. In the word *ability,* the student had difficulty dividing the word correctly into syllables. Once this was done, this word was also read correctly. In the word *balcony,* the student was able to divide the word properly but pronounced the *c* as /s/ instead of /k/ as in *cat.* Once the examiner told the student to try /k/, the student was able to identify the word.

The examiner concluded that the student's phonic ability was reasonably well developed and that given the benefit of context, the student probably would have little difficulty with word identification. (Subsequent reading of connected text confirmed this hypothesis.) The student, however, did need to develop more confidence in identifying words and become more versatile in applying variant symbol-sound correspondences. In both *refrigerator* and *balcony,* the student was unable to use alternative phoneme-grapheme correspondences to decode the words, a frequent problem for poor readers. In view of the student's overall strength, however, no intensive remedial activities were warranted.

We have now completed the discussion of informal word identification tests. To summarize the nature and use of these tests and to distinguish between simple and more complex types, see Figure 5-7.

At the conclusion of this testing, you should have gained important insights about the student's word identification skills and strategies at the intermediate level. Although more detailed evaluation requires the administration of a battery of criterion-referenced tests, the present information is often sufficient to begin instruction.

DIAGNOSIS IN CONNECTED TEXT

Because tests of isolated words do not allow the reader to demonstrate the use of semantic and syntactic abilities, students also need to be tested by reading connected text. Meaning and sentence structure make reading easier and thus permit students to identify more words. This result is readily apparent when students read a selection originally written for a younger reader. If, for example, older students with low word identification ability read a second-grade passage, their experiential and linguistic background can often compensate partly for deficiencies in word identification. Since diagnosis seeks to determine students' strengths as well as weaknesses, it is important to test words in connected text as well as in isolation.

Uses of Connected Text

If a student will be receiving special help in reading, the reading teacher might administer an informal reading inventory (IRI) in order to assess instructional level, skill development, and reading strategies. The IRI is a series of graded paragraphs. The student reads the material silently or aloud and answers questions about the text. (Since comprehension will be discussed in Chapter 8,

"Teaching Comprehension," the present description of the IRI will be limited to oral reading for the purpose of determining word identification ability.) Keep in mind that the diagnosis of word identification abilities can occur during the reading of any connected text, not simply informal inventories.

In the IRI the examiner carefully records the students' oral reading of passages, noting deviations from the text. Comments about the manner in which the text was read are also included (for example, word by word, fluently, high-pitched voice, and nervous mannerisms).

The reading is recorded on student response sheets, which contain a typed copy of the textbook passage. Figure 5-8 illustrates a recording system.

Figure 5-9 shows how the recording would appear when applied to a reading selection.

A second purpose for reading in connected text would be to determine the suitability of a specific textbook for actual use. In this situation, the student would read aloud from this text while the teacher listened carefully and recorded the student's performance. The reading might be conducted before the use of the book or it may be done at any point in the school year to determine if the student is proceeding satisfactorily. It is likely that the recording of the reading will be more "informal" than the IRI. Teachers might jot down specific impressions of the student's behavior but need not precisely code the student's rendition.

Criteria

In both the IRI and the even more informal reading from a student's textbook, similar criteria are applied to determine the student's instructional level. This is the level at which the student can perform comfortably under the teacher's direction, and yet the reading is challenging without being frustrating. The criteria include quantitative measures, the percentage of words read correctly, and qualitative assessment—such as "goodness," oral reading errors, fluency, students' risk-taking behavior, and other physical and verbal behaviors which accompany the reading.

QUANTITATIVE ASSESSMENT   The criterion which has received the most attention from educators is the percentage of words which the student reads correctly. Traditionally, the standard for instructional level for word identification has been 95 percent accuracy. That is, a student must read correctly 95 of every 100 words in connected text.

The 95 percent criterion is considerably higher than the 75 percent score necessary for instructional level on the informal word identification test. The difference is due to the redundancy of connected text, in which words such as *the, an,* and *I* are continually repeated. This redundancy makes it easier to receive a higher score, and therefore, for purposes of comparability, connected text requires a higher percentage of correct words than does the isolated word test.

The 95 percent standard has been used for many years. Its origin is credited to Emmett Betts and Patsy Aloysius Killgallon. Some authorities contend that it was based on Killgallon's study (1942) of the reading performance of forty-one fourth-grade students on an IRI (Kender, 1970). Killgallon initially reported a criterion of 93.9 percent, but it was changed to 95 percent in the final

WORD
IDENTIFICATION

1. Substitution   *hunt* / ~~hut~~

Cross out word in text and write student response above it. If substitution is immediately corrected, place a check next to it.

bank   ~~bank~~ *bunk* ✓

2. Word supplied   *dna* (howled)

Circle ~~word~~. If student asked for word, write "asked" above word. If not, write "dna," did not ask.

3. Insertion   and ∧ *the* deep

Insert caret at point of insertion and write it in.

4. Omission   shed ~~was~~ frozen

Cross out omitted word.

5. Repetition   the men were (wavy underline)

Draw wavy lines under repeated portion. If repetition occurs again, draw a second line.

FLUENCY AND PHRASING

6. Punctuation ignored   (.)

Circle the ignored punctuation mark.

7. Hesitation   long // months

Draw slash marks for each second of hesitation.

SYMPTOMATIC BEHAVIOR

8. Finger pointing   F.P. ↓

Draw vertical line with arrow next to lines in which student points and write F.P.

9. Head movement   H.M. ↓

Draw vertical lines with arrow next to lines in which behavior is demonstrated and write H.M.

10. Lip movement   L.M. ↓

(Silent read only) Draw vertical lines next to lines in which student moves lips and write L.M.

11. Audible whisper   A.W. ↓

Draw vertical lines with arrow next to lines in which student whispers audibly and write A.W.

Figure 5-8 Recording Procedures for Informal Reading Inventory

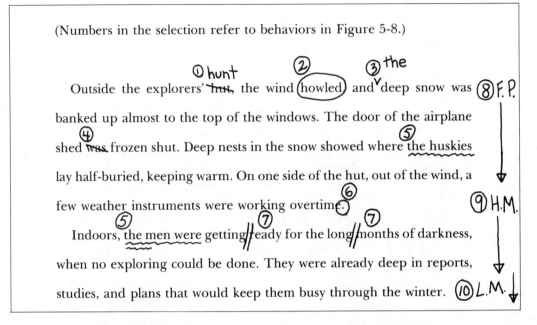

(Numbers in the selection refer to behaviors in Figure 5-8.)

Outside the explorers' hut, the wind (howled) and deep snow was ⑧F.P.

banked up almost to the top of the windows. The door of the airplane

shed was frozen shut. Deep nests in the snow showed where the huskies

lay half-buried, keeping warm. On one side of the hut, out of the wind, a

few weather instruments were working overtime. ⑨H.M.

Indoors, the men were getting ready for the long months of darkness,

when no exploring could be done. They were already deep in reports,

studies, and plans that would keep them busy through the winter. ⑩L.M.

Figure 5-9 Recording of Sample Selection   From *American Adventures* edited by Emmett A. Betts and Carolyn M. Welch. Copyright 1963 by the American Book Company. Reprinted by permission of D.C. Heath.

conclusions of the study (Beldin, 1970). Walter (1974) states that Betts set the criterion, but that the actual process by which the 95 percent figure was derived is unknown. Regardless of its origin, however, the criterion has been widely adopted for use with IRIs (Johnson and Kress, 1965).

However, despite its widespread use, this figure must be used with caution. Betts (1936) and Killgallon (1942) counted repetitions as errors. Betts, at one point, allowed students to read the selection silently before the oral reading. Since many scoring systems today do not include repetitions nor allow prior silent reading, it would seem reasonable to lower the 95 percent to take these differences into account.

Powell and Dunkeld's (1971) investigation has also raised questions about the appropriateness of the 95 percent criterion. They studied the reading performance of average students in grades one through six, identifying the highest level at which individual students achieved 70 percent comprehension. They then found the students' lowest word identification score at or below that level. The means of these word identification scores, according to Powell, varied with the reading level of the material. First- and second-grade students, for example, could tolerate an average word identification score of 85 percent and still read with 70 percent comprehension. At the sixth-grade level, Powell found 95 percent accuracy in word identification to be appropriate. In other words, young readers can make more errors in early grade-level material and still understand the selection.

Powell's most recent criterion (1978) for instructional level is as follows:

Grades one to two	87 to 93 percent	(one error in eight words to one error in sixteen words)
Grades three to five	92 to 96 percent	(one error in thirteen words to one error in twenty-six words)
Grade six and above	95 to 97 percent	(one error in eighteen words to one error in thirty-five words)

Two investigations reported by Pikulski (1974) support both the Betts-Killgallon and Powell criteria. Pikulski studied twenty-eight average second-graders in an extensive decoding program and found that they required 95 percent word identification accuracy in order to maintain 70 percent comprehension. In his second study he examined second-graders who had been referred for reading diagnosis. These students needed only to identify 83.8 percent of the words correctly to comprehend the passage. These disparate results suggest that more research will be necessary before agreement on IRI standards will be reached.

A solution to the problem is complicated by the difference of opinion about which word identification errors should be counted. Powell counts substitutions, mispronunciations, insertions, omissions, and words called for. Betts (1946) and Ekwall (1974) also count repetitions. Gilmore (1968) suggests also counting hesitations and disregarding punctuation errors. Others do not wish to count proper names as errors nor additional misreadings of words the student has already miscalled. It does little good to debate the merits of varying percentages unless agreement is reached on the types of errors which are to be counted. For this reason, we suggest it is unwise to rely too heavily on quantitative data until these differences are resolved. In other words, good judgment, in addition to quantitative data, should be exercised when determining reading levels.

MISCUE ANALYSIS   The current trend in error analysis is not to seek agreement on either countable errors or a specific criterion but to look at the errors from a qualitative perspective. Whereas in traditional error counting there exists the "all or nothing" principle—that is, the individual either makes an error or doesn't—the qualitative view rates errors on a sliding scale. Errors are graded according to how well they express the meaning of the author. Errors can thus be considered "good" errors if the deviation does not significantly change the meaning (*home* for *house*). Errors are "bad" miscues if they change the meaning of the sentence and are unlikely to make sense ("I spent the weekend at the *horse* of my friends."). From a quantitative point of view, each deviation constitutes one error. A qualitative interpretation, however, recognizes the fact that one error violated the author's meaning whereas the other did not.

Since the words *error* or *deviation* have negative connotations, the term *miscues* (Goodman, 1973) has been adopted to describe these departures from the actual text. Miscues are thus not simply signs of weak decoding ability, nor are they committed at random, but usually reflect the degree to which the reader strives for meaning and utilizes semantic and syntactic cueing systems. For example, in substituting the word *shine* for *shadow* in the sentence "All he could see was the shadow of the moon on the water," the meaning is changed, but the substitution makes sense and is consistent with the syntax of the sentence.

From this perspective, students' repetitions and self-corrections also receive a fresh interpretation. They may indicate that the readers detected dissonance between their rendering of the text and the meaning or sentence structure, and they then reread the word or phrase which did not fit the context of the sentence and substituted a more appropriate word. This is seen in a student who first read "Now but on your light and keep it on" and then spontaneously reread the sentence, "Now put on your light and keep it on."

Miscue analysis is not an isolated diagnostic teachnique but an attempt to understand the reading process itself, specifically how the reader learned to read (Goodman, 1973). It assumes that reading is a "psycholinguistic guessing game," a view which we have classified in Chapter 3, "Understanding the Reading Process," as a top-down processing of text. In a psycholinguistic orientation, readers use syntactic and semantic cues to predict graphic input, so they need only sample the print to confirm predictions.

The analysis of miscues has evolved from a research tool for studying the reading process and today is best known as a method of diagnosing word identification strategies. The initial research instrument has been simplified by Goodman and Burke (1972) and is available commercially as the Reading Miscue Inventory. Unlike the older, more traditional IRIs, miscue analysis focuses not on the student's decoding skills but on the reader's strategies—the use of the three cueing systems. Many recent IRIs have incorporated miscue analysis into their interpretation of results.

The essential steps in administering and scoring a miscue inventory will be described here. Readers who wish to study this procedure in more detail should consult the examiner's manual of the Reading Miscue Inventory.

1. The reader is called on to read aloud a selection of sufficient length and difficulty to generate twenty-five miscues. The selection is an entire story and is read in a single session.
2. The examiner records the miscues on a typed copy of the story. The student is not told unknown words but is asked to continue reading even if this requires guessing or skipping a word. In order to record the miscues accurately, the reading is taped and later replayed.
3. The student retells the story. Following the retelling the examiner asks open-ended questions designed to elicit additional information from the reader. The student receives a comprehension score on the basis of the retelling.
4. Nine questions are asked of each miscue:
   a. Is there a dialect variation in the miscue?
   b. Is there a shift in intonation?
   c. How much alike are the word and the miscue in appearance?

d. How much similarity in sound is there between the actual word and the miscue?

e. Is the grammatical function of the miscue and the text the same?

f. Is the miscue corrected?

g. Does the miscue alter the grammatical structure?

h. Does the miscue make sense?

i. Does the miscue change the meaning?

The purpose of the questions is to determine the pattern of the readers' miscues and thereby reveal their use of the three cueing systems.

5. The readers' ability to maintain meaning in their miscues is compared to their comprehension score.

Miscue analysis may uncover a number of reasons for so-called errors in word identification. The reader may overemphasize accurate word identification (for example, correcting *does not* to *doesn't*, in which no difference in meaning is involved), attempt to solve word identification problems by resorting continually to phonics, or neglect to use semantic and syntactic cueing systems. The reader may overrely on background information and reconstruct the author's message with minimal regard to the printed text.

Once the miscue pattern has been determined, remedial lessons are implemented to improve the reader's strategies so they conform more closely to a psycholinguistic understanding of reading. If students tend to ignore meaning, for example, they may be asked to read a paragraph in which a number of nonsensical items have been inserted. The guided reading of such material will make the students more aware of the need to attend to the meaning of the text.

Despite its apparent value, the reliability of the miscue scoring procedure has been questioned. Hood (1975–76) points out three weaknesses: (1) variant methods for counting the number of miscues, (2) differences about what constitutes contextual appropriateness, and (3) difficulty in determining the reader's use of graphic cues. Furthermore, Groff (1980) argues that the scoring of the Reading Miscue Inventory requires a number of subjective decisions, which reduces its reliability. Although reliability can be improved with training (Hood, 1975–76), it is unlikely that most teachers will be able to avail themselves of this opportunity.

The relationship of error patterns and reading level also raises questions about the usefulness of miscue analysis. A number of investigations have shown that students' miscues change as they move from an instructional level to a frustration level (Hood, 1978; Leslie and Osol, 1978; Williamson and Young, 1974; Wixson, 1979). At the instructional level, miscues tend to be consistent with the meaning and the sentence structure of the text. As reading becomes more difficult, the errors are more similar to the sound and visual appearance of the word. When good readers are asked to read material beyond their instructional level, the number of nonsense words and omission errors increases (Hood, 1978). The implication of these studies is that the reader's miscue patterns can be fluid rather than static. In other words, a reader's patterns depend on the difficulty of the material being read. An increase in difficulty can force a reader who used good meaning-seeking strategies at one level to overrely on graph-ophonic cues at a higher level. Hood has concluded from this observation that a shortcut to improved miscue quality is to assign the reader easy material.

A valid analysis of miscues cannot be conducted if they are drawn from a wide variety of levels both below and above the student's instructional level. Certainly it is questionable whether an analysis of miscues collected from levels significantly above a student's instructional level have much relevance for teaching students at the instructional level.

We recognize, of course, that poor readers' strategies may need improvement even when they are reading material at an instructional level. Often these students persist in using inefficient techniques (sounding out all words) or random guessing rather than attending to either context or graphophonic cues.

A more practical problem in miscue analysis is the time needed to administer the Reading Miscue Inventory (Hittleman, 1978; Hood, 1975–76, 1978; Smith and Weaver, 1978). The present Inventory usually requires a minimum of two hours to administer, score, and interpret. For this reason, it is unlikely that many teachers will use the instrument in its present form.

The potential value of miscue analysis, however, has led to the development of several abbreviated versions (Bean, 1979; Hittleman, 1978; Hood, 1978; Smith and Weaver, 1978; Tortelli, 1976). These adaptations reduce the number of miscues which must be obtained as well as the number of questions to which each miscue must be subjected. (The reader who is interested in more information about these instruments should consult the references cited.)

Although these abbreviated tests may be profitably employed in clinical settings in which the case load is relatively light, we believe the reading specialist and classroom teacher require even more practical means of diagnosing reader strategies. Therefore, we suggest the following:

1. View miscue analysis as a continuous activity rather than one that ceases after the initial diagnosis. Not only is time usually unavailable to administer the Reading Miscue Inventory, but also the use of an abbreviated version, if combined with an IRI, may result in too few miscues for a valid and reliable analysis. If, on the other hand, teachers analyze miscues every time students read aloud, patterns of errors can be detected and appropriate remedial action can be taken quickly.

2. A good measure of readers' proficiency is the semantic suitability of their miscues (Goodman, 1973), and therefore miscue analysis should focus on this dimension. To rate suitability, let's examine a student's responses to a single sentence: "After school the student raced down the street and ran into the house." If the student miscalled the word *house*, we might rank the miscues in the following manner:

   a. *home* for *house*. This is a good miscue. The student substitutes a word with a similar meaning. The student should ordinarily not be corrected for such an "error."

   b. *stable* for *house*. We'd call this a fair miscue. The miscue changes the author's meaning (unless your house resembles a stable), but the substitution makes sense. The student could have run down the street into the stable. This student should be commended for using meaning even though the miscue does not look like the original word. If students err, we would prefer they err on the side of meaning. At the same time, however, the student needs help with decoding skills. If the student were given such assistance, one of the first signs of growth would be hesitation in substituting *stable* for *house*, as the student is more aware that the visual pattern of *stable* does not provide an appropriate fit. In time, the student would attempt to insert a word which would fit both the meaning and the graphophonic requirements.

c. *horse* for *house*. This error is less satisfactory than *stable* because the substitution does not make sense even though the word looks similar and honors the syntax of the sentence. The reader needs to be encouraged to use context and perhaps would benefit from the opportunity to read easy, meaningful material. The student probably does not need more phonic instruction at this time as the miscue suggests the use of too much phonics, to the exclusion of meaning.

d. *after* for *house*. This is obviously a poor miscue. Admittedly, few students would substitute a word which makes no sense, violates syntax, and does not look like the actual word. Students who perform in this manner have developed a habit of treating reading as a random collection of words and have given up striving for meaning. This error suggests that the student has had severe difficulty in developing a sight vocabulary and has been reading too difficult material.

These four categories provide a short form of the miscue inventory with little loss of diagnostic information. Undoubtedly finer distinctions could be made. Our purpose, however, is not to provide a precise system of analysis but a practical one which can be easily used each time a teacher listens to a student read aloud. Obviously, judgments about a student's miscue pattern would be made only after extended observation rather than after one or two readings.

The miscue analysis just described is concerned with the quality of the reader's errors and supplements the quantitative score. For example, if a student scores 91 percent on word identification, which is four percentage points below the traditional standard, the quality of the miscues may determine whether the student should be considered to be at an instructional level. If miscues consist largely of insertions, omissions, and meaningful substitutions, the student may actually be reading at an instructional level, whereas miscues of lower quality, such as meaningless substitutions, may indicate the material is too difficult. If miscues are analyzed according to their quality, the debate between the Betts-Killgallon and Powell criteria becomes a less important issue.

SYMPTOMATIC READING BEHAVIOR   A third category provides additional information in determining instructional level. Symptomatic reading behavior refers to a variety of verbal and nonverbal responses which are not scored but are recorded and represent symptoms or indicators of difficulty. Punctuation, for example, is frequently ignored by the poor reader, particularly periods at the ends of sentences. This problem is often caused by material which contains too many unknown words and thereby prevents the reader from attending to the meaning of the sentence. Because they are not the cause of the problem, though they signal its presence, there is no need to remediate these symptoms themselves. The solution is not to provide lessons on attending to periods, exclamation marks, and question marks but to supply easier reading material.

Symptomatic behavior can be divided into three subcategories: (1) fluency, (2) risk-taking, and (3) physical and vocal manifestations.

Fluency refers to the reader's rhythm, phrasing, and expression. Many poor readers, of course, read in a halting, word-by-word manner, lack proper phrasing, read in a monotone, and ignore punctuation. Although their oral reading suggests that they do not understand what they are reading, the converse—that students who read with good expression are paying attention to the meaning of the text—is not necessarily true.

Risk-taking is the student's willingness to attempt to read new words. Reluctance to decode words may be responsible for a student's difficulties, but it is also likely that previous failure in reading has convinced the reader that it is better not to attempt words than to face certain failure. In addition to fear of failure, some students may not attempt words because they have become overly reliant on the teacher to tell them unknown words.

A variety of *physical* and *vocal manifestations* suggest that the reader is having difficulty. Though these behaviors cannot be scored, they should be recorded on a student response sheet, if an IRI is being used, or in the teacher's notebook. These behaviors include the following: excessive head and body movements (squirming and wriggling, nodding the head with each word), finger pointing (another symptom but not the problem itself), tense high-pitched voice and rigid posture, lip movements and audible whisper (during silent reading), rationalizations ("I can read these words most of the time, but I don't like this book"), or outright refusal to read.

From all this information it should be apparent that determining a student's instructional level is considerably more complex than simply computing the percentage of correctly read words. In summary, we suggest you look for the following items when diagnosing word identification ability:

1. Percentage of words read correctly—in the vicinity of 95 percent. Miscues include substitutions, which usually account for the largest part (D'Angelo and Wilson, 1979), words supplied, omissions, and insertions. The last two errors are minor in nature. Repetitions are not to be counted but should be noted. They may represent the student's striving for meaning and therefore are "good" miscues (Goodman, 1973). On the other hand, if repetitions are excessive, they may suggest that the student is having undue difficulty (Ekwall, 1974). Proper names are not considered errors. Also, if a student errs on a particular word more than once in the selection, only the first misreading is counted. Dialect-influenced errors are also exempt from the quantitative score.

2. Quality of miscues. Miscues consistent with the author's meaning or are meaningful are rated higher than those in which the reader substituted a word graphically similar to the word in the text but violated the meaning.

3. Symptomatic reading behavior. Note fluency, willingness to take risks, and physical and vocal behavior.

Unfortunately, no formulas are available for analyzing this information and determining an instructional level. Instead, the examiner's judgment must be the final arbiter. Essentially the teacher is seeking the best fit among a student's reading performance, placement in a text, and instructional expectations. Even all these data can determine only a tentative reading level and must be tempered by the student's ability to comprehend the material.

After administering the interview and word identification tests in isolation and connected text, the teacher has gained much more information than merely the student's instructional level. The teacher has learned something about the following:

1. The student's lifestyle, personality, self-concept, reading habits, and attitudes.
2. The word identification skills the student knows and needs to learn.
3. Student strategies in identifying words, especially the degree to which they make use of semantic and syntactic cues.
4. Symptomatic reading behaviors which indicate the student's ease in reading a text. Particularly important is the student's willingness to take risks and apply word identification skills in uncertain situations.

LANGUAGE-EXPERIENCE ASSESSMENT

Occasionally you will test students who score so low on tests of word identification that it makes little sense for them to read in conventional textual material. In these cases a language-experience assessment can be used to determine how easily they can acquire and retain vocabulary.

In a language-experience assessment students dictate a personal account to the examiner. If the student is reluctant to dictate, the examiner might suggest a topic based on information from the interview. It is preferable for students to choose their own topic, but it is better to suggest a subject and obtain an account than to forego the opportunity to observe the student reading connected text.

As the student talks, the examiner records the dictation in manuscript. When a half-dozen sentences have been dictated, the account is read to the student as the examiner points to each word. Then the student reads the account with the examiner. The student is asked to underline any known words. With a young student, the procedure is varied by reading as the student points to the words. This can determine whether the student understands the correspondence between spoken and written words, left-to-right eye movement, and return sweep.

A few of the words previously underlined (words the student says he or she knows) are written on 1-by-3-inch cards. The cards are shuffled and presented to the student for identification. After all the words have been presented, the student finds the unknown words in the original story and attempts to read them. Retention is measured by re-presenting the cards about fifteen minutes later.

The following chart can be used to evaluate informally the student's responses. No specific standards have been established for assessing this performance, but with repeated use teachers will be able to make comparisons between students and judge their readiness for formal reading instruction.

1. How willing is the student to dictate?
   resistant _____ willing
2. How mature is the student's vocabulary?
   immature _____ mature
3. How complex are the student's sentence patterns?
   simple _____ complex
4. What percentage of words was the student able to identify in context?
   0 _____ 25 _____ 50 _____ 75 _____ 100
5. What percentage of words was the student able to identify in isolation?
   0 _____ 25 _____ 50 _____ 75 _____ 100
6. What percentage of words known in isolation (question 5) was the student able to identify in isolation fifteen minutes later?
   0 _____ 25 _____ 50 _____ 75 _____ 100
7. How easily could the student find words in the story which had not been identified in isolation (question 6)?
   had considerable   found words
   difficulty _____ easily
8. Comment on other significant responses, for example, choice of topic for dictation, content, nonreading behaviors, verbal comments.

We have now completed the discussion of word identification tests in connected text. To summarize these tests and at the same time distinguish among them, see Figure 5-10.

Figure 5-10   Summary of Word Identification Tests in Connected Text

TYPE	INFORMAL READING	INFORMAL READING INVENTORY	LANGUAGE-EXPERIENCE ASSESSMENT
Material	Present text used in classroom.	Present text or selections compiled from basal reader.	Account dictated by student.
Procedure	Student reads orally to the teacher.		Student dictates to teacher who reads account *to* student and *with* student.

			Student identifies words in context and in isolation.
Purpose	To determine the suitability of a specific text and/or to assess student progress in a specific text.	To tentatively determine instructional reading level. To determine students' skills and strategies in identifying words in context.	To determine if students will benefit from systematic reading instruction and how quickly they can be expected to progress.
When to Use	When placing a student in a particular textbook or evaluating their progress in identifying words in the text.	As the first part (word identification) of a total diagnosis of students' reading ability. Ordinarily followed by evaluation of comprehension.	When students have acquired only a small sight vocabulary and cannot read in prepared connected text.
Example	Billy's teacher has determined, on the basis of a word identification test, that Billy can read at a third-grade level. She wishes to know if Billy can read the third-grade text which is used in the classroom. Later she will want to know if Billy has learned the vocabulary in this text.	From the administration of a word identification test, Ralph's teacher quickly learned that he can read fourth-grade vocabulary adequately. Now she wishes to assess this reading identification level in connected text, to evaluate the quality of his miscues and his application of phonic and structural analysis skills.	Lisa reads so few words on the preprimer list, it is unlikely she will be able to read any textbook material. At the same time her teacher needs to determine how prepared Lisa is for systematic reading instruction and to estimate how quickly Lisa might progress towards readiness, or acquire a sight vocabulary.

SKILLS MANAGEMENT SYSTEMS

Up to this point, testing of word identification skills has been conducted on an informal basis and has sought to determine students' knowledge of categories of known and unknown skills. Criterion-referenced tests found in skills management systems (SMS) have been developed to provide a more comprehensive assessment. In addition, they have the added advantage of testing students in groups rather than individually.

Skills management systems usually include the following elements:

1. A list of word identification and comprehension skills.
2. A set of behavioral objectives which state the behavior the student will demonstrate, the manner in which the skill will be assessed, and the criteria for successful performance.
3. Group pre- and posttests to determine pupils' needs as well as mastery of specific skills. Some systems make provisions for selective performance testing in an informal manner.
4. A record-keeping system for monitoring students' performance.
5. A resource file which lists commercial and teacher-made material for teaching specific skills. The file includes indexes of basal reader lessons, workbook pages, filmstrips, and so on.

These systems employ skills lists which are not empirically determined but represent the judgments of knowledgeable educators (Otto *et al.*, 1974). The skills are more or less arranged according to difficulty and/or traditional grade-level placement. Each skill has a corresponding objective; for example, the student may be asked to identify (by underlining) the common two-letter blends in real and nonsense words pronounced by the teacher. The criterion for mastery is also stated. Typically this level has been set at 80 percent.

Skills management systems have been developed by teachers in school districts as well as commercial publishers. The following commercial programs are representative of those available:

Wisconsin Design for Reading Skill Development (Otto and Askov, 1972)

Fountain Valley Teacher Support System in Reading (1971)

Prescriptive Reading Inventory (1972)

More recently, publishers of basal reading series have developed skills management systems to accompany their texts.

To explain the operation of a skills management system, we will describe the step-by-step procedures followed in implementing a typical program. This program represents no one particular system but includes features from a number of them.

1. *Testing.* Students are pretested in skills which have been keyed to behavioral objectives. Students receive tests at their instructional level. Tests are either hand- or machine-scored.

2. *Recording.* Students' scores can be recorded on a large wall chart, on individual profile cards, or in the teacher's notebook. The wall chart lists each pupil's name and the scores on each test. The teacher can then tell at a glance which students have passed a particular test. This is made even easier if all passing scores, that is, those 80 percent or higher, are circled in red. In the card system, scores for each student are listed on a separate card. The individual pupil card is particularly useful when students move from one teacher to another for instruction in different skills. Some systems employ a McBee card, in which holes beside each skill on the card are punched when the student has achieved the minimum criterion on the test. By holding a group's cards together and inserting a metal rod or skewer through the holes corresponding to a particular skill, then lifting and shaking the cards, the teacher will have on the rod only the cards of students who did not pass the test. Another system, a notebook, is useful when a teacher works with different reading groups for specific periods of the day. Each reading group and its scores are listed on a separate notebook page. This permits the teacher to identify quickly the common needs in a particular group.

When scores have been determined, the teacher can identify students who need instruction in a particular skill. Students who passed the test will be taught other skills or given independent reading or study projects.

Unlike the norm-referenced tests, which compare the student with others, a skills management system uses criterion-referenced instruments to identify the student's ability in specific skills. (A more detailed account of both norm-referenced and criterion-referenced tests can be found in Chapter 11.) In each test, particular competencies are measured rather than a general assessment of reading ability. A more distinct feature of the criterion-referenced test is its concern with the individual's absolute performance rather than relative standing among peers.

3. *Teaching.* Students who did not achieve the criterion score of 80 percent are then taught the skill. Students who in the teacher's judgment have learned the skill may be dismissed from the group before the end of the instructional cycle. Instructional cycles range from one to three weeks and are intended to allow sufficient time for most students in the group to acquire the skill.

Instruction itself is similar to conventional teaching, although one advantage claimed for a skills management system is that it encourages the use of a variety of materials beyond the basal reader lesson. These may include tapes, filmstrips, overhead transparencies, games, worksheets, and learning stations. Much of this material is housed in a central resource file and is available to all teachers. Teachers are encouraged to add activities to the collection.

4. *Posttesting.* After the teaching cycle, students are again tested on their acquisition of the skill. Those who pass the test move on to other skills whereas those who do not may receive additional instruction. At this point the testing-teaching cycle repeats itself.

The advantage of criterion-referenced tests is that they provide a comprehensive assessment of students' word identification needs and, unlike norm-referenced tests, provide results which can be directly transformed into an instructional program. Thus instruction can be individualized. Only students who need it are taught a particular skill. Originally, skills management systems were

developed by commercial firms which did not publish basal reader series. Therefore, another advantage was that a variety of basal and nonbasal material could
be used to implement the program. The word identification program freed the
teacher from using the methods and materials of a single basal reader. As publishers of basal reader series continue to develop their own management systems,
this advantage may disappear. The widespread use of basal reader programs
and the limited budget for instructional materials in most schools suggests that
skills management systems will increasingly be incorporated into a specific basal
series rather than exist as a separate, independent program which uses materials
and methods from many sources.

Despite their advantages, skills management systems have been criticized
on both theoretical and pedagogical grounds. Critics maintain that they overemphasize phonics and thereby deprive the student of language cues which
make reading both easier and more meaningful. Furthermore, these systems
divide reading into unnecessarily discrete skills and thereby violate the wholistic
nature of the reading process (Johnson and Pearson, 1975). An unintended
consequence may be the tendency to make word identification an end in itself
rather than a means for understanding printed material.

Even if the concept of a skills management system is accepted, three
questions have been raised about the validity and usefulness of criterion-referenced tests of word identification: (1) What skills are worth testing? (2) What
constitutes mastery? (3) How should word identification ability be evaluated?

English orthography consists of dozens of spelling-to-sound correspondences. Johnson *et al.* (1980) point out, for example, that sixty-one vowel clusters
(*ae, ei,* and so on) are present in our language. Since testing all correspondences
would be far too time-consuming, how shall the most important elements be
selected? Researchers in a four-year study (Johnson *et al.,* 1980) selected forty-
five spelling-to-sound correspondences for consonants and twenty-nine for
vowels on the basis of their frequency of occurrence in Venezky's (1970) analysis
of the 20,000 most common English words. The use of the most commonly
occurring correspondences, which are found in this study, can provide test-
makers with worthwhile information about students' word identification
abilities.

What constitutes mastery? In most skills management systems, the criterion for success is 80 percent. Critics have pointed out, however, that this figure
is arbitrary and that it would be preferable for standards to vary depending on
the relationship of a particular skill to comprehension. As Johnson (1973) has
shown, the mastery of subskills is not consistently related to performance in
comprehension. That is, some skills are highly correlated with comprehension
and some are not. Rather than think in terms of fixed scores and mastery, a
better approach would be to ask whether improving a low percentage on a skills
test would necessarily lead to higher comprehension. A study of the relationship
of a particular skill to comprehension might show a low correlation of .30, and
since the relationship between this skill and comprehension is small, it would not
seem advisable to spend instructional time to raise this score to the usual 80
percent.

The third question—how shall ability be assessed?—relates to the format
of the stimulus and the manner of the response. In a skills management system
students are usually (1) shown a grapheme (a letter or letters) and asked to

produce orally the corresponding phoneme (a sound) or (2) shown a picture (or read a word) and asked to write down the letters, usually beginning or ending, which they heard.

Producing a phoneme has been criticized on the grounds that it requires the individual assessment of students and therefore is too time-consuming. Furthermore, presenting isolated graphemes violates the fundamental principle that spelling correspondences are influenced by both the position of the grapheme in the word and the letters surrounding it. The practice of writing "sounds" in response to a picture or a word spoken orally by the teacher has been criticized for testing spelling ability rather than decoding skills. That is, in reading we move from a letter to its oral counterpart, but in writing, we begin with the oral and move to the written. It has been argued (Johnson and Pearson, 1975) that we cannot assume that these two processes are equivalent. In a project conducted by Johnson *et al.* (1980), this problem was resolved by presenting a synthetic word, for example, *fabe,* underlining the first letter, *f,* and then asking students to identify from the four following pictures the one that began with the same sound as the underlined letter.

A second difficulty involves the use of synthetic words. As we previously mentioned, these words are used to avoid the possibility that students already know the words on the test by sight. It is important, however, that if synthetic words are used, they are consistent with phonological and orthographic principles. We would not, for example, present the synthetic word *nlard* and ask the student to identify the first sound, because this sequence violates English orthography and may be confusing. By the same token, it would be unfair to use *aef* as a target word and ask for the sound made by *a,* expecting the student to respond with long *a.* The grapheme *ae* never occurs in the initial position as a long *a* (Venezky, 1970).

The most immediate value of the Johnson project, which resulted in the Word Identification Test Battery, is that it sets a standard by which to judge other criterion-referenced tests that attempt to measure word identification. It should also influence the development of new tests in this area. If you are inclined to use a skills management system for assessing word identification, it makes sense to employ the most technically and pedagogically sound tests available. At present, the Word Identification Test Battery would appear to represent the state of the art.

In a more practical vein, skills management systems have often been considered time-consuming and cumbersome to administer. The time needed to test, score, record, and retest not only increases the teacher's clerical work load but also reduces the time available for instruction. Excessive use of the systems has also led to the complaint that it lessens both the joy of teaching and the students' interest in reading.

However, supporters of skills management systems argue that they can contribute significantly to both effective and efficient instruction. When objectives are clearly stated, they claim, instruction is focused. Furthermore, such systems encourage efficient instruction by teaching only those students who need assistance. Students who already know particular skills can spend their time more fruitfully in other activities.

Teachers must judge for themselves whether a skills management system can help them diagnose and teach skills in word identification. Assuming that you are considering the use of a reputable system, we believe that the following suggestions can help minimize their potential shortcomings.

1. Reduce the skills list to a minimum. A judicious paring may save time in both testing and teaching without damaging the diagnostic value of the system. Do not be awed by commercial varieties. Don't hesitate to delete skills of questionable value. Our own preference, for example, is to omit skills dealing with auditory discrimination and ending consonants, among others. Since the remaining skills differ in value, we suggest you divide them into two categories: important and helpful. Those in the "helpful" category would be tested and taught only if time permitted or if students' performance in connected text suggested that a deficiency in this skill was interfering with word identification. It is very possible for a student to lack a skill on the test and compensate for this shortcoming in context.

2. No skill should be considered mastered until the student can apply it consistently (Duffy, 1978). Ample time should be given to students to apply their skills in interesting and easy trade materials, not just in basal readers. This includes time for free reading, not only after they have finished their seatwork assignments but before as well.

It follows, therefore, that teaching the skills and assessing their mastery should be done by the same person. In one school some teachers were assigned to test and teach word identification skills while other teachers conducted basal reader lessons. Under such circumstances it was difficult to assess the mastery of a skill.

3. Consider eliminating either the pre- or posttesting portions of the program. The pretesting can be eliminated if you have strong evidence that the students do not know a particular skill or that the class time would be better spent by beginning instruction and observing which students need the skill. Posttests can be dropped for those students whose proficiency is readily apparent.

Skills management systems with their criterion-referenced tests were intended to supplement norm-referenced tests since the latter provided little information of diagnostic value. Originally designed to function as an adjunct to a variety of basal readers, the current trend is to incorporate the systems into basal reader series. Advocates of such systems have stressed their value in individualizing instruction by teaching only those skills a student actually requires. Opponents have criticized the fragmentation of reading which they claim is inherent in the systems. They also believe that an unanticipated consequence of the skills management system is the tendency to view skills as ends in themselves. We believe reputable systems, if modified to meet these criticisms, can play a part in the diagnosis of word identification skills.

SUMMARY

In this chapter we stated that diagnosis involves more than the administration of tests. It also includes knowledge of reading theory and the diagnostic process.

We emphasized the use of informal instruments rather than commercial tests and stressed the need for continual observation of pupils' behavior together with the integration of diagnosis and teaching. Furthermore, we suggested that diagnosis should help you make instructional decisions and requires an understanding of the reader as a person.

To conduct the diagnosis of word identification abilities we described an interview schedule, tests of words in isolation, and reading in connected text. This battery supplied information about the reader's lifestyle and self-concept, tentative instructional level, skill development, and reading strategies in word identification. For students who are reading at a very low level, we described the use of a language-experience assessment. A skills management system was recommended for situations in which a comprehensive assessment of skills was required. We listed the components of such a system, discussed its advantages and disadvantages, and supplied suggestions for its effective use. By now, you should have a good idea of what comprises the diagnosis of word identification skills.

To summarize the use of word identification, Figure 5-11 presents common assessment problems and how each of these tests may be employed.

Figure 5-11   Summary of Word Identification Tests

WHEN YOU WISH TO	USE THIS ASSESSMENT DEVICE
1. Quickly determine students' tentative instructional level.	1. Untimed tests of words in isolation.
2. Quickly determine both students' instructional level and their skills in identifying words in isolation.	2. Flash and untimed tests of word identification.
3. Determine suitability of a specific text.	3. "Informal" reading.
4. Assess students' progress in a specific text.	4. "Informal" reading.
5. Tentatively determine students' instructional level and their skills and strategies in identifying words in context.	5. Informal reading inventory.
6. Systematically evaluate students' phonic and structural analysis skills.	6. Criterion-referenced tests.
7. Determine readiness for reading of students with limited sight vocabulary who are unable to read prepared connected text.	7. Language-experience assessment.

RELATED ACTIVITIES

1. Randomly select a dozen words from a reading passage at students' instructional level. Test the students on these words in isolation. Ask them to read in their original context any incorrectly identified words. Is there any improvement in the students' performance? If errors are made in both isolation and connected text on the same words, are the errors the same or different? What conclusions can be drawn from this testing?

2. Select one question on the student interview schedule in this chapter which involves students' interests. Ask this question of a number of good and poor readers in the classroom. Can you generalize about the responses of each group? Do they differ markedly? How might the responses influence your instructional program?

3. Assign students to read a selection aloud until a substitution miscue occurs. Let the student finish the sentence. Write down the students' response, show it to them, and ask them to make another attempt at the word. Continue writing the incorrect responses and ask for additional "best guesses." Can you determine what skills the students possess or lack? How could you confirm your impression?

4. Ask a student to read aloud increasingly more difficult selections and record the word identification errors. After each selection, ask the student to retell the story. Repeat this procedure with several children. Can you generalize about the percentage of words which must be identified correctly for the student to achieve reasonable comprehension? Repeat this activity with developmental readers at different age levels. What conclusions can be drawn from the testing?

5. Collect a number of different word identification tests which ask students to identify words in isolation. Administer each test to the same student. Repeat this procedure with other students. (To save time, begin testing at the students' presumed instructional level.) Are some tests consistently easier or more difficult than others? Could some tests be used interchangeably?

6. Administer a criterion-referenced test involving initial phonic elements which asks students to respond by writing the answer (for example, "Write the first sound you hear in these words . . .") At the completion of this test, show students a set of pseudowords or words which are not in the students' reading vocabulary and which begin with the same elements as the original written words. Ask them to sound out these words. Do their responses honor the initial phonic element? Are results from each test similar? Devise similar tests for medial elements. What conclusions can you draw?

RELATED READINGS

ALLINGTON, RICHARD L., AND ANNE MCGILL FRANZEN. "Word Identification Errors in Isolation and in Context: Apples vs. Oranges." *Reading Teacher*, 33, no. 7 (Apr. 1980), 795–800.

CUNNINGHAM, PATRICIA, M. "Can Decoding Skills Be Validly Assessed Using a Nonsense-Word Pronunciation Task?" *Reading Improvement*, 13, no. 2 (Winter 1976), 247–48.

HOOD, JOYCE. "Is Miscue Analysis Practical for Teachers?" *Reading Teacher*, 32, no. 3 (Dec. 1978), 260–66.

JOHNSON, DALE D., AND P. DAVID PEARSON. "Skills Management Systems: A Critique." *Reading Teacher*, 28, no. 8 (May 1975), 757–64.

OZER, MARK N. "Assessment of Children with Learning Problems: A Child Development Approach." In *Reading Problems, A Multidisciplinary Perspective*. Wayne Otto, Charles W. Peters, and Nathaniel Peters, eds. Reading, Mass.: Addison-Wesley, 1977.

POWELL, WILLIAM R. "The Validity of the Instructional Reading Level." In *Readings for*

Diagnostic and Remedial Reading. Robert M. Wilson and James Geyer, eds. Columbus, Ohio: Chas. E. Merrill, 1972.

SIMS, RUDINE. "Miscue Analysis: Emphasis on Comprehension." In *Applied Linguistics and Reading.* Newark, Del.: International Reading Association, 1979.

WIXSON, KAREN L. "Miscue Analysis: A Critical Review." *Journal of Reading Behavior,* 11, no. 2 (Summer 1979), 163–75.

REFERENCES

ALLINGTON, RICHARD L., AND ANNE MCGILL FRANZEN. "Word Identification Errors in Isolation and in Context: Apples vs. Oranges." *Reading Teacher,* 33, no. 7 (Apr. 1980), 795–800.

BEAN, THOMAS W. "The Miscue Mini-Form: Refining the Informal Reading Inventory." *Reading World,* 18, no. 4 (May 1979), 400–405.

BELDIN, H. O. "Informal Reading Testing: Historical Review and Review of the Research." In *Reading Difficulties: Diagnosis, Correction and Remediation,* pp. 67–84. William K. Durr, ed. Newark, Del.: International Reading Association, 1970.

BETTS, EMMETT A. *Foundations of Reading Instruction.* New York: American Book, 1946.

————. *The Prevention and Correction of Reading Difficulties.* Evanston, Ill.: Row Peterson, 1936.

BURNS, PAUL C., AND BETTY D. ROE. *Informal Reading Assessment.* Chicago: Rand McNally, 1980.

COHN, MARVIN, AND CYNTHIA D'ALESSANDRO. "When Is a Decoding Error Not a Decoding Error." *Reading Teacher,* 32, no. 3 (Dec. 1978), 341–44.

CUNNINGHAM, PATRICIA M. "Can Decoding Skills Be Validly Assessed Using a Nonsense-Word Pronunciation Task?" *Reading Improvement,* 13, no. 4 (Winter 1976), 247–48.

D'ANGELO, KAREN, AND ROBERT M. WILSON. "How Helpful Is Insertion and Omission Miscue Analysis." *Reading Teacher,* 32, no. 5 (Feb. 1979), 519–20.

DOLCH, EDWARD. *Methods in Reading.* Champaign, Ill.: Garrard, 1955.

DUFFY, GERALD G. "Maintaining a Balance in Objective-Based Reading Instruction." *Reading Teacher,* 31, no. 5 (Feb. 1978), 510–23.

DUNN, LLOYD, AND FREDERICK C. MARKWARDT, JR. *Peabody Individual Achievement Test.* Chicago: American Guidance Services, 1970.

DURRELL, DONALD D. *Durrell Analysis of Reading Difficulty.* New York: The Psychological Corporation, 1980.

EKWALL, ELDON E. "Should Repetitions Be Counted as Errors?" *Reading Teacher,* 27, no. 4 (Jan. 1974), 365–67.

Fountain Valley Teacher Support System in Reading. Huntington Beach, Calif.: Richard L. Zweig, 1971.

GILMORE, JOHN V., AND EUNICE C. GILMORE. *Gilmore Oral Reading Test.* New York: The Psychological Corporation, 1968.

GOODMAN, KENNETH S. "Miscues: Windows on the Reading Process." In *Miscue Analysis: Applications to Reading Instruction.* Kenneth S. Goodman, ed. Urbana, Ill.: National Council of Teachers of English, 1973.

GOODMAN, YETTA A., AND CAROLYN L. BURKE. *Reading Miscue Inventory Manual: Procedure for Diagnosis and Evaluation.* New York: Macmillan, 1972.

GROFF, PATRICK. "A Critique of an Oral Reading Miscues Analysis." *Reading World,* 19, no. 3 (Mar. 1980), 254–64.

HARRIS, ALBERT J. *How to Increase Reading Ability.* New York: D. McKay, 1970.

HARRIS, ALBERT J., AND MILTON D. JACOBSON. *Basic Elementary Reading Vocabularies.* London: Macmillan, 1972.

HARRIS, ALBERT J. AND EDWARD SIPAY. *How to Increase Reading Ability.* New York: Longman, 1980.

HITTLEMAN, DANIEL R. *Developmental Reading: A Psycholinguistic Perspective:* Chicago: Rand McNally, 1978.

HOOD, JOYCE. "Qualitative Analysis of Oral Reading Errors: The Inter Judge Reliability of Scores." *Reading Research Quarterly,* 11, no. 4 (1975-76), 577–98.

————. "Is Miscue Analysis Practical for Teachers?" *Reading Teacher,* 32, no. 3 (Dec. 1978), 260–66.

JACOBS, DONALD H., AND LYNDON W. SEAR-FOSS. *Diagnostic Reading Inventory.* Dubuque, Iowa: Kendall/Hunt, 1979.

JASTAK, JOSEPH F., SIDNEY BIJOU, AND SARAH JASTAK. *Wide Range Achievement Test.* New York: Psychological Corporation, 1981.

JOHNSON, DALE D. "A Basic Vocabulary for Beginning Readers." *Elementary School Journal,* 72 (Oct. 1971), 31–33.

————. "Guidelines for Evaluating Word Attack Skills in the Primary Grades." In *Assessment of Problems in Reading.* Walter H. MacGinitie, ed. Newark, Del.: International Reading Association, 1973.

JOHNSON, DALE D., AND P. DAVID PEARSON. "Skills Management Systems: A Critique." *Reading Teacher,* 28, no. 8 (May 1975), 757–64.

JOHNSON, DALE D., SUSAN D. PITTLEMAN, LINDA K. SHRIBERG, JUDY SCHWENKER, AND SANDRA S. DAHL. *The Word Identification Test Battery: A New Approach to Mastery and the Assessment of Word Identification Skills.* Technical Report 553, Wisconsin Research and Development Center for Individualized Schooling. Madison: University of Wisconsin, 1980.

JOHNSON, MARJORIE S., AND ROY A. KRESS. *Informal Reading Inventories.* Newark, Del.: International Reading Association, 1965.

KENDER, JOSEPH. "Informal Reading Inventories." *Reading Teacher,* 24, no. 2 (Nov. 1970), 165–67.

KILLGALLON, PATSY A. "A Study to Determine the Relationships Among Certain Pupils' Adjustments in Language Situations." Unpublished doctoral dissertation, Pennsylvania State College, 1942.

KLEIN, ERNEST. *A Comprehensive Etymological Dictionary of the English Language.* New York: Elsevier Publishing Co., 1966.

LAPRAY, MARGARET, AND RAMON ROSS. "The Graded Word List: Quick Gauge of Reading Ability." *Journal of Reading,* 12, no. 4 (Jan. 1969), 305–307.

LESLIE, LAUREN, AND PAT OSOL. "Changes in Oral Reading Strategies as a Function of Quantities of Miscues." *Journal of Reading Behavior,* 10, no. 4 (Winter 1978), 442–45.

LIDDELL, HENRY G., AND ROBERT SCOTT. *A Greek-English Lexicon,* rev. Henry S. Jones and Roderick McKenzie. Oxford, Eng.: Clarendon Press, 1940.

McCRACKEN, ROBERT A. *Standard Reading Inventory.* Klamath Falls, Ore.: Klamath Printing, 1966.

McNEIL, JOHN D. "False Prerequisites in the Teaching of Reading." *Journal of Reading Behavior,* 6, no. 4 (Dec. 1974), 421–27.

MURRAY, JAMES A. *A New English Dictionary on Historical Principles,* Vol. III, D and E. Oxford, Eng.: Clarendon Press, 1897.

OTTO, WAYNE, AND EUNICE ASKOV. *Wisconsin Design for Reading Skill Development: Word Attack.* Minneapolis, Minn.: Interpretive Scoring Systems/NCS, 1972.

OTTO, WAYNE, ROBERT CHESTER, JOHN McNEIL, AND SHIRLEY MYERS. *Focused Reading Instruction.* Reading, Mass.: Addison-Wesley, 1974.

OZER, MARK N. "Assessment of Children with Learning Problems: A Child Development Approach." In *Reading Problems: A Multi-Disciplinary Perspective.* Wayne Otto, Charles W. Peters, and Nathaniel Peters, eds. Reading, Mass.: Addison-Wesley, 1977.

PIKULSKI, JOHN J. "A Critical Review: Informal Reading Inventories." *Reading Teacher,* 28, no. 2 (Nov. 1974), 141–51.

POWELL, WILLIAM R. "Measuring Reading Performance Informally." Paper presented at annual meeting of International Reading Association, Houston, Tex., May 1978. ERIC, ED 155-589.

POWELL, WILLIAM, COLIN G. DUNKELD. "Validity of Informal Reading Inventory Reading Levels." *Elementary English,* 48, no. 6 (Oct. 1971), 637–42.

Prescriptive Reading Inventory. Monterey, Calif.: CTB/McGraw-Hill, 1972.

RINSKY, LEE ANN, AND ESTA DE FOSSARD. *The Contemporary Classroom Reading Inventory.* Dubuque, Iowa: Gorsuch, Scarisbrick, 1980.

SAWYER, DIANE J. "The Diagnostic Mystique—A Point of View." *Reading Teacher,* 27, no. 6 (Mar. 1974), 555–61.

SILVAROLI, NICHOLAS J. *Classroom Reading Inventory.* Dubuque, Iowa: William C. Brown, 1976.

SLOSSON, RICHARD L. *Slosson Oral Reading Test.* East Aurora, N.Y.: Slosson Educational Publications, 1963.

SMITH, FRANK. *Understanding Reading.* New York: Holt, Rinehart & Winston, 1978.

SMITH, LAURA, AND CONSTANCE WEAVER. "A Psycholinguistic Look at the Informal Reading Inventory, Part I: Looking at the Quality of Reader's Miscues: A Rationale and an Easy Method." *Reading Horizons,* 19, no. 1 (Fall 1978), 12–22.

SMITH, NILA B., AND H. ALAN ROBINSON. *Reading Instruction for Today's Children.* Englewood Cliffs, N.J.: Prentice-Hall, 1980.

SPACHE, GEORGE D. *Diagnosing and Correcting Reading Disabilities.* Boston: Allyn & Bacon, 1976.

———. *Diagnostic Reading Scales.* Monterey, Calif.: CTB/McGraw Hill, 1972.

STAUFFER, RUSSELL G. *Teaching Reading as a Thinking Process.* New York: Harper & Row, Pub., 1969.

STAUFFER, RUSSELL G., JULES C. ABRAMS, AND JOHN S. PIKULSKI. *Diagnosis, Correction and Prevention of Reading Disabilities.* New York: Harper & Row, Pub., 1978.

THORNDIKE, EDWARD L., AND IRVING LORGE. *The Teacher's Word Book of 30,000 Words.* New York: Teachers College Press, Columbia University, 1944.

TORTELLI, JAMES P. "Simplified Psycholinguistic Diagnosis." *Reading Teacher,* 29, no. 7 (Apr. 1976), 637–39.

VENEZKY, RICHARD. *The Structure of English Orthography.* The Hague: Mouton, 1970.

WALTER, RICHARD B. "History and Development of the Informal Reading Inventory." Unpublished study prepared at Kean College of New Jersey, 1974. ERIC Ed 098-539.

WEBER, ROSE-MARIE. "The Study of Oral Reading Errors: A Survey of the Literature." *Reading Research Quarterly* 4, no. 1 (Fall 1968), 96–119.

WILLIAMSON, KEON E., AND FREDA YOUNG. "The IRI and RMI Diagnostic Concepts Should be Synthesized." *Journal of Reading Behavior,* 6, no. 2 (July 1974), 183–94.

WIXSON, KAREN L. "Miscue Analysis: A Critical Review." *Journal of Reading Behavior,* 11, no. 2 (Summer 1979), 163–75.

WOODS, MARY LYNN, AND ALDEN J. MOE. *Analytical Reading Inventory.* Columbus, Ohio: Chas. E. Merrill, 1981.

6

TEACHING WORD IDENTIFICATION

Upon completion of the chapter, you will be able to

1. Discuss the implications of interactive processing for the teaching of word identification skills.
2. Explain the challenges which confront the disabled reader at each of the following levels:
    a. Sight vocabulary.
    b. Consonants.
    c. Vowels.
    d. Multisyllabic Words
3. Describe procedures for acquiring a sight vocabulary through a language-experiencing approach and trade book materials.
4. Describe procedures for teaching word identification skills at three levels:
    a. Consonants.
    b. Vowels.
    c. Multisyllabic Words.

INTRODUCTION

Have Book, Can't Read

Mike acts like many other ten-year-olds. He is of average intelligence; displays no obvious sensory (vision and hearing), cultural, or emotional difficulties; and aside from an occasional squabble, gets along well with his peers. Physically sound, he can run toe-to-toe with most students his age.

No so typical, however, is Mike's reading performance. Despite his fifth-grade standing, he is reading at a preprimer level. Furthermore, he shows little interest in reading and loathes reading instruction. Unlike his peers, Mike's reading progress is virtually at a standstill and has been for some time. And each month he is falling even further behind his classmates.

Teaching students like Mike usually requires an alternative to a basal reader approach, with which they have had only limited success. But even more important than the correct method is an understanding of the reading process. We have previously indicated that an interactive view of reading has much to offer and can help teachers make sound instructional decisions. In brief, an interactive model balances the use of both the visual and the nonvisual data in reading. Such an approach can help students who misunderstand reading and overrely on either phonics or context.

To appreciate fully the value of an interactive approach, we need to compare it with other strategies. The first approach, a "decoding emphasis," is a direct, frontal assault in which letter names and sounds are taught at the outset, followed by a heavy dose of sound blending and phonic generalizations, ending in extensive reading of connected text—that is, a bottom-up approach.

The second approach, a "meaning emphasis," stresses the use of language. In this top-down approach, semantics and syntax are emphasized, thus reducing the need to rely on visual data in identifying words. Introduction of traditional word identification skills such as phonics is delayed and deemphasized. In this method students may not be confronted sufficiently soon with the alphabetic principle.

An interactive strategy seeks to establish a more perfect balance between the nonvisual and visual aspects of reading. Although all students need help to make the most of their invisible linguistic resources, this is doubly true for those who have failed to read and who participate reluctantly in instruction. Encouraging them to use the information about language *they already possess* will help to compensate for their limited ability to process print.

We believe, therefore, that the challenge of decoding can be met by focusing on *word identification as an initial goal* but using meaningful reading material and powerful linguistic cues to accomplish that end.

Chapter Organization

Students like Mike need help in identifying words. To meet this need, we have divided word identification into four levels:

1. Sight vocabulary and context.
2. Early word identification—consonants.

    3.   Advanced word identification—vowels.

    4.   Multisyllabic words.

These levels represent four phases through which students ordinarily pass as they learn to read. In level 1, students must acquire a sight vocabulary and understand the role of context. In level 2, phonics—specifically consonant elements—should be learned. This phase may be taught concurrently with level 1 or after level 1 is well under way. Students in level 3 learn vowel sounds. Finally, in level 4, multisyllabic word identification skills are introduced.

Although students tend to progress sequentially from one level to the next, the levels—and the skills and strategies within each level—do not necessarily represent a hierarchy. The organization of this chapter simply provides a structure for teaching word identification. We recognize that students can learn these skills in different sequences, quite apart from our teaching efforts. For example, students who appear to be ignorant of vowel sounds may be able to identify multisyllabic words with ease.

LEVEL 1:
SIGHT VOCABULARY AND CONTEXT

The chief objective of level 1 is to help students acquire a sight vocabulary, a stock of high-frequency words which they can quickly identify. A second objective is to teach them to take advantage of context in identifying and remembering words. A final objective is to help them develop fluency in reading simple material. These three objectives are intimately related and should be taught concurrently. Students must be able to identify individual words quickly but they must also read fluently when encountering connected text.

Language-Experience Approach

A language-experience approach will be the primary vehicle for accomplishing the objectives of level 1. This method is sufficiently flexible to provide for both top-down and bottom-up processing.

An advantage of this approach is that it encourages the disabled reader to use considerable invisible information in processing print, thus reducing its difficulty. In language experience students read their own dictated accounts. The reading becomes easier because they possess previous information about the text.

Language experience, however, is presented as an example of how beginning reading can be successfully taught to the disabled reader rather than as the only way to reach the objectives of level 1. Although the method is theoretically sound and can be used with students of various ages and backgrounds, obviously no method is effective all the time.

The language-experience approach can be used with either a group or an individual. We will discuss its use with a student like Mike, the ten-year-old who is reading at the preprimer level, and then describe alternative strategies for group instruction. In each instance we will describe a four-day cycle, a series of

It's easier to read the page when you are the author.   (Peter P. Tobia)

coordinated activities which occur over the course of a week. As a student begins to make more rapid progress, the cycle is gradually reduced to two days, and finally a transition is made to books and other commercial material.

DAY 1   The teacher's first task is to obtain an account or story from the student. The teacher begins by explaining that these accounts will help the student to read. The student should realize that the account may be either factual or fictional. After its purpose has been explained, the teacher might ask, "What would you like to tell me?" The student can be allowed to talk about the account before beginning the actual dictation. This warm-up session helps to improve the fluency of the account. With some students it also helps if they dictate a full sentence before the teacher writes what they say. If necessary, the teacher can ask a few questions to elicit more information. The teacher should listen attentively and comment just enough to encourage the student to continue speaking. Soon, the student will be ready to dictate.

If the student is reluctant to respond, the teacher might try one of these suggestions:

1.   Give the student enough time to think of a topic. Avoid talking too quickly after requesting an account. Silence itself sometimes creates sufficient incentive for a student to dictate.

2.   Engage the student in conversation by commenting on the football emblem on a shirt or an unusual bit of jewelry, or ask about the outcome of a recent soccer game.

3.   With students' help, develop a list of topics which might be used on future occasions. On the day scheduled for dictation, the student can select from the list. The list can also be reviewed the day before dictation so the student can give some thought to a particular account.

4. Develop a picture file. Students who are reluctant to talk about themselves may talk willingly about pictures.

5. Avoid showing undue concern about a student's reluctance to dictate. One student sensed that his teacher was frustrated over his unwillingness to produce an account and found it quite effective to resist passively by not dictating. If there is such a student in your class, do not make an issue of refusal but turn temporarily to alternative activities.

6. Avoid asking, "Would you like to dictate about_____?" The student may say "No." Also, do not ask questions such as "What did you watch on television last night" in an effort to elicit dictation. Students may sense that certain topics are preferred, and they may conform out of politeness rather than genuine enthusiasm. This is particularly true with older students who tend to participate passively and need to be encouraged to express their ideas, not to echo yours.

7. Encourage students by saying, "You seem to know a lot about _____ [cars, dinosaurs, volcanoes]. Perhaps you can tell me about them."

Must teachers transcribe everything a student wishes to dictate? Occasionally students attempt to dictate a lurid account about sex, drugs, or similar topics. Teachers are not obliged to write anything which is personally offensive or which is being dictated for its shock value. A more difficult situation arises when students innocently disclose information which would create embarrassment if read by others or even later by the students themselves. Frequently this involves private family matters. The teacher should discuss the propriety of such accounts with the student. If a student wishes to confide such information, it can be done in predictation conversation and family affairs would be omitted from the actual dictation.

A related issue is whether to correct a student's usage in sentences such as "We seen the animals at the circus." We suggest that teachers edit only with great care. A student will tend to read the dictated account in the same way it was originally spoken. Confusion will result if the words have been changed. If the teacher, for example, writes *saw* for *seen* in "We seen the animals at the circus," the student may still read *seen*. In this case, we would accept the student's oral version. *Our prime purpose in obtaining these stories is to develop students' sight vocabulary, not to standardize their usage.* Calling attention to grammatical errors or altering personal language is not likely to encourage continued dictation.

A partial solution to usage errors is to read the entire account back to the students after it has been dictated and ask if they wish to make any changes. Frequently, they will detect incorrect words or unclear language and readily revise the dictation.

Words themselves should be spelled according to dictionary forms. The stability of dictionary spelling facilitates written communication. A few situations do present unusual problems. For example, a student may say "gonna" for "going to." We would write down "going to." In gray areas such as these, however, your own judgment must be exercised rather than any hard and fast rules.

Virtually all school-age students can speak in sentences, but in first attempts at dictating, some may not understand what is expected of them. It is acceptable at this point to expand student phrases to sentences. If a student, for example, has decided to talk about a fishing trip, and in order to prompt him, the teacher has asked, "Where did you go fishing?" he might reply, "in the bay." The teacher can write, "I went fishing in the bay." Once the students understands that a sentence is expected, they will usually complete the dictation in that form.

Older students need not watch the words being written unless they have a limited understanding of the nature of reading. The teacher should write as quickly as possible in order to encourage the student's flow of thoughts. Occasionally, a student in deference to the teacher's writing may slow down the dictation, robbing the account of its fluency. Say, "Keep talking. I'll catch up with you."

If the student dictates far more than can easily be recalled, the teacher may say, "We have time for two more sentences. Think how you would like to end your story." If the student has chosen a topic of epic proportions, such as detailed stories about several dinosaurs, the topic can be divided into separate chapters and continued on another day.

When the dictation is completed, the student provides a title for the account. This presents a natural opportunity to introduce the concept of main idea. Even young students can understand the concept of main idea in this setting. One student, for example, after dictating about the presents she wanted for her birthday was asked for a story title. She replied, "Call it 'The Greedy Kid.'"

When dictation is completed, the teacher reads it to the student. The read-back serves two purposes: (1) It allows the students to revise any portions which are unclear or contain improper usage. (2) The students hear the account as a whole, thereby assisting their recollection of the story on subsequent days.

The account is now read with the students. They may doubt that they can read even with the teacher's help; encourage them to try. Their reading may lag a word or so behind the teacher's, but this is perfectly acceptable. Toward the end of a sentence, the teacher's voice can be lowered. If the students continue reading, it suggests they have been attending and can use oral context. Of course, they may not necessarily be able to read these words under any other circumstances.

DAY 2   Since you may have hastily written the original dictation on day 1, rewrite the account in careful manuscript or type it on a primary typewriter. (In some circumstances, you may have done this originally.) For the beginning reader, regardless of age, leave ample space between words to help in word identification.

When typing a story, you should leave two spaces between words and two to three spaces between lines. Handwritten manuscript accounts should be similarly spaced. For elementary grade students, it matters little whether the account is typewritten or written by hand. Older students who have not acquired a sight vocabulary, however, may benefit from the "adult appearance" of a typed account since it presents none of the negative connotations associated with printing for young children and is consistent in letter size, shape, and spacing. At the same time, a primary typewriter need not be used; a typewriter with pica type is often sufficient. Large primary type may be associated with childish activities and may cause embarrassment.

Begin instruction by reading the account to the students, refreshing their memory. Then read it together with them as you did on the first day. Observe whether they are able to continue if you lower your voice at the end of sentences. If they falter, do not let them struggle but raise your voice and continue.

Ask, "Do you see any words you know?" Even a poor reader is likely to recognize at least one word. Ask them to point to any words they can identify, say each word aloud, and draw a line under it. Ask them to select additional words, say them, and underline them. Remind the students that they need not know all the words in the story. Some students may persist in underlining the words in sequence. Note this behavior—it's often a sign that the students are overrelying on oral context (or less likely, that they already know all the words!)—but do not be concerned. In subsequent activities, the known words will be separated from the unknown.

The rate of vocabulary introduction in a language-experience approach is fundamentally different from that in a basal reader program. In the language experience approach, the readers control the rate by selecting just the words they know. This eliminates the effect common to basal reader programs in which additional words are introduced on schedule regardless of whether the students are ready to learn them.

Some students may be reluctant to underline words. To encourage them, you might select a few words which you feel they know and ask, "Can you find the word _____?" Or, pointing to a word, "What do you think this word is?" Continue as long as the student responds readily to the task. This process will often convince poor readers that they *can* read.

The activities up to this point rely heavily on top-down processing, which has the advantage of making reading easy by allowing the students to draw on their own listening and speaking language background. Gradually, in the following days of the cycle, the students will be forced to attend more closely to the print itself. This flow between language meaning and visual detail continues throughout the four-day cycle and encourages the flexible use of both kinds of information.

The dictated account can also be employed to assess and/or reinforce students' phonic ability by asking them to find a word in the first line that has the same beginning sound as one supplied by you. Say, for example, "Find a word in the first line which begins like *tire*." At first, include only words they have previously identified. If they know only a few words, ask them to point to the word rather than pronounce it. For example, in the sentence "The power went out last night after we ate our supper," the students may know only the word *supper;* but if they know initial consonant sounds, they should be able to respond if you ask them to locate a word that begins like *needle*. At first, select words which begin with single initial consonants. Later, expand the activity to include other phonic elements which have been introduced (blends or digraphs).

DAY 3   On the third day read the story to the students and then with them. They should be asked to underline any known words in the story. Words

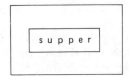

Figure 6-1 Card Window

known from the previous day should be underlined again, whereas new words will be underlined for the first time. At this point, determine how well the students can identify these words without the benefit of context. A good technique to check isolated word identification is to cut an opening in a 3-by-5-inch index card (see Figure 6-1). This "card window" (Stauffer, 1978) is moved around the page at random to check the students' word recognition. If a word is not known when shown in the window, the card is lifted to restore the context.

Through repeated practice, you can teach the students to use the card window independently. Then as you work with others, those students can practice identifying words in isolation in the window and through context by uncovering the text to check their prediction. Diligent use of this technique encourages the acquisition of a sight vocabulary.

DAY 4   In preparation for day 4, you should write the words identified in the window card on 1-by-3-inch cards. If you cannot check individually the students' knowledge of words on day 3, write, before class on day 4, all the words the student has underlined. This may result in writing more words than the student actually can identify in isolation. However, since cards can be written without the student's presence, valuable teacher-student time can be utilized for more important activities.

On day 4 distribute word cards to the students. Ask them to sort cards into two piles—known and unknown words. Mistakes in sorting may occur at first but gradually students will become more discriminating. This decision is just one of many you are asking students to make: They must select the topic for dictation, choose the words to underline, and now decide which words they know. These decisions increase their commitment to learning to read and encourage them to be more responsible for their own learning.

When all the words have been sorted, ask the students to read the words in the known pile. Allow about three seconds for a response. If students need more time, the word is not yet a part of their sight vocabulary and they will not be able to read it quickly in some contexts. If they read the word incorrectly, have them locate it in the dictated story. Some students must be shown how to move the word card across each line and down the page until they find the matching word. If they find the word and can identify it, let them keep the card for the present. Words in the unknown pile are discarded.

In subsequent days you will want to evaluate the students' retention of vocabulary. Because this testing may raise their anxieties, we have often used the following procedure. Present each word card to the student. Known words will be placed on the student's side of the desk, and all the unknown words will be placed on the teacher's side of the desk. When all the word cards have been presented, the teacher and student count the words in their respective piles. The person with the most words is declared the "winner." If the lessons have been conducted properly and paced appropriately, the student will invariably have collected more words than the teacher. If the student does not, the teacher should alter teaching procedures and/or slow down the pace of instruction.

As an optional activity, the teacher may invite the student to "win back" words in the teacher's pile by looking up words in the original account. All words identified in this manner can be credited to the student. The activity is conducted more formally with older students but is effective with all ages.

In the beginning of the language-experience approach, known words can be kept in an ordinary envelope with the student's name on it. Each story is numbered and dated and a corresponding number is placed on the back of each known word card. The first story and cards are numbered *1,* the second *2,* and so on. This system allows a student to locate words quickly once numerous stories have been dictated.

As students progress, they will use different cues to identify words. At first, they may remember a word by its location in the story. Later they will be able to use the words surrounding the unknown word to help them. Sensitivity to length and letters, beginning with the initial letter, soon develops. When words are more familiar, but still unknown at sight, students may begin turning to the appropriate story for assistance but mentally race ahead and call it out before they see it in context. This is another sign of progress and suggests a growing reliance on the visual features of the word.

If students indicate they can identify words from other sources (cereal boxes, road signs, and so on), write out word cards in a different colored ink to distinguish them from words in the dictated stories.

Obtain a new dictated account every four days, but as the student progresses, the dictating cycle can be gradually reduced to two days by selectively omitting steps in the procedure. After four days, move onto another story; do not belabor an account until every word is learned. High-frequency words will occur in subsequent stories, and words of low frequency are relatively unimportant in beginning reading.

Since all students construct their own book, dictated accounts should be bound together for use in later lessons. The simplest binding is formed by punching holes in several sheets of manila paper, fastening the sheets together with paper fasteners, and attaching colored construction paper for a cover. Dictated accounts are usually typed or written on separate paper and then pasted onto the manila pages. Additional pages may be inserted as they are needed. A more durable option is to place the stories in sturdy composition books.

Students can also construct their own books by using standard book-binding techniques. These books take longer to construct but are attractive and durable and enhance the status of language-experience stories. Directions for constructing books such as these can be found in Weiss' *How to Make Books* (1978). Dictated accounts for students beyond the elementary grades, including adults, are typed on full 8-½-by-11-inch sheets of paper and inserted in a plastic binder with pressure clamps.

Figure 6-2 illustrates a page from a language-experience book.

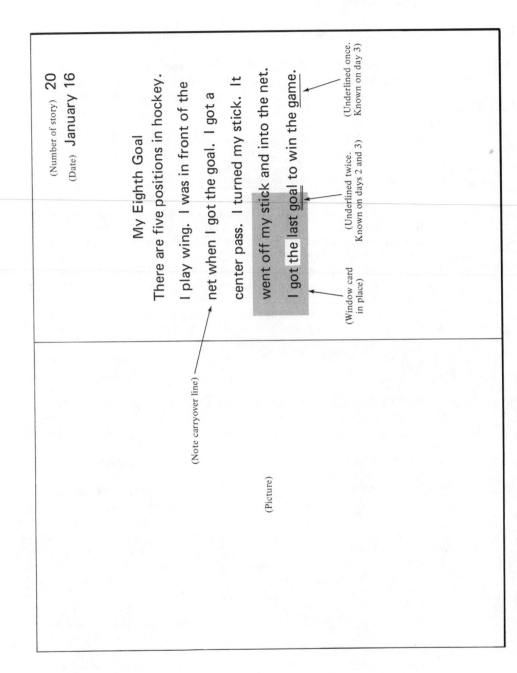

(Number of story) 20

(Date) January 16

My Eighth Goal

There are five positions in hockey.
I play wing. I was in front of the
net when I got the goal. I got a
center pass. I turned my stick. It
went off my stick and into the net.
I got the last goal to win the game.

(Note carryover line)

(Picture)

(Window card in place)

(Underlined twice. Known on days 2 and 3)

(Underlined once. Known on day 3)

Figure 6-2 Open Pages in a Language-Experience Book

ILLUSTRATING THE DICTATED ACCOUNT   Primary-age students should be encouraged to illustrate their dictated accounts, as this helps them remember the topics. For example, students may be unable to use story context to identify a word because they do not remember the account. The picture frequently jogs their memory. Older students are usually less interested in drawing pictures, and the decision to illustrate should be left to the discretion of the teacher and the student.

The preceding language-experience activities were designed for an individual student who needs to develop a basic sight vocabulary. Variations of this approach are helpful in working with a group of students.

Group Dictation

The individual dictated account is highly effective since the students read their own personalized meaningful text. However, primary-age students who have gotten off to a slow start in reading can benefit from group dictation. The advantage of the group is twofold: Pressure on individuals is reduced because the teacher's attention is divided among several children. Second, students can learn a good deal about reading by watching their peers perform—dictating sentences, underlining words, and so on. Students who are reluctant to dictate, for example, can watch their more confident classmates and discover vicariously that this activity can be rewarding.

Group procedures differ slightly from individual instruction. On day 1 of the four-day cycle, for example, the teacher presents a stimulus to the children—a highly motivating concrete item that students can see, feel, manipulate, and perhaps even smell or taste. The stimulus can be food—apples or popcorn—or an animal—rabbit, hamster, gerbil, or goat. Science experiments or activities which develop naturally from other curricula are also appropriate. Just as relevant are significant news events. Students are eager to dictate about space flights or presidential elections, but current events need not have nationwide significance. When a small rural schoolhouse burned to the ground, what do you think the students talked about soon after being assigned to new quarters? In choosing stimuli, be sensitive to parental values. In some communities, stimuli relating to particular religious holidays may be objectionable. Family rules about eating may influence the use of food stimuli. On the other hand, do not restrict an individual's freedom to dictate about personal or family beliefs and practices.

Students should be led in a discussion of the stimulus, perhaps calling attention to its attributes, its uses, and the categories to which it belongs. If the stimulus is a bag of apples, you can help students talk about their shape, color, texture, and taste; how they are used in food; and their relationship to other kinds of food. Students then dictate sentences which are recorded on large chart paper. Approximately six sentences can be dictated about a single stimulus. Try to elicit a sentence from each student, but do not force a child to contribute.

The following account (Figure 6-3) is an example of a group story.

The steps for the first two days follow procedures for individual stories except that the teacher leads the group in rereading the story. Students underline the known words on the chart. On day 3, a copy of the story is distributed to each student, words are underlined, and window cards are employed to check

> **OUR PETS**
>
> Lisa said, "My hamster gathers everything in his cage and puts it in a corner and makes a nest out of it." Troy said, "My dog likes to lick. He always eats his heart worm pill." Rachel said, "I'm getting a white bunny with light brown spots." Kristen said, "My dog King likes to eat steak everyday and she licks herself when she is finished."

Figure 6-3 A Group Language-Experience Account

Figure 6-4 Basic Language-Experience Cycle

INDIVIDUAL DICTATION	GROUP DICTATION
Day 1	**Day 1**
1. Discussion of stimulus	1. Presentation of stimulus
2. Dictation	2. Discussion
3. Rereading	3. Group dictation
	4. Rereading
Day 2	5. Underlining known words—I (chart)
1. Rereading	
2. Underlining known words—I	**Day 2**
3. Phonic assessment/instruction	1. Rereading
4. Illustrating account	2. Underlining known words—II (chart)
	3. Phonic assessment/instruction
Day 3	4. Illustrating account
1. Rereading	
2. Underlining known words—II	**Day 3**
3. Card window check	1. Distribution of individual copies
	2. Underlining known words—III
Day 4	3. Card window check
1. Word cards—self-assessment	
2. Word cards—teacher assessment	**Day 4**
	1. Word cards—self-assessment
Day 5	2. Word cards—teacher assessment
New dictation or review	
	Day 5
	New dictation or review

words in isolation. On day 4, word cards are distributed and students sort them into known and unknown categories before they are checked by the teacher.

A transition from group to individual stories should be made as soon as possible since those individual accounts make greater use of a student's personal language and experience. Students begin individual dictation when they have participated actively in all phases of group dictation and are learning and retaining vocabulary.

A combination of group and individual teaching techniques can be used if you introduce a stimulus to the group, discuss it with the children, and then take dictation from individuals rather than from the group. Students should dictate out of the hearing range of other students because they may mimic one another's ideas.

This completes the presentation of the basic steps in group and individual language-experience stories. Figure 6-4 summarizes these procedures.

Language Experience and Textbooks

A language-experience approach is ordinarily designed to help students develop a basic sight vocabulary and see the relationship between language and print. When this objective has been accomplished, a transition to conventional reading material is made. One exception is the use of an experience approach with textbook assignments for underachieving readers. A typical problem in the middle grades is the inability of students with low reading levels to read grade-level materials efficiently. If they are capable of understanding the material and simply lack the ability to identify the words, language-experience procedures can be helpful.

The following procedures are suggested to help students deal with textbook assignments.

1. Read the selection to a small group of students. (This procedure is easily adapted for use with an individual.)
2. Ask each student to remember at least one idea from the reading.
3. In a student-led discussion, have them decide which ideas are most important to use and the sequence in which they should be organized.
4. The teacher, meanwhile, reads related selections to other groups of students and then returns to take dictation from the first group.
5. Students dictate to the teacher, and copies are distributed the following day to each group in the classroom. All students receive a copy of each account. The teacher reads each dictated account to the whole class and then they read them together. Individual students may volunteer to read an account aloud.
6. Each group prepares a set of questions based on the dictated text. In turn, each group asks another group one of these questions. The responding group discusses the question, agreeing on a single answer by consensus or majority vote. The teacher or a panel of student judges evaluates the accuracy of the answers. The teacher may later discuss the appropriateness of particular answers.

7. The accounts may be read chorally on later days.
8. For testing purposes, the students are responsible for the information on the dictated accounts.

In this section we have reviewed the steps in the basic language-experience cycle. Reading for meaning, or top-down processing, has been given primary attention through the experience and language the student brings to the task. At the same time, we have encouraged students to focus on the print itself, a bottom-up, or decoding, orientation. When these procedures are used together, they facilitate interactive processing of the text.

Retention of Sight Vocabulary

Some students have trouble remembering words. An important tool for helping them remember difficult words is the word card. These should be reviewed daily. Words which cannot be identified immediately are "looked up" in the dictated account. When approximately two dozen words have been acquired, students are asked to construct word-card sentences. In this activity the word cards are laid out in sequence across the desk. For example:

Dana	can	ride	a	bicycle.

Students can be shown how to build the first sentence and then are asked to substitute other word cards in the sentence. Other proper names, for example, can be inserted for Dana: [*Jared, Ronnie, Terri*] . . . *can ride a bicycle*. This gives the student practice in reading the same word several times but makes minimal reading demands because only one word in the sentence is changed. Occasionally words can be inserted which add humor to the sentences, for example, *Dana can eat a bicycle*. Students who are anxious about reading deserve a bit of comic relief.

Numerous activities can facilitate the review of word cards. If duplicates are made, they can be used to play card games such as Concentration, Old Maid, and Go Fish. In addition, word cards can be used to play many board games by putting each student's cards in a pile and requiring a student to pick a word from the pile and read it before moving his or her piece. The number of letters in the word can determine the number of spaces the student is allowed to move. In this manner, the cards replace dice or spinners. A worthwhile variation of this game is to prepare cards which contain these words in phrases and sentences. This step enables context to be used in word identification.

When a student's envelope overflows with cards, transfer them to a word bank, a plastic or wooden recipe file box for 3-by-5-inch cards. Insert alphabetic dividers in the box to separate the words by initial letter. As an optional step, place small coin envelopes between the dividers and have students file their cards in these envelopes to insure that the cards do not shift position. See Figure 6-5 for a description of this equipment.

When the card collection swells, it is more efficient to review the cards by

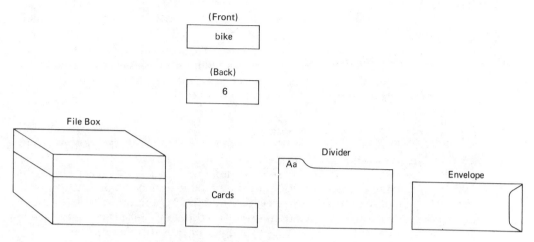

Figure 6-5 Components of the Word Bank

establishing a systematic schedule of recontact rather than rely on word-card sentences. On Monday, students may review words beginning with *a, b, c,* and *d;* On Tuesday, additional letters may be reviewed; and so on. The constant review of the words helps students attend to word detail and perceive patterns in letter order. If a word is not known, the student is taught to turn the card over, check the story number on the reverse side, and find the word in the original account. In this manner, the student is given functional practice in the use of context cues, an important objective of level 1.

As a general rule, we would expect students to identify immediately about 70 percent of the words in their bank and be able to decode another 10 to 15 percent through context. If students forget too many of these words, be ready to adjust your teaching procedures. The following steps may be taken to improve retention:

1. Take more care in giving word cards to students. Insist that they be able to read a word in the window card before a card is distributed.

2. Keep words from a particular story in a separate envelope and review them frequently before allowing them to be transferred to the larger word-box collection. This "holding tank" approach makes it easier to check the word in context because all words in that envelope relate to the same story. It also allows students to concentrate on a set of words before they are scattered among the alphabet where they will be reviewed less frequently.

3. Provide for systematic rereading of old stories, not necessarily to learn all the words but to retain familiarity with a story. This will facilitate the use of context.

4. Encourage students to review their words with other students. Their

partner, of course, must keep alert so that no credit is given for miscalled words.

5. If a word is persistently miscalled, make a check on the back of the card. If a word is checked three times, discard it, or place it in the teacher's file box under the student's name. Periodically, the students may review these cards to see if they can repossess them.

Word cards reinforce and test students' retention and measure the ability to transfer knowledge from one setting to another. If students know words in isolation, they are more likely to know them in a variety of settings.   ·

Students frequently overrely on context to unlock words. Facile in memorizing a language-experience account, they feel little need to attend to words themselves. The use of word cards in which students are temporarily deprived of context helps to redirect their attention to word detail. Here they can practice identifying words solely on the basis of length and distinctive features.

More immediate feedback can be provided by recording the student's incorrect responses to a word (Stauffer, 1978). Joseph, for example, was unable to read the word *Patty*, but he was encouraged to think of a word which looked like it. He replied with *Betty*. The teacher wrote *Betty* below *Patty* and said, "This is what you said." Now Joseph replied with *Petty*. The teacher wrote *Petty* and repeated, "This is what you said." Each time Joseph compared the original stimulus, *Patty*, with his latest guess. The predicting continued as Joseph said *Pet*, *Pat*, and finally *Patty*. Each time the teacher encouraged Joseph to hypothesize, but the teacher never asked him to sound out the word or apply a phonic rule. Direct instructions to the student may be appropriate under some circumstances, but this technique stimulates students to apply the orthographic and phonic knowledge they already possess.

To retain words, students also require many opportunities to read connected text. Students can reread their experience stories aloud to themselves, the teacher, a classmate, secretary, custodian, visiting dignitary, aide, volunteer, kindergarten students, students at a lower grade level, or anyone else who will listen. If duplicate copies of the story are sent home, they may also be read to parents, siblings, aunts, cousins, and guests. Continual reading is the best way to synchronize the semantic, syntactic, orthographic, and phonic cueing systems and develop the automatic decoding (LaBerge and Samuels, 1974) which frees students to attend more carefully to the meaning of the text. This is particularly important when they begin to read stories other than language-experience accounts. Furthermore, the experience stories students choose indicate how they feel about themselves as readers. Students unsure of their ability will often return to their first story, which is usually short and is familiar. As they become more confident, however, they will begin to read other stories more often.

Enrichment Activities

The student who is struggling to read can easily become bored, tired, or frustrated. Having a collection of enrichment activities on hand in order to maintain a student's interest will make both teaching and learning more enjoyable. Here are some suggestions:

1. Students are delighted to read their dictated accounts from a large classroom screen. Make an overhead transparency of a dictated account and display it with an overhead projector.
2. Take pictures of students, preferably with a self-developing camera, and have students talk about the pictures.
3. Many schools have access to a videotape recorder. Students can tape various school activities and dictate a story as the tape is played back.
4. Use a tape recorder. Students may be reluctant at first to talk into a microphone, but with time and practice, this often becomes a favorite activity. Dictated accounts can be recorded and played back at the end of the period or day, providing tangible evidence of the day's accomplishments.

Transition to Books

Students need help to read accounts and books written by others. With this new material, they are deprived of much previous knowledge of the text, and reading thus becomes more difficult. This fact is dramatically illustrated by students who can read their dictated stories fluently but who read hesitantly when faced with relatively easy material written by others. At the same time, teachers can help students to realize that the same word identification strategies which worked so well for them with language-experience stories can be used in reading conventional books.

Here are some specific suggestions on how to move students from language-experience accounts to other printed material.

When a word appears prominently in an experience story, make available books which contain these words either in their title or text. For example, if a group made applesauce or a student told of an apple-picking experience, you might display the book *Ten Apples Up on Top* (LeSieg, 1961), a humorous account of animals who compete in juggling apples, or the delightful *Apple Pigs* (Orbach, 1979), in which a family is deluged by a harvest of apples. Students do not need to read these books in their entirety. It is sufficient that they identify any words in the book they know. Students will undoubtedly notice the word *apple*, the first step in preparing them to read books on their own.

Students can also begin the transition by reading each other's dictated accounts. Stories about the same topic are easier to read and highly motivating. The student who originally dictated the account is usually willing to assist the reader.

Assign students to survey magazines and newspapers for words they can read. If known words occur in large type, they may be cut out and pasted on construction paper. Words in small type can be marked with a transparent marker.

Once students have acquired a sight vocabulary of approximately 100 to 150 words, are able to read their experience stories fluently, and have learned to use context, they are ready for more demanding transitional activities. Now the teacher's task is to help them learn words which occur frequently in children's texts but which have not appeared in their dictated accounts.

Begin this process by assessing students' current knowledge. Place words from a high-frequency vocabulary list on index cards and ask students to identify them. When the student misses five words, the testing ceases and these five words are used in dictated sentences.

Several high-frequency vocabulary lists can be used for this purpose:

Dolch Basic Sight Vocabulary (Dolch, 1936).
188 Words of More than 88 Frequencies (Durr, 1973).
Basic Elementary Reading Vocabularies (Harris and Jacobson, 1972).
A Basic Vocabulary for Beginning Readers (Johnson, 1971).
Great Atlantic and Pacific Sight Word List (Otto and Chester, 1972).

Some authorities proclaim the virtues of one list over another, but we believe the words on any of these lists overlap sufficiently to serve your purposes. If a graded list is chosen, such as the Harris and Jacobson or Johnson, use only the first-grade words. It is sufficient to teach students the first 200 words in the Otto and Chester list of 500. When words of highest frequency from lists such as these have been learned, words of lower frequency can be mastered in a much more enjoyable manner through extensive reading.

The use of trade (library) books intensifies at this point. These books encourage reading because they are not perceived like basal readers, are humorous, frequently contain fewer words per page—a very real motivating force for a poor reader—and can be read in one sitting. Furthermore, their interest level is sufficiently high so that older students reading at a preprimer level will read a trade book even though they would reject a basal text of the same reading difficulty. Trade books substitute for basals at least until the students can read a basal commensurate with their interest. Trade books, of course, are never eliminated from the program; they continue to provide high-interest reading material throughout the student's reading program.

For primary students, you can bypass the typical basal material for the entire first-grade program and move into a basal, if desired, at the beginning of grade two. With older students, high-interest low-readability magazines such as *Sprint, Action,* and *Reader's Digest* can be used along with trade books in making the transition to a basal text. Again, the use of a basal can be postponed until the student's vocabulary and the interest level of the basal text are comparable. The lower interest level of a basal reader may lead you not to use it with some students, particularly in remedial teaching. On the other hand, the graded vocabulary of a basal can facilitate the acquisition of unknown words. In addition, students at the same instructional level can discuss the same selection, a valuable comprehension technique. If group dicussion can be accomplished solely with trade books, however, they may be used in place of a basal series.

Trade books can be used effectively by selecting a book such as *Bears in the Night* (Berenstain, 1969) which contains considerable action, makes good use of context cues, and has a simple text. The first page reads, "In bed," and shows a picture of several bears tucked in bed. If you were using such a text you could ask students either to read the text aloud or to identify any words they knew. Students are likely to know the word *in* as a sight word, and contextual and picture cues will help them identify *bed.*

Students with a minimal sight vocabulary should be able to read this book comfortably. If they struggle, however, the book can be put aside and additional time devoted to developing a more adequate vocabulary through experience stories. If students can read it easily, continue as long as their attention can be sustained. If possible, complete the reading of the entire book in one sitting as this helps build the students' confidence.

Students who can move rapidly through texts such as these now begin to realize that perhaps they too are readers. Their success with simple stories is more convincing evidence of their ability than any praise you can offer. You might also try introducing the same book to two students, assigning them to read alternative pages. Or if another student is unavailable, you can read every other page. In either event, the burden on the disabled student is reduced, and reading progresses rapidly.

If trade books are included in the program, students will acquire a sight vocabulary of high-frequency words, develop fluency, practice word identification strategies, and equally important—learn to enjoy reading. Try arranging these books according to difficulty. If students are progressing slowly, have them read additional books at the same level of difficulty before moving on to harder material.

Figure 6-6   Summary of Sight Vocabulary and Context Emphasis

PHASE	COMMENT
I. The basic four-day cycle	Four days is the usual time devoted to a single account. The cycle can be slowed to five days to provide more time for review or speeded up to two days if students are making rapid progress.
II. Retention activities	Interspersed with the ongoing basic cycle, these activities make heavy use of word cards and rereading old stories.
III. Enrichment	Sustaining student interest is a vital part of any corrective/remedial program. Many activities employ A-V aids such as tape recorders and cameras.
IV. Transition to books	Students learn high-frequency words which have not appeared in language-experience stories and read numerous easy trade books, individually and with other students.

Summarizing Level 1

In level 1, the student develops a sight vocabulary and concomitantly learns to use context as a word identification strategy. A language-experience approach has been advocated as an appropriate means to accomplish both objectives. Students who read experience stories realize that their account must make sense, and they learn to distinguish between random responses and informed guessing, a distinction which has previously eluded them.

Finally, repeated reading of language-experience stories and trade books provides an opportunity to integrate semantic, syntactic, and phonic cueing systems. When this phase is completed, students are ordinarily reading at the first-reader level.

Figure 6-6 on page 131 summarizes the major features of the emphasis on sight vocabulary and context.

LEVEL 2: CONSONANTS

Word Identification Strategies

In level 1, you sought to help students build a sight vocabulary, use context, and develop reading fluency. These objectives are continued in level 2, but emphasis is now placed on helping students use the syntactic and semantic cueing systems in reading material beyond the experience-story level. And although attention to visual information through phonics is maintained, our approach is now more formal. In level 1 we assumed that students could teach themselves a good deal about the reading process, including orthographic and phonic cues. Now we proceed deliberately to help a student decode words.

When students encounter unknown words, they should be taught a dependable, efficient strategy for identifying them. The general steps in this procedure are the following:

1. Use the context or overall meaning of the sentence by asking students to skip unknown words, read to the end of the sentence, return to the troublesome word, and try to fill in a word which makes sense. This use of meaning reduces the number of possible alternatives. If the students are still uncertain of the word's identity, they should proceed to step 2.

2. Use the phonic cues, but only to the extent necessary, in conjunction with context. That is, phonics should not replace context but complement it. Students should not routinely "sound out" words, letter by letter. "Sounding out" entire words is seldom necessary and is an inefficient strategy. As necessary, direct students' attention to the initial elements and inflectional endings such as *ing, ed,* and *s.*

3. If these strategies cannot help students decode unknown words, tell them to ask the teacher or a classmate for help.

The success of a predicting strategy relies on not only the students' skill but also their willingness to take risks. Risk-taking is influenced by two factors: (1) the appropriateness of the material and (2) the cost of making a mistake. If the text has been written with careful regard for language and meaning clues and the students are reading at their instructional level, they are more likely to make good use of semantic and syntactic cues and risk a guess. If, on the other hand, the students know too few of the words at sight, the text does not provide meaningful cues, and previous experience has not prepared them for this selection, they are less likely to risk a prediction. Furthermore, even if the circumstances invite a well-thought-out guess, students are not likely to attempt to decode if the consequences of failure are too high. We suggest the following techniques to encourage risk-taking:

1. Give students credit for a reasonable, though incorrect, guess.
2. Frequently ignore the miscue, no matter how serious, in hopes that as the reader continues subsequent context will lead him or her to correct the error.
3. Avoid interrupting the reading. Wait until the entire page or selection has been read before helping the student with the miscalled words. This strategy is particularly useful when anxiety rather than skill deficiency is inhibiting students' willingness to predict.

Reading meaningful connected text under a teacher's direction helps students develop context skills. Sometimes, however, you must employ alternative activities to accomplish this objective. One useful strategy is the use of the cloze technique. In a cloze activity, every *n*th word is deleted and students attempt to achieve closure by filling in the missing word. To accomplish closure, they use cues in the sentence. Ordinarily, in testing, exact replacements of words are required; synonyms for missing words are usually not allowed. For instructional purposes, however, credit is given for synonyms. The sequence of cloze activities described here (Hauser, 1979) begins at an aural level and moves gradually to actual reading exercises of increased complexity. In these exercises, every seventh word is deleted.

The steps in this cloze technique are as follows:

1. Read cloze selections to students and discuss their responses. Encourage students to evaluate the appropriateness of their responses on the basis of syntax and semantics. The discussion session is an important feature of cloze instruction as it helps students develop sensitivity to language and meaning cues.
2. Present cloze sentences in writing and have students choose from three words to fill in the deletion.
3. Again present cloze sentences, but have the students select replacements from a list of words, equal to the number of sentences. List these words apart from the sentences.
4. Present cloze exercises but supply the initial letter of the desired replacement. This forces students to attend to visual detail as well as meaning.
5. Ask students to read selections of two to three paragraphs with every seventh word deleted. No lists or initial letters are supplied. They must supply the missing words.

PHRASE POOLS   Phrase pools (Spiegel, 1978) are another device to help students attend to meaning. In a phrase pool, a student selects one phrase from each of the three "pools" to form a sentence. Three sentences are constructed, and a phrase may be used more than once.

1	2	3
The funny goat	cut the hay	in the morning
A happy farmer	ran after me	in the woods
The bright sun	makes me hot	in the summer

As the students participate in these activities, they will be less likely to regard reading as a list of words strung randomly across the page but will rapidly begin to correct their miscues, an early sign of growth. Both good and poor readers use the context before the word, but it has been our experience that poor readers tend not to honor context after the miscue. As poor readers improve in word identification, they too become more sensitive to subsequent context. Students who continue to be oblivious to their errors may be helped by passages which contain gross absurdities: "We had a good lunch today at school. First we ate meat loaf and pages in books. Then we drank a big glass of windmill." Or "Tom went fishing in the lake last night. The sun was hot. She caught two big pencils." Very often such material can encourage a student to attend more carefully.

SKIPPING WORDS   Allowing students simply to skip words is sometimes acceptable, particularly if little meaning is lost. Of course, some students have developed such an aversion to reading they would gladly skip whole sentences if given the opportunity! For this reason a balance must be maintained between a rigid word-perfect position and license to make wholesale deletions in the text.

TELLING THE WORD   Telling students a word is justifiable under certain circumstances. If students have exhausted all the meaning, language, and word identification skills at their command and still are unable to identify a word, supply the word. Students who have experienced long-term failure may be unable to give sufficient attention to a word until they have achieved more success in reading. It is far better to tell them the word than to have them deplete their limited energy. Finally, if it is apparent that the limited context of the word or its unusual structure presents considerable difficulty, supply the word at the outset rather than let students waste valuable time struggling to decode it. This applies also to words which are unlikely to be in the readers' listening vocabulary. Words of foreign extraction, particularly names of people or places, fall into this category. If, on the other hand, students have the skills to identify a word, encourage them to do so rather than tell them the word. Your students will gain a great deal of confidence if encouraged to demonstrate their own competence.

ROLE OF PHONICS AND ORTHOGRAPHIC CONSIDERATIONS   A second objective of level 2 is to teach the consonant elements. Before teaching consonants, an understanding of the writing system or orthography is helpful.

(Orthography is concerned with the manner in which we represent oral language in written form.) A study of English orthography reveals that some of its supposed irregularity is due to its representation of both meaning as well as speech. Although this may place beginning readers at a disadvantage, it does have the beneficial effect of forcing them to rely on meaning. Thus, little would be gained by changing the orthography to reflect only the transcription of speech.

Furthermore, though English orthography does not exhibit a perfect one-to-one correspondence between graphemes and phonemes, regularity does exist between clusters of graphemes and their corresponding phonemes. A young reader, for example, was unable to identify the word *through* in the phrase *through the woods.* He insisted that the word could not be *through* because it had a *g* at the end. The student failed to understand that the *cluster* of letters *ough* translates into speech, not the *g* alone. In English orthography, this translation considers both the position of the letter in the word and the letters surrounding it.

Regularity also exists in letter sequences themselves, regardless of phoneme-grapheme correspondences. The concept of "legal" sequences is tacitly understood by the proficient reader. For example, *q* is always followed by *u;* the cluster *km* is "illegal" unless each letter belongs to a separate morpheme as in *milkman;* some clusters can appear at both the beginning and ends of words (*sh* as in *ship* and *rash*), but others are limited to either the beginning or end. We can have *bl* as in *blank,* but *bl* cannot end a word.

The predictability of letter sequences helps the reader to identify words (Venezky and Massaro, 1979). If a three-letter word begins with *th,* for example, a vowel must follow. In English, the most likely possibility is *e.* If a word begins with *sp,* a limited number of options are available, for example, a vowel—*spi(t), spe(nd), spo(t), spu(d)*)—or a three-letter cluster with *sp* followed by *l* as in *split* or *r* as in *spray.*

Some authorities believe that reading instruction should help students become aware of the predictable nature of letter order at a tacit level. An informal, effective approach, is to expose students to a wide variety of words in print to enable them to hypothesize about letter sequences and then receive sufficient feedback to confirm or reject these predictions.

The complex nature of written language does suggest implications for the teaching of phonics. First, students should be taught to apply phonics in close conjunction with other cueing systems. The variability of the English alphabetic code requires support from syntax and semantics. Second, phonic elements should be taught within the context of specific words because the sound value of letters depends on surrounding letters and their position in the word. Third, the reading of connected text is a good way to teach students about the predictability of letters within words. Niles *et al.* (1977) suggest that a reciprocal relationship exists between an awareness of this regularity and learning to read. That is, as beginners learn to read, they begin to see letters in patterns and at the same time this knowledge facilitates their reading growth.

METALINGUISTIC DEVELOPMENT   Unfortunately, a phonic system in any language presents additional problems for the reader. Consider that from an historical perspective, written language began with picture writing and gradually evolved to ideographic forms, in which objects and ideas could be represented by stylized symbols. The final step in this progression was the familiar alphabetic system. Each system along the way meant a move away from the direct representation of meaning by means of pictures and abstract drawings to an intermediate representation. That is, in our system, the letters represent sound and the sound is related to meaning. In effect, phonology has come between meaning and corresponding pictures or ideographs. This arrangement, which may have been motivated by a desire to help the writer, obviously makes it easier to convey information with a limited number of symbols, an invaluable feature in typewriters or printing presses.

This development, however, requires beginning readers to think of words apart from their representation of meaning or their communicative function. The beginning reader, despite a rich oral language, lacks this "metalinguistic" awareness, an ability to think about language apart from its function.

Evidence of students' metalinguistic immaturity is their limited ability to segment or break up the flow of speech, which appears to run like water over a dam. The child, of course, can separate speech into words and even syllables, but the spoken word is not easily divided into separate speech sounds. Nor does the beginning reader know how the oral language corresponds to words in print. At first, even the concept of *word* itself is unclear. Beginners may understand the need to match speech and print, but they may believe the first word in oral language stands for an entire line of print.

The difficulty in segmenting speech is readily apparent at the acoustical level where a three-letter word with three phonemic elements, for example, *sat,* consists of one continuous flow of speech. That is, if we were to tape-record the word *sat,* we could not cut the tape to separate the three elements. Our best attempts would result in sounds which did not correspond to the sounds in the original word. It is only our slowly acquired knowledge about words and phonemes which allows us to perceive a word correctly. The beginning reader, however, has difficulty in relating discrete letters to segments of speech because these segments are closeted within a word.

A first step in teaching phonics is to develop the understanding that speech is composed of separate sounds, a concept which eludes many disabled readers. Ironically, reciprocity exists here also, because students must understand the segmentation of speech to learn important word identification skills and they must read in order to appreciate this concept.

Henderson (1979) has suggested that students develop metalinguistic awareness in distinct stages. At the preschool stage, they lack an adult sense of a word but can distinguish a word from a picture. As they begin to read, they realize letters are important constituents of words, but their concept of a word is still unclear. When they have acquired a respectable sight vocabulary, they start to understand that letters are related to phonemes, at least in beginning and ending positions. At the beginning of grade two, the student becomes more sensitive to vowels.

Problems arise when instruction runs ahead of the student's developmental level. If, for example, students do not understand the concept of a *word,* it does little good to teach them letter-sound phonics, for they have insufficient learning to which to relate these correspondences. Henderson says, "He has no place to put them . . . [because] for him words [at this stage] have no beginning or end" (p. 21). In the letter-name stage, initial consonants can be profitably taught, and vowels can be introduced when the student shows an awareness of the internal structure of words.

TEACHING CONSONANT ELEMENTS   Since students vary in their understanding of these concepts, the introduction of systematic phonic instruction will also vary. With some students teachers can begin teaching initial consonants in level 1 when the students know a single word beginning with that element. With other students, it is preferable to delay instruction until they have acquired three or four words beginning with that element. This usually occurs at the onset of level 2.

Systematic instruction in phonics should also consider a student's affective state. Disabled readers have often had difficulty in learning phonics. In view of past failure, the student's conceptual difficulty with phonics, and the low interest in this skill, it is sometimes best to delay phonics instruction until the student has gained a better understanding of reading and has acquired more confidence in his or her reading ability.

A delay in teaching phonic elements does not mean phonics is ignored. Your first objective is to help the students apply the phonic skills they already know. Most students today, although they may have limited word identification ability, have been exposed to a good deal of phonics and frequently possess more phonic skills than they can effectively use. Their knowledge is usually isolated from actual reading, however, and has not been integrated with the more valuable semantic and syntactic cueing systems. Thus, it provides little help in decoding connected text. The student is like the starving recluse surrounded by cartons of unopened food.

Harold typifies the student who scored high on phonic knowledge but low on application. He insisted he couldn't read the word *remember,* but when queried about his word attack strategies, Harold replied, "Divide the word into syllables and sound out each syllable." The teacher suggested that Harold follow his own advice, and after Harold had worked through the word a few times, he was able to identify it. The teacher did nothing more than ask Harold to apply existing skills. This is not to suggest that all students have sufficient phonics skills but fail to apply them. We do believe, however, that lack of application is a common problem and should be dealt with before teaching new phonic elements.

In summary, we have described the phonic system, examined the potential obstacles confronting a student, and suggested that the first step is to help the students apply the skills they already possess. The objective for level 2, learning consonant elements (single consonants, blends, and digraphs) can now be discussed in detail. See Figure 6-7 for a list of these elements.

Specific steps in teaching consonant elements have traditionally included letter names, visual discrimination, auditory discrimination, association, production, substitution, and application. These steps are now described.

SINGLE CONSONANTS			CONSONANT DIGRAPHS	
One Sound	*Two or More Sounds*	CONSONANT BLENDS	*One Sound*	*Two Sounds*

b	m	c (came	bl	sc	ch	ng	th (those
c	n	face)	cl	sk	gh	nk	thin)
d	p	g (go	dl	sm	ph		wh (what
f	r	gem)	fl	sn	sh		who)
h	t	s (hiss	gl	sp	shr		
j	v	rose	pl	st	thr		
k	w	sugar)	sl	sw	sch		
l	x	x (box	br	tw	(schwa)		
	y	exit	cr	spl			
	z	xylophone)	dr	scr			
			fr	spr			
			gr	str			
			pr	sch (school)			
			tr				

A consonant blend is a cluster of two or three consonants that are blended together to make one sound but that do not lose their separate identities. A consonant digraph is formed when a cluster of consonants produce one sound and the sound is a new sound—the separate letters appear to lose their individual identities.

Figure 6-7 Consonants Consonant chart from *Reading Instruction for Today's Children,* second edition, by Nila Banton Smith and H. Alan Robinson, copyrighted 1980, 1963, by Prentice-Hall, Inc. Reprinted by permission.

LETTER NAMES   You need not teach the letter names until students are taught initial consonant sounds. Knowledge of letter names does not help a student read better (Venezky, 1975) but reflects a child's interest in reading, which in turn may reflect parental encouragement and overall intellectual maturity.

VISUAL DISCRIMINATION   Most students can make adequate visual discriminations among words when they enter first grade. In some instances they may not be able to distinguish between isolated letters such as *b* and *d* or *q* and *p*, but you can remedy this problem by placing these letters in words. Since there is limited utility in discriminating between isolated letters, little instruction in visual discrimination is ordinarily required.

AUDITORY DISCRIMINATION   Students are traditionally taught to discriminate among spoken words in terms of beginning, medial, and final elements. Two words may be presented, such as *toy* and *bike,* and students will be asked to tell if these words begin with the same sound. A more advanced exercise requires students to determine which two of three spoken words begin with the same sound, for example, *ball, sip,* and *bat.* Similar exercises can be conducted with blends, digraphs, and vowels.

It has been reasoned that students must hear differences among speech sounds in order subsequently to relate letters to these sounds. If they cannot discriminate auditorily between the initial sounds of *tire* and *radio,* how will they be able to match the letter *t* with its appropriate speech sound? It would seem, therefore, that ample practice in auditory discrimination should be given in the early phases of reading instruction. Evidence exists, on the other hand, to suggest that we should rethink the role of auditory discrimination. Consider the following:

1. Eimas *et al.* (1971) have shown that children younger than one month of age can discriminate between syllables such as *pa* and *da.*
2. Students who do poorly on the Wepman Auditory Discrimination Test (Wepman, 1973) can subsequently repeat the test items correctly. A subject who says that *pat* and *bat* are the same word can repeat each word correctly after the tester pronounces it (Blank, 1968).
3. Hammill and Larsen (1974), in a literature review of auditory behavior, found a correlation of only +.26 between auditory discrimination and reading ability. Although this was statistically significant, the correlation remains too low to be of practical value.
4. When children enter first grade, their phonological and speech production ability approaches adult levels of development (Carroll, 1960; Erwin and Miller, 1963).
5. It is questionable whether the usual auditory discrimination processes are improved by traditional discrimination activities. Moe (1972) concluded that students' skill in this area tended to develop apart from instruction.
6. Auditory discrimination tests such as the Wepman include items which discriminate against students who speak with a black dialect (Geissal and Knafle, 1977).

How can we reconcile the apparent conflict between research and practice? Many authorities have concluded that we have misinterpreted students' difficulty with auditory exercises. Since students can talk, they must have reasonably developed auditory ability. One problem may be caused by an inability to understand test directions. Many students, for example, have only a limited understanding of key terms such as *same, beginning sound,* and *word.* When told to "Clap your hands when I say a word with the same beginning sound as *ball,*" they may not comprehend what is expected of them. This difficulty may also be related to overall intellectual maturity.

We believe that virtually all students have sufficient auditory discrimination to learn phonics despite their frequent inability to complete successfully auditory discrimination tasks. Teachers should usually omit auditory activities and proceed directly to instruction in the association of letters and sounds.

ASSOCIATION   Two procedures can be used for associating phonemes (sounds) with graphemes (letters). In the first, students need to know only one sight word which begins with the element you want to teach. If the student knows the word *something* as a sight word, for example, it is written down and you can say, "I am going to say some words. If a word I say starts like *something,* draw a line under the first letter of the word." Say these words: *soda, soup, sip, ball, soon, tiger,* and so on. Initially, it's a good idea to give more positive than negative examples, which helps a student develop a set for the beginning *s.* When negative examples are used, select words that differ considerably from *s* words. Avoid the *sh* digraph, as in *show,* or even a word like *baseball* as the medial *s* may confuse students.

When students know two or more sight words, write them in vertical columns on the chalkboard or a piece of paper. For example,

something
here
ball

Then say, "Underline the beginning letter of the word which starts like the word I say: *horse, bomb, soda, house,*" and so on. To increase involvement, supply all the students with a list of the words and ask them to mark their individual copies. If copies are covered with acetate sheets and marked with a crayon or similar marker, they may be reused.

In this association step, two elements of the word are matched—the visual appearance and the beginning sound. The student sees the beginning of the word *something* and focuses attention on the beginning sound. The student quickly generalizes that words which begin like *something* have the same initial sound as other words beginning with the letter *s.* Most students who have completed a year of school, regardless of reading level, possess a fair understanding of single initial consonants.

Your phonic lessons should employ questions rather than lengthy explanations. As a rule, try not to speak more than three consecutive declarative sentences without asking a question or issuing a command. It is far better, for example, to ask, "Does *ball* [spoken] begin like *bug* [written]?" than to say, "Notice that *ball* begins like *bug.*" At the same time, avoid giveaway questions in which the desired answer is obvious, such as "Do you all hear the /b/ sound in *ball*?" You must determine how well students are learning the element; this is difficult if you do most of the talking.

Avoid isolating consonant sounds. This practice distorts the sound by adding a vowel to it. Speak in terms of the sound at the beginning of *ball* rather than the *buh* sound. The order in which consonants are taught is not critical, although students should know at least one word beginning with that element before attempts are made to teach the element. The procedures used with single consonants can also be applied to blends and digraphs. Although most students with a year of school will be familiar with single consonants, they may have difficulty with blends and digraphs. Selecting elements for instruction is not simply following a prescribed list but observing which elements students attend to or ignore in actual reading.

Some students may need more examples of beginning consonants before they are able to make the association between letters and sounds. When this is the case, three words from a student's sight vocabulary might be presented:

said

see

something

You might say, "Look at these words and listen to me say them. What two things are alike about them?" If this question presents too great a challenge, say, "What do you see about the words that is the same? Now listen as I say each word. What do you hear about them that is the same?"

PRODUCTION   The production step tests the student's skill in associating auditory and visual symbols. If the sound-symbol relationship of *s* is being assessed, for instance, you can say, "Tell me some other words which begin like *soda*." These words can be written down to reinforce the association of the letter with the sound. As a variation, write the stimulus word *said* or the letter *s* and ask students to produce other words which begin like *soda* or the *s*. Some students, of course, may respond correctly because they have memorized words beginning with that letter, so be careful when evaluating an *s* at this stage. Since producing a word is more difficult than selecting a correct response from a number of choices, as in the association step, producing words with the element should not be used until the element has been learned.

SUBSTITUTION   Once students have mastered a few associations of consonants, substitution can be introduced. You might present the known word *hat* and say, "Take away the *h* from *hat* (erasing the *h*), put in *s* (write *s* before *at*) and you have _____." The word *hat* can be stressed so that students can use the rhyming cue. If students know other consonants, additional words may be formed. The blending of a beginning sound with ending units or phonograms presents a challenge for students, and therefore this skill must be practiced regularly over a period of days or even weeks.

APPLICATION   Finally, students must be able to apply phonic generalizations in reading connected text. Students who know *ride* and encounter *tide* should be able to decode *tide* by means of substitution techniques. If they do not notice the similarity between the two words, they can be asked to think of a word which looks like *tide*. If this suggestion does not help, write *ride* below *tide* and see if they can decode the word without further help. Each time you provide assistance, you will want to note if they can identify the word with less help.

Structural Analysis

The inflectional endings of *-s, -ed,* and *-ing* as well as *-'s* can be taught in level 2. These elements are best taught as the need arises rather than through a predetermined set of lessons. Students will learn these skills more easily if they are taught in context, since language cues reinforce these skills. In the sentence

SKILLS AND STRATEGIES	COMMENTS
1. Using context	Students are taught to use context by reading to the end of the sentence before employing other word attack strategies. They now apply context clues in reading material which they have not written.
2. Skipping words	If used judiciously, skipping words is acceptable and often can relieve anxiety over word-perfect reading.
3. Telling the word	Students should be told the unknown words when they have exhausted their own resources and when neither context nor phonics is likely to be successful.
4. Teaching consonant elements	The key skills in learning the consonant elements are (1) association of phonemes and graphemes, (2) substitution, and (3) application.

Figure 6-8 Summary of Level 2

"The donkey was pulling the cart," the syntactic cues help with the decoding of *pulling.*

Figure 6-8 summarizes the skills and strategies taught in level 2.

LEVEL 3: VOWELS

The objectives of level 2, using context to identify words in printed material and learning consonant elements, continue in level 3. Level 3, however, emphasizes vowel sounds. Clinicians who work with disabled readers frequently report that these pupils know many consonant elements but little about vowels beyond the rote statement that they are *a,e, i, o, u,* and sometimes *y.* Unfortunately, the relationship between knowledge of vowels and reading ability is not straightforward. Ignorance of vowels does not always lead to poor decoding ability, and some students with a healthy knowledge of vowels still struggle to identify words.

You're probably curious to know what role vowels do play in learning to read. We believe formal knowledge of the various vowel sounds is not absolutely necessary, but neither should vowels be dismissed completely. Some students become so frustrated in learning vowels that other methods of word identification should be pursued. Vowels are not ends in themselves, and therefore we should not insist on mastery of this skill if word identification can be achieved in other ways. On the other hand, specific attention to vowels may be warranted because they occur in the medial position of words, and it is here that students frequently have the most difficulty in decoding.

The Complexity of Vowels

Vowels are usually taught after consonants because they provide the reader with less information in identifying words. If you knew only the consonant elements in G—rg— W—sh—ngt—n, you would have little difficulty identifying a well-known president. If, on the other hand, you knew only the vowels, —eo—e —a—i—o— would present a much more formidable challenge. If the reader has the benefit of context, vowel skills are not crucial in most instances. Furthermore, letter-sound correspondences of vowels are considerably more complex than similar correspondence of consonants. With consonants, the phoneme-grapheme correspondence is fairly consistent. With vowels, however, there are not only at least two phonemes related to each of the vowels (long and short vowels) but also the value of a vowel is influenced considerably by its position in the word and the letters around it. The letter *o*, for example, represents different sounds in each of these words: *hot, goat, horse, house, hoot,* and *toy.* The variability of vowels is also related to the use of dialect. The word *pen* according to standard pronunciation has a short *e* vowel, but in some dialects, the word is pronounced as if it were a short *i.* Also, in some sections of New England the *ar* in *car* is pronounced with a short *o* so that *party* sounds like *potty.* Under these circumstances, statements about vowel sound-letter correspondences should be made cautiously, and standard pictures in which *a* stands for *apple, e* for *elephant,* and so on should be used with discretion. This is especially true in working with students whose pronunciation deviates from standard speech. Students' difficulty with vowels does not necessarily involve pronouncing the vowels but rather focusing on vowels embedded within words, relating one letter to a variety of sounds, and if they speak with a dialect, responding correctly to assignments which assume a standard pronunciation.

Synthetic Approach

Two approaches may be used in teaching vowels. The first is a synthetic technique in which word parts are blended into a whole. Its advantage is that students can sound out words quickly by learning a limited number of elements, such as the short *a, e,* and so on. The disadvantage is that the interpretation of vowels depends on their position in a word and the letters around them, and thus a synthetic approach, if used exclusively, may hinder a student from making an appropriate decision about which sound to attach to a particular vowel. If a synthetic approach to learning vowels is employed, the following procedures may be used:

1. Write a number of sight words with the short *a* sound such as

hat

map

tap

Ask students to identify similarities among these words. Elicit the response that the words all have the letter *a* and that the *a* in the words represents the same sound. Ask if they know the name of this particular sound of *a*. If not, tell them that it is the short *a*. Produce the short *a* in isolation (see cautions about dialect) and ask students to repeat it after you. The key words listed, *hat, map,* and *tap,* may be used to help the student remember the short *a*.

Short vowels are frequently introduced first because they are more regular and occur in more words. When long vowels are introduced, a variety of patterns are used, such as double vowels—for example, *goat*—and vowel-consonant-*e* (VCE) patterns—as in *like*.

2. Help students produce the short *a* sound, but if they speak a dialect, permit them to render the sound in their own dialect. If you are in doubt about how they produce vowels, listen carefully as they normally say words such as *fat* and *tap*. In order for vowel instruction to be effective, you must be aware of their pronunciation of these sounds. Don't confuse them by substituting a vowel sound which deviates from their normal pronunciation. If you are working in a group in which students pronounce vowels differently, it may be necessary either to teach vowels by using key words such as *hat*, which each student can pronounce in his or her dialect, or to deemphasize the teaching of vowels in a group.

3. Assign blending exercises in which students are shown consonant-vowel pairs such as *sa* and *ta*. Endings are then added so that students realize the activity leads to real words. Blending, of course, can also deal with each letter separately, although it is not possible to isolate most initial consonants without distorting their sound. Technically, consonant-vowel pairs such as *sa* result in an open syllable (syllable ending with a long vowel), but in practice students are not likely to be confused because open syllables are generally taught at a later time.

4. The order in which vowels are introduced is unimportant, though we suggest you do not teach the short *e* and short *i* back-to-back since students frequently confuse them. This is especially true of speakers of dialect, to whom words like *pin* and *pen* are homophones.

5. Students should employ synthetic blending techniques when meaning cues are insufficient and they are unable to decode the word by means of consonant substitution or more analytic methods. In the word *bit*, for example, consonant substitution can be used to identify the word, whereas it is more efficient to apply synthetic procedures to the word *kept* unless the student knows a word or word part with a similar pattern.

6. The long vowels are usually taught next. The distinction between long and short vowels does not refer to the duration of the sound in words; some short vowels (*u, i, e*) are held longer than some long vowels (*o, e, a*). For this reason there has been a movement to label the short and long sounds *glided* and *unglided,* respectively, to emphasize the manner in which they are produced. This terminology may be technically more accurate, but it has not replaced the more familiar terms in most textbooks and basal reader programs.

Since the long vowel sounds are the same as the letter name of the vowel, readers already have some acquaintance with them. To teach these sounds, write known words on the board, such as *cape, rate,* and *bake,* and ask students how these words are alike. Through questioning, elicit the fact that each word contains the letter *a*, that each *a* represents the same sound, and that this sound is the same as the name of the letter. Label these *a*'s the long vowel sound of *a*. Continue in a similar manner with other long vowels. However, you should carefully pace instruction in order to assure overlearning. For this reason, it helps to begin each lesson with a review of the previous day's lesson. This step reinforces the new skill and helps the teacher evaluate the students' progress.

Unlike the short vowel, which ordinarily appears in a consonant-vowel-consonant (CVC) pattern, the long vowel may occur in the VCE pattern, as in *hope,* as well as in vowel digraphs such as *oa* and *ai*. Students thus must learn more than one long-vowel pattern.

7. The variety of vowels in our orthography has led to the formulation of generalizations to help students decide which vowel sounds to choose in a word. One familiar rule is "two vowels go walking," which states that if two vowels are side by side, as in *boat,* the first one does the "talking" (is long) and the second is silent. Unfortunately, this generalization is true only 45 percent of the time. Words such as *chief* and *said* are exceptions (Clymer, 1963). Obviously, so many exceptions exist to this rule that its value is questionable. Of course, it can be improved by restricting it to certain pairs of vowels, such as *oa,* but in doing so, the rule becomes more complicated. Thus we are confronted with a dilemma: easily learned general rules are often undependable, but the technically more accurate statements complicate learning and often lead to such a preoccupation with rules that students (and teachers) lose sight of more valuable word identification strategies and their application.

To further complicate matters, some "rules" function quite well only if we calculate the percentage of words which follow the rule compared to the total number of words in a specified corpus of words. Consider the rule "When *a* is followed by *r* and final *e,* expect to hear the sound heard in *care*." This rule applies between 90 percent and 100 percent (Caldwell *et al.,* 1978) of the time when -*are* words are compared *to the number of words in which the* -*are element appears.* However, when the comparison is made between -*are* words which follow the rule and the number of words with this element in *typical connected text,* the percentage falls to 16. Thus, in actual reading the rule has much less utility. The reason for this low figure is that the word *are* itself accounts for 84 percent of the exceptions. In sum, few rules exist which are both simple and sufficiently dependable in connected text. Caldwell *et al.* have identified just three vowel generalizations and seven consonant generalizations which meet this criterion. The vowel generalizations are

1. When the letter *i* is followed by the letters *gh,* the *i* usually stands for its long sound and the *gh* is silent.
2. In *ay* the *y* is silent and the *a* is long.
3. Words that have *ee* have a long *e* sound.

Versatility

We believe the best course to follow is to teach students to be versatile. For example, if students encounter an unknown word and try a short vowel sound and it does not produce a word they have heard, they should try other alternatives, such as the long sound. To encourage versatility, write a word, such as *chief,* which does not conform to the "two vowels go walking" rule and allow students to test alternative sounds until a word is produced which they have heard. The objective of activities of this type is not simply to name the word but also to develop the habit of testing hypotheses. You can help students by valuing a willingness to "play around" with alternative sounds rather than stressing precise word identification.

The vowel elements are listed in Figure 6-9. In level 3 it is sufficient to teach formally the long and short vowels. Other vowels can be learned from words which the student knows by sight, as the *ow* in *town,* the *r*-controlled vowel in *car,* and so on, and should be taught as they are needed. It's questionable, for example, to present a lesson on the *oi* sound unless students have difficulty with a word containing *oi.* In that case call attention to other words they know with that element, and if necessary, provide systematic instruction in that element as suggested for the short and long vowels. If, on the other hand, words with *oi*

Figure 6-9 Vowels Vowel chart from *Reading for Today's Children* by Nila Banton Smith and H. Alan Robinson, copyrighted 1980, 1963, by Prentice-Hall, Inc. Reprinted by permission.

LONG	SHORT	SCHWA (ə)	OTHER SOUNDS	OU SOUNDS
ā (ate)	a (at)	a in above	ä (father	bough
ē (be)	e (end)	e in parcel	far)	cow
ī (ice)	i (it)	i in pencil	ér (term	journey
ō (open)	o (hot)	o in lemon	bird)	though
(show)	u (up)	u in circus	ô (order	through
ū (mule)	y (bicycle)		often	touch
(few)			all	
y (by			awe)	
candy)			oi (oil	
			boy)	
			ú (put	
			wood)	
			ü (rule	
			move	
			blue	
			loose)	

The most common sounds are represented on this chart. For exceptions to the patterns represented and for rarely used sounds, pupils will need to refer to the pronunciation guide of a dictionary and carefully interpret the diacritical marks. A most important concept is that there is not always a one-to-one phoneme-grapheme relationship—note that the ô sound may be applied to *all* and the ü sound may be applied to *move,* for example. The vowel patterns that result in only one vowel being pronounced are not represented in the chart, although they may be long, short, or schwa. Examples: rāin, cōat, bāy, cert*a*in, bread, frēe, liēn, brēak.

sat	bed	fall	fowl	her
sing	big	saw	bus	hair
set	lip	tel(l)	fil(l)	pal
sit	mud	deck	bite	tied
hot	lid	nice	mes(s)	few
him	den	tick	Tom	fire
top	hug	clif(f)	poke	hear
ran	hut	sink	tore	real
say	far	cob	tow	tea
sad	hem	sod	cast	bee
jam	cup	fog	cane	care
sun	mate	tub	meat	deaf
tin	tent	cuf(f)	glas(s)	boat
rap	test	rush	Bev	cue
sand	rake	table	kind	too
tack	hide	sight	toss	out
sum	lock	mis(s)	team	pound
tab	made	Ron	most	cure
bag	came	for	rol(l)	nature
told	cape	ful(l)	bone	fur
rash	face	fact	pale	fir
fish	sang	taf(f)y	save	raid
	sank	cook	rove	auto
	song	nation	folly	boil
			sage	

Figure 6-10 Glass Common Letter Clusters in Whole Words Glass Common Letter Clusters from *Teaching Decoding as Separate from Reading* by Gerald G. Glass. Copyright 1973 by Adelphi University Press, Garden City, New York. Reprinted by permission.

continually appear in the students' reading but they can decode them through context and consonant sounds, do not dwell on the *oi*.

Variability

The inconsistency of vowels and the need to observe their position in the word and the letters surrounding them force the reader to read from right to left. In the word *torn*, for example, we cannot determine which sound to apply to the *o* until we look at the letter *r* following it. This, of course, limits the effectiveness of a system in which vowel sounds are learned in isolation and applied without consideration of their context. One solution is to use a cluster approach in which a vowel such as *o* is not taught in isolation but as part of one of the following clusters: *ot, oat, or, oist*. In effect, the cluster would be taught as a unit with consonant sounds substituted at the beginning or end of the word. Words with the VCE pattern would not be taught as a generalization but would be related to words such as *rake, hide,* and *cape,* which have been taught previously.

APPROACHES	COMMENT
Synthetic	Involves the blending of separate elements. For example, *b–a–t*.
Analytic or letter cluster	Requires student to learn a stock of word parts, for example, *oist*, as units and compare these with related parts of unknown words, *moist*.
Generalizations	The unreliability and limited utility of vowel generalizations suggests that students should approach unknown words with trial and error. Flexibility in word attack should be emphasized rather than vowel "rules."

Figure 6-11   Summary of Level 3

Glass (1973) has listed 119 of these units or clusters. (See Figure 6-10 for the complete set.) This approach is likely to be of more value with older students who possess a larger sight vocabulary than with younger students who know fewer words. As in the teaching of consonants, begin with a cluster for which the student already knows a sight word. If the cluster *ot* is to be taught, a sight word such as *hot* could be used. Possible steps in teaching would be the following:

1. Present a known sight word which contains the cluster.
2. Remove the initial consonant.
3. Help the student pronounce the cluster.
4. Show the student how additional words can be created by adding consonants to the beginning of the word. The procedure is similar to consonant substitution except that a deliberate emphasis is placed on learning specific clusters which can be generalized to other words.

Figure 6-11 summarizes the approaches used in level 3.

LEVEL 4: MULTISYLLABIC WORDS

Problems with Multisyllabic Words

Students who have overcome the challenge of earlier levels and can now decode most monosyllable words may still stumble over words of more than one syllable. One reason for this difficulty is that multisyllabic words are not simply combinations of syllables; additional rules of correspondence (complex phonic rules which take into account a variety of factors such as position and surround) are required (Groff, 1977). For example, the letter *a* needs seven rules of correspondence in one-syllable words but an additional eight rules if it appears in multisyllabic words. We do not advocate teaching any of these rules, but they do demonstrate that multisyllabic words are more than combinations of one-syllable words.

Syllabication

A traditional solution for identifying multisyllabic words calls for dividing them into syllables and then applying phonic generalizations to each syllable. Correct syllabication thus becomes a prerequisite to applying phonics. In the word *zombie,* for example, if the word were divided incorrectly between the *o* and the *m,* the first syllable, according to a common phonic rule, would be open. Vowels in open syllables are long, and as a result, the word would be mispronounced. (A syllable ending in a vowel is called an open syllable, as the first syllable in *savor.*)

Rules for dividing words into syllables rely primarily on visual inspection. The three most common are as follows:

1. When two consonants come between two vowels, as in *supper* or *lumber,* divide the word between the two consonants: *sup-per* (VC-CV pattern).
2. When a single consonant comes between the two vowels, divide the word after the first vowel, as in *ba-con* (V-CV pattern).
3. When a word ends in a consonant followed by an *le,* as in *cable,* the final syllable is made up of the consonant and the *le* (Cle pattern).

Since disabled readers often have difficulty with multisyllabic words even after they have mastered one-syllable words, practice in applying these rules is inevitably a part of the reading program in the middle grades.

Traditional syllabication rules, however, have been criticized in recent years. Although students should understand the concept of a syllable and be able to divide words into syllables, present instruction, some authorities claim, leaves much to be desired. The following criticisms have been directed at the teaching of syllabication:

1. The traditional word divisions of syllables do not relate to the manner in which the word is pronounced but reflect the conventional practices of the print setter. In the word *better,* for example, the VC-CV rule divides the word between the two *t*'s. The dictionary main entry does show that the word is divided in that manner, but a second entry which reflects the word's pronunciation shows that the first syllable ends after the sound of *t* (there is only one sound of *t* although there are two letters). If students pronounce the word with two *t*'s, the pronunciation will be distorted.
2. Students (and adults as well) usually decide on syllabic divisions *after* saying the word; that is, they see the word, work out its pronunciation, and then divide it into syllables on the basis of the pronunciation. Yet the very reason for dividing the word into syllables is to help identify it. One implication is that students should not be asked to divide words they can already read.
3. A syllable is a unit of speech, not a unit of written language. Since the division of syllables at the oral level is imprecise, the written word cannot

be marked off neatly by reference to an oral counterpart. This statement suggests that it will be equally difficult to create rules for the written syllable when the oral syllable is in doubt. In practice, however, this concern is not critical, as only an approximation to a word in the reader's speaking vocabulary is necessary in order to decode it.

4.   Proper syllabication of words requires many more rules than the student is ever taught. The present rules, by simplifying the problem, may mislead the student.

What are the implications of these criticisms? One view is that once students have understood the concept of a syllable and the value of dividing words into parts, it is best to teach them to employ trial and error rather than rely on any rules at all. They should attempt various divisions until they can match the written word with a word in their listening vocabulary. If the word is not in their listening vocabulary, a common problem with disabled readers, then neither syllabication or phonics will help. (Very often we struggle with readers over the identification of a multisyllabic word only to discover that they have not heard the word before.) A quick, though by no means ideal, solution is to ask the students to find the word in the dictionary and use the pronunciation key and diacritical marks to decode it. In the long run, the students may need to acquire a larger listening vocabulary if they are to identify these words efficiently. Remember that in all those word identification strategies, the student is to use context first to narrow the possibilities.

Compare-Contrast Theory

A final nail in the coffin of conventional practice is provided by research (Cunningham, 1979) suggesting that students do not actually follow school rules for syllabicating a word and sounding it out. On the contrary, if readers do not know a word, they analyze it into the largest parts they can handle and compare these parts to words or word parts they already know. Readers then recombine the word parts until a whole word is achieved for which there exists an acoustic and/or semantic match.

If students were attempting to identify the word *circumstance*, they would try to deal with the largest possible unit. In this case, if they knew *circumference*, the word might be broken into two parts—*circum* and *stance*. The second syllable, *stance*, might be related to the similar whole word, to *dance*, or to *stand*, with a substitution of the final *ce*. If, on the other hand, the students could not deal with the *circum* as a unit, they might relate *circum* to *circus*, and by substitution, get *circum*. Or they might relate *cir* to *circus* and *cum* to *cup*, and by substitution, to *cum*.

The syllabication process in the traditional sense would not precede the application of phonics but would occur together with the identification of word parts. The students would attempt to recombine parts until a word resulted which they had heard before. If the first recombining did not result in a known word, the students would consider other combinations. If the word were not in their listening vocabulary, of course, they would have difficulty achieving closure.

To help students identify multisyllabic words, Cunningham *et al.* (1981) suggest steps similar to the following:

1. Show students words like *charter, defer,* and *ferment* and ask them to find two cards from the following collection—a tangible word store—with similar parts.

   he *went* *her* *can* *car*

   Students then pronounce "store words" and multisyllabic words.

2. Increase students' tangible word store by adding words such as *in, at, then, it,* and *is.* Show words such as *bitter* and *bandit* and again ask students to match them with similar words in the tangible store.

3. Continue adding words to the tangible store and repeat the procedure in the first two steps. By this time students should be able to unlock numerous multisyllabic words.

4. Assist students to realize that known one-syllable words can be used to help identify multisyllabic words. Encourage them to use this strategy in their everyday reading assignments. Consult Cunningham *et al.* (1981) for a list of tangible store words and practice words.

One worthwhile approach in teaching this strategy to a small group is to place a premium on experimentation. In addition to the individual procedures just described, the teacher might list at one side of the board words or word parts which could be used to help identify the multisyllabic words. If the word *concentrate* were the stimulus, the following words could be listed: *content, concern, connect, center, train,* and *trade.* Students working in small teams would attempt to decode the word. In the discussion, they would defend the pronunciation they chose. Each team should work until they could reach consensus or agree by majority vote and then report their decision to the entire group. They should cite reasons for their choice, including the use of words or word parts which were helpful to them. The correct answers would then be supplied by the teacher. Rather than give points for correct answers only, credit could also be given for approximations and sound reasoning. The scoring system might look like this:

3 points—correct word
2 points—very close
1 point—partly correct
0 points—not close at all!

The first team to collect fifteen points would be declared the winner.

Accents

Accents, along with syllabication, are a part of most reading programs. Unfortunately, no reliable rules exist for determining proper accent. Thus, students should be taught the concept of accent—with which they are already familiar at a tacit level—but need not complete exercises in accenting. They can be told to try the accent on the first syllable first as this is its most common location in English words. If this strategy is not successful, other syllables can be given the accent until closure is attained.

Affixes

Prefixes and suffixes, usually taught at this level, differ from syllables in that they represent meaning. Thus, whereas knowledge of affixes might help in word identification, they also aid comprehension. In words such as *subway, submarine,* and *subterranean,* the affix *sub-* can help the reader determine the word's meaning. Our preference is not to teach meanings of affixes in isolation but to deal with them as they occur and to use context as a first clue to meaning. If an affix appears more than once, the meaning can be best taught inductively by discussing words with the same element, for example, *zoology, geology.* In teaching affixes for word identification, a comparison of the stimulus word with known words or word parts can be employed.

Students' word identification needs beyond this point will usually require the use of a dictionary. Many of the unknown words will not be in the students' listening vocabulary, and the dictionary provides diacritical markings whereby the word may be sounded out. Of course, the dictionary also provides a meaning for the word. In a sense, the use of the dictionary signals an increasing focus on word meanings, concepts, and comprehension in the reading program and a relative deemphasis on word identification.

Figure 6-12 summarizes the various approaches to teaching multisyllabic words.

Figure 6-12 Summary of Level 4—Multisyllabic Words

APPROACHES	COMMENTS
Traditional syllabication	It is questionable whether the traditional rules for dividing words into syllables are sound and whether students actually use these rules.
Compare and contrast	An alternative to traditional syllabication, the reader compares unknown parts of words with known words or word parts. The word *robot,* for example, can be identified by means of *rope* and *got.*
Accents	As a general rule, students should apply the accent to the first syllable and then use trial and error if this approach is not successful.
Affixes	Affixes are meaning units which can aid both word identification and meaning. Words can be identified through a compare-contrast theory.

Activities

In time, remedial students resist a steady diet of skill-building activities. The following activities can provide variety and sustain interest.

Every pupil response. To involve as many students as possible, use the every-pupil-response technique in which students are given a set of cards whose content will vary with the skill under consideration. If you are teaching consonant digraphs, for example, students might have the *th, wh, ch,* and *sh* cards on their desks. Call out words beginning with those sounds and have each student hold up the appropriate card. At a glance you can determine which students understand the skill. Those who tend to rely on their classmates' responses can be seated toward the front of the group to minimize copying. Later they can receive additional instruction on this skill.

Stop. To help students make the association between letters and sounds, write a word on the board and tell students you will say a list of words. Each time a word begins with the same sound as the word on the board, they are to call out "stop." If this activity is too noisy or overstimulates the group, use the every-pupil-response technique and have them hold up a "stop" card.

Picture cards. In teaching phonics, use pictures of common objects. A good source are old readiness workbooks or first-grade workbooks. Cut these pictures out, glue them to index cards, and use them in playing matching games (find all the pictures which begin like *pizza* does) or games such as Concentration. Card games like Go Fish and Old Maid can also be converted into phonic activities by using cards in which letters are matched to pictures of an object with the corresponding initial consonant.

 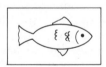

Overhead pictures. Place word identification activities on acetate sheets and project them onto a chalkboard with an overhead projector. Students can draw lines on the board matching pictures and initial consonants. The sheets can be reused. As a variation, use actual objects whose identity can be determined by silhouette.

Taped worksheets. Phonic worksheets can provoke cries of "oh, no, not another one" if used continually. As a variation, tape-record directions to a worksheet which has been covered with heavy acetate. Taped material should include directions, the purpose of the activity, and correct answers. Students listen to the directions, turn off the tape while they complete the page, and return to the tape for the correct answers. Have students mark responses with a crayon which can be rubbed off with a moist tissue so the sheet can be reused.

Object phonics. Use objects which represent sounds in words such as initial consonants. Objects can be brought in by students after you help them develop a suitable list. Some appropriate objects might be a bar of soap for *s,* a book for *b,* a candle for *c,* and so on.

Word sorts. Use word sorts (Gillet and Kita, 1979) with groups of eight to ten students. Word sorts can begin with picture sets which students can categorize by concept, such as foods, colors, farm or circus animals, and advance to phonic activities in which the teacher places two cards on the chalk tray

and asks students to sort their pictures (provided by the teacher for this exercise) into three groups—those which begin like *lamp* or like *sun* and those which begin with neither sound. Later, additional picture cards are placed on the chalk tray

but this time students categorize a set of word cards, matching the initial sounds of the picture with the beginning sound on the word card.

As a final activity, students can be subdivided into groups of three to four, word cards are handed out to each student, and they are asked to categorize these cards in any manner they wish. When the sorting has been completed, students attempt to name the categories devised by their peers. Categories can include both meaning and phonic features.

Dismissal. Dismiss students from the reading group by saying, "All those with first names beginning like _____ may leave the group." This not only provides a quick phonic review but excuses students in an orderly fashion. Later, students may be asked to produce a word with a particular element before leaving the group. Be sure you provide alternative tasks so the last student in the group doesn't have to come up with another word in a category already depleted.

Keys. Help students construct consonant and vowel keys (Stauffer, 1978) on which they record a key word, a word in their sight vocabulary which includes a particular phonic element. These words are placed on cards which stand or are taped on the student's desk and serve to remind students of phonic elements. The key functions best when it is developed by students after they have learned a new element.

Squares. Games such as checkers, tic-tac-toe, and bingo can be converted to word identification activities by placing word cards or phrases on the squares. Students must read the word or phrase before putting their piece in that square.

SUMMARY

This chapter began with a description of a nonreader, a student whose primary problem was word identification. We suggested that a solution to his difficulty lay in helping him to use both meaning and decoding skills—in proper balance. The use of semantic and syntactic information would make reading easier, and attention to orthography and phonic cues would provide needed precision and foster independence in word identification.

We stated that acquiring successful word identification strategies presented the student with four challenges: (1) Acquiring a sight vocabulary and using context, (2) applying consonant and (3) vowel sounds, and (4) unlocking multisyllabic words. A language-experience approach was suggested as one way to help students learn and respond quickly to high-frequency words. We presented step-by-step directions for teaching at these four levels, pointing out limitations in certain traditional practices, such as auditory discrimination and syllabication, and advocating other strategies, such as compare-contrast, which should prove helpful with multisyllabic words. Throughout this chapter we pointed out specific behaviors for teachers to observe and suggested adjustments in instruction to meet student needs more adequately.

We closed the chapter with a list of suggestions which should provide both variety and enrichment in learning to identify words. If students like Mike receive such assistance from concerned teachers who understand the reading process and display a certain amount of creativity in improvising other theoretically sound techniques, we are convinced that the reading problems of such students can be substantially reduced.

RELATED ACTIVITIES

1. Record a language-experience account from students of different ages and reading levels on a similar topic, for example, pets, sports, family. Compare the language of the students in terms of vocabulary and sentence structure. Compare their ability to read the account with you and to you.

2. Identify an unknown phonic element in which the student knows a sight word containing that element. Teach it by using the procedures in this chapter.

3. Conduct auditory discrimination exercises with students of the same age who differ in the size of their sight vocabulary. Are these two variables positively related? If so, what might account for the correlation? What are the limitations of such a conclusion?

4. Conduct an individual language-experience cycle with one student. What adjustment might be made in the use of these techniques to improve their effectiveness with this particular student?

5. Use the compare-contrast strategies in this chapter to teach students several multisyllabic words which they cannot identify in either context or isolation.

6. Examine several basal reader series and compare and contrast the procedures for teaching vowels. What are the advantages and disadvantages of each method? Use these procedures to teach a number of brief vowel lessons. What procedures appear to be the easiest and/or the most effective?

7. A decoding emphasis in beginning reading has been recommended by several reading authorities since some research indicates that students in decoding programs achieve higher reading levels in the primary grades. Does this advantage continue throughout the elementary school years? Locate and evaluate research on this topic. Good sources are Jeanne Chall, *Learning to Read: The Great Debate* (New York: McGraw-Hill, 1967); and R. Corder, *The Information Base for Reading* (HEW Final Rep., Project No. 0-9031) (Berkeley, Calif.: Educational Testing Service, 1971 (ERIC Document Reproduction Service No. 054-922).

8. Review the research on the value of pictures in teaching word identification. Then observe classes in beginning reading to determine how pictures are actually used in instruction. Are the research procedures similar to classroom practice? What can you conclude?

RELATED READINGS

ADAMS, MARILYN. *Beginning Reading: Theory and Practice.* Champaign: Center for the Study of Reading, University of Illinois, 1977.

CHALL, JEANNE S. *Learning to Read: The Great Debate.* New York: McGraw-Hill, 1967.

CHOMSKY, CAROL. "When You Still Can't Read in Third Grade: After Decoding, What?" In *What Research Has to Say About Reading Instruction.* S. Jay Samuels, ed. New-ark, Del.: International Reading Association, 1978.

RESNICK, LAUREN, AND PHYLLIS A. WEAVER, EDS. *Theory and Practice of Early Reading,* Vols. 1–3. Hillsdale, N.J.: Lawrence Erlbaum, 1979.

STAUFFER, RUSSELL G., JULES C. ABRAMS, AND JOHN J. PIKULSKI. *Diagnosis, Correction, and Prevention of Reading Disabilities,* New York: Harper & Row, 1978.

REFERENCES

BERENSTAIN, STAN, AND JAY BERENSTAIN. *Bears in the Night.* New York: Random House, 1969.

BLANK, MARION. "Cognitive Processes in Auditory Discrimination in Normal and Retarded Readers." *Child Development,* 39, no. 4 (Dec. 1968), 1,091–1101.

CALDWELL, EDWARD C., SANDRA R. ROTH, AND RALPH R. TURNER. "A Reconsideration of Phonic Generalizations." *Journal of Reading Behavior,* 10, no. 1 (Spring 1978), 91–96.

CARROLL, JOHN B. "Language Development." In *Encyclopedia of Educational Research.* Chester W. Harris, ed. New York: Macmillan, 1960.

CLYMER, THEODORE. "The Utility of Phonic Generalizations in the Primary Grades." *Reading Teacher,* 16, no. 4 (Jan. 1963), 252–58.

CUNNINGHAM, JAMES W., PATRICIA M. CUNNINGHAM, AND SHARON V. ARTHUR. *Middle and Secondary School Reading.* New York: Longman, 1981.

CUNNINGHAM, PATRICIA M. "A Compare/Contrast Theory of Mediated Word Identification." *Reading Teacher,* 32, no. 7 (Apr. 1979), 774–78.

DOLCH, EDWARD. "A Basic Sight Vocabulary." *Elementary School Journal,* 36, no. 6 (Feb. 1936), 456–60.

DURR, WILLIAM. "COMPUTER STUDY OF HIGH FREQUENCY WORDS IN POPULAR TRADE JUVENILES." *Reading Teacher,* 27, no. 1 (Oct. 1973), 37–42.

EIMAS, PETER D., EINAR R. SIQUELAND, PETER JUSCZYK, AND JAMES VIGORITO. "Speech Perception in Infants." *Science,* 171, no. 3968 (Jan. 22, 1971), 303–306.

ERWIN, SUSAN M., AND WICK R. MILLER. "Language Development." In *Child Psychology,* 62nd Yearbook, National Society of the Study of Education. Chicago: University of Chicago Press, 1963.

GEISSAL, MARY ANN, AND JUNE D. KNAFLE. "A Linguistic View of Auditory Tests and Exercises." *Reading Teacher,* 31, no. 2 (Nov. 1977), 134–41.

GILLET, JEAN WALLACE, AND M. JANE KITA. "Words, Kids and Categories." *Reading Teacher,* 32, no. 5 (Feb. 1979), 538–42.

GLASS, GERALD. *Teaching Decoding as Separate from Reading.* Garden City, N.J.: Adelphi University Press, 1973.

GROFF, PATRICK. *Phonics: Why and How.* Morristown, N.J.: General Learning Press, 1977.

HAMMILL, DONALD D., AND STEPHEN C. LARSEN. "The Relationship of Selected Auditory Perceptual Skills and Reading Ability." *Journal of Learning Disabilities,* 7, no. 7 (Aug./Sept. 1974), 429–35.

HARRIS, ALBERT J., AND MILTON D. JACOBSON. *Basic Elementary Reading Vocabularies.* New York: Macmillan, 1972.

HAUSER, CAROL. "Action Research for the Improvement of Reading Comprehension through the Use of Cloze Procedure." Unpublished Field Project, Rhode Island College, Providence, Rhode Island, 1979.

HENDERSON, EDMUND H. "Developmental Concepts of Words." Mimeographed. Charlottesville: University of Virginia, 1979.

JOHNSON, DALE D. "A Basic Vocabulary for Beginning Reading." *Elementary School Journal,* 72, no. 1 (Oct. 1971), 29–34.

LABERGE, DAVID, AND S. JAY SAMUELS. "Toward A Theory of Automatic Information Processing in Reading." *Cognitive Psychology,* 6, no. 2 (Apr. 1974), 293–323.

LESIEG, THEODORE. *Ten Apples Up on Top.* New York: Random House, 1961.

MOE, ALDEN J. "An Investigation of the Uniqueness of Selected Auditory Discrimination Skills Among Kindergarten Children Enrolled in Two Types of Reading Readiness Programs." *Dissertation Abstracts,* 32 (1972), 6,295 A.

NILES, JEROME A., AILEEN GRUNDER, AND CAROL WIMMER. "The Effects of Grade Level and School Setting on the Development of Sensitivity to Orthographic Structure." In *Reading: Theory, Research and Practice.* P. David Pearson, ed. Clemson, S.C.: National Reading Conference, 1977.

ORBACH, RUTH. *Apple Pigs.* New York: Collins Publishers, 1979.

OTTO, WAYNE, AND ROBERT CHESTER. "Sight Words for Beginning Readers." *Journal of Educational Research,* 65, no. 10 (July–Aug. 1972), 435–43.

SMITH, NILA BANTON, AND H. ALAN ROBINSON. *Reading Instruction for Today's Children,* 2nd ed. Englewood Cliffs, N.J.: Prentice-Hall, 1980.

SPIEGEL, DIXIE LEE. "Meaning-seeking Strategies for the Beginning Reader." *Reading Teacher,* 31, no. 7 (Apr. 1978), 772–76.

STAUFFER, RUSSEL G., JULES D. ABRAMS, AND JOHN J. PIKULSKI. *Diagnosis, Correction and Prevention of Reading Disabilities.* New York: Harper & Row, 1978.

VENEZKY, RICHARD L. "The Curious Role of Letter Names in Reading Instruction." *Visible Language,* 9 (Winter 1975), 7–23.

VENEZKY, RICHARD L., AND DOMINIC W. MASSARO. "The Role of Orthographic Regularity in Word Recognition." In *Theory and Practice of Early Reading,* Vol. 1. Lauren B. Resnick and Phyllis A. Weaver, eds. Hillsdale, N.J.: Lawrence Erlbaum, 1979.

WEISS, HARVEY. *How to Make Books.* New York: Thomas Y. Crowell, 1978.

WEPMAN, JOSEPH. *Wepman Auditory Discrimination Test.* Chicago: Language Research Associates, 1973.

7

DIAGNOSING COMPREHENSION

Upon completion of the chapter, you will be able to

1. Discuss the influence of world knowledge in the comprehension process.
2. Distinguish between norm-referenced and criterion-referenced tests.
3. Discuss uses and limitations of norm-referenced and criterion-referenced tests.
4. Construct, administer, score, and interpret a cloze test.
5. Construct, administer, score, and interpret an informal reading inventory.
6. List and explain reasons for poor comprehension.

At the weekly staff meeting at Lincoln School, Mrs. Marks was discussing Susan's need for a diagnostic reading evaluation: "We have struggled for years to teach this child the basics—sight words, phonics, and structural analysis—and we thought we had succeeded. We had hoped that Susan, who is now in fourth grade, would be able to read at grade level, but she doesn't seem to understand her reading assignments. We need a thorough diagnosis of her reading ability, particularly in the area of comprehension."

DIAGNOSING COMPREHENSION

It certainly makes sense to analyze Susan's comprehension ability. The time and energy spent diagnosing Susan's difficulty will enable her teachers to correct the comprehension difficulties as efficiently as possible.

The Influence of World Knowledge

Before discussing the diagnostic process it will help to reexamine the influence of world knowledge, or nonvisual information, on comprehension. World knowledge represents the past experiences and concepts which students bring to the printed page and which enable them to make sense of the text. The presence of world knowledge explains why illiterate adults can comprehend stories written for young children even though they miscall many of the words. They compensate for their lack of word identification ability with an abundance of prior information about the text—information about the world which they have gained through life experiences.

The existence of world knowledge means that diagnosing comprehension becomes a complex task. World knowledge interacts with the information in print and makes it difficult to distinguish between an alleged reading difficulty and students' understanding of the world.

This means that statements such as "She doesn't understand" must be made cautiously. Susan may understand a great deal when reading cooking recipes, photography magazines, and manuals on the care and feeding of goats. She may not understand, however, whenever the reading material covers topics for which she possesses insufficient background information, such as the Arctic, the Boer War, and atomic particles. In this sense, we all have a degree of reading difficulty. For each of us, some areas of life are totally unfamiliar and, hence, more difficult to comprehend.

The important question teachers must ask themselves is whether the students' inability to understand a reading assignment is caused by insufficient world knowledge or lack of specific reading skills. A prime example is the college student who requests help from instructors in the school's reading and study skills center. The reading staff may be prepared to teach reading and study strategies but may require help from subject-matter specialists in strengthening the student's conceptual background.

The influence of world knowledge also has implications for comprehension instruction since we never really "master" comprehension as we do word identification skills. Once students know the vowel generalizations, for example, they need not relearn them at a higher level. Comprehension skills, however, are never mastered (though we may grasp the concepts of main idea, drawing conclusions, and so on) because our ability to comprehend is influenced by the difficulty of the material (readability, conceptual difficulty, and so on). As soon as we think we "know" main ideas, inference, or any other comprehension skills, we can be given reading material which is conceptually more demanding and, hence, less comprehensible.

Diagnostic Assumptions

All diagnostic techniques for evaluating students' comprehension are laden with assumptions. Three assumptions in particular should be carefully examined if valid conclusions are to be reached about students' reading ability. The assumptions deal with word identification, capacity for improved comprehension, and quality of comprehension instruction. We will discuss these three before describing specific testing procedures.

ADEQUATE WORD IDENTIFICATION ABILITY   The first assumption is that students like Susan can identify words proficiently. Some authorities question whether there really are students with well-developed word identification skills who still fail to comprehend. Calfee, *et al.* (1976), Golinkoff (1975–76), and Canney and Winograd (1979) believe that most poor comprehenders are preoccupied with word identification and thus are unable to devote sufficient attention to the text. Furthermore, Matz and Rohwer (1971) have concluded that students with comprehension problems in reading do not suffer from a general comprehension problem. All these studies imply that the culprit in many so-called comprehension problems may not be reading comprehension at all but weak decoding skills. One of the first steps in a diagnosis, therefore, is to evaluate students' abilities in identifying words. If word identification skills are not sufficiently developed, intensive efforts to diagnose or remediate comprehension are premature.

CAPACITY FOR IMPROVED COMPREHENSION   A second assumption is that reading comprehension can be significantly improved. If Susan, for instance, is presently comprehending at a level commensurate with her overall intellectual ability, it may be unrealistic to expect her reading comprehension to exceed that level—except, of course, in specific instances in which she can take advantage of considerable background experience. (An individual intelligence test along with expectancy formulas such as described in Chapter 2, "Students with Reading Problems," can help determine the present limits of Susan's comprehension ability.) If Susan scored substantially below average on the intelligence test, we would not expect her to comprehend at grade level. This does not mean that her general intellectual functioning cannot be improved. Assistance in developing this competency, however, must precede or be conducted concurrently with comprehension instruction.

QUALITY OF COMPREHENSION INSTRUCTION   Finally, we need to evaluate Susan's present instructional program. We shouldn't assume that she has been receiving exemplary or even adequate instruction. Durkin (1978) who observed reading instruction in grades three to six, defined comprehension instruction as "something the teacher does or says to help children understand or work out the meaning of more than a single isolated word" (p. 8). After spending hours observing classroom instruction, she concluded that minimal comprehension instruction was actually taking place in those grades. Teachers devoted a majority of their scheduled instructional time to giving assignments, checking assignments, and questioning students. The questioning consisted of isolated, single queries rather than a series of questions to help students understand the reading material. Students' responses were judged right or wrong with little attempt to determine the reasons for incorrect answers. In brief, instruction followed an "A and A" method—*Assign* and *Assess*. Durkin's study suggests that no evaluation of students' comprehension ability is complete without a thorough examination of their present instructional program.

NORM-REFERENCED TESTS

Now that we have examined the assumptions about word identification, capacity, and the quality of instruction, we can discuss specific comprehension tests. Even if teachers rely heavily on observing pupils' behavior in diagnosing comprehension, they will undoubtedly want to make considerable use of more formal evaluative instruments. The hundreds of tests presently available can generally be divided into two types: norm-referenced tests and criterion-referenced tests. Both types have similar content but differ in that norm-referenced tests are designed to compare students' performance with one another. The criterion-referenced measures, on the other hand, are intended to compare students to a predetermined level of performance, regardless of their relative standing with each other.

Characteristics

Since norm-referenced tests are intended to compare students with one another, we cannot evaluate an individual's behavior until we determine how his or her score compares with other students who have taken the test. If a student, for example, had answered sixty-seven of ninety-three items correctly on the reading subtest of the Primary II Stanford Achievement Test, at the end of the school year, we would conclude that the student achieved a percentage score of 72: hardly impressive. However, if we compared this performance with others who took the test at that grade level, we would learn that sixty-seven correct responses was the average score for students with a grade level of 2.9. Thus, with 72 percent of the items answered correctly, the student would be reading at grade level.

Simply put, norm-referenced tests compare an individual's performance, not simply with any group, but with the scores of a norming sample of students representing a range of geographic regions, community sizes, and socioeconomic levels. These individuals are tested and their scores are subjected to statistical analyses to determine the norming sample's central tendencies and spread of scores. Further analyses convert the raw scores into grade equivalents, percentiles, stanines, and normal curve equivalents. An explanation of each type of score can be found in Chapter 11, "The Evaluation of Reading Tests and Programs."

Types of Norm-Referenced Tests

There are many ways to categorize norm-referenced tests. We feel that a meaningful approach is to separate them into survey tests and diagnostic tests since that is how reading teachers frequently use them. Since their uses vary considerably, we will explain how they might help teachers improve their evaluation of reading comprehension. We will limit our discussion to those parts of the test which purport to measure comprehension.

SURVEY TESTS—USES AND LIMITATIONS   The survey test is usually group-administered. There are exceptions, however, such as the Peabody Individual Achievement Test (Dunn and Markwardt, 1970) which is administered individually. These tests require students to read short passages and complete the passage by choosing from a series of words. An example of this type of item is shown in Figure 7-1. Examples of reading comprehension tests of these types are the following:

Stanford Reading Tests (1973)
Metropolitan Reading Tests (1978)
California Reading Tests (1977-78)
Gates-MacGinitie Reading Tests (1978)
Iowa Test of Basic Skills—Reading Test (1978-79)

Figure 7-1   Sample Sentences and Multiple Choice Questions from Stanford Achievement Test, Primary II, Reading Comprehension   Reproduced by permission from the Stanford Achievement Test: 7th Edition. Copyright 1982 by Harcourt Brace Jovanovich, Inc. All rights reserved.

Reading Comprehension

SAMPLE

Rick picked some apples.
He put them in a

A   **truck   box   pail   basket.**
    ○   ○   ○   ●

The apples will be used to make

B   **lemonade   pies   soup   pictures.**
    ○   ○   ○   ○

The items in these tests cover a variety of topics and reading skills. The reading subtest of the Stanford Achievement Test, Primary II, contains paragraphs about television, goats, tools, shopping, trumpets, window washers, and gulls. Students are expected to interpret inferential material by identifying main ideas and drawing conclusions. Knowledge of vocabulary is also necessary. Results, however, are not subdivided into specific skills but are instead reported in the form of a single score.

Survey tests can serve a number of useful educational purposes. First, they can function as rough indicators of a school's or system's achievement in comprehension. For example, they either confirm the impression of administrators and teachers that students are making satisfactory progress or reinforce suspicions that reading achievement is declining. Although low scores warn the educational community of impending or existing problems, they do not diagnose the cause.

Second, survey tests are often used to select students who need special assistance. Compensatory reading programs for disadvantaged children as well as programs for the learning disabled usually require placement to be based on objective test data. These group-administered survey tests provide a convenient means to determine eligibility.

Finally, survey tests fulfill the need for political accountability. Continued community and federal support for reading programs is facilitated when it can be demonstrated that students have made gains on tests. At the same time, critics can use low scores to support their accusations that tax money is being squandered. Despite the fact that schools cannot always claim sole credit for high scores, nor are they entirely responsible for low scores, the test results provide ammunition for those who wish either to defend or to attack the school's reading program.

If survey tests are used for either curriculum evaluation or political accountability, there is no need to give them to every student. Instead, it is sufficient to sample the student body and test only selected students. In this way, time and money would be saved and students would be spared needless testing. When this procedure is used, though, only group results at the school or system level would be reported.

Unfortunately, survey tests provide little assistance in developing specific instructional programs for students like Susan. Most survey tests are group instruments and are better suited for describing the collective performance of individuals at the classroom, school, and district level. They are less accurate in assessing individual behavior.

Also, since survey tests measure reading on a global level it is difficult to determine a student's specific comprehension strengths and weaknesses. Even if specific test items were analyzed, it would be impossible to determine if reading skills were confounded with world knowledge. Did Susan, in other words, incorrectly answer an item because of a skill deficiency in word identification or comprehension or because she lacked background information? If Susan lacks sufficient world knowledge, it would seem appropriate to enrich her background. But specific remediation in this area presents a thorny problem since test items may include information ranging from dancing lessons to electrical current theory. Moreover, only a few questions are asked about each topic. In other curriculum areas with more limited content, a review of individual items may be helpful. If students are tested on map-reading skills and err on questions of latitude and longitude, for instance, this information may have direct diagnostic implications. Reading, however, is essentially a process and therefore can involve any subject. Even if only reading skills were analyzed, it is unlikely that a sufficient number would be available in any one skill to make any reliable judgments about the student's performance.

A third problem with survey tests is that students with reading problems tend to score higher on a group reading test, in terms of grade equivalents, than on typical classroom reading material (Harris and Sipay, 1980). In survey tests, students can increase their score by guessing. Hence, if they are placed in material according to a standard reading test score, they are likely to be frustrated. Furthermore, a grade equivalent score does not measure students' ability to meet particular grade-level standards. It merely compares students with one another. A grade equivalent of 5.6, for example, simply means that a student correctly answered as many questions as the average student who was in the sixth month of the fifth grade.

A final criticism of survey tests is that they have been constructed to function in a manner similar to intelligence tests. It is generally accepted that if two tests are otherwise equal, the one that can make finer distinctions between individuals is preferable. In an attempt to maximize the spread of scores and differentiate among students, test questions have been included which load heavily on the same factors found in intelligence tests. As a result, the reading tests have come to resemble intelligence tests, making it difficult for instructional programs to raise test scores substantially (Thorndike, 1973–74).

DIAGNOSTIC TESTS—USES AND LIMITATIONS   Diagnostic reading tests, like survey tests, compare an individual's score with the norming sample. They differ, however, in that they attempt to measure specific reading abilities rather than global performance.

Some well-known tests in this category, most of which are administered individually, are the following:

> Gray Oral Reading Tests (1963–67)
> Gilmore Oral Reading Test (1968)
> Durrell Analysis of Reading Difficulty (Durrell, 1980)
> Stanford Diagnostic Reading Test (1976) (This test is administered in a group.)

Figure 7-2 shows a sample selection from the Gilmore Oral Reading Test.

An individually administered test is usually more useful for diagnostic purposes since students are asked to recall answers to comprehension questions rather than to select a correct response from an array of possible answers. In addition, the examiner is better able to observe important behaviors such as motivational level, anxiety, and coping mechanisms. Individual tests also allow the examiner to listen to the student read orally, and hence, word identification skills and strategies can be evaluated. This sometimes helps determine whether

Gilmore Oral Reading–B

4. Tom and Ned live near a large city park. They often visit it with their playmates. In the park are many shady maple trees. There is a pleasant picnic ground on the hill, and the valley below has a pretty little pond. The girls always enjoy watching the boys while they sail their tiny boats in the water. Mother and Father enjoy picnics in the park.

TIME_____Seconds

__1. What kind of trees grow in the park?
__2. Where is the picnic ground?
__3. What is in the valley?
__4. What do the boys do at the pond?
__5. What do Mother and Father like to do in the park?

NUMBER RIGHT _____

ERROR RECORD	Number
Substitutions	
Mispronunciations	
Words pronounced by examiner	
Disregard of punctuation	
Insertions	
Hesitations	
Repetitions	
Omissions	
Total Errors	

Figure 7-2 Grade Four Passage from Gilmore Oral Reading Test Reproduced by permission. Copyright 1951 by Harcourt Brace Jovanovich, Inc., New York, NY. All rights reserved.

poor comprehension is attributable to deficiencies in word identification. On the other hand, an individual test requires more time to administer. An entire class of students can be tested with a group test in the same time that it takes to give one individual test.

An important question related to assessment is how well these tests diagnose comprehension. An examination reveals that in most instances diagnosis focuses on word identification. When students make word identification errors on the Gilmore Oral Reading Test, for example, errors are classified as substitutions, mispronunciations, insertions, hesitations, repetitions, or omissions. Diagnosis of comprehension, on the other hand, is conducted at a global level. An answer is simply marked right or wrong.

Another limitation of the majority of these instruments is that they test only for literal comprehension. Only the Stanford Diagnostic Reading Test evaluates both literal and inferential reading (at level 2 but not level 1). If a test restricts itself to one level of comprehension, its diagnostic function is severely limited.

Another limitation is the lack of norms. The Gray Oral Reading Test, for example, asks students questions about passages, but the norms are based on time and the number of oral reading errors rather than comprehension. The Durrell Analysis of Reading Difficulty provides norms for the silent reading test but not the oral.

A final problem is passage dependency, which refers to the student's need to read the passage in order to answer the comprehension questions. Sometimes the wording of a question allows the reader to answer correctly without reading the selection. The Durrell Analysis of Reading Difficulty, for example, asks the following questions: "What does [the kitten] drink?" "What did the boys do when the sun went down?" "What did the boat hit?" Likely answers are that the kitten drank milk, the boys went to sleep, and the boat hit a rock—and these can often be determined without actually reading the passages.

In sum, diagnostic reading tests usually provide more information than survey tests, particularly when the former are individually administered. However, many have limited use because they measure only literal information. Some do provide limited norms in comprehension, though. Before using a test of this type, it would be wise to consult the checklist for test evaluation in Chapter 11, "The Evaluation of Reading Tests and Programs," and Buros (1968 and 1975).

Cloze Tests

Another type of norm-referenced test is the cloze test. Based on the concept that individuals seek closure, the test requires the reader to fill in deleted words from a passage rather than answer specific questions. In the typical cloze selection, every fifth word (narrative material) or tenth word (expository selection) is replaced by a blank space of standard length. The test requires vocabulary knowledge and an ability to use context.

A typical cloze test is constructed by selecting a passage of at least 250 words to allow twenty-five deletions in either every fifth or tenth word. The passages represent material which students would ordinarily be asked to read. Usually the first sentence of the passage contains no deleted words. Deletions begin with the second sentence.

Students are instructed to fill in the blanks with words that make sense, and they are given credit only for exact word replacements. Accepting synonyms creates a scoring problem because evaluators may disagree about the appropriateness of a synonym. Furthermore, allowing words other than exact replacements increases the time necessary to score the test.

The student's score on the test is the percentage of correct words compared to the total number of deletions. Different standards have been used to interpret the results. They vary with the test which was used to determine the students' reading levels and to which the cloze scores were then related. Bormuth (1968), for example, employed a modified version of the Gray Oral Reading Test. The use of various anchoring tests accounts for the discrepancy in scoring criteria. The following criteria represent two scoring systems:

	BORMUTH (1968)	ALEXANDER (1969)
Independent level	57	62
Instructional level	45–56	48–61
Frustration level	44	47

With this information, teachers will be able to determine whether a particular passage can be read with understanding by students in a particular class. If, for example, a teacher wishes to determine how well students can read their social studies text, one or more representative passages can be chosen for use in a cloze test. Cloze passages should be chosen from more than one section if the text varies significantly in difficulty.

If a large majority of students achieved instructional level standards, this book would be suitable for the class as long as the teacher directed the reading. On the other hand, if most of the students achieved an independent level on the cloze tests, the chapters could be assigned for independent reading. If a large portion of students were unable to read the book, the teacher would have to either provide alternative learning opportunities (visual aids, projects, experiments, discussion, reading to students) or select easier material. If the material in which the students were tested was similar in difficulty to other materials used by the class, the results could be generalized to these texts.

Although overall scores are best used to determine a group's ability to handle particular selections (Estes and Vaughan, 1978), responses of specific individuals can be used diagnostically. Discussing with students the reasons for their incorrect answers can help the teacher understand the breadth and depth of the readers' vocabulary and their word identification strategies. In some cases a synonym may have been substituted, such as *big* for *huge*. In other instances a student may have even inserted a word which indicated more sophistication than the text required, such as *miniature* for *little*. In reviewing students' answers, group discussion can help sensitize the students to subtle differences in word meaning. In the discussion session it is preferable for students to defend their responses, some of which may be quite reasonable, before the teacher reveals the exact replacement. This practice encourages students to think through the reasons for a chosen word. Answers can also be evaluated on a qualitative basis, ranging on a continuum from exact replacement to inappropriate replacement. This activity illustrates the close relationship of diagnosis to remediation. On the one hand, the teacher is becoming more aware of the student's vocabulary level, and on the other hand, the discussion session helps the student be more sensitive of word meaning.

The cloze test has an important advantage over conventional tests. Cloze tests are easily constructed and scored. Thus, they can be made from a variety of textbooks or other reading material with minimum effort. The creation of time-consuming questions as well as uncertainty about their quality are also avoided. As a result, teachers need not hope that results on a social studies passage can be generalized to the science text. With cloze they can also quickly create, administer, and score a passage from the science text itself.

One disadvantage of the cloze test, particularly with elementary-school students of low reading ability, is that some will find the test frustrating to complete regardless of the difficulty of the material or preparation for the task. Cloze tests require students to supply answers to a minimum of twenty-five missing words. Even if students are encouraged to spell words as they sound, many will find this a tedious chore. In addition, some students with limited language facility will feel constrained by tests which require them to rely heavily on semantic and syntactic clues. When students grudgingly participate in the testing, it may not be a valid measuring device despite its obvious convenience.

The cloze is best suited for determining whether groups of students can read a wide variety of textbooks. The differences between the basal reader and these texts as well as the differences among content area texts themselves require testing in specific areas, and the cloze is an appropriate device for this purpose.

CRITERION-REFERENCED TESTS

The limitations of norm-referenced tests, both the survey types and those which purport to be diagnostic, have led to the development of criterion-referenced tests. In this section we will examine the characteristics and construction of criterion-referenced tests, their usefulness in making educational decisions, and their limitations.

Comparison with Norm-Referenced Tests

Criterion-referenced tests differ from norm-referenced tests in several ways. The former are not designed to compare students' relative standing with their peers but instead assess their ability to perform specific tasks. In a criterion-referenced test, for example, a student might be asked to identify a topic sentence. Proficiency would be determined by the percentage of correct responses. With many of these tests, the minimum acceptable score is 80 percent. Thus, students' individual scores are judged in relation to the established criterion rather than to a norm group's average score. It is conceivable that all or none of the students would reach the mastery figure.

The development of criterion-referenced tests begins with the identification of specific educational objectives. The listing of these objectives may parallel the division of comprehension into discrete subskills, such as main idea; drawing conclusions; sequence; using context; detail; and reading at the literal, inferential, and critical levels. Some norm-referenced tests also include items involving many of these skills, but comprehension is measured on a global basis rather than in terms of specific skills.

The intent of criterion-referenced tests, to measure mastery of specific objectives, influences the selection of items. A norm-referenced test attempts to select test items which maximize the difference among individuals. Since developers of criterion-referenced tests are not concerned with the dispersion of scores, items are not restricted to any particular range of difficulty. If we expressed the difference between norm- and criterion-referenced tests graphically, the norm-referenced test would be depicted by the familiar bell-shaped curve

in which scores are dispersed equally around the mean. The criterion-referenced tests, by contrast, would produce a curve—after instruction—

with a pronounced negative skew. Ideally, most scores would fall at the high end of the continuum since most students would "master" the test.

Uses of Criterion-Referenced Tests

We have repeatedly argued that tests should help teachers make instructional decisions. For this purpose, criterion-referenced tests are usually superior to norm-referenced ones. If students are tested on separate comprehension skills, it can be readily determined which skills have been learned. Teachers can then focus instruction on those skills in which individuals cannot demonstrate sufficient proficiency. Proponents suggest that the individualization which is made possible by the use of criterion-referenced testing should lead to more efficient instruction.

Another potential advantage is increased student motivation. Motivation improves because students are informed of the objectives of instruction, work only on needed skills, and receive periodic feedback about their progress.

Many criterion-referenced tests measuring comprehension have been organized into skills management systems (SMS). As with SMS in word identification, behavioral objectives are developed, tests are prepared to assess mastery of the objectives, and students are tested in comprehension skills before and after instruction. Some SMS that assess comprehension are the following:

> Fountain Valley Teacher Support System in Reading (1971)
> Prescriptive Reading Inventory (1972)
> Wisconsin Design for Reading Skill Development (1977)

Skills management systems usually include a variety of comprehension skills. The following skills, for example, are included in the Wisconsin Design for Reading Skill Development: word parts (affixes), context clues, details, paraphrase, central thought, relationships and conclusions, and sequences.

Selecting Criterion-Referenced Tests and Skills Management Systems

In order to select criterion-referenced tests or SMS of high technical quality, the following questions might be asked: (1) Do the test items measure the intended objectives? (2) Is the students' performance from one testing to another consistent in the absence of instruction? and (3) Are students who receive instruction able to score higher than those who have not been instructed? A complete checklist for conducting an evaluation of SMS can be found in *How to Teach Reading* (Otto *et al.*, 1979, pp. 70–71).

Issues in Evaluating Comprehension Skills

In addition to concerns about test selection, teachers should be aware of specific issues involving the evaluation of comprehension. We have already mentioned that the diagnosis of comprehension is complicated by the presence of world knowledge. It is not easy to determine whether a student fails a criterion-referenced test because of a skill deficiency or lack of background knowledge. For this reason we suggested that comprehension skills are never really mastered. In the interest of accuracy the term *mastery* should be used with caution. When it is employed, it should mean no more than that the student has demonstrated sufficient competence in a skill at one level either to move on to the same skill at a higher level or to receive instruction in another skill.

Another problem, which involves all tests of comprehension but is more pronounced in criterion-referenced tests, is whether comprehension is a unitary or global process or whether it is composed of many discrete subskills. And if discrete subskills do exist, how many are there? And what are they? Authorities differ; opinions can be arranged along a continuum. At one end are those who believe that comprehension is composed of numerous subskills. At the other are those who contend that comprehension is essentially a unitary phenomenon and cannot be subdivided.

Many Subskills (e.g., Ginn's 360 primary reading series lists 49 subskills) (Rosenshine, 1977)	Three or Four Subskills 1. General verbal ability 2. Explicit comprehension 3. Implicit comprehension 4. Appreciation (Lennon, 1962; Rosenshine, 1977; MacGinitie, 1973)	Unitary Process (Thorndike, 1973–74)

In view of these differences, a number of solutions have been proposed. Farr (1971) believes that it would be far better to organize comprehension in terms of specific tasks—for example, locating a program in a television guide—rather than to wait for conclusive evidence in support of specific factors. Rosenshine (1977) suggests that since a high correlation exists among reading skills, one skill is probably just as effective as another in promoting overall comprehension. He does add, however, that students tend to learn those skills which they are taught. This statement would argue for emphasizing instruction in skills that are considered most helpful.

Though differences of opinion do exist, the weight of the evidence and the judgment of authorities suggest that a relatively small number of skills—probably less than a half dozen—can be differentiated. Furthermore, agreement exists on three points:

1. Vocabulary constitutes a good deal of reading comprehension (Anderson and Freebody, 1979). When the influence of vocabulary is removed, the remaining factors account for a small part of the process.
2. Aside from vocabulary, the best differentiation of comprehension is between understanding explicit and implicit information.
3. It is questionable whether the skills of comprehension can be organized into a hierarchy in which the mastery of basic skills is a prerequisite to learning advanced skills (Simons, 1971).

In light of these views, we find Cramer's solution (1978) appealing. He has organized comprehension into four categories: (1) literal or explicit, (2) implicit or reasoning, (3) word meaning, and (4) appreciation. The traditional comprehension skills are listed under one of these categories (see Figure 7-3).

EXPLICIT (LITERAL)	IMPLICIT (REASONING)
Main idea (stated)	Inference
Factual questions	Prediction
Sequence (stated)	Application
Following directions	Cause-effect
Restating information	Interpretation
Finding proof	Evaluation
Recognizing details	Contrast
Recalling details	Purpose setting
Locating information	Comparison
	Generalization
WORD MEANING (VOCABULARY)	Extrapolation
	Recognizing propaganda
Denotation	Main ideas (implied)
Connotation	Drawing conclusions
Multiple meanings	Critical reading
Contextual meanings	Creative reading
Compounds	
Synonyms	APPRECIATIVE (AFFECTIVE)
Antonyms	
Homonyms	Mood
Homographs	Tone
Root words	Characterization
Prefixes	Beauty
Suffixes	Humor
Word origin	Values (personal)
Idioms	Feelings
Slang	Opinion
Figures of speech	
Classification	
Metaphor	
Simile	

Figure 7-3 The Four Basic Components of Comprehension   From *Writing, Reading and Language Growth* by Ronald L. Cramer. Copyright 1978 by Charles E. Merrill Publishing Company, p. 206. Reprinted by permission.

In Cramer's system, however, we need not become too concerned about distinguishing among skills within a category. In implicit skills, for example, inference and drawing conclusions may overlap somewhat. Lessons in both skills can be taught, but it is not essential to differentiate between them. A diagnostic program which followed this plan would evaluate student abilities in the four broad areas but would not concern itself with measuring each of the subskills which falls under the major areas.

Because disagreement about the number and kind of comprehension skills is reflected in the construction of available SMS, we suggest the following:

1. After selecting an SMS of high quality, use only those tests which help to make instructional decisions. Do not administer a test simply because it has been included in the test battery. If the curriculum places little value on teaching sequence, for example, do not test students on this skill.

2. If testing time is limited, administer the tests in order of importance to the school's instructional program. Evaluate the less important skills informally during actual instruction and only as times allows.

3. Select at least one test from the literal meaning category and two or more from the inferential category. The precise skills which are chosen will depend on the available instructional material, the broad curriculum goals and philosophy of the school, and a teacher's personal inclinations. As for vocabulary, specific words are not tested, but it is possible to assess students' use of context in determining word meaning.

INFORMAL READING INVENTORIES

The informal reading inventory (IRI) is a unique instrument which we have arbitrarily categorized as a criterion-referenced test. It has traditionally been used to interpret comprehension. In its simplest form the IRI consists of a series of graded passages and accompanying questions. The student reads the passages orally or silently and then answers the questions.

Purpose and Reading Levels

The purpose of the IRI is twofold: to identify students' four reading levels: independent, instructional, frustration, and potential; and to identify students' needs in word identification and comprehension.

The generally accepted standards for each of the four levels are as follows:

Independent level. This is the level at which students understand virtually all the material they read, and they can complete reading assignments without a teacher's assistance. In word identification, they exhibit few if any errors. Their oral reading is usually fluent and they show no signs of frustration.

Instructional level. The instructional level is the range in which students can function well under a teacher's direction. Students understand most of the material, and with a teacher's assistance they are able to progress to an independent level. They know most of the words but may require occasional assistance from the teacher. Signs of frustration are not present.

Frustration level. At this level students understand little of the reading selection. Their word identification ability is inadequate. Students will read only with great effort and undue stress. Even with ample assistance from the teacher, they are not able to read with adequate comprehension. Signs of frustration, such as finger pointing, lip movement, and head movement, are readily apparent.

Potential level. At the potential level (also called the listening comprehension level) students can understand the reading passages if it is read by the teacher. The student is not required to read but instead listens.

The IRI can help to identify strengths and weaknesses in both word identification and comprehension. As students read orally, the quantity and quality of their miscues can be analyzed. Answers supplied to comprehension questions can help teachers understand the students' experiential background as well as their ability to read at the literal and inferential levels.

The popularity of the IRI is due to its ability to assess a wide variety of reading and reading-related behaviors. It measures not only comprehension but also word identification, fluency in oral reading, ability to attend, interest in reading, response to frustration, risk-taking behavior, and overall strategies. In a sense, the IRI represents "one-stop" testing.

Rationale and Development of the IRI

The rationale for the IRI is to simulate a guided reading lesson. In a traditional reading lesson, the teacher assigns pages to be read silently. After reading the passage, students are asked questions about it. Some form of oral reading frequently follows. The IRI, although not identical to the typical reading lesson, provides a similar opportunity to gather information about students' word identification and comprehension. To the extent that the selection and the testing procedures are like those employed in the reading class, the results can be generalized to everyday performance. The IRI, then, is essentially a series of miniature reading lessons.

Originally, the IRI was used informally. The teacher would select a passage from a textbook, ask the student to read a few paragraphs, either orally or silently, and then pose questions about the content. The student would read from a series of increasingly more difficult texts if the teacher's purpose was to place the student in an appropriate text or reading group. If the purpose was to measure a student's growth in a particular text, a similar procedure would be used.

Over the years, however, the IRI has become more formalized. Today, college professors and teachers create IRIs which specify the passage's length and readability and the number and type of questions. In addition, complex scoring procedures are used for the analyses of word identification and comprehension errors.

Commercial Versus Informal Inventories

One result of the growing formalization of the IRI is the commercial inventory. This test is not necessarily drawn from a basal series, but it uses selections from numerous sources whose readability is determined by one of the widely used formulas, such as the Dale-Chall (1948) or Spache (1970). Suitability of interest for a particular grade level is also considered. Questions attempt to cover a variety of reading skills, such as literal comprehension, inferential comprehension, main idea, cause and effect, and vocabulary. Directions are carefully spelled out, as in standardized tests, and the scores are subjected to detailed analysis.

The commercial inventories have been criticized for not accurately assessing students' performance in the regular classroom text. If the IRI material is easier than the classroom text, students' performance will be inflated and they will be overplaced. On the other hand, if the IRI is more difficult than the classroom material, the student will be underrated in reading ability. The solution, according to some authorities, is to use actual classroom materials as informal inventories.

A case, however, can be made for IRIs which are not taken from texts in classroom use. First, a reading program should not be intended to teach a student to read only a particular basal reader. Therefore, if only these basal texts are used, we may misinterpret the students' performance. Mike, for example, was a first-grade student who performed differently on the reading specialist's IRI than on the classroom basal reader. In the latter, Mike was reading at the first-reader level, and his teacher believed that he was keeping up with the reading group. The IRI, drawn from different material, showed that Mike read well only at a primer level. Since the discrepancy might have been caused by different vocabulary, the reading specialist tabulated Mike's word identification errors and found that every one of these words had appeared in Mike's school material. The specialist concluded that Mike was able to read the words in his text because these stories were frequently reviewed until Mike had virtually memorized them. He had not learned the words sufficiently well to identify them in other settings. In this instance it was important that Mike be tested in material other than school texts.

A second reason for using a commercial or home-made IRI is related to the creation of questions. It is time-consuming to construct good questions for every new selection. Furthermore, there are distinct advantages in using the same questions repeatedly: not only does it save time but also it will help the teacher evaluate students' responses. In asking the same questions many times teachers will develop standards for acceptable answers. Also, the repeated use of the same questions will help the teacher distinguish between common and novel answers, which can provide insight about the students. Finally, the use of these questions with many students will enable the teacher to identify and revise confusing questions.

The best solution, we believe, is to administer a prepared IRI to students with reading difficulty and then evaluate their ability to read in the school's basal reader. The prepared IRI will provide sufficient diagnosis of reading level and reading needs, but the students' own material, which can be tested more informally, can help the teacher place them more precisely in the appropriate basal text—assuming they have not been previously taught from this text. A comparison of performance in each set of materials can help determine whether the students have learned to read school texts well enough to transfer this reading ability to materials they have not previously encountered.

Construction

Teachers can either purchase a commercially prepared IRI or construct their own. The following commercial IRIs are available:

Analytical Reading Inventory (Woods and Moe, 1981)

Diagnostic Reading Scales (Spache, 1981)

Durrell Analysis of Reading Difficulty (Durrell, 1980)

Standard Reading Inventory (McCracken, 1966)

Diagnostic Reading Inventory (Jacobs and Searfoss, 1979)

The Contemporary Classroom Reading Inventory (Rinsky and de-Fossard, 1980)

Informal Reading Assessment (Burns and Roe, 1980)

Classroom Reading Inventory (Silvaroli, 1982)

Basic Reading Inventory (Johns, 1981)

Although it is easier to buy a published IRI, teachers can benefit from developing their own. First, they will be better able to evaluate IRIs because writing and rewriting questions will make them more aware of the qualities of good questions. This is particularly true if questions are criticized by a knowledgeable reading professional such as a college instructor or an experienced reading specialist. Second, teachers may be more willing to revise weak questions if they were originally responsible for them. (Poor questions should be revised on commercial IRIs as well.) Fine-tuning the instrument can lead to more valid judgments about students' comprehension.

SELECTIONS   To begin constructing an IRI, select two basal reader passages at each level from the primer through sixth grade. (Any material, of course, can be used for an IRI, but the use of graded materials simplifies the selection process.) Choose a series which is neither the most difficult nor the easiest on the market. If in doubt, consult with experienced teachers who have used the series. Preprimer selections can be omitted because the comprehension demands at this point are minimal. Reading ability at the preprimer can be adequately evaluated with word identification and language-experience assessments. If junior high students are frequently tested, add passages at the seventh- and eighth-grade levels. These selections should include literature, social studies, and science. Beyond eighth grade, the concept of grade level becomes meaningless. Higher reading levels can be better assessed by a cloze test in specific reading texts.

Selections should increase in length with the grade level. The following are suggested lengths at each level (Stauffer *et al.*, 1978):

LEVEL	NUMBER OF WORDS
Primer	60–75
1	75–100
2	100–125

LEVEL	NUMBER OF WORDS
3	125–150
4	150–175
5–6	175–200
7–8	200–225

It is best to select passages from the very beginning of an account and to end the selection with a complete paragraph. Do not terminate the account so abruptly that the reader is overly concerned about the outcome.

Choose selections which are likely to be of interest. If students prefer active, outdoor activities, for example, choose selections of this type.

Another consideration is the amount of information the selection contains. Since several questions will be asked about each passage, select passages which contain sufficient information for this purpose. An account with considerable dialogue, for example, is unlikely to provide a sufficient source of questions. At the same time, avoid selections heavily laden with detail. They often place too high a burden on the student's memory.

Two passages, each from a separate selection, should be chosen at each level and should be of comparable difficulty and interest. Do not take selections from the same story; students may confuse the selections or use information from the first selection to help answer questions on the second passage. In either event the test results will be affected.

QUESTIONS Next, develop comprehension questions. Write five questions at the primer level, seven at the first-reader level, and ten questions at grades two through eight. Some selections may appear to contain insufficient information, and you may need to reduce the number. However, this will reduce the test's reliability, so try to select passages with sufficient information and then work diligently to develop the required questions.

The questions should cover three areas: literal comprehension, inferential comprehension, and vocabulary. The number and type at each level are as follows:

LEVEL	FACT	INFERENCE	VOCABULARY
Primer	2	2	1
First	3	3	1
Second to eighth	4	4	2

In developing questions, observe the following rules:

1. Questions should cover the entire passage rather than a portion of the passage. This practice is likely to enhance the recollection of the story.
2. Whenever feasible, ask questions in the order in which the answers occur in the story.
3. Questions should deal with significant information in the passage. Do not ask trick questions or questions dealing with minute detail. Do not

ask students to recall long lists of items. Avoid questions such as "What was the name of the boy in the story?"—unless the name itself is an important element in the plot.

4. Avoid questions which can be answered with a yes or no response. You can, however, ask a two-part question in which the first part asks "Did Jack fall into the water?"; then follow up with "How do you know?" Credit is given only if both parts of the question can be answered correctly.

5. Avoid questions which can be answered solely from a picture clue or the student's background information. Determine whether any of the questions could be answered without reading the text at all. (Of course, if an individual has sufficient world knowledge, for example, an adult reading a third-grade selection, that is a great advantage.)

Vocabulary questions present a particular dilemma. On the one hand, vocabulary is a critical component of comprehension. On the other hand, many vocabulary questions are "passage independent," because they can be answered without referring to the passage at all. For example, for the question "What is copper?" students' responses may not be based on information in the story but on prior knowledge. For this reason you should take care in interpreting vocabulary questions. One solution is to compute scores without the vocabulary questions when answers to these questions would either raise or lower the instructional level.

Despite their limitations, vocabulary questions do have value. Responses can often enrich a teacher's understanding of students. The child who says that copper is "the orange stuff you rip out of empty houses" comes from a different background from the one who describes copper as a soft metal with an atomic number of 29. Also, it has been our experience that students who consistently miss vocabulary questions often have difficulty with content area material in the intermediate grades and may have problems conceptualizing.

6. Ask convergent rather than divergent or open-ended questions. Convergent questions can be scored more objectively. The need to restrict questions to convergent types, of course, limits the usefulness of the IRI since comprehension instruction should make considerable use of divergent thinking. We also prefer not to use main idea questions ("What would be a good title for this story?") as their scoring is too subjective.

7. Do not provide information in an earlier question which can be used to answer a later question.

8. Be sure that two questions do not ask for the same information.

9. In vocabulary questions, do not ask students to name a word which has a particular meaning: for example, "What word in the story means the same as _____?" Rather, ask "What does _____ mean?" Vocabulary questions can include expressions or figures of speech such as "What does the phrase 'as the crow flies' mean?"

Individual testing allows the teacher to probe for additional information. (Peter P. Tobia)

Administration

The IRI consists of two sets of material: a copy of the story for the student to read and a copy for the teacher on which to record the student's responses. The teacher's copy is double-spaced to allow room to record word identification miscues. Students can read the passage from their copy or from an actual textbook. It is preferable to use the actual texts because this can indicate the students' familiarity with books. If the text itself is used, begin by telling the students the page number of the story and asking them to locate it.

The first selection to be read should be at least one grade level below the tentative instructional level as indicated by the informal word identification test. That is, if this test suggests a third-grade level, begin with the second-grade IRI selection. This practice will help determine the student's independent level, the level at which the student can understand the material without a teacher's assistance.

The first selection at each level is read orally; the second, silently. Inform the students that they are to read the selection aloud and be prepared to answer questions about the passage. While they read, note responses on your copy by coding word identification and related behaviors.

Next, ask the questions that accompany the passage. Write down the answers in the margin of the teacher's copy and evaluate them later. In evaluating answers, you may wish to give partial credit if the student demonstrates some understanding but answers imprecisely.

If words were supplied during the oral reading to enable the students to answer particular questions, decide whether to give credit for those answers. Use judgment concerning whether they could have answered the questions without help in word identification.

If you are uncertain about whether a student has answered a question completely, say, "Tell me more." Probing will frequently determine whether the student actually knows an answer.

In addition to scoring for correct responses, analyze incorrect answers. Do they indicate lack of specific background experiences, faulty reasoning, difficulty remembering facts, or simply an inability to identify words?

If you suspect the students are not attending sufficiently to the selection or understand more than they can recall, repeat each incorrect question after all have been asked once and tell the students to search the passage for the answer. This step may help you to distinguish between students who don't understand the passage and those who had difficulty remembering the material. Do not, of course, give formal credit for these answers.

Continue testing by asking the students to read the silent selection for that level. Remind them that you will ask questions at the conclusion of the reading. As they read, note whether they move their lips, whisper audibly, point with their fingers, or exhibit any other signs of frustration. These are not problems in themselves, but they may be symptomatic of reading difficulty. Also note how carefully the students are reading. Are they mouthing each word, reading with ordinary care, or skimming lightly over the passage? Poor readers often have more difficulty attending to silent reading. As an additional measure, ask the students one other question in which they must locate the answer in the passage and read it aloud. Note if they are able to focus quickly on the desired line, they systematically reread the entire selection until the line is found, or they move around the page in a random fashion. Mark the words or lines which they read. Note whether they read the appropriate sentences or too much material.

Assign additional oral and silent selections until the students are able to answer only 50 percent of the questions correctly or have considerable difficulty in word identification. Occasionally a student's reading becomes so halting that it is unnecessary actually to ask the questions for the oral section; you can often assume that the student would miss at least half of them. In addition, when comprehension on the oral selection is close to 50 percent, you need not ask the students to read the silent selection if they have previously read less well on the silent selection than on the oral. On the other hand, if the readers have consistently scored higher on previous silent selections, ask them to continue with the silent passage.

By this point you have gathered information which can determine the students' independent, instructional, and frustration levels. You can also determine the students' potential level by means of a listening comprehension test. Its purpose is to determine how well the students could read if word identification were not a problem. The term *potential* does not imply a permanent ceiling on the students' reading but indicates the limits of their present reading ability if they were motivated, knew all the vocabulary, and possessed the necessary word identification skills. The test is administered by reading selections to the students and then asking the IRI questions. The highest level at which a student scores 75 percent or more is the potential level.

The potential level can also be determined through an individual intelligence test and expectancy formulas (as discussed in Chapter 2, "Students with Reading Problems.") We believe the intelligence test provides a more valid assessment of potential because it measures a wider range of information. It has also been our experience that the intelligence test provides a higher potential. The lower score on the listening test may be caused by poor listening habits. In the absence of an intelligence test, however, the listening assessment can quickly determine whether we should be expecting the students to read beyond their present level and how wide a gap exists between present ability and potential.

Scoring

The quantitative scoring of comprehension is determined by computing the percentage of correct answers at each grade level. If, for example, students correctly answered eight out of ten questions at the fifth-grade level, they would receive a score of 80 percent. These numerical scores constitute one part of the information needed to diagnose the students' reading ability.

The following scoring system has traditionally been used to determine the students' comprehension levels:

READING LEVEL	PERCENTAGE SCORE
Independent	90–100
Instructional	75–89
Frustration	0–50

Scores between 50 and 75 fall below the instructional level but above the frustration level. Students who score in this range would probably receive some benefit from the reading material, but progress would be slow. In all cases, quantitative scores are only guides to determining levels and must be interpreted in light of the students' overall response.

Interpretation

In addition to the percentage scores, the following information is also of value:

1. *The type of question answered correctly.* In general, students have more trouble with inference questions than questions which require recall of literal information. Therefore, lower scores on inference questions do not necessarily provide significant diagnostic information. If students consistently answer literal questions correctly and fail to answer inferential questions, however, their instruction may have been limited to word identification and literal comprehension. This interpretation is often substantiated when the student comments that "The story didn't say" when you ask an inference question. The student means that the test does not state the answer explicitly and therefore the question cannot be answered. In these instances, it is advisable to ask the question again and have the student reread the passage to find the answer. This "second look," in which the student is pressed to find the answer, can tell you how easy it is for the student to comprehend at the inferential level. As for vocabulary questions, errors of this type may reflect lack of exposure to reading and written language and an insensitivity to word meaning—or all of these.

2. *Motivational level.* Ordinarily, a student will attempt to perform well during the initial testing. However, some students will be so anxious about being

tested that their performance will become depressed. On the other hand, some students will hasten to complete the test. All these behaviors suggest what may occur in the classroom.

3. *Response to frustration.* Carefully observe the students' behaviors as the test becomes more difficult. Again, their conduct during the test may predict how they respond to frustrating experiences in the classroom.

4. *Speed.* Speed of reading is not formally evaluated, but extreme levels may be symptomatic of other difficulties. Slow reading suggests limited word identification abilities and/or an overly precise word identification strategy. Rapid reading accompanied by good comprehension is commendable, but when comprehension is low, the student may view reading as decoding to speech—or is ill at ease in reading and wants to terminate the testing.

5. *Word identification versus comprehension.* The relative strength of word identification and comprehension provides helpful information about students' reading ability. If the word identification score is low and comprehension is low, we might suspect that the student's limited word identification ability is depressing comprehension scores. A thorough diagnosis of comprehension would be difficult until the students improve their ability to read the words. If word identification is limited but comprehension is evident, the students may be relying largely on world knowledge. This strength, however, can dissipate as reading levels increase. The students may eventually reach a point at which they will not be able to read satisfactorily with their present word identification ability. An exception is students in the intermediate grades who are reading for meaning but perform poorly in oral reading. Their miscues ordinarily are of high quality and thus often distinguish them from the poor reader. If their word identification is high but comprehension remains low, the students may be preoccupied with the words, are not attending to the meaning of the text, or possess limited background information.

Case Study

The interpretation of the IRI can best be illustrated by an actual case study. We offer this example to illustrate how teachers need to review quantitative and qualitative behavior in reading and related areas and to seek to understand the dynamics of the student's reading.

Karen was a ten-year-old fourth-grader who was referred for testing to the school reading specialist because her teacher was concerned about her poor progress. Throughout the testing Karen was friendly and cooperative. During the initial interview she said that she read trade books when assigned schoolwork had been completed. She had recently finished *Henry Huggins* by Beverly Cleary (1950). On the word identification test Karen received the following scores:

LEVEL	FLASH	UNTIMED
PP–1	100%	100%
2	92	100
3	68	88
4	56	84

Karen's scores suggest a low third-grade reading level. Furthermore, her ability to analyze words was adequate at grade four despite a low score in sight vocabulary. Additional analysis showed that she possessed a good command of phonic skills. On the IRI Karen received the following scores:

| LEVEL | IDENTIFICATION | COMPREHENSION | |
		Oral	Silent
3	97%	85%	85%
4	94	30	60

On the IRI, Karen performed well in word identification at both the third- and fourth-grade levels (97 and 94 percent, respectively). Her scores suggest that she is able to make effective use of context. If we were to set an instructional level on the basis of word identification and oral reading, she could undoubtedly handle fourth-grade material. Comprehension, however, dropped off to a frustration level at grade four. This loss of meaning might have been predicted by her miscues in grade-four material. Although the errors were few in number, most of them changed the author's meaning and involved words which did not make sense.

An analysis of Karen's comprehension errors at the fourth-grade level showed that she consistently missed vocabulary questions and most inference questions. Thus, if we evaluated her performance solely on the basis of word identification, oral reading, and literal comprehension, she could read in grade-four material. However, if she were expected to deal with inferential questions and understand vocabulary, her instructional level would be grade three. Appropriate placement therefore would be influenced by the teacher's expectations.

How well might we expect Karen to read? Her scores on the Wechsler Intelligence Scale for Children—Revised (WISC-R) fell in the below-average range of intellectual functioning. Thus, Karen's reading level approaches her present potential. In other words, Karen is reading about as well as we might expect, and intensive remedial instruction is not warranted. If the intelligence scores had been in the average or above-average range, we might have looked more intently at motivational, cultural, or instructional factors.

The test results suggest that Karen needs to be given more opportunities for inferential thinking. Essentially this consists of asking Karen to relate her world knowledge to information supplied by the text. Specific strategies for encouraging inferential thinking are described in Chapter 8, "Teaching Comprehension."

On the basis of her low vocabulary scores, we suspect that Karen will have difficulty acquiring concepts in social studies and science and will need to be paced more slowly in these areas. She will also benefit from the use of experiential approaches rather than strictly verbal methods which emphasize lecture, discussion, and reading. Certainly oral reading and literal comprehension exercises should be reduced if not eliminated.

Limitations

Although the IRI can be an effective diagnostic tool, its usefulness is constrained by (1) the vagueness of the concept of grade level, (2) the interest level of the student, (3) the student's world knowledge, and (4) problems in the differentiation of comprehension.

One difficulty in developing a valid IRI is uncertainty about grade level itself. The problem is related to a number of factors. First, no standard exists for determining grade level. Most readability formulas use only vocabulary and sentence length and do not adequately take into account concept depth and density—the abstractness of the concepts as well as their number in a given selection. At present there is no agreement that the present formulas can or should determine grade level. In addition, readability formulas assume that shorter sentences are easier to read despite Irwin's finding (1980) that two short sentences are sometimes easier to read when they are connected by a conjunction which expresses the relationship between them.

Confounding the lack of suitable criteria for defining grade level is the variation in basal readers. The basals produced in the 1970s are generally more challenging than those written in the 1950s. Even today, publishers' standards differ. It is well known that a student who can read at grade three in one basal series may have difficulty reading the grade-three book in another series, and that within a "second-grade" book, stories may range from grade one to four in readability.

The problem of grade level is compounded by disagreements concerning the criteria for adequate comprehension. Betts (1946) set a criterion of 75 percent for instructional level, but Powell (1978) has set lower standards at all levels (55 percent for grades one to two, 60 percent for grades three to five, and 65 percent for grade six). Powell claims that the traditional criterion is arbitrarily high and was influenced by standards used in examinations for licensing teachers. Spache (1976) believes that a minimum of 60 percent should be acceptable in determining a student's instructional level.

We believe the solution lies in developing a satisfactory match between the test and classroom instruction; that is, that the material must be comparable in difficulty in both places. It need not, however, be the same material. Second, the teacher's standards should determine how well students are expected to perform in comprehension. If a teacher, for example, expects students to read only the words and answer literal questions, standards can be lower. Although we believe that IRIs should assess higher-level thinking skills, the instrument itself is servant, not master, of the reading program and should measure the students' ability to achieve local objectives, not determine those objectives.

The appropriateness of any percentage figure can be determined only by comparing the test and the test criteria with actual instructional practices. Since expectations vary among teachers, it is unlikely that any uniform answer can be given to this question. Each teacher will need to set IRI requirements to fit local expectations.

A second limitation of the IRI is that students' reading comprehension is often influenced by their interest in the material (Asher *et al.*, 1976). If students are extremely interested in a passage, they may work diligently to complete and understand difficult selections. On the other hand, if they are indifferent to a selection, they may perform poorly.

Teachers cannot control the students' interest, but they can take three steps to minimize the negative effects of its lack:

1. Select passages on the basis of interest in addition to technical considerations such as length, quantity of information, and grade designation.
2. If a student receives an unexpectedly low score, assign an alternative selection at the same level to determine if interest is a significant factor.
3. If the students' performance appears to be heavily influenced by the level of interest, allow them to choose which of the two selections at a grade level they wish to read. This self-selection process may motivate them to perform at an optimal level.

As we have said repeatedly, reading comprehension is influenced by the student's world knowledge. A student who possesses a good deal of prior information on a particular topic is likely to score higher in comprehension on an IRI selection dealing with that subject than a student with less background information. A student can also compensate for limited word identification skills by bringing a wealth of prior experiences to the text. The influence of world knowledge suggests that the content of the IRI should be similar to the material in the classroom. If an IRI is selected from a narrative passage in a basal reader, it may not predict reading comprehension in a social studies or science text. A student may be unable to read the material because of limited background in specific concepts and generalizations. This problem persists even if content IRIs are used—unless the content is similar to material in classroom use.

A fourth problem with an IRI is its limited ability to differentiate comprehension ability. That is, even though IRIs label questions according to type (for example, literal or inferential) or subskill (main idea or detail), these questions may not necessarily measure what they purport. Schell and Hanna (1981) analyzed commercial IRI questions and concluded that they are not always objectively classifiable, that questions in one category may be more difficult than those in another, that some questions may be independent of the passage, that the reliability of each category is unknown, and that research does not support the division of comprehension into several skills. At best, differentiation of comprehension, we believe, should be limited to factual, inferential, and vocabulary, and care should be exercised in making judgments about strengths and weaknesses even in these areas.

SUMMARY

In this chapter we reviewed two types of comprehension tests: norm-referenced and criterion-referenced. The most familiar norm-referenced instruments are the standardized survey tests. These devices serve best in evaluation of curriculum and reflect the progress of groups of students rather than individuals. Such evaluations fulfill political as well as educational purposes, but they are of limited value in diagnosing the comprehension needs of poor readers.

The second type of test, criterion-referenced, include reading skills tests, which are usually part of a skills management system, and informal reading inventories (IRIs). The criterion-referenced tests in reading skills provide more diagnostic information, but they are limited since content also influences comprehension.

The IRI, a type of criterion-referenced test, is a multifaceted instrument which assesses word identification skills and strategies and comprehension. It can also be used to evaluate motivational levels and attitudes. The IRI attempts to simulate a conventional reading lesson in which the student reads and answers questions. Although the very informal inventories can be used to assess students' performance in their own textbooks, the IRI has evolved into a more formal clinical tool. In order for it to be effective, a match must exist between the instrument and instructional expectations. Despite its lack of psychometric rigor in comparison to norm-referenced tests, the IRI can be an invaluable, all-purpose device in the hands of a knowledgeable teacher.

After reading this chapter, teachers should be prepared to conduct a diagnosis of students' comprehension ability, including the selection or construction of appropriate instruments and their administration, scoring, and interpretation. The diagnosis, however, is just the first half of the task. It is necessary to become acquainted with specific practices for remediating students' difficulties. This help is provided in Chapter 8, "Teaching Comprehension."

RELATED ACTIVITIES

1. Select a norm-referenced reading survey test currently used in the schools. Examine the comprehension questions and determine the background experience students would require to answer these questions. Compare this requirement with the curriculum for the grade at which the test is administered.

2. Administer a norm-referenced test to a student and then discuss the answers with the student. When questions have been answered incorrectly, try to determine whether the mistake is due to deficiencies in word identification, skills, or world knowledge.

3. Prepare an IRI according to the procedures in this chapter. Administer this test and a commercial inventory to at least one student. Examine the results. Also compare the results with the student's present instructional placement. If a marked variation exists between the tests and the student's reading level, try to determine the reason.

4. Gather a number of commercial IRIs as well as your own test, if you have constructed one. Determine how many questions students can answer on the basis of available pictures and/or background knowledge.

5. Compare students' performance on an IRI in which comprehension is measured by specific questions as well as a retelling of the account. What are the advantages and disadvantages of each approach? Did the students perform markedly different under these two testing formats?

6. Administer a comprehension test from a SMS. Discuss the results with students to determine if errors were caused by deficiencies in word identification, skills, or world knowledge.

7. Examine a number of criterion-referenced tests which are used to evaluate main ideas. How are they alike? How are they different? Do tests at the same level appear to vary in difficulty? If they do, how might you explain the differences? What are the implications for diagnosis?

8. Administer a listening comprehension test and use the following procedures to determine an estimated intellectual quotient:
   a. Convert the grade level for listening into a mental age by adding five years and two months. If a student, for example, can comprehend through listening at the third-grade level, the comparable mental age would be 8.2.
   b. Compute the intelligence quotient by inserting the appropriate figures in the formula: IQ equals mental age divided by chronological age.

Compare this IQ to the one on an individual intelligence test. Repeat the procedure with several students to determine if you can generalize about the relationship between expectancy based on intelligence tests and on listening comprehension tests.

RELATED READINGS

POWELL, WILLIAM. "Measuring Reading Performance Informally." Paper presented at annual meeting of International Reading Association, Houston, Tex., May 1–5, 1978 (ED 155-589).

ROSENSHINE, BARAK. *A Consideration of Skill Hierarchy Approaches to the Teaching of Reading.* Champaign: Center for the Study of Reading, University of Illinois, 1977.

STAUFFER, RUSSELL G., JULES C. ABRAMS, AND JOHN J. PIKULSKI. *Diagnosis, Correction, and Prevention of Reading Disabilities,* New York: Harper & Row, 1978. Chaps. 4 and 5.

TUINMAN, J. JAAP. "Determining the Passage Dependency of Comprehension in Five Major Tests." *Reading Research Quarterly,* 9, no. 2 (1973–74). 206–23.

REFERENCES

ALEXANDER, H. W. "An Investigation of the Cloze Procedure as a Measuring Device to Identify the Independent, Instructional and Frustration Level of Pupils in the Intermediate Grades." Doctoral dissertation, University of Illinois. Ann Arbor, Mich.: University Microfilm, 1969, No. 69-10, 625.

ANDERSON, RICHARD, AND PETER FREEBODY. *Vocabulary Knowledge and Reading,* Reading Education Report No. 11. Champaign: Center for the Study of Reading, University of Illinois, August 1979.

ASHER, STEVEN R., SHELLEY HYMEL, AND ALLAN WIGFIELD. *Children's Comprehension of High- and Low-Interest Material and a Comparison of Two Cloze Scoring Methods.,* Technical Report No. 17. Champaign: Center for the Study of Reading, University of Illinois, November 1976.

BETTS, EMMETT. *Foundations of Reading Instruction.* New York: American Book, 1946.

BORMUTH, JOHN R. "Cloze Test Readability: Criterion Reference Scores." *Journal of Educational Measurement* 5, no. 3 (1968), 189–96.

BURNS, PAUL C., AND BETTY D. ROE. *Informal Reading Assessment.* Chicago: Rand McNally, 1980.

BUROS, OSCAR K, ED. *Reading: Tests and Reviews.* New Brunswick, N.J.: Gryphon Press, 1968.

———. *Reading: Tests and Reviews II.* Highland Park, N.J.: Gryphon Press, 1975.

CALFEE, ROBERT C., RICHARD ARNOLD, AND PRISCILLA DRUM. "A Review of 'The Psychology of Reading' by Eleanor G. Gibson and Harry Levin." (Proceedings of the National Academy of Education, Vol. 3, 1976, 1–80.)

CALIFORNIA READING TESTS. Monterey: California Test Bureau/McGraw-Hill, 1977–78.

CANNEY, GEORGE, AND PETER WINOGRAD. *Schemata for Reading and Reading Comprehension Performance.* Technical Report No. 120. Champaign: Center for the Study of Reading, University of Illinois, 1979.

CLEARY, BEVERLY. *Henry Huggins.* New York: Morrow, 1950.

CRAMER, RONALD L. *Writing, Reading and Language Growth: An Introduction to Language Arts.* Columbus, Ohio: Chas. E. Merrill, 1978.

DALE, EDGAR, AND JEANNE S. CHALL. "A Formula for Predicting Readability." *Educational Research Bulletin,* 27 (1948), 11–20, 37–54.

DUNN, LLOYD M., AND FREDRICK C. MARKWARDT. *Peabody Individual Reading Achievement Test.* Circle Pines, Minn.: American Guidance Services, 1970.

DURKIN, DOLORES. *What Classroom Observation Reveals About Reading Comprehension Instruction.* Technical Report No. 106. Champaign: Center for the Study of Reading, University of Illinois, October 1978.

DURRELL, DONALD D. *Durrell Analysis of Reading Difficulty.* New York: The Psychological Corporation, 1980.

ESTES, THOMAS H., AND JOSEPH L. VAUGHAN, JR. *Reading and Learning in the Content Classroom.* Boston: Allyn & Bacon, 1978.

FARR, ROGER. "Measuring Reading Comprehension: An Historical Perspective." In *Twentieth Yearbook of the National Reading Conference,* pp. 187–97. F. P. Green, ed. Milwaukee: National Reading Conference, 1971.

FOUNTAIN VALLEY TEACHER SUPPORT SYSTEM IN READING. Huntington Beach, Calif.: Richard L. Zweig, 1971.

GATES-MACGINITIE READING TESTS. Lombard, Ill.: Riverside Publishing Co., 1978.

GILMORE ORAL READING TEST. New York: Psychological Corporation, 1968.

GOLINKOFF, ROBERTA M. "A Comparison of Reading Comprehension Processes in Good and Poor Comprehenders." *Reading Research Quarterly,* 11, no. 4 (1975–76), 623–59.

GRAY ORAL READING TESTS. New York: Psychological Corporation, 1963–67.

HARRIS, ALBERT J., AND EDWARD R. SIPAY. *How to Increase Reading Ability.* New York: Longman, 1980.

IOWA TESTS OF BASIC SKILLS. Lombard, Ill.: Riverside Publishing Co., 1978–79.

IRWIN, JUDITH W. "The Effects of Explicitness and Clause Order on the Comprehension of Reversible Causal Relationships." *Reading Research Quarterly,* 15, no. 4 (1980), 477–88.

JACOBS, H. DONALD, AND LYNDON W. SEARFOSS. *Diagnostic Reading Inventory.* Dubuque, Iowa: Kendall/Hunt, 1979.

JOHNS, JERRY L. *Basic Reading Inventory,* 2nd ed. Dubuque, Iowa: Kendall/Hunt, 1981.

MCCRACKEN, ROBERT A. *Standard Reading Inventory.* Klamath Falls, Ore.: Klamath Printing, 1966.

MACGINITIE, WALTER H. "What Are We Testing?" In *Assessment Problems in Reading,* Walter H. MacGinitie, ed. Newark, Del.: International Reading Association, 1973.

MATZ, ROBERT D., AND WILLIAM D. ROHWER, JR. "Visual Elaboration and Comprehension of Text." Paper presented at Annual Meeting of the American Educational Research Association, New York, 1971.

METROPOLITAN READING TESTS. New York: Harcourt Brace Jovanovich, Inc., 1978.

OTTO, WAYNE, ROBERT RUDE, AND DIXIE LEE SPIEGEL. *How to Teach Reading.* Reading, Mass.: Addison-Wesley, 1979.

POWELL, WILLIAM. "Measuring Reading Performance Informally." Paper presented at Annual Meeting of IRA, Houston, Tex., May 1–5, 1978 (ED 155–589).

PRESCRIPTIVE READING INVENTORY. Monterey, Calif.: CTB/McGraw-Hill, 1972.

RINSKY, LEE ANN, AND ESTA DE FOSSARD. *The Contemporary Classroom Reading Inventory.* Dubuque, Iowa: Gorsuch Scarisbrick, 1980.

ROSENSHINE, BARAK. *A Consideration of Skill Hierarchy Approaches to the Teaching of Reading.* Technical Report No. 42. Champaign: Center for the Study of Reading, University of Illinois, December 1977.

SCHELL, LEO M., AND GERALD S. HANNA. "Can Informal Reading Inventories Reveal Strengths and Weaknesses in Comprehension Subskills?" *Reading Teacher,* 35, no. 3 (Dec. 1981), 263–68.

SILVAROLI, NICHOLAS, J. *Classroom Reading Inventory,* 4th ed. Dubuque, Iowa: W. C. Brown, 1982.

SIMONS, HERBERT D. "Reading Comprehension: The Need for a New Perspective." *Reading Research Quarterly* 6, no. 3 (Spring 1971), 338–63.

SPACHE, GEORGE D. *Diagnosing and Correcting Reading Disabilities.* Boston: Allyn & Bacon, 1976.

_____. *Diagnostic Reading Scales.* Monterey, Calif.: CTB/McGraw-Hill, 1981.

_____. *Good Reading for Poor Readers,* rev. ed. Champaign, Ill.: Garrard, 1970.

STANFORD DIAGNOSTIC READING TEST. New York: Psychological Corporation, 1976.

STANFORD READING TESTS. New York: Psychological Corporation, 1973.

STAUFFER, RUSSELL G., JULES C. ABRAMS, AND JOHN J. PIKULSKI. *Diagnosis, Correction and Prevention of Reading Disabilities.* New York: Harper & Row, 1978.

THORNDIKE, ROBERT L. "Reading as Reasoning." *Reading Research Quarterly,* 9, no. 2 (1973–74), 135–47.

WISCONSIN DESIGN FOR READING SKILL DEVELOPMENT. Minneapolis, Minn.: Interpretive Scoring Systems/NCS, 1977.

WOODS, MARY L., AND ALDEN MOE. *Analytical Reading Inventory,* 2nd ed. Columbus, Ohio: Chas. E. Merrill, 1981.

8

TEACHING COMPREHENSION

Upon completion of this chapter you will be able to

1. Explain the concept of schema and its relationship to comprehension.
2. Discuss the role of word identification in comprehension instruction.
3. Describe a model procedure for teaching comprehension skills.
4. Explain the purposes of, and list the steps in using, the directed reading-thinking activity.
5. Describe procedures for modifying students' world knowledge.
6. Discuss the concept of ultimate comprehension and its implications for instruction.

All the students in Mrs. Allen's reading group are having difficulty in comprehension, but they appear to be suffering from different kinds of problems. A survey of the group reveals that

Fred would probably understand his reading assignment if he had better word identification ability.

Karen views reading as the conversion of print into speech; she is rarely concerned about the meaning of the text.

Bob can answer literal questions but is mystified when asked to do inferential thinking.

Rose was once told that people who make up their minds should not change them. She persists in holding a particular view even though the textual evidence suggests another interpretation.

Craig is street-wise, but at the same time he is unfamiliar with many of the concepts and generalizations it is assumed elementary-school students know.

When Hope is asked to interpret a passage, she tends to ignore the printed information and overrely on her own experience.

Bruce has no difficulty comprehending, but he seldom makes the effort. His problem is largely a matter of attitude rather than cognitive deficiency.

CHAPTER ORGANIZATION

These seven problems, although not exhaustive, do represent four major types of comprehension problems. Type 1 involves word identification. Fred doesn't know the words, whereas Karen, who can decode, is unable to move beyond the words to meaning. Type 2 problems are related to comprehension skills. Bob is limited to interpreting the text at the literal level, and Rose is unwilling to adjust her interpretation as new information becomes available. Type 3 problems involve world knowledge. Craig has had experiences beyond his years, but he lacks the specific background which schools value. Hope tends to overrely on her well-developed background. Bruce's lack of motivation represents the fourth type of difficulty.

In this chapter we will examine three of these four difficulties:
1. Problems involving word identification.
2. Problems relating to comprehension skills.
3. Problems involving world knowledge.

Problems of motivation will be discussed in Chapter 9, *"Motivating Students to Read."*

All three categories will be better understood if they are studied in light of what we know about world knowledge or schema. We will first explain the concept of schema, relate the theory to the three difficulties, and then suggest specific strategies for dealing with each.

Understanding involves bringing meaning to the book.

SCHEMA

The Meaning of Schema

According to a schema view of reading, comprehension is dependent on information we possess before we read a particular page. The only way to comprehend printed material is to associate the words in the text with what we already know. This idea, which has had a long history (Durkin, 1980), suggests that reading comprehension is more than extracting information *from* a text: it requires the reader to bring information *to* the text. Renewed interest in schema (the plural is *schemata;* the word originally meant form or structure; today it refers to cognitive structure) during the past decade rests on this fundamental idea and attempts to explain how prior knowledge influences our understanding of what we read.

Schemata are similar to concepts in that they are ideas or abstractions about various aspects of life. Schemata are the "idea" units in which world knowledge is stored in memory and serve as the "building blocks" of the human information processing system (Rumelhart and Ortony, 1977). Each schema represents a theory of some part of the world. Together, they comprise one's personal view of reality (Rumelhart, 1980).

Since schemata are building blocks of knowledge, we possess vast numbers in our cognitive structure—schemata for dogs, for love, for eating at a restaurant—the schemata related to goals like eating at a restaurant have been called scripts (Schank and Abelson, 1977)—for pizza, and for a gothic novel or a fugue. These schemata emphasize the generic concepts in memory, not the recollection of specific past experiences. Memory of past experiences is called episodic memory (Tulving, 1972). If we examined our schema for "a trip to the ocean," for example, we would find that it consists of many concepts or subschemata such as tides, sand castles, suntan lotion, starfish, and salt water. The schemata, though rooted in experience, are represented at a generic or conceptualized level rather than memory of a specific day at the ocean.

Our schemata for trips to the beach and a variety of other phenomena are laid down in the memory according to a definite structure. They are not bits and collections of information strewn around the mind like the boots and clothing in a cluttered hall closet. The particular arrangement for a schema is hierarchial. This organizational form is like a child's set of cylinders or boxes in which each smaller container can be nested inside the next larger one. The schema comparable to the largest container resides at the top level and is general enough to include every concept or subschema in its group. The schema for the human body, for example, is sufficiently general to pertain to the member elements, face, arms, legs, trunk, and so on. Figure 8-1 presents a simplified and partial schema of the human body.

Figure 8-1   Simplified and Partial Schema of the Human Body

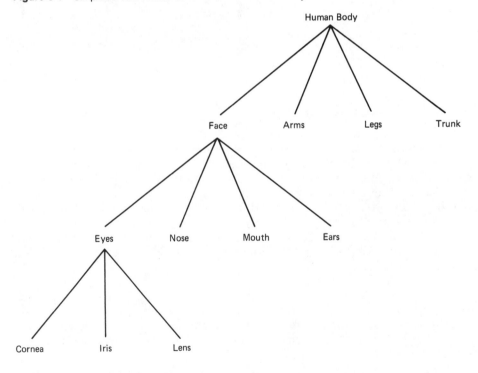

As we proceed down the schema, that is, from general to specific, the number of elements increases, and at the same time, the subschemata become narrower in nature. If we continued to follow a downward track, we would eventually end with a "unique perceptual event" (Adams and Collins, 1977) which could no longer be subdivided. If we were to reverse direction and proceed upward beyond the human body schema, we would encounter higher order schemata, such as mammals.

Schemata are not only linked in a vertical fashion but also contain a description of the relationship to other schemata at the same level and at levels below and above them in the hierarchy. For this reason the linking among schemata is often called a network. In the schema for family, for example, the relationship of mother and father are explained. Schemata would also describe the relationship between cats and dogs, men and women, gasoline and cars, and laws and courts, as well as less obvious relationships such as dental care and high sugar concentrations in children's breakfast cereals. As human beings we are constantly forging and refining these connections. In fact, much of our comprehension of the world requires us to think in terms of the relationships among concepts. We are interested not only in starfish and salt water oceans but also in how these two concepts are related. This proclivity for seeking out connections between the familiar and the new is the basis for learning.

A schema also contains rules or features which characterize a particular concept (Smith, 1975). In order to distinguish a goat from a dog, for example, we first need to identify the features of each concept. Some of these features must be unique to the concept. If our rules for goats and dogs, for example, only included the number of legs, we would not be able to tell them apart. These unique rules are called *distinctive* features (Smith, 1975).

Schema and Reading

Schema theory assumes that the printed text itself conveys no meaning (Adams and Collins, 1977). It simply provides the reader with a set of directions for reconstructing the author's meaning. To effect this reconstruction, readers must supply information from their schemata. The words in the text are like the buttons on a pushbutton telephone; they connect us with a multitude of information but do not contain meaning in themselves.

If our perception of a page is not directly related to the letters and words, what is their role? The letters and words are merely electrochemical signals stimulated by visual patterns of light and dark. Before they reach the brain, they undergo several transformations. As a result, the coded message which reaches the brain is considerably different from the original stimulus. The text thus provides direction, but an individual's schemata supply the other ingredients from which the perception is constructed. This perception is analogous to cooking. The recipe provides the instructions, but the cook must supply the ingredients.

Although meaning does not reside in the text, neither is the meaning of the text entirely in the schema. Meaning results from an interaction between an abstract schema and the visual data. The outcome is a specific, concrete representation of knowledge.

In the schema-theoretical view, both the writer and the reader share the responsibility for adequate comprehension. Writers must not only anticipate their readers' schemata but also activate the appropriate schemata. Writers could be familiar with your schemata but write so ambiguously that you could not interpret their message. Bransford and Johnson (1972) deliberately gave subjects this message:

> If the balloons popped, the sound wouldn't be able to carry since everything would be too far away from the correct floor. A closed window would also prevent the sound from carrying, since most buildings tend

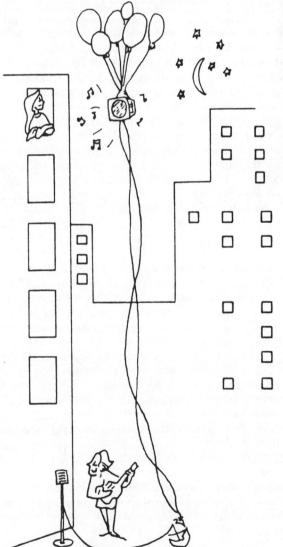

Figure 8-2 Picture to Accompany "Popping Balloons" From J. D. Bransford and M. K. Johnson, "Contextual Prerequisites for Understanding Some Investigations of Comprehension and Recall," *Journal of Verbal Learning and Verbal Behavior,* 11, no. 6 (December 1972), 718. Reprinted with permission.

to be well insulated. Since the whole operation depends on a steady flow of electricity, a break in the middle of the wire would also cause problems. Of course, the fellow could shout, but the human voice is not loud enough to carry that far. An additional problem is that a string could break on the instrument. Then there could be no accompaniment to the message. It is clear that the best situation would involve less distance. Then there would be fewer potential problems. With face to face contact, the least number of things could go wrong. (p. 718)

The readers found that the message was difficult to remember unless it was accompanied by a picture to help activate the desired elements. Before you look at the figure, (Figure 8-2) try to interpret the passage and mentally draw a picture which would account for the information in the text. This exercise will make apparent how difficult comprehension is when a schema is not activated.

If authors must anticipate the readers' schemata and provide sufficient textual information, the readers must possess adequate schemata. If, however, readers lack schemata, the teacher must prepare them for reading a new story or textbook chapter. This readiness step is intended to either add new schemata or extend and refine the existing schemata so they can be activated by the text.

Since readers' schema on the same topic can differ, readers may interpret the same sentence in a variety of ways. Trabasso (1980) supplies this example:

Mary had a little lamb. What do you think of:
1. Its fleece was white as snow.
2. She spilled gravy and mint jelly on her dress.
3. The delivery was a difficult one and afterwards the vet needed a drink. (p. 5)

In expository text or technical materials—such as a chemistry lab manual, a handbook for defusing unexploded bombs, or written directions for assembling a ten-speed bicycle—a much narrower band of interpretation is permitted.

Comprehension

Proponents of schema theory contend that comprehension occurs by a process called *instantiation*. According to this view, schemata are composed of variables or slots (Minsky, 1975). When the slots have been filled with information from the text, the schema is instantiated and comprehension takes place. Suppose, for example, someone began observing an athletic contest and suspected that it was baseball. In order to comprehend the situation as a game of baseball, the person would need a schema for baseball games. This schema might contain subschemata such as bases, batters, pitchers, catchers, and a baseball. The individual would need to fill the slots or variables in these subschemata by applying the rules or attributes of the schema. If we saw a person swinging a wooden club at a round sphere, the batter subschema might be slotted or instantiated. The process would continue as slots in other subschemata were filled. If the size of the ball did not conform to the "size" variable in the ball schema, the observer might be forced to conclude that the game was not baseball at all, draw upon a softball game schema, and repeat the process. When the schema matched up with the available information, the situation or event would be comprehended. Thus, quality of comprehension is influenced by the fit between the schema of the reader and the schema which the writer assumed the reader possessed (Adams and Bruce, 1980).

In reading, the filling of slots is first activated by information contained in the text. Since no text is totally explicit, however, the activated schema must supply information for filling slots. An account about a baseball game may not reveal the fielding position of the fourth batter in the lineup, but with a well-developed schema for playing position and lineup order, the reader might suspect that the batter was an outfielder. In situations in which the information is not activated by the text, the reader must rely more heavily on schemata.

Filling in slots from schemata is required in inferential thinking. Here the text provides some, but not all, of the needed data. Students need to be aware that it is possible to draw on particular world knowledge to supplement print just as they can usually determine how many legs are on a table without actually seeing all of them.

The mechanism for filling slots—and thus comprehending—is *hypothesizing*. In hypothesizing, readers generate schemata which they hope will conform to their prior expectations as well as to the textual information. They then test these hypotheses by searching for evidence to confirm them. For this reason Rumelhart (1980) says that schemata are like theories which we keep testing. We say in effect, "I'll test my baseball theory to see if it accounts for the information I am receiving. If the baseball theory cannot be slotted perfectly, I can either accept it as the best available fit or activate and test another hypothesis."

Since many theories may be hypothesized, an interactive process is employed to direct the traffic and channel the reader's predictions. This mechanism activates a schema from both a top-down and a bottom-up perspective. These sources have also been called *conceptually driven* and *data driven* (Bobrow and Norman, 1975).

In order to illustrate this process, let us examine the following passage.

A man wearing a brown suit entered a store one morning intent on buying shoes.

Here the subschemata *shoe* and *store* may activate the schema *shoe store*. *Shoe store* is now a theory which must be tested. Since shoe and store activated shoe store, which lies on a higher or more general level, we say that the reader has engaged in bottom-up processing; this activation is data driven. The reader, now equipped with the shoe store schema, will attempt to fill slots in this schema at lower levels. This process is conceptually driven.

The man picked up a number and and waited to be served.

This sentence is consistent with the practice of selling shoes in some stores.

Finally the clerk asked for the man's size.

This also is consistent with the shoe store theory. Shoe size as a subschema can be slotted.

> He provided the clerk with the information and said, "I will take two."

The reader, in filling slots for shoe store, may wonder why the man did not ask to be fitted, but it is possible that the customer knew his size and was in a hurry. The reader might question why the customer did not ask for a pair of shoes; however, asking for two shoes would fit the shoe store theory but asking for one or three would not.

> "That will be $75," said the clerk. "That's rather expensive for such a small size," thought the man, "but the old shoes are wearing thin."

The comment about money is appropriate for a shoe store purchase, and since some shoes are very expensive, the price is not extraordinary. The comment about size presents a problem. Although some variation in pricing exists, small shoes should not cost more than medium-size shoes. The remark about thin shoes, on the other hand, is consistent with the theory, as is the man's additional comment,

> "I do not want to be out on some rainy night with shoes in that condition. It could cause problems."

The effect of weather on feet with worn shoes comes into play here.

> "I remember being stopped by a police officer with shoes in that condition. He said that I had better replace them before I had an accident."

The shoe safety subschema can slot the remark about the dangers of worn shoes, but the warning by the police officer seems out of place. Laws do not apply to worn shoes. This raises doubt about the shoe store theory.

> "But I had better replace them before I have an accident. All right, I will take two, but I will put them on myself. I've got the tools in my trunk."

At this point the reader may reject the shoe store schema. Although the man could certainly put on his own shoes, he shouldn't require tools other than a shoehorn; even this is not likely to be found in the trunk of a car.

Depending on the reader's schemata, other hypotheses may have been activated as the story proceeded. The shoes may be brake shoes or they may be tires. You could evaluate the brake shoe or tire theory by rereading the account and seeking lower-level information—another example of top-down processing. Both top-down and bottom-up processing would be occurring simultaneously, and for this reason it is termed an interactive process.

Much inferential thinking can also occur in this text. How did the man get to the store? Until the last line we are given little information to answer this question. The reference to trunk, however, and the realization that the shoes are either brake shoes or automobile tires could lead us to conclude that he arrived by car. Of course, the text does not make this explicit. It is only as our auto supply store schema is activated and trunk is associated with automobiles that we infer the answer. The schema itself has filled the slot.

In summary, bottom-up processing occurs initially as data in the text activate lower-level schemata such as shoe and store. Once this process is underway, schemata at increasingly higher levels are filled until the shoe store schema is activated. At this point, top-down processing may come into play. It samples the text for confirmation of the shoe store schema. Some information, such as the color of the man's suit, may be ignored as it is not pertinent to the task of confirming the shoe store hypothesis. Bottom-up processing would still continue, helping to keep the reader "honest." It is particularly helpful when readers find information which is new or does not match their top-down predictions.

Top-down processing plays an important role when bottom-up information is insufficient to result in a decision. It helps the reader to decide between two or more possible interpretations. At the conclusion of the story, the reader may not be able to decide between brake shoes and tires on the basis of explicit statements in the text. A schema could be activated, however, on the basis of two clues: (1) the policeman is more likely to observe worn tires than worn brake shoes; and (2) it is more likely that the person would replace his tires than his brake shoes.

Though schemata have been portrayed in static terms—as if they were unchanging—in reality, they are continually in a state of flux. They must adjust or accommodate in order to understand new information. Accommodation occurs by accretion (adding new facts), modifying existing schemata (refining or tuning), and creating new schemata (restructuring) (Rumelhart, 1980).

In this section we have described the basic features of a theoretical schema and can now proceed to relate it to the three types of comprehension problems, including specific strategies for improving students' understanding. As we stated at the beginning of this chapter, a schema can shed light on the comprehension process and enable us to help students with a variety of deficits.

WORD IDENTIFICATION

Poor Comprehenders and Word Identification

The comprehension difficulties of some students are related to their deficiencies in word identification. Fred knew too few words, which made it difficult for him to use bottom-up processing to activate a schema. Fred will comprehend only if he learns the words or compensates for his inadequacies by bringing a wealth of knowledge to the printed page. In oral reading, for example, Fred may stumble through the text, but with appropriate background information he may read with adequate comprehension. This often occurs with students who read texts designed for much younger students for here they are able to offset their limitations in word identification. Unfortunately, students' abilities to compensate diminish as the concept level of the text moves beyond their experiences.

Fred's problem is common among poor comprehenders—students with inadequate comprehension ability often possess weak decoding skills (Golinkoff, 1975–76). In reading isolated words, poor comprehenders have more trouble identifying unfamiliar words, and they also read familiar words more slowly than students with good comprehension. The difference between good and poor comprehenders persist in connected text. Furthermore, students with poor comprehension correct fewer word identification errors that alter the author's message (Weber, 1970).

Automaticity and Context

One conclusion which could be drawn from the weak decoding ability of poor comprehenders is that word identification should precede comprehension. In fact, Samuels (1979) makes just such an argument. He claims, on the basis of a behavioral analysis of reading, that decoding must occur before comprehension. The reader, he feels, cannot attend to more than one aspect of reading at a time, and therefore decoding skills must be mastered at an automatic level before the reader can give sufficient attention to comprehension. Only as decoding reaches the level of "automaticity" will the student be able to process information in a top-down manner. The principles of automaticity would apply to the young beginning reader as well as to the older student who is a poor decoder.

Automaticity suggests that students should practice decoding often, such as repeated reading of large amounts of easy materials. Extensive practice should enable them to read text in phrases and clauses, which would eliminate the word-by-word reading in which they perform as if they were reading a list of randomly selected words rather than a meaningful message. According to Samuels, students who need to attend only minimally to words could then focus on comprehension.

As compelling as this argument is, undue stress on automaticity may interfere with decoding for meaning. That is, automaticity may accurately describe word identification but not reading (Kintsch, 1979). By erecting a two-level model of reading in which word identification is a prerequisite to meaning, attention to meaning is delayed. It is possible that meaning delayed is meaning denied. We prefer, therefore, that students deal with meaning at the outset. All reading instruction should impress upon students the long-range view of reading as a meaningful activity.

Furthermore, meaning should be introduced early because it helps word identification. According to schema theory, information from print as well as the individual's cognitive structure help the reader to identify words. Students who read an account to which they can relate their personal experiences can use meaning, in the form of context, to assist in word identification even as words activate meaning. Therefore, although we usually view decoding as a means to comprehension, word identification and comprehension exist in a reciprocal relationship to one another and should not be separated.

In summary, teachers will often need to develop students' decoding skills in order to improve their comprehension. But these processes are not mutually exclusive. Meaning, in the form of context cues, can facilitate the identification of words. It can be employed concurrently with traditional decoding skills and need not be delayed until after word identification has reached the level of automaticity. Furthermore, context is the first comprehension strategy which should be taught; instruction in using meaning can begin with the child's first word. Skill in using context or semantic cues prepares students for more complex comprehension tasks.

Encouraging the Use of Context

Specific strategies to encourage the use of context include the following:

1. When students read in connected text and cannot identify a word, tell them to skip it, read to the end of the sentence, and use the meaning of the sentence to reduce their uncertainty. A decision on the word should be tempered by phoneme-grapheme considerations, but attention should not be directed to phonics until meaning cues have been exhausted.

2. Use cloze procedures to encourage students to use context cues. Arrange cloze deletions so that nouns and verbs are deleted instead of using an nth word deletion pattern. In addition, discuss the students' choices in order to point out differences in word meaning and the cues which can be used to select words for particular contexts.

3. If students encounter unknown words and are hesitant to decode them because their initial prediction is not consistent with the word's graphophonic cues, cover the word and encourage them to list a number of words which might make sense in that setting. At first, accept all words which fit the context even if they alter the author's message. Later, give credit only for substitutions consistent with the meaning of the text. After initial predictions have been made, uncover the word and have students select the prediction consistent with the visual information.

Chapter 6, "Teaching Word Identification," described a balanced system for helping students develop a reading vocabulary. If necessary, review this chapter on how word identification skills can be taught.

Mental Set

Unlike Fred, whose weak decoding skills limits his comprehension, Karen performs poorly on comprehension tasks despite adequate word identification skills. Students like Karen often have a misguided notion about the nature of reading and believe it is sufficient to pronounce words aloud correctly. For this reason they see no need to approach reading as a thinking or problem-solving task. Their preoccupation with words and oral reading inhibits the activation of a schema.

To solve this problem, teachers need to change students' mental set by encouraging them to look beyond the words to the message of the writer. If an inappropriate mental set is their only problem, it can be corrected with a minimum of difficulty. Several teaching strategies can be employed to accomplish this goal:

1. Reduce oral reading to a minimum. If students do extensive oral reading long after they have developed an initial sight vocabulary, they will

conceive of reading as the fluent pronunciation of words and will not attend to the meaning of the message. If students are reluctant to stop reading orally, set limits on this activity. Even if material is to be read aloud, ask students first to read it silently.

2. When assigning silent reading, give students a purpose. Although pupil-established purposes are best, teacher-set purposes are preferable to none at all. Assess the students' reading through questioning rather than oral reading. The students' responses will usually reveal whether they have understood the material.

3. Frequently provide students with written instructions to encourage them to attend to the meaning of the message. The school day is filled with many opportunities for using functional directions; teachers need not employ contrived workbook exercises or tasks such as directing students to walk to the green wall and touch their toes with the thumb of their right hand. Here are just a few examples of written directions which you can use:

    The first three students who answer five questions correctly in today's assignment can use the listening stations. We have a new tape today, "Call of the Wild."

    Open your book to page 15. Read the first sentence and ask yourself who this person reminds you of.

    Turn to the table of contents of your book and find the story which begins on page 63. Be ready to tell what you think this story will be about.

    When you finish underlining the words you know in your story, put the new word cards in the file box.

    Read your new words to yourself and when you know them, raise your hand.

    When you finish reading page 17, you can go to your regular classroom.

    When the bell rings, all students riding bus 23 will leave the room first.

4. Encourage students to ask questions. Unfortunately, teachers usually ask all the comprehension questions, leaving the student to play a passive role. The ReQuest procedure, reciprocal questioning (Manzo, 1969), can help students participate more actively in the questioning process. In this procedure, the teacher and students take turns questioning one another. The teacher's questions also serve as a model for appropriate questioning behavior.

To begin using the ReQuest method, select a reading passage and ask students to read the first sentence silently. Tell them that you will ask a question about this sentence. When students have finished reading, ask your question. Then say, "Now you may ask me a question about the sentence." (If the first sentence contains little information, have the students read and ask a question about the second sentence.) The procedure continues with you and the students asking each other questions. If you are working with a group of students, they can be allowed to ask three questions for every question you ask. Both you and the students must attempt to answer questions accurately. If a question cannot be answered from the passage, the respondent must say, "The sentence doesn't give the answer to that question." At first, alternate questions by sentences. Later have students read whole paragraphs and then alternate questions until the text in the paragraph is exhausted.

It is sufficient to use this technique for the first two or three paragraphs of the story. After that point, the students have usually read enough of the story to respond to purpose-setting questions such as "What do you think will happen next?"

The ReQuest procedure is particularly helpful for students who are unwilling to read more than a few lines at a time. Even the most recalcitrant reader will usually answer a question about a single sentence. Often these students will be motivated to finish a story once they have completed the initial paragraphs. Questioning the teacher also gives students a sense of importance and they will read intently in order to evaluate the teacher's answers.

Beginning readers of all ages, who often have difficulty attending to several lines at one time, can benefit from use of the ReQuest procedure. It permits them to proceed on a line-by-line basis while maintaining a high level of motivation. If students have difficulty asking questions from text material, initiate reciprocal questioning by using personal questions such as "What's your favorite color? What do you like to eat? What do you do after school?" Have students ask you similar questions. This technique helps students make the transition to asking questions from written material.

Silent reading, purpose setting, and ReQuest can help to shift students' attention to the meaning of the text. Throughout this chapter other strategies will encourage a thoughtful attitude toward reading. At first students may resist comprehension tasks for they may have received considerable satisfaction from oral reading. With persistence, however, teachers can show them that becoming engrossed in a story and satisfying their curiosity about its outcome can be even more rewarding.

SKILLS

The two remaining problem areas in comprehension, skills and world knowledge, are interrelated. Difficulty in using a skill is often influenced by the quality of students' background information. Therefore, skills cannot be exercised in a vacuum but must be linked to specific content. For this reason we never really master comprehension skills; our ability to understand is always constrained by the content in which we are applying the skill. In order to give each problem sufficient attention, however, we will deal with skills and background knowledge separately, always recognizing that in the final analysis they interact and that certain instructional strategies can be employed to correct deficiencies in either skills or world knowledge.

The Role of Comprehension Skills

Reading is a problem-solving process, but the problems which require solving vary in nature. One problem may be to determine the central thought of a paragraph; another, to identify details supporting that idea; and a third, to draw conclusions on the basis of information provided by the text and schema.

Solving these problems requires different skills—just as a carpenter uses a variety of skills to cut wood, bore holes in it, plane its surface, and sand it smooth. Skills enable us to make effective use of our schema though the underlying process of reconstructing a message on the basis of visual and nonvisual information remains the same. The visual information activates higher-level schema, and hypotheses at higher levels seek confirmation from information at lower levels.

Some students appear to lack the skills to solve particular reading problems although they have adequate schemata. To extend our earlier analogy, consider a carpenter sitting on a pile of wood but lacking the skills to saw, drill, plane, and sand it. In a like fashion, some students possess appropriate skills but are not aware that they apply to reading. A student, for example, may be adept at predicting outcomes in social situations or on the athletic field but may have difficulty using the same skill in reading.

To gain better insights into how to teach important comprehension skills allow us to offer some suggestions. First, however, we need to ask a more basic question related to comprehension.

How many comprehension skills are there? In Chapter 7, "Diagnosing Comprehension," we pointed out that there is considerable disagreement about the precise number of comprehension skills. Opinions range from several dozen to the view that reading comprehension is essentially a global process and cannot be subdivided into component parts. Our view falls between these two extremes and parallels that of Cramer (1978), which believes that comprehension can be organized into four parts: explicit (literal comprehension), implicit (reasoning), word meaning (vocabulary), and appreciative (affective). (See Figure 7-3 for a listing of these categories and accompanying subskills.) The first three areas will be discussed in this chapter.

Explicit Comprehension Skills

Reading comprehension instruction has traditionally emphasized explicit or literal skills. Guszak (1967) found that teachers' questions focus largely on the literal level. In a guided reading lesson, many questions follow the "who did what, when, and where" pattern. Even "why" and "how" questions which appear to go beyond the literal level can often be answered correctly by referring to explicit information in the text.

Literal questions often make minimal demands on the thinking ability of students. Children can often answer these questions by simply matching words in the question to those in a single sentence in the passage. If the text asks, "What is the process by which plants manufacture sugar?" the student can skim the passage for words like *plants, manufacture,* and *sugar,* find the sentence that reads "Plants manufacture sugar by the process of photosynthesis," and answer correctly without any idea about the meaning of the term *photosynthesis.* It is questionable whether any comprehension has occurred or whether the student is merely using word identification and rudimentary linguistic skills to arrive at the answer.

Although literal comprehension tasks are both overused and misused, they do have value. We will discuss and evaluate several such skills and suggest procedures for teaching them. The outline of skills in Figure 7-3 provides the structure for this discussion.

MAIN IDEA   At the literal level, this skill is seldom needed because a main idea is not a literal task unless the passage explicitly states, "The main idea of this paragraph is _____." The inclusion of a topic sentence at the head of a paragraph does not constitute a literal main idea.

SEQUENCE   Students are frequently asked to put a story's events in chronological order. Just as often, teachers deplore students' inability to complete these tasks successfully. Sometimes the problem is not the students' sequencing ability at all but their remembering the events themselves. A partial solution is to reduce the events which they are to arrange in order. If the exercise lists eight events, for example, reduce it to four.

Another solution to students' sequencing problems is to minimize chronological sequence and emphasize mechanical sequence, which is more important. In mechanical sequence the events must occur in a particular order if the outcome is to be successful, for example science experiments, gardening, cooking, and construction. Mechanical sequence is more concerned with cause and effect or consequence than with temporal order. Fortunately, most such tasks allow us to refer to written directions, such as cookbooks and instructions for assembling or constructing objects. Furthermore, many uses of mechanical sequence do not even occur in written material though they often play an important role in construction tasks, such as carpentry, in which the worker must often reason out the appropriate order of activities without the aid of written directions. In summary, mechanical sequence relies on reasoning rather than sheer memory of events and thus is more important than chronological sequence.

READING FOR DETAILS   Skill in following directions can help students distinguish between significant and unimportant detail. Often students are content to grasp the gist of a passage, rationalizing that the specific facts in the text are only minor details. In following directions students learn that details such as addresses, names of individuals, telephone numbers, and quantities of ingredients can spell the difference between success and failure. The young cook who substitutes baking soda for baking powder in a doughnut recipe soon appreciates the need for attending to details.

Attention to detail can spell the difference between life and death for older students who work in hazardous surroundings. One illiterate adult was shocked when he first learned to read because he frequently smoked under a sign which said "No Smoking in this Area—Dangerous Fumes." Other natural situations that can be capitalized on to teach this skill are to have students fill out coupons for prizes, refunds, and free literature which appear in newspapers and magazines.

Recalling detail plays an important role in literal comprehension when details support main ideas. As students read, therefore, they should be seeking support for their hypotheses in the details of the text. This top-down processing can occur naturally when we ask students to offer proof for their ideas. If the students claim that their predictions about a story's outcome were correct, they should be required to read the lines or sentences which support their contention. In this manner they can be introduced to the relationship between central thought and supporting details.

Implicit Comprehension Skills

Implicit comprehension involves reasoning in which students fill in or instantiate slots from their schemata rather than from textual information. If a person reads a story in which the trees' leaves are turning red, orange, and brown, and is asked what service a car will require shortly, that reader would need to consult both a fall season and an automobile schemata. If the reader lives in the colder climates and has a well-developed cooling system schema for cars, one reply might be that it was time to check the car's antifreeze.

What should be taught in implicit comprehension? In Chapter 7 we suggested that it was not necessary to test or teach all seventeen skills listed under implicit comprehension (see Figure 7-3). First, it is difficult to distinguish among many of these skills. Second, teaching more than a dozen separate skills presents logistical problems in monitoring progress and providing instruction. For this reason we propose to reduce the seventeen skills to three major categories: (1) general inference, (2) purpose setting, and (3) main idea. This arrangement will allow teachers to focus on the most important inferential skills.

GENERAL INFERENCE   The first category consists of skills such as inference, cause and effect, and drawing conclusions although it is not necessary to differentiate among them. The important consideration in general inference is that students confront questions for which the text does not provide explicit answers.

Students are often mystified by assignments which require inferential thinking although they are adept at answering literal questions. This condition can usually be traced to instruction which has overemphasized recall of specific facts and details. Because students have been conditioned to expect all answers to be explicitly stated in the text, they are at a loss when encountering inferential questions. Several strategies can be used to help them interpret the text at the inferential level.

1. The most straightforward solution is to start asking students to answer inferential questions. The earlier mentioned ReQuest procedure can be used for this purpose. Begin with literal questions and when students are familiar with the procedure, ask questions at the inferential level as well. It is to be hoped that they will model the teacher's question-asking behavior and try to ask their own questions at this level. The ultimate goal, of course, is to influence the questions students raise as they read their assignments. An awareness of questioning at this level is a first step in comprehending between-the-lines information. The teacher can then model a strategy for answering inference questions by "thinking out loud" the steps used to arrive at the answer.

2. You need not develop special material for developing inferential thinking. Much material is already available. In assigning workbook pages, for

Figure 8-3 Reading and Thinking Reprinted by permission of the publisher. From *Reading and Thinking, Book II*, by Arthur J. Evans. Copyright © 1979 by Teachers College, Columbia University. All rights reserved.

Drops of rain began to show on the windshield and soon the windshield wipers were switched on. We closed the windows and kept going.

We left the town behind, then the last straggling houses, and the road got much worse. It was some moments before we realized that we had a flat tire.

Dad pulled up at the side of the road, and after some hesitation David took the jack out of the trunk and raised the front of the car. Dad is very good with tools, and soon had the tire off, while I was loosening the spare tire.

In a few minutes we were on our way. But we were soaked to the skin.

1. What steps were necessary to change the tires?

    _____

    _____

    _____

2. Was it raining hard?

    _____

3. Which tire was punctured?

    _____

4. Were they near a garage?

    _____

5. Had they more than one wrench?

    _____

    _____

    _____

6. Was there some air in the spare tire?

    _____

    _____

example, select those which ask questions at the inferential level. A good example of material for developing inferential thinking is *Reading and Thinking* (Evans, 1979). (See Figure 8-3 for a page from this workbook series.) Note how students are required to relate background information to the text.

3. In order to lessen demands on students who are not acquainted with inferential tasks, allow them to complete assignments in teams of two to three students with the requirement that they arrive at one answer for each question.. When the answers are corrected, it is important that the reasons for all answers are discussed.

In summary, stress inference of all kinds without differentiating between skills such as drawing conclusions and cause and effect. Undoubtedly logical distinctions can be made, but we feel that these differences elude struggling readers—and frustrate many of them. Neither do we wish to burden teachers with unmanageable lists.

MAIN IDEA   The main idea or central thought requires special attention. As students read expository texts they must absorb and retain vast amounts of information. Reading paragraphs and larger units in terms of a central thought helps them to organize and summarize this information. If students read each sentence in isolation, their memory of the text will be hampered. Since we cannot assume that students who are taught main ideas in narrative accounts will automatically transfer this skill to expository writing, specific instruction in textbooks may be required.

Teaching main ideas is complicated by the fact that the term *main idea* has been interpreted in a number of ways (Pearson and Johnson, 1978). It can refer to the gist of an account (the story or paragraph is about rabbits) or the central thought (rabbits need to reproduce rapidly in order to survive as a breed.) Students (and their teachers) may be confused by main idea tasks because they refer to different behaviors.

Despite differences in interpretation, *main idea* implies a categorization or classification of elements and requires abstracting an idea from specific statements. This means that a student's ability to generate main ideas depends on understanding the concepts in the passage as well as familiarity with the skill.

Teachers may wish to convey the following information to students about main ideas:

1. Paragraphs often contain central thoughts which sum up information in the passage. Sentences in the paragraph usually consist of details which support the central thought.
2. Main ideas are usually stated in a topic sentence or implied by the paragraph as a whole.
3. Topic sentences are often the first or last sentence in the paragraph.
4. Paragraphs follow a variety of forms. The most common are listed here:

TOPIC SENTENCE FIRST

topic sentence   *Many superstitions have grown up from lack of understanding.* Because people did not understand comets, they came to think of them as signs from the gods that disaster was on its way. Because no one understood the electrical conditions causing lightning and thunder, they considered them angry displays of the gods.

TOPIC SENTENCE LAST

When the day is a very cold one, water changes to ice. When the day is a hot and dry one, water changes so that it flows off into the air. When a pan of water is put on a hot stove, the water changes to steam that we can see above the pan. If this steam hits a cold dish, we can see water on the dish. *Water can change in many different ways.*

topic sentence

MAIN IDEA IMPLIED, NO TOPIC SENTENCE

Trees provide people with food—from fruit to nuts. Sap from trees can be made into delicious syrup. Wood and bark from trees provide us with homes, furniture, paper and telephone poles. Toothpicks, yo-yos, pencils, and rowboats are other products often made from trees. (Early, Canfield, and Karlin, 1979, p. 70)

Instruction in these skills would occur over a period of time and would be determined by both students' need and readiness. Need means the student requires the skill in order to make progress. Readiness refers to the student's intellectual and motivational receptivity. A student may need the skills, but may not be prepared to learn them. One pupil, for example, may need main ideas in order to read more efficiently, but suffers from considerable deficiencies in word identification which need to be corrected first. Another would also benefit from instruction in main ideas but loathes reading so intensely it is preferable to concentrate first on developing an interest in reading.

Informal instruction in main ideas can begin at early reading levels by the use of three procedures: (1) Ask students to develop titles for language-experience stories which they have dictated. If they are reading a basal reader or trade book, ask them to supply alternative titles and help them evaluate their choices. If students have difficulty with this assignment, provide three or four choices, asking them to select the best title and defend their choice. (2) Before reading a story, ask students to use the title to predict its content or outcome. When the story has been read, ask them to evaluate the title. How well did it describe the actual account? (3) Play games like Target in which you pick a familiar topic, such as motorcycles. Each student in turn must make a statement about the topic. At a more sophisticated level, write generalizations or topic sentences, such as "motorcycles are fun" or "motorcycles are dangerous," and ask students to supply supporting details.

When students are ready for more systematic instruction in main ideas, the following model may be employed. (The model can be easily adapted for teaching other comprehension skills, too.)

1. Introduce the skill. Questioning and modeling are two techniques which can be used to introduce a variety of skills. Questioning directs students to think about a passage in a particular way. It is particularly useful if teachers ask a *series* of questions, building on previous responses, rather than asking isolated questions. In this manner questions can be adjusted to the students' present level of skill development.

    Questioning techniques, however, are not always sufficient in helping students learn specific skills. They may need to be shown more directly how to identify information such as main ideas. In these instances, modeling may also be employed. In modeling, teachers present a task in skill learning and then "think aloud" as they search for an answer. In this manner the teachers allow students to look in on their thought processes.

2. Supervise practice in which students are assigned a limited number of exercises. Students can be allowed to work in teams of two to three. Check answers in a group session. Students not only state their answers but defend them as well. The teacher discusses the answers and the students' reasoning, helping them to understand why a particular answer is correct while trying to understand their point of view.

3. Assign independent work. When students complete their assignments hold a group session in which feedback is provided.

4. Teach application. In future reading activities, students should be expected to apply their skill. One technique is to keep a list of skills which have been introduced. As reading material is selected for reading, determine which skills might be applied in these selections. Although reading selections would be chosen for their relevance to the school curriculum and their meaningfulness to the students, take advantage of the selection's potential for applying specific skills.

Worksheets can be used to practice skills, but vary the activities in order to maintain the students' interest. If the main idea exercises provide multiple-choice answers, have students arrange the choices according to plausibility. Also, ask students to change words in the choices in order to change an answer of low plausibility into one of high plausibility.

A second variation is to supply the students with the correct answer but require them to find support for it in the passage. In subsequent lessons, students can be expected both to answer the question and to find supporting evidence in the text.

Let us suppose that we plan to teach students to identify the main idea of a paragraph by locating the topic sentence. The first step would be to present a topic sentence that is much more general than the other sentences in the paragraph. Here is one suggested activity teachers may find helpful. Begin by composing a paragraph such as the following:

> Henry ate a lot of food today.
> For breakfast Henry ate three bowls of cereal.
> Henry ate four sandwiches for lunch.
> A big steak, three potatoes, and two helpings of vegetables were eaten by Henry at supper.

Print each sentence on a separate index card. Distribute the cards to students and ask them to read their sentence aloud. Ask the other students to determine which sentence tells about all the others. As an alternative, ask the students who think they are holding this sentence to hold up their cards. If there is disagreement, ask students if the selected sentence tells about all the other sentences in the set. When the correct sentence has been identified, ask students to defend their choices. Repeat the procedures with other paragraphs until the students demonstrate an understanding of the concept. Label the identified sentences as the topic sentences.

If modeling were used as a teaching strategy, the teacher would say something like this aloud: "Let's see. I must find one sentence that tells about the rest—the main idea. I can't use the breakfast sentence because that discusses only one of the three meals. That's also true of the lunch and supper sentence. Let's see if the remaining sentence, "Henry ate a lot of food today," would fit. The word 'today' includes all the meals. 'A lot of food' can certainly refer to all three meals as well. That's the sentence I'll pick as the main idea."

In steps two and three, provide the students with paragraphs containing a well-defined topic sentence. Tell them that topic sentences are frequently found at the beginning or end of paragraphs. Initially, avoid using paragraphs which follow a structure to which students have not been introduced. Materials for all these exercises can be found in workbooks, teacher's manuals, worksheets, and resources material which accompany skills management systems.

In the application step, direct students to specific paragraphs in their textbooks, particularly in expository material, and ask them to identify the topic sentence. Limit paragraphs to those which place the topic sentence at either the beginning or end of the paragraph. As more complex forms are introduced, a wider variety of paragraphs can be used. Later, as students read extensively in textbooks, show them how main ideas can help them organize their thinking and retain information.

Teaching main ideas can be tedious unless teachers provide a variety of stimulating activities. Following are some further ideas which they can use in practice:

1. When students finish a story, ask them to supply a one-sentence summary. Duplicate summary sentences and ask the class to select the most appropriate one. As a variation, have the students write the summary in telegraphic form, in which the main idea is expressed in as few words as possible. Give credit for brevity as well as accuracy.

2. Cut out newspaper articles, separate the headlines from the story, and have students match headlines with the articles. To increase the difficulty of the task, limit stories to the same general topic, such as sports or world or local news.

3. Give students a story without a headline and ask them to select the most appropriate headline from four choices. Later, ask them to supply their own headlines.

4. When students are ready to be introduced to paragraphs with an implied main idea and no topic sentence, distribute copies of the following paragraph and ask them to work in pairs to determine the main idea. To add interest, write your interpretation of the main idea in code. After students have written a few of their statements on the board, help them to unlock the coded sentence. Here is an example of a paragraph with an implied main idea.

> When volcanoes erupt, many animals may be killed by the heat. People in the area can be severely burned. Many plants are covered with volcanic ash and do not survive. Acres of trees are toppled.

The main idea, in coded form, is as follows:

vlao srhr flya | ocne aeam uxzb

To decode the sentence, ask two students to come to the board and alternately write down one letter from each side of the dividing line until all the letters are exhausted. When they are finished, the message should look like this: *volcanoesareharmfulxyzab*. By dividing the sentence into words and dropping the letters *xyzab*, which were added only to fill out the last groups, the sentence would read, "Volcanoes are harmful." This statement can now be compared to the students' version. They need not be exactly alike but should convey a similar thought.

PREDICTION   The third category of implicit comprehension skills consists of a number of related skills which we have labeled *prediction*. They include purpose setting, prediction, evaluation, critical reading, recognizing propaganda, and creative reading. Teachers themselves might be required to use all these skills if asked to read an article called "Measuring Student Readiness for Beginning Reading." The teacher might, for example, declare a purpose for reading: "I will read to see if the article contains anything new about this topic. I am already familiar with readiness tests and checklists so I will disregard those topics if they should appear. I predict that if any new information is presented, it will deal with very informal assessment techniques or criterion-referenced testing." The teacher now reads critically, evaluating the suggestions against external norms such as practicality and the time and effort necessary to implement them. Since one person's truth can be another's propaganda, the reader would probably analyze propaganda techniques if the author's views differed sharply from the reader's. The reader might ask whether the author presented information fairly and completely, used logical arguments, and avoided slanted vocabulary. Finally, the reader would read creatively by asking questions such as "Can I use this information in my first grade or kindergarten classroom?" If the reader is a specialist or consultant that person might ask, "How can I use this information to help teachers in my school improve the testing program?" If the article focuses on a problem rather than its solution, the reader may read creatively by devising solutions to the problem. We should help students use these skills as they read also.

The purpose-setting and predicting aspects of inference have much in common with the schema theory of reading. In both cases the reader generates hypotheses and evaluates them against information in the text and existing schema. For this reason we need not teach the process, for students have been using it for years. Learning to talk, for example, requires a child to hypothesize about rules of language and to seek confirmation. Our task is to help students apply the same problem-solving process in reading.

A predicting and purpose-setting stance contrasts sharply with approaches in which students are cajoled to memorize everything they read. Furthermore, it places the emphasis properly on the process of problem solving rather than on the product—the correct answer (Collins and Smith, 1980). A "right answer mentality" can inhibit students from wrestling with ideas and developing or testing hypotheses. Predicting involves more risk but is likely to be of greater long-term value.

The following are a number of activities in which prediction and evaluation play important roles:

1. In completing many comprehension activities, students are usually asked to read a passage and then answer accompanying questions. Turn the procedure around by asking them to read selected questions first and predict the answer. This works best if the question provides a multiple response, allowing students to evaluate the plausibility of the possible answers before reading the passage. (Questions 4, 5, 7, 8, and 9 in Figure 8-4 can be used for this purpose.) Students will now be reading to confirm their predictions rather than trying to remember everything in the text.

2. To help students follow directions to worksheets, ask them to predict instructions on the basis of a survey of the page. When predictions have been made, supply the actual directions orally or in writing.

3. Before students view filmstrips or films, embark on a field trip, or attend a concert or play, ask them to predict what they will see and hear. After the event, review the predictions.

In all these activities, the leading question is "What do you think?" This divergent query encourages students to speculate, to hypothesize, and to play with possibilities before settling down to find the correct answer. It also relieves students of the need to be right. Too often, as Stauffer (1969) has said, students are intimidated by the tyranny of the right answer.

A question students should be frequently asked is "Why do you think so?" (Stauffer, 1969). Here they must defend their thinking with specific facts. Questions like this and the one in the previous paragraph are like a paragraph

Figure 8-4 **Reading for Concepts** Reprinted from *Reading for Concepts, Book D,* by W. Liddle, copyright 1970, with permission of Webster/McGraw-Hill.

1. Most of our water supply comes from
   a. oceans.
   b. wells.
   c. springs.
   d. rivers and lakes.

2. The word in paragraph 2 that means *dirty* or *not safe to use* is

   _____

3. The words "a dying lake" in paragraph 3 refer to

   _____

4. The story does not say so, but it makes you think that
   a. we have an endless supply of fresh water.
   b. all kinds of life need fresh, clean water.
   c. polluted waters are beautiful.

5. Our rivers are often polluted by
   a. detergents.
   b. fish.
   c. rocks.
   d. lakes.

6. It is easy to make polluted water safe again.
   Yes   No   Does not say

7. On the whole, this story is about
   a. polluted water.
   b. washing clothes.
   c. going fishing.

8. We must learn to take care of the water we now have because
   a. factories need time to learn how to make water.
   b. we must have water to use in the future.
   c. the first settlers used up most of the water.

9. Which of these sentences do you think is right?
   a. Water pollution is a problem today.
   b. Our water is still clean and safe.
   c. Suds from detergents help clean polluted water.

which begins with a topic sentence telling what the author thinks, followed by supportive material explaining why he or she thinks that way.

Students who have difficulty changing their mind when confronted with new evidence benefit from predicting activities because it forces them to make use of the information in the text. Since many predicting activities take place in a group, students must convince not only their teacher concerning the correctness of their views but also the toughest jury of all—their peers.

Students can be encouraged to defend their thinking through team learning (Dunn and Dunn, 1972), in which they work in small groups on a given assignment. Tasks requiring inferential thinking are best because they make greater demands on schema and allow for more personal interpretations. Students decide on answers by consensus or majority vote. To reach agreement, students must defend their answer and convince other members on the team of its reasonableness. Another benefit of this technique is that it allows teachers to observe the discussion and determine students' background knowledge as well as their reasoning skill. Deficiencies which have been noted can be corrected later. Team learning is particularly helpful with students who have failed. Because students work with their peers rather than alone, they may begin to model the problem-solving strategies of others in their group.

Vocabulary and Context Skills

The final implicit comprehension skill involves the use of context in determining the meaning of words. Learning new vocabulary usually involves concepts, but from a skill viewpoint, students need to learn how to approximate a word's meaning from the words around it. Although teachers need not systematically teach students the clues used to identify word meaning, they should be aware of them so they can point them out to students when the need arises. The following are the major context clues found in reading material:

1. *The experience clue.* If students have had the appropriate personal experience they will be able to figure out the meaning of *automobile* in the sentence "Our family rode in our new *automobile* on our summer vacation."
2. *Definitions.* Authors use definition clues in various ways. They may use the direct approach as in "A *toggenberg* is a breed of goat." "To *loath* means to dislike intensely." In some instances, a clue covers two sentences: "A *cat's claw* is a specialized tool. It is used to draw nails out of wood." The first sentence provides the general category, and the second sentence specifies the use of the tool. Definitions are also indicated by means of apposition. "Babe Ruth batted in the clean-up spot, the fourth place in the lineup."
3. *Synonyms.* Often the word is explained in a subsequent sentence. "The woman bought a *monteith* at the auction. She was surprised to acquire the large silver punch bowl at such a low price."
4. *Compare and contrast.* "Unlike the *former corrupt* administration, the new one is very *honest.*" "All the executive wished for his vacation was *peace* and *tranquility.*"

In this section we have discussed the skills of reading comprehension—those abilities which help readers make the most of their knowledge. We divided these skills into three categories: literal, inferential, and use of context to determine word meaning. Literal skills focus on specific facts and details which either provide significant information (as in directions) or serve to support more general levels of information (as in main ideas). Inference includes a variety of skills but can be condensed into a general level, a main idea category and a purpose-setting category. In all three types, the reader must rely much more on schemata than in literal comprehension. Finally, readers need to be made aware of the role of context in helping to determine the meaning of unknown words.

PROBLEMS RELATING TO WORLD KNOWLEDGE

Earlier in this chapter we discussed a student who lacked appropriate background information and another who overrelied on her personal experiences and frequently misinterpreted the intended message of the writer. Both problems involve world knowledge, or schemata. Students must possess ideas in their cognitive structure which can be matched with information in the text if understanding is to result.

Three implications flow from this schema theory of reading. First, reading teachers need to maximize students' use of their existing schemata. Second, teachers must teach students to balance the use of schemata and textual information. Some students must acquire more adequate schemata whereas others should make greater use of the text in activating schemata and confirming hypotheses. Third, teachers must try to improve students' schemata by requiring the reader to modify a schema to comprehend the new information. In this section we provide suggestions for accomplishing these three tasks.

Making the Most of Existing Schemata

Students must be helped to make the most of the schemata they already possess. One method is to employ the Directed Reading-Thinking Activity (DRTA) (Stauffer, 1969).

DIRECTED-READING THINKING ACTIVITY   The DRTA follows a three-step procedure:

1. Students gather increasingly greater information about a story, relate it to their schema, and then predict the story's outcome.
2. They read to find evidence confirming their predictions.
3. They are expected to evaluate their hypotheses by citing specific facts from the text. In narrative accounts, purposes are reset as additional evidence from the story is gathered. In expository selections all purposes are established before reading begins.

The teacher guides the process by asking two kinds of questions: "What do you think?" and "Why do you think so?" Variations of these questions might be "What do you think this story will be about?" "What do you think will happen next?" "What do you think _____ will do now?" "Why did you say that?" "Why do you think _____?" The precise wording depends on both the nature of the events and the students' predictions.

The teacher also asks students to confirm their predictions by reading lines or sentences from the pages which have been read. If the student says, "I was right about my predictions," the teacher replies, "Can you read a line [or lines] to prove your point?"

The entire process influences students in a number of ways. In order to hypothesize, they must call up considerable background knowledge. In this manner the *DRTA* maximizes their use of their schemata. In addition, the teacher continually presses students, particularly those who overrely on schema and disregard the text, to "tell us more about your ideas." As students extend themselves beyond the actual evidence, they challenge each other's predictions and conclusions. The teacher encourages reaction by asking, "Do you all agree with Bob's ideas?" "Do you agree, Helen?" "Why do you agree [or disagree]?" The group dynamics help students change their interpretation in light of new or conflicting evidence. Finally, the *DRTA* heightens motivation by asking students to commit themselves publicly to a point of view. Students read, not to satisfy the teacher's purposes, but to vindicate themselves. It is their intellectual credibility which is being evaluated. Voting is frequently used as a technique to insure commitment to a particular point of view.

The teacher serves as moderator, making few statements but continually asking questions, always pushing students to draw on background and story clues to predict future events. The teacher's questions are designed primarily not to check comprehension but to force students to defend and expand on their own views. For this reason Stauffer (1969) describes the teacher as an "intellectual agitator."

The teacher's questions do not hop from one point to another but follow a line of thought and pursue students in the Socratic manner. Each time students respond they are asked another question, which presses them still further to defend their views. Because teachers often have difficulty asking questions in this manner, we frequently invoke the "rule of three," which states that you cannot make more than three statements in succession without asking a question. This rule inhibits the tendency to lecture students and encourages a questioning strategy.

While the teacher serves as moderator and agitator, members of the group act as the jury. They evaluate each other's predictions and subsequent interpretations, using as a norm both their own schemata and information in the text. A student, for example, may say, "I was right in my prediction." The teacher may reply, "How do the rest of you feel about that?" Other students, who also have stated their views, are usually quick to respond. Even when the group assents to an incorrect conclusion, the teacher should continue the reading in the expectation that subsequent evidence in the story will serve as a corrective. Students who disagree on a point can be asked to read a line (or lines) in the text to support their view. Sometimes students will pore over the page unable to find their proof and finally confess that they were mistaken. In other instances students skim quickly over the page, locate the appopriate lines, and with the look of triumph, proudly announce they have found their answer.

Students will occasionally encounter material in stories which they don't understand. Resist the temptation to immediately explain the difficult sections. If the problem is minor, it will have little bearing on the story and may even be clarified by subsequent events. On the other hand, if the story requires a schema far beyond the students' intellectual level, it is unlikely that a quick explanation will suffice. Just as explaining a joke seldom leads to laughter, an explanation will rarely be adequate to develop the necessary concepts. Take time at a later date to develop the students' background.

To explain how the DRTA functions, consider a story entitled "A Train Races an Airplane" (Stauffer *et al.,* 1960). The story takes place in 1927 as Charles Lindbergh returns to the United States from his record-breaking flight to Paris and is greeted by crowds of well-wishers. The actual race involves transporting the films of his triumphant arrival in Washington, D.C., to New York City, where crowds are anxiously waiting to see the films.

The first step is to prepare students for any unknown vocabulary which they might encounter. Traditional methods meet this need by introducing the "new words"—those words which have not previously appeared in the series. You can omit this practice and instead emphasize strategies for decoding unknown words. The precise steps depend on the amount of prior instruction in word identification; in this third-grade story it might consist of three steps:

1. Read to the end of the line and see what word makes sense.
2. Use phonic cues. Start with beginning sounds, then the ending sounds, and finally the medial sounds. Use only as much information as necessary to reach a decision. (In higher grades, students would employ additional skills such as looking for word parts in multisyllabic words, using affixes, consulting the glossary, and so on.)
3. Ask the teacher for assistance.

Another preparatory step suggested in many basal reader manuals is to make several introductory remarks about the story's plot. These statements are intended to provide necessary background and to motivate students to read the account. However, this kind of readiness is usually unnecessary in narrative accounts which are within the students' instructional level. Also, they force the teacher into a lecturing rather than a questioning mode, frequently reveal the plot, and underestimate students' ability to do their own thinking. Motivation can be developed more effectively by helping students set their own purposes for reading.

At this point, in this lesson, help students establish their purposes for reading. One approach is to ask them to turn to the table of contents and silently read the name of the story which begins on page 98. (Do not ask a student to read the title aloud because the students should read for themselves.) Now ask, "What do you think this story will be about?" (At first, your questions will be quite general. As the story proceeds, you can ask for more specific questions. Avoid questions such as "Have you ever been on a train or an airplane?" You are not interested in their travel experiences but whether students can use these experiences to help them predict the story's outcome.) Students may reply, "It is about a race." Follow with another question, such as "Who do you think will win?" The following questions might also be raised: "Why do you think the airplane [or train] will win?" "Do the rest of you agree?" "What do you think?" Subsequent questions will depend on students' answers to the initial queries. Following are typical questions and answers to the story that one of us witnessed.

Teacher:	Who do you think will win?
Pat:	The airplane.
Teacher:	Why?
Pat:	Planes are always faster than trains. I took a plane to Chicago last year and it took only an hour. My father said that a train would take a couple of hours.
	[Another student might comment that planes are not always faster.]
Teacher:	How fast do you think an airplane can fly?
	[The teacher is pressing the student. Can Pat support her thinking on grounds other than her father's opinion?]
Pat:	Maybe 500 miles an hour.
Teacher:	Do the rest of you agree with Pat's ideas?
	[No response]
Teacher:	What do you think, Bernie?
Bernie:	Well, a plane can fly faster, but maybe the weather is bad and so the plane couldn't take off at all. My grandfather was supposed to fly to see us, but it was snowing and he had to take the bus for the last part of the trip.
	[The student is relating his experience to the story.]
Teacher:	What do the rest of you think?
	[Again no response. Most members of the group are still unwilling to commit themselves. Some are reluctant because they always like to be correct and want more information before risking a prediction. Others who have had difficulty in reading do not wish to expose themselves to additional failure. The DRTA, by not providing immediate feedback, increases anxiety for both groups because they must maintain their views for several pages before learning if their predictions are correct. When students are reluctant to participate, ask questions such as "Do you agree?" rather than "What is your prediction?" To overcome students' objections that they do not know the answer, stress that you are asking what they think—what is their best guess.]
Teacher:	Let's take a vote. How many think the train will win? The plane?
	[The truth is not determined by majority vote, but voting forces students to commit themselves publicly.]
Teacher:	Now read the first three pages of the story to see if you were correct in your predictions [see Figure 8-5].
	[Explain that predictions need not be correct. Incorrect hypotheses are equally valuable. It is important, of course, for the students to know, after reading, whether their prediction was accurate.]

Students now read the first three pages. Books are closed when they finish reading. If possible, call individual students who finish first to your side and ask, "Were you right? How do you know?"

In the year 1927, the train run from Washington, D.C. to New York City was often in the news. It was the fastest run on the whole Pennsylvania Railroad. Some said it was the fastest ride in the country.

The owners of the Pennsylvania Railroad were happy about all this. They wanted people to know about their railroad.

The people who traveled each day from Washington, D.C. to New York were also happy. They liked to make the trip as quickly as they could.

1927 was also the year a young man made a great trip in an airplane. Starting from New York City, he flew across the Atlantic alone.

People thought it couldn't be done. They thought a man would never fly the Atlantic alone.

But one young man thought he could do it. Charles Lindbergh believed he could fly the Atlantic alone—and he did.

For a day and a night the people in the United States listened carefully to their radios. Would Lindbergh make it across the Atlantic? Everyone cheered when he arrived overseas.

Then Lindbergh made a return trip across the Atlantic. This time he traveled in a special ship ordered by the President.

Lindbergh was a great man now. Everyone wanted to see him. He was in the news in almost every country.

Many people traveled to Washington, D.C. to see Lindbergh arrive in the United States. All the streets were crowded. Everyone wanted to see the President welcome Lindbergh home.

Many other people couldn't travel to Washington, D.C. They waited to see moving pictures of the President and Lindbergh. The pictures were to be taken in Washington and then shipped all over the country.

Figure 8-5 "A Train Races an Airplane" From "A Train Races an Airplane," pp. 98–100 in *Across the Valley,* edited by Russell G. Stauffer. Copyright © 1960 by Holt, Rinehart and Winston. Reprinted by permission.

Teacher:	Were you right?
Bernie:	It didn't say yet.
	[This is a valuable lesson for students to learn—that because the prediction is made, the answer will not necessarily be found.]
Teacher:	[To entire group] What do you think now?
Pat:	I think that maybe the train will win.
Teacher:	Why do you think so?
	[The teacher is not willing to let students change their mind without a reason. Students are continually trying to determine the correct answers by observing teachers' verbal and nonverbal behavior. Perhaps Pat thought that it was too obvious that the plane would win and so she switched to the train.]
Pat:	Well, it says that the race was in 1927. That's a long time ago. I don't think planes were very fast then.

Teacher:	How fast do you think they could travel at that time?
Pat:	About 100 miles an hour.
	[Teacher doesn't agree or disagree.]
Teacher:	And the train?
Pat:	About 50 miles.
Teacher:	Then which one would win?
	[Pat realizes the problem with her reasoning. She's either going to have to change the speeds or return to her original idea. The teacher leaves Pat to think through the problem and turns to others in the group.]
Teacher:	How about the rest of you? Do you want to stay with your original idea or change it?
Tom:	I don't think we can tell. We don't even know where they raced to. [Tom is resisting a commitment until the nature of the race is disclosed. In response, you could ask, "What would you need to know before you were willing to make a prediction?"]
Teacher:	Let's read the next page.

The students continue to predict, read, and evaluate their predictions.

Toward the end of the story some students note that the train travels at a rate of two miles a minute, calculate that this means 120 miles an hour, and argue that the speed supports the train hypothesis. They also mention that the train has a photography laboratory aboard in which the film is being developed as the train races toward New York City. Other students counter that the train travels at two miles a minutes "at times" and not all the time. They feel that the train is still too slow even if the pictures are being developed.

Before reading the final two pages, students are asked again who they think will win. Another vote is taken. The teacher asks, "Those who favor the train, what are your reasons?"

Pat:	The plane is faster because it can go over the mountains.
Bernie:	The train will win because it goes two miles a minute and they are getting the pictures ready in the train's darkroom. [Other students contribute different ideas or agree with the previous speakers.]
Teacher:	Read the last page to find out [Figure 8-6].

The students read the final page. Shouts of "I knew it would be the train" mingle with groans from those who supported the plane. Virtually everyone demonstrates audibly that they understood the outcome.

Teacher:	What did you find?
Sara:	It was the train.
Teacher:	Can you read a line to prove it?
Sara:	"The train won the race after all."
Bob:	That's not fair. The plane got there first. It didn't say anything about getting the pictures to the movies. [The nature of the outcome is in dispute despite the sentence in the text.]

While Engine 460 was roaring along toward Wilmington, the plane passed overhead. The pilot flew low over the train as if to say "hello." Then on he went to New York City.

The airplane arrived ahead of the train. But the pictures it was carrying were not yet ready for showing. The newsmen went to work on them as soon as the plane landed.

In the meantime, Engine 460 arrived from Washington, D.C. with pictures all ready to show. These were rushed to the moving picture houses.

The pictures carried by train were seen two hours before the pictures that came by airplane. The Pennsylvania Railroad was the winner of the race after all.

Figure 8-6 Continuation of "A Train Races an Airplane" From "A Train Races an Airplane," p. 104 in *Across the Valley,* edited by Russell G. Stauffer. Copyright © 1960 by Holt, Rinehart and Winston. Reprinted by permission.

Teacher: What do the rest of you think? Why?
[It is not necessary to settle the matter. The important point is to press adherents of each view to present cogent reasons in support.]

The lesson concludes as the teacher mentions that she has a few books on the history of trains and planes and that some students might like to find out how fast trains and planes could travel in 1927. Others may wish to make a chart showing the fastest speeds of man, animals, planes, cars, trains, rockets, and so on.

In subsequent lessons, you could check sight vocabulary, give decoding lessons, and ask the class to reread the story to identify the clues suggesting that the train would win. If students displayed conceptual deficiencies during the reading, these could also be refined.

In future stories, you could vary the amount of reading done before predicting. In some accounts students would read half of the story before predicting the outcome. Another procedure is to look at all the pictures and then predict the story. The number of interruptions in the story and their locations also depend on the plot development.

The DRTA requires you to attend closely to students' responses. In order to react to them rather than become preoccupied with your own plans it is *sometimes* helpful to make only minimum preparations for a story. Minimum planning includes reading the story to yourself, deciding at which points to have students make predictions, and arming yourself with "What do you think?-Why?-Prove it" questions. When you meet with the students, listen carefully to their responses and build your questions on their responses.

ADAPTING THE DRTA TO THE NEEDS OF THE PROBLEM READER The DRTA can be especially effective with the problem reader if a few procedures are modified:

1. Whenever possible, focus students' attention on one question throughout the story. In "The Train Races the Plane" the question was "Who

will win?" For students who are having trouble with comprehension, this is preferable to asking broader questions such as "What do you think the story will be about?" Questions that focus can be identified by determining the central problem or conflict.

2.   Limit the number of predictions. It is not necessary for every student to make a personal prediction. Purpose setting can be accomplished by asking a few students to predict and allowing others to adopt one of these hypotheses. The chief concern is whether students have committed themselves to a purpose.

3.   Delay a request for predictions until students are well into the story. Most students are hesitant to predict on the basis of limited evidence, especially those who have experienced failure. Use the ReQuest procedure at the beginning of the story or read the first few pages to the students.

4.   Rewrite portions of high-interest stories at the students' instructional level. In one instance a teacher rewrote portions of the story "Blue Beard" (Johnson, 1969) at the second-grade level. The teacher read portions of the original version to them while the students read selected paragraphs in a simplified version. The students' paragraphs were placed on separate sheets. Purposes were set as in an ordinary DRTA. (Figure 8-7 presents one selection from the original and rewritten versions.)

An advantage of this technique is that the students' interest can be sustained since reading by the teacher allows the story to move quickly. The combination of a listening-reading format with a DRTA, will probably increase the students' motivation. Finally, students will have an opportunity to hear selections of literary quality which often they are unable to read in the original version.

The DRTA can also be used to help students who are unwilling to change their minds when confronted with evidence contrary to their initial perceptions. Before reading the story "Master of the Mountain," students were asked whether they thought a mountain climber would be able to reach the peak of the Matterhorn safely. All agreed that he would succeed and they persisted in this view even when the story, which had been rewritten by the teacher, contained deliberate clues to the contrary. (The mountain climber was very old, had recently broken bones, was alone, and so on.) Only when students read the final page and learned of the mountain climber's fatal fall did they appreciate the need to attend to the evidence at hand. From a schema point of view, the students may have lacked a well-developed schema for tragic endings and thus were unable to use the information in the text which suggested such an outcome. Although the students were unsuccessful in correctly interpreting this story, the teacher can use their failure to help them develop an adequate schema or to attend more carefully to specific information in the text.

The DRTA can also be used with expository material by altering the procedures for securing predictions. In "Lobstering," for example, a young author discusses his family's lobstering business (*Social Science Reader*, 1974). The

ORIGINAL

So overcome with curiosity was she that, without reflecting upon the discourtesy of leaving her guests, she ran down a private staircase, so precipitately that twice or thrice she nearly broke her neck, and so reached the door of the little room. There she paused for a while, thinking of the prohibition which her husband had made, and reflecting that harm might come to her as a result of disobedience. But the temptation was so great that she could not conquer it. Taking the little key, with a trembling hand she opened the door of the room.

SIMPLIFIED

So she left her friends and ran down the cellar steps. She stopped at the

door. She knew her husband would be mad if she opened the door. But she

couldn't help it. She took the little key. Her hand shook. She opened the

door of the room.

Figure 8-7   **Blue Beard: Original and Simplified Versions**   From *Perrault's Fairy Tales*, translated by A. E. Johnson. Copyright 1969 by Dover Publications, 1969. Reprinted by permission.

students are to make all predictions before reading the story. Once they have read the title and looked at the first picture, they can be asked to predict the following:

1. The location of the story.
2. The minimum age a boy is allowed to go out alone on his boat.
3. The bait used to catch lobsters.
4. Dangers in lobstering.
5. Size of the daily catch.
6. Kind of boat used for lobstering.

These categories represent important information in the account and are first discussed informally, with the teacher asking questions such as "Where do you think this story took place?" Students are given ample time to draw on their own experiences. They may remark that they know a good deal about lobstering because they once went on their uncle's boat and he showed them how to catch lobsters. Their experiences may differ from the boy's in this particular account but they can help them predict the story. On the other hand, students who have little familiarity with lobstering would be less able to make accurate predictions. This should not prevent them, however, from setting purposes.

These six categories are then written across the board, and the teacher systematically records the students' responses so they can be referred to after the story has been read. The students read the entire four-page selection without interruption. The teacher reviews the students' predictions by asking if they were correct. Students are also asked which predictions could not be confirmed from the story and whether it contained any significant information about which they had not predicted. This information is also recorded under the appropriate category. If some questions about the story are still unresolved, the students can locate this information in other reference material.

In summary, the DRTA is a versatile tool for activating students' world knowledge and directing the comprehension process. It works effectively with both narrative and expository accounts and can be adapted to the needs of students who are having difficulty. The emphasis in the DRTA is not simply on arriving at correct answers but on working through a process, common to all learning, of hypothesizing and reading for confirmation.

Accommodation

When we focus on word identification skills in remediating comprehension difficulties, we are assuming that students possess adequate schemata and that comprehension will occur if they can obtain access to their world knowledge. According to this process, students interpret the text in light of their present schemata.

However, sometimes students must alter their cognitive structure if comprehension is to take place. This process, which Piaget calls *accommodation,* has been also termed *learning* (Smith, 1975). Learning occurs by adding new facts, changing existing schemata, or creating new schemata. Once accommodation takes place, readers are able to comprehend the text by relating their revised knowledge of the world to it.

THE ROLE OF BOOKS   In schools, reading has traditionally played an important role in learning or accommodation. Reading, in fact, often appears to be the chief avenue of learning. On the very first day of school students are given books which represent the school curriculum. Throughout the year they are assigned stories and chapters in these texts and are tested on their content.

There are good reasons for relying heavily on a textbook curriculum. Books represent an economical means of conveying information. They are certainly less costly and time-consuming than many real life experiences, experiments, field trips, movies, and audiovisual aids. Books can transport the reader to the past and to distant lands beyond our reach. In a few sentences books can state a concept that would take hours to present by experiential approaches.

Under many conditions, books and related reading matter can help students to learn. If the student knows the word and has reasonably developed comprehension skills and the schema assumed by the author, learning can take place.

Books can even facilitate learning if students lack some knowledge or skills. Students can often understand the author's message and gain new information if the teacher carefully guides the reading, asks appropriate questions, and provides brief explanations. Books can also help if students are attempting to learn concepts at a high-school level or higher but possess only a limited background. If students, for example, are studying the anatomy of the eye, they may be helped by referring to an elementary textbook account of the same subject.

If too great a disparity exists between the reader's schema and the schema which the writer had anticipated, reading alone may be insufficient. Guided reading and brief explanations cannot always breach the gap, and easier books of the proper kind may not be available. In this situation students may need considerable instruction before reading the text if they are to learn from it.

How can students be helped to learn under these circumstances? As a general rule, new information will be better learned and remembered if it can be integrated with existing schemata. For this reason the best overall advice for building background is to help students link the old, familiar information to the new information which is to be learned. Perhaps you have visited a construction site and seen poured concrete slabs from which iron rods protrude. These rods help to tie the existing concrete with concrete which will be poured at a later date. Without these rods, the old and new sections would separate under stress. This process is similar to relating old information to new. Note that this example is useful only if you have seen concrete slabs and iron rods. If you have not, we have not related the new concept with your present schema.

ANALOGIES   Analogies are often employed to help students form the mental connections between familiar and new information. In an analogy we say, "*A* is like *B* in the following way." If we were trying to explain racquetball, we might say that it is like tennis—a ball hit with a paddlelike instrument. We frequently add contrasting information: in tennis, players hit the ball over a net and toward one another, but in racquetball both players hit the ball against a wall.

Analogies are used to explain more complex concepts as well. In explaining symbiosis, we might say that it is like helping your friend finish her paper route so she can help you repair your bicycle.

Analogies, like all strategies which attempt to link the old and new, are effective only if the teacher is aware of some aspect in the reader's schemata which is similar to the new concept. Very often teachers are unable to use analogies effectively because they know too little of the reader's background. Perhaps you have had the experience of asking for directions shortly after moving into a new city and the individual responded by asking if you were familiar with a particular landmark known by all the city's natives—"Do you know the old cheese factory on Route 51?" When you reply negatively, the direction-giver must now try again to evaluate your present familiarity of the city before he can provide the information you require. It doesn't help to learn that your destination is two miles past the cheese factory unless you are already familiar with that location. The need to link the old with the new explains why a teacher who is familiar with the student's background can often be as effective as the teacher who knows a great deal more about the subject matter itself but less about the student.

Building Background

In this section we will approach the problem of providing sufficient background in a variety of ways—acquaintance with vocabulary terms, vocabulary enrichment, and concept formation. These tasks are interrelated and distinctions between them are not always clear-cut. We have divided them into three categories because they vary in complexity and require different approaches.

VOCABULARY TERMS   Vocabulary terms are those for which students know the underlying concept but are unfamiliar with the language, such as occurs when adults who speak another language are learning English. They may be familiar with many of the concepts in the new environment but lack English words for them. Young children may know a concept but are unfamiliar with the appropriate terms. This was evident in the case of the second-grader who was having trouble with the algorithm 16 plus 5. The teacher kept repeating "Add 6 and 5, bring down the one, and carry the one." When the child continued to look puzzled, an aide who was more familiar with the local idiom, said, "Let me show him. Bring down the 1 and tote 1." The child replied "Now I get it. Why didn't you say that in the first place?" Fortunately, linking the old with the new in these situations is relatively easy. It usually means providing the students with familiar words to help them learn the new ones.

Learning vocabulary terms does not mean that students should look up words in the dictionary—at least not all the time. Hunting up words, writing their definitions, and using the words in a sentence is of limited value for several reasons:

1. It is not very interesting if done on a routine basis, particularly by students who are having difficulty and already lack interest in reading.
2. Students may not learn the meaning of the word from the definition because of unfamiliar terms in the dictionary meaning.
3. Students can appear to know the word's meaning by simply memorizing the definition.
4. Individual words may have several meanings, and the precise interpretation depends on the context in which it is embedded.

Rather than using dictionary definitions, you can help students understand word meaning by comparing and contrasting words with other words. Use familiar synonyms and antonyms to help students learn the new term. If the student does not know the meaning of *dense* and context is of little value, you can say that it means the same as *thick*. If the unknown word is *deficient,* you can say that it means the opposite of *enough*. The specific context, of course, will narrow the intended meaning, but synonyms and antonyms can approximate its meaning.

VOCABULARY ENRICHMENT   A more complex vocabulary problem exists when students understand the basic meaning of a word but need to enrich that meaning. School lessons which can enrich vocabulary development include the use of

1. Antonyms.
2. Synonyms.
3. Figures of speech.
4. Homographs (read, read).
5. Homophones (fare, fair).
6. Multiple meanings of words (the many meanings of *run* as in *home run, run* in a stocking, *run* on the bank).

The following activities can be used for this purpose:

1. Delete nouns, verbs, and adjectives from sentences and ask students to fill in as many words as possible for a specific deletion. Discuss the choices, calling attention to the differences between the words. In the sentence, "The boy _____ home," students might insert *walked, hopped, skipped, romped, crawled, bicycled, trotted, jogged.*

2. As students read selections, note the common words which are used in a variety of ways. Write these words in sentences and see if students can use the context to interpret them. Suppose the word *high* appeared in a story. Here are other meanings of high: high and dry, high and mighty, high-class, high gear, high-handed, high hat, high jinks, high sounding, hightail, highway, highway robbery. An excellent source of multiple meanings can be found in *A Dictionary of Idioms for the Deaf* (Boatner and Gates, 1966).

3. When a figure of speech appears in an account, occasionally ask students to illustrate its literal sense. Then use the expression in two or more additional sentences to help students generalize its metaphorical meaning.
   a. He was scared during the bombing raid but kept a stiff upper lip.
   b. Their boat was going down quickly but the captain kept a stiff upper lip.
   At this point, you may want to ask students the definition of the phrase. After they have developed their hypotheses, supply the following sentence and ask them if their meaning is appropriate: "Father was having trouble getting the car started but he kept a stiff upper lip."

4. Use words orally in a meaningful but informal context before a reading lesson in which the words occur. This may help the students to interpret the words' meaning when they encounter them in print.

Our personal preference in enriching vocabulary is to discuss words that have appeared in the students' reading lessons rather than create special vocabulary lessons. Since the meaning of a word is bound by context, this principle is violated when vocabulary activities are developed in isolation. Even if the word appears in a sentence in a worksheet, the context provided by a narrative or expository account is often lacking.

We suggest that teachers draw up a list with the following categories and note whether the students' present reading assignment can be used to develop vocabulary meanings. The following is based on a story from a sixth-grade basal reader (Durr, 1974) about the formation of a volcano.

> Synonyms: *legends, dense.*
>
> Antonyms: *violence.*
>
> Figures of speech: *Volcanoes are like windows.*
>
> Homographs: None appear in this account.
>
> Homophones: *through, threw.*
>
> Multiple meanings: *cone, crust, funnel, depression.*

CONCEPT FORMATION   Concept formation is an essential part of learning. It enables the reader economically to classify a complex world and thus organize it into more easily manageable categories.

Concepts are more difficult to learn than mere facts since they stand for a class of objects, not specific entities.

Identifying a sheep, for example, requires an individual to see beyond a specific animal, to know the attributes of "sheepness" and to apply these correctly to animals who vary in size, shape, ear formation, and disposition—and still qualify as sheep.

Concepts are also elusive since they can never be completely known. I can know the game of tennis, for example, in that I can distinguish it from all other games, including those which employ a paddlelike implement and a net. But I can also know the game from first-hand experience as I try to serve or return the ball. I can know the game at another level as I study its history, its rules, and its famous matches. One implication for learning is that students need to not only learn concepts but also continually refine and extend those they already possess.

Although concepts are important in reading to learn, stories in the elementary grades contain relatively few concepts which are so essential or so far beyond the understanding of students that the story is incomprehensible without them. In the story "The Train Races an Airplane," students displayed numerous erroneous concepts about airplanes, trains, and geography and yet were able to follow the plot adequately and fulfill their purposes. The correction of misunderstandings and the extension and enrichment of concepts can thus be delayed until the story is completed.

It is more likely that the students will have difficulty with concepts in expository material which they encounter in textbooks such as social studies and science. It is at this level that students who appeared to breeze through the primary grades now find it difficult to read their textbooks with understanding. In these instances instruction in concept formation is often necessary, before as well as after the reading of a selection.

To improve the teaching of comprehension we will suggest procedures for essential concepts.

The first step is to identify the important concepts in a particular selection. If you are using a textbook, these concepts may be listed in the teacher's edition or placed in boldface type or italics in the text. In a basal reader, essential concepts will be far fewer, but you will need to look through the text and determine which ones are prerequisites for comprehension. In one basal reader, understanding one story depended on distinguishing between root vegetables and leafy vegetables. The story concerned an elf who was eating a farmer's crops. The clever farmer solved the problem by allowing the elf to harvest that part of the plant which grew above ground one year and which grew below the ground the following year. The tricky farmer then proceeded to grow potatoes in the elf's above-ground year and lettuce in the elf's below-ground year. This left the farmer with the more desirable parts of the plants in both years. The students required considerable help with the concepts of root and leafy vegetables before they were able to understand the story.

Since many more concepts may be introduced than students can assimilate without getting cognitive indigestion, you may need to employ a "post holing" approach, in which attention is focused on a limited portion of the curriculum. In social studies, for example, it might be preferable to study a few periods of history well rather than superficially survey 200 years of events in a single school year. This method can thus enable students to deal with subject matter at a conceptual rather than a rote memory level.

When important concepts have been identified, it is helpful to determine how well students already understand these ideas. For the basal story about root and leafy vegetables, students' backgrounds will differ, and all students will not need the same instruction. Students who live on a truck farm in which potatoes and lettuce are grown will ordinarily require less preparation than those in an urban environment. Informal diagnosis can be conducted by selecting a few representative concepts, writing them on the board one at a time, and saying, "Tell me what you know about this word" or "What words do you think of when you see the word I have written?" By recording the students' responses and asking additional questions about these terms, you can approximate their level of understanding and gear the teaching of concepts accordingly.

It is generally assumed that students need some experience with a concept in order to learn it. Too often the phrase "provide experiential background" suggests nothing more than a field trip. Unfortunately, the number of concepts to be learned, the high cost of transportation, and its time-consuming nature place limitations on the field trip as an important device for providing background. Fortunately, a variety of other experiences can be employed: movies, filmstrips, dramatizations, interviews, experiments, models, pictures, cassette tapes, reading to students, diagrams, and chalkboard drawings. If students need experience with root and leafy vegetables it might be ideal to visit a farm and actually harvest potatoes and cut a head of lettuce or cabbage, but sufficient experience could be conveyed by a classroom garden or movies or filmstrips.

Experience with a concept is a necessary condition to learning it, but students must also be helped to examine their experiences through observation and language. That is, teachers need to talk to children about their experiences. If students are to learn the concept of Holstein cows, for example, they must not only see or view pictures of the cows but also note their coloration and other distinctive features. Some students (and adults also) can go through many experiences such as this without noticing these distinctions unless someone calls their attention to them.

Concepts can be learned in a variety of ways, but the most general strategy is to try to relate the new concept to one which the student already knows, to build on the experience. If we are introducing students to root and leafy vegetables, we can begin with the known concept of vegetables. If Holstein cows are being presented, students' knowledge of cows is a starting place. A study of metamorphic rock can begin by reviewing the nature of igneous and sedimentary rock.

Up to this point we have indicated that concept formation requires experience of some kind, an examination of the experience (in which teacher and students talk about it), and a connection of the new information to previously existing concepts. We suggested that analogies could be employed to link the unknown with the known. Beyond these general guidelines for concept formation lie specific models such as the Concept Attainment Model (Joyce and Weil, 1972), the Taba Model (Taba, 1967), the Ausubel Model (Ausubel, 1968), and the Suchman Inquiry Model (Suchman, 1967). Space permits only a brief description of the Concept Attainment Model. For a detailed discussion of all these models, consult Eggen *et al.* (1979).

Concept attainment is an inductive model in which the student is provided with examples or exemplars (both positive and negative) of a concept and is helped to abstract appropriate attributes. To accomplish this task, students hypothesize about the concept and receive feedback from the teacher.

If we wished to apply the model to learning the concept of root vegetables, for example, we could write the following words on the board:

> potatoes—yes
> lettuce—no

In this instance, potatoes is a positive exemplar of the concept and lettuce is a negative exemplar. Students are told to think of an idea in which potato is an example but lettuce is not. Students might then generate hypotheses such as the following:

1. Brown vegetables.
2. Round vegetables.
3. Vegetables with skin.
4. Vegetables which grow underground.

The teacher would then supply another exemplar:

> carrots—yes

Students would be asked to evaluate their first four hypotheses. They might reject the first three, reasoning that none apply to the carrot, which is a positive exemplar. If students could come to no decision, additional examples would then be presented, both positive and negative, until they agreed on the concept. The label, root vegetables, could then be supplied. Students could also be asked to list the attributes of the concept. This step would help those students who did not understand the common features of vegetables like potatoes and carrots. The teacher's role is not to tell students that they are right but to supply sufficient exemplars so students can decide for themselves that they are correct.

The success of the process would depend, of course, on students' familiarity with the exemplars, which themselves are concepts. If students had seen carrots only in a can, it is unlikely they could generate worthwhile hypotheses.

In this section we have dealt with accommodation, the concept that cognitive structure must often be altered if comprehension is to occur. Accommodation, or learning, operates along a continuum in which at one end it is necessary only to supply a new label—a vocabulary term—to an old concept to situations in which the concept itself is unknown or little understood. Reading can sometimes facilitate accommodation, but in other instances concepts must be developed before a selection is read. In general, the new information must somehow be linked to the old. Analogy is a commonly used approach for tying the known and unknown together. Specific models have also been developed to teach concepts. In concept attainment, students are given positive and negative exemplars, they hypothesize about the concept, and then they are supplied with additional exemplars which help to confirm, reject, or revise the original concept. Concept formation is particularly crucial in dealing with subject matter material, and concepts often must be taught before the reading; however, concept enrichment with most stories can be delayed until after the selection has been read.

ULTIMATE COMPREHENSION

We have discussed comprehension instruction at length without attempting to define it, for doing so in a meaningful way is difficult. Usually we resort to other words which add little understanding to the term. We could say, for example, that *comprehension* means to understand the text. This response, however, only raises additional questions. What does it mean to understand? Does it imply that the reader should understand everything in a reading assignment or is it sufficient to understand 75 percent of the material? Then, what does it mean to understand 75 percent?

In some instances, of course, it is easy to determine the meaning of *comprehension*. If the material consists of directions for assembling a radio or bike or a recipe for baking a cake, we could say that the reader has comprehended if the completed radio receives all local stations with reasonable fidelity, the bike rides smoothly in all twelve gears, and the cake is gobbled up in short order. In most other situations, however, the evaluation of comprehension is likely to be more subjective, as is the meaning of *comprehension* itself.

We believe that a solution is to view comprehension as a relative matter. That is, quality of comprehension is always relative to the readers' purpose. If the readers have accomplished their purposes, they have understood the selection. As Smith (1979) has said, reading is getting answers to your questions. This means that reading is a highly personal matter. No one can pass judgment on an individual's comprehension unless one understands the individual's purposes. If two people are reading a sports story one may want to learn the final score of a game. When she discovers that the Clippers defeated the Eagles 61 to 56, she is satisfied and has comprehended. The second individual may want to know why the Clippers were able to upset their rival. Neither individual can judge the other's comprehension by her own purposes.

To understand fully students' problem with comprehension, we must first know the questions they are asking of the text, for the quality of their questions determines their comprehension. In other words, students' comprehension begins with knowing the right questions. If students cannot ask the right questions, or are not motivated to ask any questions at all, they are unlikely to obtain the correct answers. In many instances, of course, the "right questions" include those determined by the teacher. In this case students need to learn the questions important to the teacher. This does not eliminate the need for students to ask their own questions; comprehension is expected to continue long after an individual completes formal schooling.

In order to ask appropriate questions students must know something about a subject. In fact, the more they know, the more likely they will be able to ask high-quality questions. If, on the other hand, the students know little about the subject, their questions will reflect their inadequacy and so will their comprehension. Teachers frequently observe this phenomenon in the classroom when students claim they don't know enough about a topic even to ask questions.

If students do possess adequate background, they must develop the habit of aggressively asking appropriate questions of the text. This view contrasts with indiscriminate reading in which the reader attempts to hold in memory everything that is read. The instructional program should provide generous opportunities for students to raise their own questions—particularly about topics of importance to them. One approach is to use a self-selection or individualized reading (Stauffer, 1969) in which the following procedures are employed:

1. Students select a topic of interest to them.
2. Students list questions which they hope to have answered by the reading material they select.
3. Students read to answer questions—though they will be learning incidental material as well.
4. Students' questions will change as they read. Some questions will be answered; others will be eliminated because they cannot be answered with available resources or are no longer interesting. New questions will be raised as additional reading is done.
5. Students read additional material in order to answer these questions.
6. Students eventually report their findings to the other students, selecting from the wealth of information they have gained that which they believe will be of interest to their peers and will answer their questions about the topic.

7. Students are evaluated on the quality of their questions as well as their diligence in seeking answers and their success in finding them.

This technique will not necessarily raise the quality of questions but it can teach the student to take a more active role in raising and answering questions which are important to them.

Ultimate comprehension suggests that comprehension is a relative condition of determining one's own purposes for reading and that it occurs before the reading, during it—as the reader asks new questions—and at the completion of the selection—as the reader asks if the purposes have been accomplished, whether the information is of any value, and whether additional information is needed. It is called "ultimate" because reading to fulfill the teacher's purposes is a temporary condition. Eventually the reader will be responsible not only for knowing the answers, but equally as important, for raising the questions.

SUMMARY

In this chapter we suggested that you view reading comprehension problems from three perspectives: (1) decoding deficiencies, (2) skill limitations, and (3) difficulties related to background information. We argued that problems in all three of these areas are linked to the quality of students' schemata.

Decoding problems must be resolved before serious attention is given to comprehension, but the two processes are never separate. Comprehension in the form of context should be employed from the outset of instruction. Skills help students take advantage of the knowledge they possess. In comprehension, important skills include reading for detail (significant facts or facts supporting the main idea), inferences (main idea, purpose setting, critical reading, creative reading, and general inference), and using the context to determine the meaning of words. Skills cannot function without sufficient schemata or background information. Teachers must first activate this knowledge by using activities such as the DRTA and see that students acquire the appropriate vocabulary and concepts before, during, and after the reading lessons. Comprehension requires students to ask appropriate questions, and ultimately these questions must be their own. Appropriate questioning, which relies on adequate background, is a necessary condition for achieving comprehension.

RELATED ACTIVITIES

1. Direct the reading of a story by means of a DRTA. If possible, ask someone familiar with the technique to observe the lesson and comment on your teaching. Then observe that individual teaching the same story to another group of students and compare the lessons.
2. Select a fairy tale and rewrite selected paragraphs so they can be read by students reading below grade level. Conduct a DRTA with these disabled readers, reading portions of the story to students and having them read the simplified versions.
3. Select a chapter from a content area text (science or social studies). Identify important vocabulary and generalizations in the chapter and suggest ways of teaching them.

4. Interview a variety of adults about their vocational and personal reading habits. Determine the comprehension skills or abilities required of them, and develop activities for teaching these skills.

5. Identify one concept in a science textbook. Develop a series of nonreading activities to teach it. Write reading material at an easy level to supplement and extend the concept.

RELATED READINGS

ADAMS, MARILYN J., AND ALLAN COLLINS. *A Schema-Theoretic View of Reading Comprehension.* Champaign: Center for the Study of Reading, University of Illinois, 1977.

DURKIN, DOLORES. *What is the Value of the New Interest in Reading Comprehension?* Champaign: Center for the Study of Reading, University of Illinois, 1980.

HERBER, HAROLD. *Teaching Reading in Content Areas,* 2d ed. Englewood Cliffs, N.J.: Prentice-Hall, 1978.

PEARSON, P. DAVID, AND DALE D. JOHNSON. *Teaching Reading Comprehension.* New York: Holt, Rinehart & Winston, 1978.

RUMELHART, DAVID. "Schemata: The Building Blocks of Cognition." In *Theoretical Issues in Reading Comprehension.* Rand J. Spiro, Bertram C. Bruce, and William F. Brewer, eds. Hillsdale, N.J.: Lawrence Erlbaum, 1980.

SMITH, FRANK. *Comprehension and Learning.* New York: Holt, Rinehart & Winston, 1975.

REFERENCES

ADAMS, MARILYN, AND BERTRAM BRUCE. *Background Knowledge and Reading Comprehension.* Champaign: Center for the Study of Reading, University of Illinois, 1980.

ADAMS, MARILYN J., AND A. COLLINS. *A Schema-Theoretic View of Reading Comprehension.* Champaign: Center for the Study of Reading, University of Illinois, 1977.

AUSUBEL, DAVID. *Educational Psychology: A Cognitive View.* New York: Holt, Rinehart & Winston, 1968.

BOATNER, MAXINE T., AND JOHN E. GATES. *A Dictionary of Idioms for the Deaf.* West Hartford, Conn.: American School for the Deaf, 1966.

BOBROW, D. G., AND DONALD A. NORMAN. "Some Principles of Memory Schemata, Representation and Understanding." In *Studies in Cognitive Science.* D. G. Bobrow and A. M. Collins, eds. New York: Academic Press, 1975.

BRANSFORD, JOHN D., AND M. K. JOHNSON. "Contextual Prerequisites for Understanding. Some Investigations of Comprehension and Recall." *Journal of Verbal Learning and Verbal Behavior,* 11, no. 6 (Dec. 1972), 717–26.

COLLINS, ALLAN, AND EDWARD E. SMITH. *Teaching the Process of Reading Comprehension.* Champaign: Center for the Study of Reading, University of Illinois, 1980.

CRAMER, RONALD L. *Writing, Reading and Language Growth.* Columbus, Ohio: Chas. E. Merrill, 1978.

DUNN, RITA, AND KENNETH DUNN. *Practical Approaches to Individualizing Instruction.* West Nyack, N.Y.: Parker Publishing, 1972.

DURKIN, DOLORES. *What Is the Value of the New Interest in Reading Comprehension?* Champaign: Center for the Study of Reading, University of Illinois, 1980.

DURR, WILLIAM K., ED. *Galaxies.* Boston: Houghton-Mifflin, 1974.

EARLY, MARGARET G., ROBERT CANFIELD, AND ROBERT KARLIN. *Reaching Out, Reading Skills Workbook 11.* New York: Harcourt Brace Jovanovich, Inc., 1979.

EGGEN, PAUL D., DONALD P. KAUCHAK, AND ROBERT J. HARDER. *Strategies for Teachers—Information Processing Models in the Classroom.* Englewood Cliffs, N.J.: Prentice-Hall, 1979.

EVANS, ARTHUR J. *Reading and Thinking, Book II.* New York: Teachers College Press, 1979.

GOLINKOFF, ROBERTA M. "A Comparison of Reading Comprehension Processes in Good and Poor Comprehenders." *Reading Research Quarterly,* 11 (1975–76), 623–59.

GUSZAK, FRANK J. "Teacher Questioning and Reading." *The Reading Teacher,* 21, no. 3 (Dec. 1967), 227–34, 252.

JOHNSON, A. E., TRANS. *Perrault's Fairy Tales.* New York: Dover, 1969.

JOYCE, BRUCE, AND M. WEIL. *Models of Teaching.* Englewood Cliffs, N.J.: Prentice-Hall, 1972.

KINTSCH, WALTER. "Concerning the Marriage of Research and Practice in Beginning Instruction." In *Theory and Practice of Early Reading,* Vol. 1. Lauren B. Resnick and Phyllis A. Weaver, eds. . Hillsdale, N.J.: Lawrence Erlbaum, 1979.

MANZO, ANTHONY V. "The ReQuest Procedure." *Journal of Reading,* 13 (Nov. 1969), 123–26.

MINSKY, M. "A Framework for Representing Knowledge." In *The Psychology of Computer Vision.* P. M. Winston, ed. New York: McGraw-Hill, 1975.

PEARSON, P. DAVID, AND DALE D. JOHNSON. *Teaching Reading Comprehension.* New York: Holt, Rinehart & Winston, 1978.

RUMELHART, DAVID E. "Schemata: The Building Blocks of Cognition." In *Theoretical Issues in Reading Comprehension.* Rand J. Spiro, B. C. Bruce and W. F. Brewer, eds. Hillsdale, N.J.: Lawrence Erlbaum, 1980.

RUMELHART, DAVID E., AND ANDREW ORTONY. "The Representation of Knowledge in Memory." In *Schooling and the Acquisition of Knowledge.* Rand J. Spiro and William E. Montague, eds. New York: Lawrence Erlbaum, 1977.

SAMUELS, S. JAY. "How the Mind Works When Reading: Describing Elephants No One Has Ever Seen." In *Theory and Practice of Early Reading,* Vol. 1. Lauren B. Resnick and Phyllis A. Weaver, eds. Hillsdale, N.J.: Lawrence Erlbaum, 1979.

SCHANK, ROGER C., AND ROBERT P. ABELSON. *Scripts, Plans, Goals and Understanding.* Hillsdale, N.J.: Lawrence Erlbaum, 1977.

SMITH, FRANK. *Comprehension and Learning.* New York: Holt, Rinehart & Winston, 1975.

———. *Reading Without Nonsense.* New York: Teachers College Press, 1979.

Social Science Reader. Pleasantville, N.Y.: Readers Digest Press, 1974.

STAUFFER, RUSSELL G. *Teaching Reading as a Thinking Activity.* New York: Harper & Row, 1969.

STAUFFER, RUSSELL G., ALVINA TREUT BURROWS, AND MILLARD BLACK. *Across the Valley.* Philadelphia: John C. Winston, 1960.

SUCHMAN, J. *Inquiry Box: Teacher's Handbook.* Chicago: Science Research Associates, 1967.

TABA, HILDA. *Teacher's Handbook to Elementary Social Studies.* Reading, Mass.: Addison-Wesley, 1967.

TRABASSO, TOM. *On the Making of Inferences during Reading and Their Assessment.* Champaign: Center for the Study of Reading, University of Illinois, 1980.

TULVING, E. "Episodic and Semantic Memory." In *Organization of Memory.* E. Tulving and W. Donaldson, eds. New York: Academic Press, 1972.

WEBER, ROSEMARIE. "A Linguistic Analysis of First Grade Reading Errors." *Reading Research Quarterly,* 5 (1970), 427–51.

9

MOTIVATING STUDENTS TO READ

Upon completion of this chapter you will be able to

1. Distinguish between the disinterested and the discouraged reader.
2. Describe nonconventional, nonbook activities for arousing interest in reading.
3. Explain the procedures for conducting team-learning activities.
4. Discuss techniques for publicizing and creating demand for books.
5. List arguments for and against the use of reading games.
6. Describe techniques for encouraging students who lack confidence in their ability to read.

Reading is an intellectual process, but at the same time we can never underestimate the importance of a positive attitude. Noam Chomsky (1970), the famed linguist, recognized this truth when he said

> The dominant factor in successful teaching is and will always remain the teacher's skill in nourishing, and sometimes arousing, the child's curiosity and interest and in providing a rich and challenging intellectual environment in which the child can find his own unique way toward understanding, knowledge and skill.

Consider the role of attitudes in the following cases:

Ralph appears to be highly motivated: he plays an aggressive game of hockey, manages a newspaper route and works hard to keep his motocross bike in running order. Unfortunately, his motivation seems to melt away when it comes to reading. Though he *can* read, he seldom does.

Tina, like Ralph, doesn't like to read either. Unlike Ralph, however, Tina has struggled to acquire the basic reading skills. After years of failure, though, she has just about given up the fight. She is convinced that she will always be a poor reader and lately she has neglected to use even the limited reading ability she does possess.

Ralph and Tina are "D and D" students—disinterested and discouraged. Their lack of motivation is a more serious problem than their inability to learn the skills of reading. In fact, teachers often find that their most difficult task is to motivate students with little interest and to encourage those who have lost hope in their ability to read. Some teachers would even claim that teaching reading skills to the worst illiterates is not difficult at all—if you can motivate them to work.

Students like Ralph and Tina may not have always been disinterested and discouraged. When they first entered school, they expected to read and to enjoy it. As they continued through the grades, however, something went wrong; perhaps unrealistic stories about make-believe children were unappealing, the spit and sputter of phonics made no sense, or maybe they struggled in vain to keep up with the pace of instruction. Maybe their parents never read to them, or perhaps they lacked readiness skills for reading. At this point it is unimportant how they lost interest nor does it help to seek a scapegoat. The point is, they lack the motivation to read and we must help them to regain it if they are to reach their reading potential.

The focus of this chapter is to help teachers motivate disinterested and discouraged students. Improving motivation can help students reach their reading potential and thus satisfy civic, vocational, and personal needs. They may never love classical literature or spend their evenings reading poetry, but they can learn that books provide a great deal of enjoyment and satisfaction and can be a resource in time of need.

Because motivational problems can be of two types, we are dividing this chapter into two parts, First, we discuss students like Ralph who can read but choose not to. Second, we consider Tina and other discouraged students whose low estimate of their reading ability inhibits them from trying. Specific activities will be suggested to make reading more satisfying for both groups. The suggestions for motivating disinterested students can also be used with discouraged students. When students view themselves as incompetent readers, however, we also need to help them believe that they can learn.

THE DISINTERESTED READER

Disinterested readers are those who possess some reading skills, are not suffering from any particular deficiency in word identification or comprehension, but are reading too little to achieve their reading potential. There are innumerable reasons for lack of interest, but they probably can be reduced to two principal factors: the value placed on reading and the nature of past reading instruction. If reading is not valued in the students' home, school, or community, they are not likely to develop an avid interest in books. Methods of instruction may also influence their attitude. A program, for example, can achieve good results in skill acquisition but may accomplish this goal at the expense of developing interest.

To develop interest does not mean that the student's chief loves, such as baseball, fishing, or motocross, must be sacrificed but that the student must make room for reading within an existing lifestyle. Essentially, this is done by linking the student's present interests to reading—which in turn suggests that the instructional program should be just as concerned with its effect on students' interests as it is in its success in building a sight vocabulary and developing phonic and comprehension skills. In the following section, basic strategies for dealing with these readers are described.

Basic Strategies

The basic strategy for dealing with disinterested students is to make reading more satisfying, by either extrinsic or intrinsic means. Extrinsic satisfaction is shown when the student finds reading tolerable because it becomes associated with highly desirable rewards. For example, a teacher might give students material rewards: "Read three books and you'll earn a star or be allowed a special privilege like extra time in the gym."

Sometimes teachers feel strongly about the need to provide extrinsic rewards for reading because they believe that students will be unwilling to cooperate under any other circumstances. We are sympathetic with teachers who must deal with recalcitrant and defeated students in this manner. Indeed, extrinsic rewards may sometimes be necessary. Following a systematic schedule of rewarding students, such as behavior modification, rather than reinforcing students in an indiscriminate fashion will improve the effectiveness of this strategy. More information on this subject can be found in *How to Use Contingency Contracting in the Classroom* (Homme, 1970) or *Help! These Kids Are Driving Me Crazy* (Carter, 1972). We hope, however, that more intrinsically satisfying reading activities can be employed as soon as possible, for we believe that reading should be its own reward.

In order to help disinterested students, we must resolve problems relating to school books, school assignments, and the school curriculum. In the following section we will describe techniques for dealing with these three problems.

Nonbook Approaches

Frequently, students with motivational problems find textbooks dull as well as difficult. They feel that these books are a pale reflection of the world they know. Accordingly, they participate grudgingly in any type of reading lesson. These students may have also learned that their textbooks are too difficult to be truly enjoyable. For these reasons, teachers should require reading materials other than just basal readers and school textbooks. Students should read more trade (library) books, paperback books, newspapers, magazines, and language-experience stories. These materials have few of the negative connotations associated with basal readers or textbooks and can appeal to a far wider range of interests and reading levels. Many of these materials can be read in a single sitting, and therefore the student can experience the joy of completing a whole book with a minimum of time and effort.

Students with severe negative feelings toward books may need to be taken out of books—at least temporarily—and provided with a variety of alternative reading material. The following are some nonbook alternatives.

Typed stories. Students whose aversion to books increases in direct proportion to their thickness may be willing to read a single story if it is printed on separate sheets of paper with wide margins and generous space between lines.

Signs. If you teach in an urban environment, tour the neighborhood and have students read as many signs as they can. Keep a record of these words and add them to a list during the school year. Use the words for word analysis and vocabulary exercises.

T-shirts. Many students wear vivid T-shirts to school, often with an abundance of words. In many areas you can arrange to have these shirts printed to your specifications. If this is not possible, wear and encourage students to wear preprinted shirts.

Display buttons. Printed buttons are widely distributed to publicize commercial products ("Buy Sassy Soda") or political candidates ("Vote for Mr. Right"), to promote various causes ("Clean Up the Bay"), or as a means of self-expression ("I am a Pisces"). Collect, wear, and display these buttons and encourage your students to contribute to the collection. If your school has its own button printer, make personalized buttons for yourself and your class.

Menus. Ask a local restaurant for used menus. If ready-made menus are not available, copy the menu from a fast-food restaurant and duplicate copies for the class. In either instance, allot students a hypothetical amount of money and ask them to select a meal with this sum. With older students, you can specify that the meal must contain a dessert, a vegetable, a beverage, or the four basic food groups.

Traffic signs. In our automobile-dominated world, traffic signs abound. Even very young children often can identify signs by their distinctive shape before they are able to actually read the words. Help students to list signs which they see to and from school. Write these words on a "Sign Chart." To add interest, arrange a scavenger contest to see which students are the first to find a particular sign such as "Yield" or "Merging Traffic."

Record jackets. Collect record jackets of popular songs. These can be placed on the chalk tray at the beginning of the reading period. Students who know a specified number of words on each jacket may take the jacket from the tray. The game continues until all the jackets have been removed. If a listening center is available with headsets, students may be allowed to listen to the records in the jackets.

Bumper stickers. Encourage students to bring in actual bumper stickers. Conduct informal discussions on the meaning of such stickers as "Support Your Right to Arm Bears" or "Back the Bottle Bill."

Bottle caps. Collect bottle caps and periodically dump the collection onto a tabletop. Students can take turns reading words on the caps. They may be allowed to keep the caps if they can read them.

Beach towels. A current trend is to have words or phrases printed on large beach towels. Periodically display a few towels on the classroom wall and encourage students to bring in their own towels. If the towel is placed near the door, students can be asked if they can read the words as they leave the class.

Candy bars, food wrappers, and cereal boxes. Instead of throwing away these wrappers and food containers, set them up on a bulletin board for students to identify words they know. If you wish to use this material in a more formal manner, give student teams a large box of assorted candy bar wrappers, food wrappers, and cereal boxes and see which team can identify the most words.

Unusual locations. Look for words in unusual locations. One soda-can manufacturer printed riddles on the bottom of cans—but on the inside. When the can had been emptied the teacher asked the students to read the riddle.

Rubber stamps. Visit your local stationery store and buy a few rubber stamps with such words as PAID and FIRST CLASS. Ask businesses to donate their old stamps. Perhaps you could order a few new stamps with current words or expressions the students are fond of. Let them use these stamps to decorate blank sheets of paper.

Label maker. Bring in a label maker and make labels for words which students can read. Allow them to request additional labels to place on their personal possessions.

These ideas and materials certainly do not constitute an entire reading program but they can provide the first steps to motivate students who resist reading from books.

Write-Less Assignments

A second motivational problem of many problem readers concerns written assignments. Too often students are asked to complete written assignments when they have finished textbook pages. Eventually, they associate reading with writing, and since they often have as much difficulty with writing as reading, their resistance to reading increases. The problem is exacerbated when teachers evaluate students' reading ability by their written performance. If the students have limited ability to express themselves in writing, this can further depress their interest in reading.

One solution to this problem is to reduce the amount of required writing a student must do after completing reading assignments. One helpful technique is to change the order of assignments. Usually, students are asked to read material and then complete a related written task. When they finish the written assignment, they are frequently allowed to do free reading. Reverse this procedure by asking students to do free reading first. When they have finished their free reading, they may complete their usual reading and writing assignments. Many students quickly realize that they can avoid the written assignments entirely by spending their time in free reading. If they do, you have gained in two ways—students are reading more and the burdensome written assignments have been reduced.

In many instances, writing assignments can be eliminated without any deleterious effects on students' reading. Furthermore, students' writing energy can be reserved for more valuable exercises in which self-expression is encouraged. If students do not take advantage of the opportunity to read, of course, they can be required to complete their usual assignments. On the other hand, conscientious reading can be a legitimate means of avoiding writing assignments. It is to be hoped that some students will read avidly and their example will encourage others.

If written assignments follow reading, the amount of writing should be kept in perspective. It is far better to read one paragraph and write a one-word answer than to read a few sentences and be asked to write a paragraph. It is even more beneficial to read several paragraphs and merely check the correct answer. These assignments, of course, may take less time for the students to complete, as writing by hand is often a tedious chore. Simply keeping students busy with writing assignments, however, exacts a high price, since it can foster negative attitudes toward reading.

Functional Reading

A third barrier to reading satisfaction involves the curriculum itself. The school's goals and the students' interests are often so divergent that it is difficult for the student to get excited about reading. The school may be trying to acquaint students with the geography of the sub-Sahara, but the student is interested only in the geography of the local minibike trail. One solution to this problem is to increase the meaningfulness of reading by using reading tasks which are related to real-world situations. Following are descriptions of several functional reading tasks which attempt to improve students' motivation.

Be sure that the materials you are using are up-to-date. If you are using a television guide, for example, students will not be interested in last year's programs. For the same reason, we dislike prepared workbook materials which simulate functional reading material. No matter how well they are prepared, they lack the touch of reality which comes from using this season's baseball cards or today's newspaper.

ACTIVITIES Collect baseball cards—they are readily available in the spring—and play baseball bingo. Distribute several cards to each student and ask questions such as "Who did the following?"

Had 25 runs batted-in for the Phillies in 1975.
Played with the Dodgers in two world series.
Has a lifetime earned run average of 3.93.
Was the Red Sox Most Valuable Player for 1979.

Questions can vary in difficulty depending on the reading ability and baseball knowledge of the students. For those with limited ability ask questions which match players and positions with teams, for example, "Which player is a catcher for the Yankees?" Students turn cards face down if they have the appropriate card. The first player with all cards face down is the winner.

Popular song titles can also be used to develop interest in reading. Take either a list of the top forty records or advertisements listing popular records and tapes and make up exercises in which students match clues to specific record titles. Clues are related semantically to the song titles. Here are a few examples:

SONG TITLES	CLUES
1. Auto American	____Clock Watcher
2. Morning Train	____Sit Down
3. Wine Light	____50 Wheels
4. Just the Two of Us	____Liquid Sun
5. Too Much Time	____AM Travel
6. I Can't Stand It	____A Pair

Movie ads can be used in a similar manner. Cut out small movie ads, paste them on 8½-by-11 sheets, and duplicate. Using the procedures for song titles, give students clues and ask them to identify the movies.

Applications and coupons of all kinds also make interesting reading and are readily available through the mail, in magazines, and in stores. Some coupons offer free material such as travel literature or refunds on purchases. Select those which meet the interests and reading levels of your students. Help students complete the forms and then follow through by mailing or submitting them. This material is particularly useful in encouraging students to read for detail.

Many states issue a state highway map. By obtaining multiple copies, you can develop exercises in which students read maps in order to solve problems. One activity is "Lost," in which individuals become disoriented and do not know where they are. They can, however, identify the communities around them. If you were using a map of the United States, for example, individuals might see Chicago to the north, Memphis to the south, Louisville to the east, and Kansas City to the west. In what city might our lost persons be located? (The answer is St. Louis.) When you use a state or city map, begin with places familiar to your students.

Another enjoyable activity is to help students read airline schedules. Then have the students respond to questions such as these:

1. What is the earliest flight out of New York City to Chicago?
2. When does this flight arrive in Chicago?
3. What is the first-class fare for this flight?
4. You would like to leave for Los Angeles immediately after school. What flight would you take?

Today's students watch a good deal of television; for the disinterested reader these long hours of viewing often come at the expense of reading. Since students are going to watch television, try to correlate reading exercises with it. Here are some activities that may appeal to your students.

Make available multiple copies of television viewing guides and have students locate the programs they intend to watch on a particular day or evening. Identify one program which is likely to be watched by most of the students. The next day, all the students who viewed the program can dictate a group account about it. Use the finished account to play Request. This is a game in which you and the students alternately ask each other questions about the program. On other weeks, watch the program yourself, select significant vocabulary terms used on the show, and discuss these words with the students. Include new meanings of familiar words and figures of speech. A related activity can be conducted with television commercials. Play a matching game in which the students must match a popular phrase in the commercials with a product or service and a brand name.

Because students often express interest in specific programs, write to the Television Reading Program (Capital Cities Communications, Inc., 4100 City Line Avenue, Philadelphia, Pennsylvania 19131) for information about scripts of popular programs. Use these scripts to supplement the regular reading program.

Set up a bookshelf with trade books about current television programs. Make these books available while these shows are still popular.

If your school owns videotape equipment, allow students to share the books they have read on closed circuit television.

Students' musical interests can be used to motivate reading. Begin by playing a current favorite on the phonograph. Let the students sing the song if they wish and react to the beat. Prepare an overhead transparency of the lyrics and point to the words as the record is being played. When students can read the lyrics in context, use a large window card—a paper with a rectangular hole—to isolate words and phrases. Duplicate copies of the song for each member of the class. First play the record and let the students follow along. Finally ask them to read the words without the benefit of the record and check word identification ability by isolating phrases and words.

Newspapers have endless motivational uses. The following ideas may appeal to your students:

Find the league standings for baseball, basketball, hockey, and football and plot the home cities of each team on a map of the United States and Canada.

Give students a single story or column from the sports page and a highlight marker. Have them highlight all the words they know.

Tell students to find the weather report and locate the highest and lowest temperatures in the United States for the previous day.

Give students a description of a house, car, motorcycle, or pet and have them search the classified section for an item which fits your specifications. For example, "I want a motorcycle for no more than $400." "I would like a used Sunfish sailboat and will pay no more than $700."

Very often students are unmotivated to read because they do not believe that reading makes any difference in their lives.

Periodically, hand out or write on the chalkboard a set of directions for the day's or week's activities. Include special events or surprises: "We've got a new collection of elephant joke books. They are on the shelf next to my desk. You may read them instead of doing your workbook assignment." "Monday only: students who read a trade book this period are excused from their written assignment." "On page 23 of your workbook, do questions 1–20 but skip all the even-numbered items."

TEAM LEARNING   To encourage active participation in these reading assignments, use a team-learning approach. (Team learning also reduces the amount of reading material you will require as each team requires only one copy of the selection.) In team learning, students are assigned to groups of two to five students; they try to reach agreement on assigned questions, either by consensus or majority vote. The team discussions precede decision making and force students to defend their views before other students. During the discussions the teacher can observe and evaluate the students' background knowledge as well as their thinking skills. When most teams have completed an assignment, answers are discussed in a group session. Team learning encourages students to cooperate with one another, which often motivates students who would be unwilling to complete a task on their own. Team-learning activities are not limited to functional reading but can be used with any reading assignment.

More elaborate team-learning procedures have been developed by the researchers at Johns Hopkins University (Slavin and DeVries, 1979). The techniques were originally developed to help students in recently desegregated classrooms work more effectively together. Research has shown that team learning can improve students' learning and enhance their interpersonal relations. In team learning students at different levels of ability help one another learn—and temper the "caste" system which often develops when students are grouped by ability.

The Johns Hopkins researchers employ three different procedures: Teams-Games-Tournaments (TGT), Student Teams-Achievement Division (STAD), and Jigsaw. Space permits only a brief description of these activities. For additional information, including a teacher's manual and an introductory filmstrip, write to Johns Hopkins Learning Project, 3505 North Charles Street, Baltimore, Maryland 21218.

In Teams-Games-Tournaments, students cooperate with fellow team members and later compete with members of other teams. Thus poor readers receive help from their teammates, contribute to the team's success, and receive valuable peer approval. Procedures for TGT are as follows:

1. Teach a reading task in the usual manner.
2. Divide the class into teams of four to five members so that teams are balanced by ability, sex, and race.
3. Provide each team with practice material on the task. If students have been taught a lesson on main ideas, they will be given material related to this skill. Team members work in pairs and help one another develop proficiency in the skill by completing the practice material.
4. At the end of the practice period, which varies in length, assign team members to tournament tables. Tournament table assignments are ho-

mogeneous. The top three students (who belong to different teams) are assigned to the first table, the next three to the second tables, and so on.

5. Give students at each table a task related to the week's practice material.

6. The student at each table who scores the highest number of points on this task earns six points for his or her team, the second highest earns four points, and the lowest player earns two points. This means that the poorest students on a team can contribute in the tournament as much as to the team's success as the best student on that team—which makes everyone a valued member. Since students are competing against their equals, their expectancy of success is greater than if they were competing against more able students.

7. Compute team scores for each tournament and establish team standings. Publicize the results in a newsletter. Continue the tournament for several weeks, keeping cumulative scores on each team's performance.

Student Teams-Achievement Division differs from TGT in that students take individual quizzes rather than participate in tournaments. Like TGT, team members help one another learn the skill, and students are compared only to students like themselves.

Jigsaw, a third approach, is more suitable for studying specific content material. In Jigsaw, a topic is divided into separate sections. Students study a particular section with members of other teams. If the class is studying the life of Abraham Lincoln, for example, some students work on his boyhood, another group on the middle years, and a third on his presidency. They then return to their own teams and teach other members the material they have learned. All students take a quiz at the end of the unit. Though students are evaluated on the basis of their individual scores, rather than team effort, team members help each other learn the material instead of relying solely on their own resources.

Publicizing Books

Functional reading activities are immensely helpful in motivating disinterested students, but at some point teachers will want to encourage students to read trade books. A good story is not only satisfying but also gives considerable more practice in reading than do functional reading activities or even basal readers. It is an accepted truism that we learn to read by reading a good deal, and full-length books fill that need.

One way to begin is to conduct a public relations campaign on behalf of books. The following are suggestions to entice the disinterested to pick up a book and read.

Read aloud to the students. Ordinarily, the books read will be those the students cannot read for themselves but which they can understand and enjoy. Occasionally, read a book that they could read on their own if they were sufficiently motivated. Instead of reading the complete book, though, read just enough to whet their appetite and then leave the book on a nearby table or bookshelf. Don't force them to read the book. Instead, allow students to select it of their own accord.

As space permits, set up a special reading area in a corner of the classroom. Furnish this area with a rug, rocking chair, pillows, bookshelves, and a generous supply of books, particularly paperbacks. Book areas can also contain cassettes and headphones for listening to stories on tape and filmstrip viewers in which students can look at filmstrips about children's literature.

When books are being ordered, allow students to assist in the selection process. Develop criteria with them, allot them a definite dollar figure, provide catalogs, and have them choose specific titles.

Establish an identification collection. Using a bulletin board and a bookshelf, display pictures or objects which can be identified with the help of a set of accompanying books. Birds, rocks, trees, fish, and cars are some appropriate categories for identification.

Build a reference shelf. In order to impress students with the value of books for locating information, set up a reference shelf with the following material: dictionary (several levels of difficulty), telephone directory, map, bus schedule, television guide, address books, newspaper, *Guiness Book of World Records* (1982), and an almanac.

Invite an author. Ask the school or local librarian if an author of children's books lives in your area, particularly one who writes books which your students might enjoy. Invite the author to speak to the class about these books and the events which inspired them.

Nothing succeeds like an engrossing
book in encouraging students to read.
(Peter P. Tobia)

Create a "good for" bulletin board in which you display books which can help students with personal interests, such as playing baseball or hockey, learning to fish, fixing bicycles, baking cookies, and so on. Books can be placed on a shelf below the bulletin board.

If students do not own books of their own, help them start a home library. Collect old boxes and have students cut off the front, leaving a sturdy bookcase. Decorate the sides with contact paper or old wallpaper samples. Distribute one or more paperback books to each student and have them take the bookshelf home. In order to make books available to students, encourage your school to operate a "Reading Is Fundamental" campaign so all students will be supplied with a book. For information about Reading is Fundamental (RIF), contact RIF at 475 L'Enfant Plaza, Washington, DC 20560.

Place a bulletin board where students frequently line up—perhaps on the classroom door—and ask them to provide advertisements in which they try to "sell" books they have enjoyed. Set aside a shelf in the room for these "For Sale" books.

Laughter not only is good medicine but also can develop healthy readers. Set up a humor shelf in the classroom, filling it with humorous stories and joke books. Periodically introduce one of these books or read a few jokes to the students. Here are a few of the titles you might consider:

Mishmash and Uncle Looey (Cone, 1968).

Oh, How Silly (Cole, 1970).

Five Men Under One Umbrella and Other Ready-to-Read Riddles (Low, 1975).

Going Bananas: Jokes for Kids (Keller, 1977).

Knock, Knocks: The Most Ever (Cole, 1976).

A Chocolate Moose for Dinner (Gwynne, 1976).

Funny Bone Dramatics (Carlson, 1974).

Students often become interested in books when they make one themselves. Directions for making a variety of exotic books are supplied in Weiss' *How to Make Your Own Books* (1974).

Tape record the initial portions of some books. Students are often motivated to finish the book on their own. An excellent collection for stimulating primary students' interest in books is *Instant Readers* (Martin, 1970). Students listen to tapes of these books while following in the text. The tapes, with musical accompaniment, help students learn the text.

Matching Students with Books

Success in motivating students to read depends on helping them find appropriate books. In this section we discuss the types of books and specific titles which might be used with reluctant readers. Space permits us to introduce just a fraction of this worthwhile material. We hope that these suggestions will demonstrate that books in print do meet a vast range of interests, needs, and reading levels.

Taking students to ballgames is possible, but you can also make available the dozens of books on baseball. If you teach in New England, for example, you will find many children rooting for the Boston Red Sox. They may enjoy *The*

Ballpark—One Day Behind the Scenes at Fenway (Jaspersohn, 1980), which describes the stadium where the Red Sox play; it relates in detail the park's operations from dawn through game time. And regardless of the team your students support, the *Baseball Encyclopedia* (Reichler, 1979) is certain to answer many of their questions. It contains the records of every major league player as well as world series and team statistics. One caution about books dealing with sports figures: players come and go with such rapidity that today's star is tomorrow's unknown. Most young students are familiar with current players but are usually unacquainted with—and uninterested in—past favorites. Purchase only books that are up-to-date.

Some of your students may not like to read but they love to draw. In *Dinosaurs* (Emberley, 1980), students are taught how to draw creatures from the past, like the Stegosaurus. They might also enjoy *Ed Emberley's Big Green Drawing Book* (1979), in which they can draw 198 different pictures with nine basic shapes; or *Ed Emberley's Great Thumbprint Drawing Book* (1977) in which fingerprints provide the basis for a variety of pictures.

The creation of homemade first readers is also a worthwhile undertaking (Steinberg, 1976). Write stories for beginning students, using their names, their current heroes, and the vocabulary of their basal reading series. Each day add new stories to the collection. Staple the stories together or help students put pages in a book which they can bind. Use a language-experience approach to teach the vocabulary so that students will have learned many of the words before the introduction of the books.

Pop-up-books (Random House) can motivate primary students who have seldom been read to and have not experienced the joy of books. The movable pages in these books are activated by pulling tabs and turning wheels. Animated story characters generate interest without the need to actually read the books. You can read for students while they operate the pages. The books, of course, are fragile and will not tolerate excessive abuse. Teach students to manipulate the books with care and supervise their use.

Would your students like to present a puppet show? In *How to Have Fun Making Puppets* (1974) the author explains construction procedures for easy or elaborate puppets and gives tips on staging puppet shows. Books like this give students an opportunity to follow directions, an important reading skill.

Many students are enthralled with anything that rolls on wheels, and numerous books are available to satisfy this interest. Books like *Wheels* (Radlauer, 1976) are especially appropriate as they are short, well illustrated in full color, and contain a text of between two and four lines on each page written at a low-primary reading level. At a slightly more difficult reading level but with the same colorful illustrations are books like *Motorcycles* (Radlauer, 1967), one of a set of books about cars, cycles, horses, and dune buggies.

For students who prefer flying, show them the *Paper Airplane Book* (Simon, 1976), in which a detailed account about how to construct paper gliders is provided. If students cannot read the entire text, read portions to them. Regardless of who does the reading, this is an opportunity to demonstrate the usefulness of books. This book also deserves a place on your "how to" book display.

Students are often intrigued by magic tricks. *Magic Secrets* (Wyler and Ames, 1967) is written at a primary level, but it can help students become adept at performing magic feats.

Some disinterested students would rather work with their hands than read. *Model Cars and Trucks and How to Build Them* (Weiss, 1974) allows them to do both. Here they are introduced to building model cars and trucks with simple tools. A similar book is *How to Build a Better Mousetrap Car . . .* (Renner, 1977).

Learning to write in code also appeals to many students who wish to communicate secretly with their friends. The following books contain simple to complex codes:

> *Secrets with Ciphers and Codes* (Rothman and Tremain, 1969).
> *Codes and Secret Writing* (Zim, 1948).
> *Codes and Ciphers—Secret Writing Through the Ages* (Laffin, 1964).
> *The Kids' Code and Cipher Book* (Gordon, 1981).
> *How to Write Codes and Send Secret Messages* (Peterson, 1970).

Students are often asked to learn social studies or science by reading fact-filled textbooks. As an antidote to possible dullness, introduce them to trade books involving historical fiction. These books help students to see behind dates and places, to identify with historical figures, and to experience the emotions of the times. If students are studying the Revolutionary War, for example, the conflicts and issues of that period can come alive if viewed from a human perspective. The following books, written at a variety of reading levels deal with the Revolutionary War:

> *Johnny Tremain* (Forbes, 1943). A handicapped boy aids the cause of the revolution.
> *Sam the Minuteman* (Benchley, 1969). The opening battle of the Revolutionary War.
> *Jack Jouett's Ride* (Haley, 1973). Thomas Jefferson is warned that the British are pursuing him.
> *Deborah Sampson* (Felton, 1976). A woman soldier in the war.
> *The Scarlet Badge* (Hays, 1963). Other perspectives on the war.
> *My Brother Sam Is Dead* (Collier and Collier, 1974). Family conflicts over the war.
> *Six Silver Spoons* (Quackenbush, 1971). Paul Revere's ride; for the young reader.

Any library for disinterested (and discouraged) readers should include a number of high-interest, low-vocabulary books. These books meet the need of students whose interests far exceed their reading ability or who need many books at their independent level if they are to find reading a satisfying experience. If books are part of a series, select, if possible, specific titles rather than the entire collection since the quality of books can vary.

Resources for Locating Books

The following materials can help you find books of all kinds for disinterested students.

The New Hooked on Books (Fader, 1977).

Read for Your Life (Palmer, 1974).

How 2 Gerbils, 20 Goldfish, 200 Games, 2000 Books and I Taught Them How to Read (Daniels, 1971).

Good Reading for Poor Readers (Spache, 1974).

Easy Reading Book Series and Periodicals for Less Able Readers (Graves *et al.*, 1979).

"Children's Books for the Remedial Reading Laboratory" (Adams, 1976).

Two other sources might also be consulted even though they contain books not chosen specifically for the needs of the disinterested reader. They can serve, however, to acquaint you with new material which may be of interest to your students. Each October issue of *The Reading Teacher* contains "Children's Choices," a collection of new fiction and nonfiction trade books chosen annually by school students. In addition to this annual list, every issue contains reviews of current trade books and thus can be a valuable resource. Subscriptions can be ordered by writing to the International Reading Association, 100 Barksdale Road, Newark, Delaware 19711. Another good listing is the periodical *Bulletin of the Center for Children's Books*, published by the University of Chicago Press. Subscriptions can be obtained by writing to the *Bulletin* at the University of Chicago Press, 5801 Ellis Avenue, Chicago, Illinois 60637.

Activities to Encourage Reading

The following activities can help bring students and books together.

Sustained silent reading, also known as uninterrupted SSR, or the uninterrupted reading period, is a motivational device in which students read for a set amount of time each day without interruption, and without written assignments or book reports. The rules for sustained silent reading are simple: (1) students should have sufficient material to read during the allotted time (this is not the time to hunt up a book or walk to and from the library corner); (2) they read for the entire period. According to the McCrackens (1978), the activity works best if the teacher reads as well. They concluded that the most important factor to encourage reading was the teacher's behavior. If the teacher read diligently, so did the students. If the teacher shared a book with the class, the students followed the example.

If you want to improve students' motivation, do not require written book reports. The most you should expect of reluctant readers is to keep a record of the books they have read. This will help them appreciate the extent of their reading. Books can be recorded on index cards and kept in the teacher's file box or recorded informally; in one class the teacher distributed sheets filled with cars and students wrote the titles of completed books over the cars and then colored them.

Often students can be enticed to read a book if they are told that you would like their opinion about it. If you are sincere, periodically ask them to review a book for you—no written reports; simply a brief oral reaction. Questions such as "What did you think of the book?" "To whom would you recommend it?" "Do you think _____ might like it?" would be appropriate to ask at this time.

Telling a story by using a flannel board and felt figures (Ross, 1973) is another way to motivate students. Ask student volunteers, using the same felt characters, to tell the same story or another one. Transcribe the story as the students dictate but limit the account to one page, which eliminates the tendency of children to ramble. When the dictation is completed, read it to the students and then reread it with them. Subsequent steps would depend on the needs of the readers. The students could simply read the account and take it home, place it in a group or individual book, tape-record it, or underline words from it and study them in isolation.

"Cooks" who teach reading may find *Welcome to the Food for Thought Restaurant* (Coutu and Karmozyn, n.d.) a valuable resource for teaching reading through recipes. This booklet provides a detailed and inspiring account of two third-grade teachers who sought to improve students' reading ability, particularly their ability to follow directions. The reading material consists of directions for preparing meals and recipes for cooking specific dishes. A year-long project, the students bought food and prepared a series of meals throughout the school year. The following recipe, Friendly Dog Salad (Figure 9-1), was their first attempt.

Figure 9-1 Friendly Dog Salad

FRIENDLY DOG SALAD

Ingredients: 1 lettuce leaf
1 canned pear half
1 canned prune
2 canned mandarin orange segments
1 maraschino cherry
1 raisin

Directions:
1. Wash 1 lettuce leaf and pat dry with paper towel. Place on salad plate.
2. Place 1 pear half cut side down on the lettuce leaf.
3. Cut the prune lengthwise in half with a knife and take out the pit. Place one of the prune halves at the large end of the pear half for the ear.
4. Scoop out a tiny hole in the pear half for the eye with a teaspoon. Place one raisin in the hole.
5. Cut the maraschino cherry in half. Place one half at the top of the narrow end of the pear half for the nose.
6. Use the mandarin orange segments for the collar.

Many books on reading methods contain ideas for encouraging independent reading. Browse through them for ideas that suit your particular situation. *How to Teach Reading* (Otto *et al.,* 1979) contains an especially fine collection in Chapter 11, "Individualizing Reading Instruction."

The Role of Games

Games are sometimes suggested as worthwhile motivators for the following reasons:

1. Games appeal to students' competitive nature and thereby distract them from their concern about their inadequate reading ability. For example, students who might balk at attempting to identify a word may persevere when competing against their classmates.
2. Games can make drill more enjoyable. Children often need considerable repetition in order to retain vocabulary and skills. Because drill is often dull work, conducting it in a game format can make it less arduous.
3. Games can help teachers evaluate students' performance. By observing students' behavior in a game, teachers can assess their ability to identify words or apply particular skills. In one classroom a student repeatedly complained that she couldn't remember words. Then she trounced her classmates and the teacher in a variation of Concentration. The game was a better test of her memory than any formal instrument.

Games, however, have a number of shortcomings:

1. Games don't teach. If students don't know a word or a skill, they can spend considerable time in a game and never learn it.
2. Games often require students to encode (process speech to print) rather than decode (process print to speech). In Quizmo, for example, students are given bingolike cards and place markers on letters which match words read by the teacher. If the teacher reads the word *tiger,* for example, the student would place a marker on the *t.* In this game the stimulus is oral, whereas in reading the stimulus is written. Thus, students are spelling and not reading.
3. Games often take too long to complete. It may be more efficient to accomplish an objective by direct instruction. It is distressing to see twenty minutes being used to play a game when the same objective could be accomplished in a five-minute exercise.
4. Games often present words or skills in isolation, but students may really need opportunities to apply the skills they have learned in meaningful reading.
5. Games operate with fixed rules which all students are expected to follow. Rigid rules, however, represent the antithesis of diagnostic teaching, for in teaching we continually change the "rules" in order to meet students' needs.

Before using reading games, ask yourself the following questions:

1. Is the game likely to improve students' motivation or will they be just as motivated without it?

2. Do the students possess the knowledge and skill to participate mean-
   ingfully in the game or are they destined to always lose a particular
   game—not a very motivating thought.
3. Do the benefits of the game justify the time necessary to play it?
4. To what extent is the game like reading itself? Does it employ decoding
   or encoding? Does it require the students to apply skills in context or
   practice them in isolation?
5. Can the rules of the game be changed periodically to take into account
   students' changing needs?

Our own preference is to minimize the role of prepared games. Balance
the use of prepared games, both the teachermade and commercial variety, with
ad hoc "paper plate" games created on the spot and disposed of at the conclusion
of the lesson. Suppose, for example, you were working on vocabulary meanings
and students were finding the activity uninteresting. You might quickly devise
the game Fake It. That is, you write a sentence on the board and underline a
vocabulary term from the lesson. Then you take three index cards and write the
meaning of the underlined word on one of them. The other two cards are left
blank. Three students pick the cards from the teacher. The student with the
definition states it, and the other students invent plausible meanings. (These
students may or may not know the meaning of the original word themselves.)
The group attempts to determine which person stated the real definition. Depending on the students' responses to the activity, the rules can be modified.

THE DISCOURAGED READER

Self-Concept

Students' reading behavior is regulated by their image of themselves as
readers. If students consider themselves disabled, they will perform accordingly.
Their reasoning might go something like this: "Disabled readers lose in the
game of reading. I am a disabled reader. Therefore, I will lose if I play the
game." Since one seldom plays a game in which there is no hope of winning, they
cease to play.

Readers' low self-concept also leads them to deprecate their positive
reading behavior and be unduly swayed by their errors. This effect is frequently
seen when students read a passage aloud. They may read the first few sentences
flawlessly, but instead of thinking that they are improving, they may regard their
good performance as a matter of luck rather than skill. Soon they make a few
miscues. These misreadings remind them that they are, after all, poor readers.
Rapidly, their confidence drains away and they stumble through the remainder
of the text, hurrying to finish like a person running through a punishing
gauntlet.

This self-concept, which exerts such a powerful influence on behavior, is
like an identity or a name. Once we obtain a name we hang on to it dearly, for we
would rather maintain a secure though destructive self-image than be left in

doubt about who or what we really are. Like shoes, we often prefer the old worn-out pair rather than new, more protective footwear.

One implication of our need for security is that our self-concept changes slowly, if at all. We should not think, for example, that a few words of praise or a pat on the back will change discouraged students into confident readers. Students may even reject praise which is inconsistent with their self-image.

Though self-concept is resistant to change, we must make the attempt to modify it. Students will participate actively and willingly in reading activities and will read extensively on their own only if they believe they are capable of succeeding. In this section we make several suggestions to help students develop faith in their ability to read. These suggestions can be employed concurrently with activities to develop interest in reading.

Students' low self-esteem can discourage teachers as well. It is difficult to listen to students who mumble about their "dumb" reading behavior day after day without being influenced by their laments. Because you may need many fresh ideas to renew your spirit as well as to encourage your students, we suggest that you read *100 Ways to Enhance Self-Concept in the Classroom* (Canfield and Wells, 1976).

Activities to Aid Self-Concept

One way to improve quickly a child's self-concept is to teach a skill which has none of the negative associations connected with reading. Card games such as those described in *Deal Me In* (Golick, 1973) are excellent activities to bolster low self-concepts. Knots, magic tricks, or scientific experiments are also useful. Success in these new activities can often help strengthen students' confidence in their ability to learn. At the same time it enables you to build trust. As students learn to trust you, they will be more willing to follow your suggestions and participate in reading lessons, to take risks necessary for learning, and to read extensively on their own.

Encourage students whenever possible by showing them that you care about their progress. Encouragement is ". . . an action which conveys to the child that the teacher respects, trusts and believes in him and that his present lack of skills in no way diminishes his value as a person" (Dreikurs *et al.,* 1971, p. 66). Here are some ways to encourage students.

Recognize students' efforts with comments like "You have been trying hard" or "You have worked a long time on this page."

Distinguish between praise and encouragement. Encouragement is expressed while the student is struggling to succeed. "Keep going . . . you are making progress" are words of encouragement. Praise, on the other hand, occurs when the task is completed. Praise, unfortunately, is sometimes misunderstood by students. The child may associate praise with acceptance. If you praise me, you accept me. If you criticize me, you reject me. Furthermore, students may feel under pressure to win your continued acceptance. They realize that what you give today in praise can be withdrawn tomorrow through criticism. This may leave them in a state of anxiety. As a result, students may resist praise rather than to have their hopes alternately raised and dashed by praise and criticism.

Reimer (1967) has listed several comments to use in encouraging students:

You have improved in _____.
You can help us by _____.
Let's try together _____.
We think you can _____.
I am sure that you can straighten this out.

When you do offer praise, comment objectively on the students' performance rather than make global remarks. Say "You read the whole page with only two mistakes" instead of "You did a good job today." This helps the students themselves to conclude that they did a good job.

It is difficult to convince some students that they are capable of improvement after years of failure. Even when they read well, they may reject their performance as a sign of progress because they are reading easy material. Therefore, it's helpful to collect information about their performance over an extended period of time in order to change their self-image. Records enable the students to see their accomplishments—how many books read, skills completed, words learned—and how the level of difficulty has increased since instruction was begun. In reviewing a student's record, avoid evaluative statements such as "Your record shows that you're doing good work," but say "You read twenty-six books this year." Let students draw their own conclusions.

Another way of encouraging students is to tailor your standards to fit their needs. When students are discouraged, lower your requirements, or they may balk at participating at all. (One measure of progress in working with discouraged students is their willingness to return for instruction with at least as much motivation as they brought to the previous lesson.) You need not, for example, correct every error for a student to progress. When a student is reading aloud, it's probably best to make no comments at first about miscues unless the student requests help or hesitates. Later, call attention only to miscues which affect comprehension. Finally, when the student's self-image has improved, you can move on to less important miscues.

Few rewards are more satisfying than working hard on a task and seeing an improvement in one's own ability. For students to experience this feeling they may need to practice something many times, just as a musician repeatedly rehearses a piece of music. For example, students may be asked to participate in reading a play to an audience. This is an excellent opportunity for them to read the lines several times and receive helpful feedback from the teacher. When they actually do read to the audience their performance should reflect their improved ability, and even more important, they will have gained confidence in themselves.

An important facet of instruction teachers shouldn't overlook is helping students take responsibility for their own learning. Too often poor readers live in a continual state of dependency. Like invalids, they are constantly helped to complete a task. This well-intentioned help can make them more rather than less dependent. To counter this tendency, distinguish between your responsibilities as a teacher and the students' obligations. In word identification, for example, a teacher must teach strategies for dealing with unknown words but students must apply them. In a language-experience approach, the teacher must take dictation from the students, but they must look up words in previous stories to help recall them.

Self-respect comes not only from helping oneself but also from assisting others. One useful strategy is to assign older students to read to younger ones. Even primary students can read to kindergarteners. Help students select appropriate material and practice it thoroughly. The opportunity to contribute to someone else's education can also help students improve their own reading.

Modifying Common School Practices

In addition to these suggestions, we can propose three changes in school practices that can help to enhance a student's self-concept. They deal with oral reading, grouping, and report cards.

Round-robin oral reading, in which students take turns, is often a humiliating experience for the struggling readers. Other pupils may make disparaging remarks about their performances, continually correct errors, and tell them unknown words before they have a chance to work out identification for themselves. It is little wonder that some students dislike reading and have low opinions of themselves as readers. It is important, therefore, to eliminate this practice and replace it with more positive experiences. One alternative, when oral reading is warranted, is to ask students to read privately to you. Second, students should always read the material silently before reading aloud. Third, insist that they practice the material sufficiently before reading in a group. It is assumed, of course, that they are reading material at their instructional level. Finally, forbid students to criticize other students' reading.

In ability grouping students often take on the characteristics of the reading group to which they have been assigned. If they belong to the "low group," they may act out their role as low performers. Less may be expected of them because of their placement. To counter this tendency, organize groups on other bases than simple ability. Team-learning groups permit students of low ability to mix with other students. Students can be invited to sit in with higher groups as an invited guest as they begin to make progress. Individualized reading projects allow students to read according to their interests and bring them into contact with other students with similar interests. A variety of groupings helps to break down the walls which segregate disabled readers from their peers.

Grading practices, particularly report cards, present a third challenge for the teacher who wishes to improve students' self-esteem. Students who have been told that they are improving are often disappointed when they find unsatisfactory grades on their report cards, which compare them to peers or to arbitrary standards.

At the school or system level one solution is to add descriptive information to the report card. Explain students' standings as they relate to grade-level standards, but also indicate the students' progress in reaching those standards. One way to do this is to indicate the level at which the students are reading and whether they are making satisfactory growth at that level. Another alternative is to divide each grade level into at least four sections so that the report will indicate the unit the students are reading. The mark 3 2/4, for example, means that the student is reading the second of four units in the third-grade basal text. In this manner, a student's report card would be more likely to show progress from one reporting period to the next.

Encourage the school or system to supplement the formal report card with parent-teacher conferences. Grades reflect only a narrow aspect of students' performance and often fail to indicate small improvements in reading. A face-to-face meeting with parents can help provide a more balanced and more encouraging description of a student's behavior. To maximize the benefits for the students, invite them to the conferences if they are mature enough to participate.

In this section we have argued that some students resist reading because they doubt their own ability to learn. Erasing this doubt, then, becomes just as important as teaching the skills of reading. You can stimulate the necessary self-confidence by encouraging students' efforts, not merely praising their accomplishments. We have also offered suggestions for modifying school practices in oral reading, grouping, and grading.

SUMMARY

Teaching reading demands more than instruction in cognitive skills. It requires dealing with students' feelings, attitudes, and interests. In this chapter we looked at two types of students whose negative feelings can impede their reading growth—the disinterested and the discouraged. For disinterested students who can read but do not like to, we suggested that you begin with nontraditional reading material such as buttons and beach towels, deemphasize writing assignments, and use functional reading selections. We described how to use everyday materials from airline schedules to television guides, listed numerous ways to whet students' appetites for reading books, and pointed out that your task was to match students with appropriate trade books. We described several off-beat books which might appeal to students with particular interests. Finally, we talked about discouraged readers who perform according to their self-perceptions and need to believe they can learn to read. We listed several techniques for helping these students and stressed the importance of encouraging rather than merely praising them.

RELATED ACTIVITIES

1. Design and implement a behavior modification schedule to increase students' recreational reading.
2. Conduct and evaluate an uninterrupted sustained silent reading program.
3. Develop a functional reading activity and assign students to complete the activity by means of a team-learning approach.
4. Read the article "Teacher Praise: A Functional Analysis" by Jere Brophy in the *Review of Educational Research*, 5, no. 1 (Spring 1981), 5–32. Then observe teachers' use of praise

in a corrective-remedial setting. Compare Brophy's observations with your own. What are the implications for improving the effectiveness of praise?

5. With the help of teachers, administrators, and athletic leaders, identify coaches of school and community teams who have been recognized for their ability to motivate their players. Observe these coaches during a game and analyze their motivational strategies. To what extent are these strategies worthwhile? Can they be applied to students with reading problems? How?

6. Observe classes for students who are having difficulty in learning. Record the teacher's comments and behavior which may affect students' self-concept as learners. Show how teaching procedures in these settings could be modified to enhance students' self-esteem.

RELATED READINGS

ALLINGTON, RICHARD L., AND MICHAEL STRANGE. "The Problem with Reading Games." *Reading Teacher,* 31, no. 3 (Dec. 1977), 272–74.

BEANE, JAMES A., RICHARD P. LIPKA, AND JOAN W. LUDEWIG. "Synthesis of Research on Self-Concept." *Educational Leadership,* 38, no. 1 (Oct. 1980), 84–89.

GORDON, THOMAS. *Teacher Effectiveness Training.* New York: McKay, 1977.

GAMBRELL, LINDA B. "Getting Started with Sustained Silent Reading." *Reading Teacher,* 32, no. 3 (Dec. 1978), 328–31.

NATCHEZ, GLADYS. *Gideon: A Boy Who Hates Learning in School.* New York: Basic Books, 1975.

REFERENCES

ADAMS, IRENE. "Children's Books for the Remedial Reading Laboratory." *The Reading Teacher,* 30, no. 3 (Dec. 1976), 266–70.

BENCHLEY, NATHANIEL. *Sam the Minuteman.* New York: Harper & Row, 1969.

CANFIELD, JACK, AND HAROLD C. WELLS. *100 Ways to Enhance Self-Concept in the Classroom: A Handbook for Teachers and Parents.* Englewood Cliffs, N.J.: Prentice-Hall, 1976.

CARLSON, BERNICE W. *Funny Bone Dramatics.* Nashville, Tenn.: Abingdon, 1974.

CARTER, RONALD D. *Help! These Kids Are Driving Me Crazy.* Champaign, Ill.: Research Press, 1972.

CHOMSKY, NOAM. "Phonology and Reading." In *Basic Studies on Reading.* Harry Levin and Joanna P. Williams, eds. New York: Basic Books, 1970.

COLE, WILLIAM. *Knock Knocks: The Most Ever.* New York: Watts, 1976.

———. *Oh, How Silly.* New York: Viking, 1970.

COLLIER, JAMES L., AND CHRISTOPHER COLLIER. *My Brother Sam Is Dead.* New York: Four Winds, 1974.

CONE, MOLLY. *Mishmash and Uncle Looey.* Boston: Houghton-Mifflin, 1968.

COUTU, LINDA, AND MIKE KARMOZYN. *Welcome to the Food for Thought Restaurant.* Burrillville, R.I.: Mimeo, n.d.

DANIELS, STEVEN. *How 2 Gerbils, 20 Goldfish, 200 Games, 2000 Books and I Taught Them How to Read.* Philadelphia: Westminster, 1970.

DREIKURS, RUDOLF, BERNICE B. GRUNWALD, AND FLOYD C. PEPPER. *Maintaining Sanity in the Classroom: Illustrated Teaching Techniques.* New York: Harper & Row, 1971.

EMBERLEY, ED. *Ed Emberley's Big Green Drawing Book.* Boston: Little, Brown, 1979.

———. *Ed Emberley's Great Thumbprint Drawing Book.* Boston: Little, Brown, 1977.

EMBERLEY, MICHAEL. *Dinosaurs! A Drawing Book.* Boston: Little, Brown, 1977.

FADER, DANIEL. *The New Hooked on Books.* New York: Putnam's, 1977.

FELTON, HAROLD W. *Deborah Sampson: Soldier of the Revolution.* New York: Dodd, Mead, 1976.

FORBES, ESTHER. *Johnny Tremain*. Boston: Houghton-Mifflin, 1943.

GOLICK, MARGIE. *Deal Me In*. New York: Jeffrey Norton, 1973.

GORDON, NANCY. *The Kids' Code and Cipher Book*. New York: Holt, Rinehart & Winston, 1981.

GRAVES, MICHAEL F., JUDITH A. BEOTTCHER, AND RANDALL A. RYDER. *Easy Reading Book Series and Periodicals for Less Able Readers*. Newark, Del.: International Reading Association, 1979.

Guiness Book of World Records. New York: Sterling Publ. Co., 1982.

GWYNNE, FRED. *A Chocolate Moose for Dinner*. New York: Dutton, 1976.

HALEY, GAIL. *Jack Jouett's Ride*. New York: Viking, 1973.

HAYS, WILMA P. *The Scarlet Badge*. New York: Holt, Rinehart & Winston, 1963.

HOMME, LLOYD. *How to Use Contingency Contracting in the Classroom*. Champaign, Ill.: Research Press, 1969.

How to Have Fun Making Puppets. Mankato, Minn.: Creative Education Society, 1974.

JASPERSOHN, WILLIAM G. P. *The Ballpark—One Day Behind the Scenes at a Major League Game*. Boston: Little, Brown, 1980.

KELLER, CHARLES. *Going Bananas: Jokes for Kids*. Englewood Cliffs, N.J.: Prentice-Hall, 1977.

LAFFIN, JOHN. *Codes and Ciphers—Secret Writing Through the Ages*. New York: Abelard-Schuman, 1964.

LOW, JOSEPH. *Five Men Under One Umbrella and Other Ready-to-Read Riddles*. New York: Macmillan, 1975.

McCRACKEN, ROBERT A., AND MARLENE J. McCRACKEN. "Modeling Is the Key to Sustained Silent Reading." *The Reading Teacher*, 31, no. 4 (Jan. 1978), 406–408.

MARTIN, BILL, JR. *Instant Readers* (Series). New York: Holt, Rinehart & Winston, 1970 .

OTTO, WAYNE, ROBERT T. RUDE, AND DIXIE LEE SPIEGEL. *How to Teach Reading*. Boston: Addison-Wesley, 1979.

PALMER, JULIA R. *Read for Your Life*. Metuchen, N.J.: Scarecrow, 1974.

PETERSON, JOHN. *How to Write Codes and Send Secret Messages*. New York: Four Winds, 1970.

QUACKENBUSH, ROBERT. *Six Silver Spoons*. New York: Harper & Row, 1971.

RADLAUER, ED. *Motorcycles*. Glendale, Calif.: Bowmar Publishing, 1967.

———. *Wheels*. Glendale, Calif.: Bowmar Publishing, 1976.

REICHLER, JOSEPH L., ED. *The Baseball Encyclopedia*. New York: Macmillan, 1979.

REIMER, CLINT. "Some Words of Encouragement." In *Study Group Leader's Manual* by Vicki Soltz. Chicago: Alfred Adler Institute, 1967.

RENNER, AL. G. *How to Build a Better Mousetrap Car and Other Experimental Science Fun*. New York: Dodd, Mead, 1977.

ROSS, RAMON, R. "Frannie and Frank and the Flannelboard." *The Reading Teacher*, 27, no. 1 (Oct. 1973), 43–47.

ROTHMAN, JOEL, AND RUTHVEN TREMAIN. *Secrets with Ciphers and Codes*. New York: Macmillan, 1969.

SIMON, SEYMOUR. *The Paper Airplane Book*. New York: Penguin, 1976.

SLAVIN, ROBERT E., AND DAVID L. DEVRIES. "Learning in Teams." In *Educational Environments and Effects*. Herbert J. Walberg, ed. Berkeley, Calif.: McCutchan Pub. Co., 1979.

SPACHE, GEORGE D. *Good Reading for Poor Readers*. Champaign, Ill.: Garrard Pub. Co., 1974.

STEINBERG, ZIM. "Batman Books: Homemade First Readers." *The Reading Teacher*, 29, no. 7 (Apr. 1976), 676–82.

SUTHERLAND, ZENA, ED. *Bulletin of the Center for Children's Books*. Chicago: University of Chicago Press.

WEISS, HARVEY. *How to Make Your Own Books*. New York: Thomas Y. Crowell, 1974.

———. *Model Cars and Trucks and How to Build Them*. New York: Thomas Y. Crowell, 1974.

WYLER, ROSE, AND GERALD AMES. *Magic Secrets*. New York: Harper & Row, 1967.

ZIM, HERBERT S. *Codes and Secret Writing*. New York: Morrow, 1948.

10

INDIVIDUALIZED EDUCATIONAL PLANS AND CASE STUDIES

After reading this chapter, you should be able to

1. Explain how reports can be used by school personnel, parents, and individuals in referral agencies.
2. List ten guidelines to follow when writing reports for students with reading problems.
3. Describe the purposes and guidelines for writing individualized educational plans and case studies.
4. Identify the similarities and differences of the two types of reading reports: individual educational plans and case studies.

Each day, local, state, and federal regulations are demanding more time and effort from school personnel, resulting in a voluminous amount of paperwork by all professionals who service students with physical or educational handicaps. Today, teachers who work with children having reading difficulties should expect to spend at least a portion of their time completing forms and writing reports. Gone are the days when the reading teacher simply asked classroom teachers to "send me your students who can't read." Now documentation is needed to substantiate which students are most in need of reading instruction, to dismiss students from programs, and to verify that students are making progress. This chapter attempts to convince teachers that documenting their efforts and writing reports isn't nearly as difficult as it may first appear.

THE AUDIENCES FOR REPORTS

One of the first questions teachers must ask when writing reports is "Who am I writing this report for?" A natural audience would be other teachers in the school(s), and sometimes parents ask for a report of their child's reading ability or progress. Obviously, a report sent home to parents will differ in substance and style from one sent to a teacher down the hall. Occasionally, a pediatrician or a neurologist may solicit a report. A clearly written report will help the child as well as the professional requesting the information.

Teachers should understand that the type of report may vary, and for this reason it is important to look at several different documents.

The reading teacher works with parents and other professionals in devising a plan for instruction.

School Reports

Ms. Good had been sending three of her students to the reading special-ist's room for help three times a week. After several months, however, the reading teacher began to feel that there was little correlation of instruction between her efforts and Ms. Good's. The specialist had undoubtedly given an assortment of tests and had developed some ideas about the students' abilities. Yet Ms. Good seemed to be insensitive to the kinds of instruction these students really needed. How can reading teachers offer suggestions without offending the classroom teachers and all of the other Ms. Goods they must work with?

Put yourself in the specialist's position. One of your first steps should be to ask yourself whether you and the Ms. Goods of your system are able to communicate freely with one another. Simply stated, can the two of you sit down and talk professionally without either of you feeling intimidated or threatened? If not, that's your first hurdle. Unless you have good rapport with other teach-ers, written reports will be cooly received at best, and at worst, discarded in the corner wastebasket. The key word is *communication*. If you already have a good working relationship with your coworkers, you're halfway there. If interpersonal problems exist between you and the staff, they must be overcome. Solving com-munications problems is complex and really beyond the scope of this book, but we can suggest three excellent resource books for anyone who needs to under-stand more about working with adults:

> *On Becoming a Person* (Rogers, 1961).
> *Toward a Psychology of Being* (Maslow, 1962).
> *Parent Effectiveness Training* (Gordon, 1970).

These books are available in paperback editions and would be worthwhile addi-tions to any professional library.

Meanwhile, back to our situation at hand. If you and Ms. Good are on speaking terms, now is the time to approach her—in a nonthreatening fashion—and explore how the two of you might work more closely together. Whatever you do, don't open your discussion with a question such as "How is Robert doing on his short vowels?" Ms. Good (1) may not know what a short vowel is, (2) hasn't covered that skill yet since it's not introduced in the basal reader workbook for another three weeks, or (3) couldn't care less. A more palatable beginning might be a comment such as

> Robert has been doing so well these past two weeks. He's finally seeming to catch on to what we're doing. "Brenda [Ms Good], if I send some work back to the room with Robert, could you see that he works on it in his spare time and brings it with him the next time he comes to reading class?"

If Ms. Good consents, you're on the right track. If she doesn't under-stand the intricacies of teaching short vowels, she won't be placed on the defen-sive since you will be doing the teaching. And if she hasn't covered that skill in class yet, Robert will have a chance to show all his friends how smart he really is once he returns from your room. If Ms. Good couldn't care less, maybe your conscientiousness will have a positive effect and encourage her to become more involved with Robert and his needs.

It should be obvious that working with teachers requires sensitivity as well as perseverance. In some instances, you may be invited into a teacher's classroom to help instruct students learning a specific skill. In other situations, your presence may be threatening to the teacher. You need to be sensitive to how you are perceived by other teachers. Usually, a relaxed, easygoing style will win the confidence of your coworkers. Given enough time, even the most insecure teachers will see that you are there to help them, not to evaluate their effectiveness.

One way to gain the confidence of fellow teachers and to open the channels of communication is to send bimonthly written reports to the classroom teachers of each of your students (see Figure 10-1). These reports briefly describe your teaching efforts and implicitly reveal that you want to cooperate with other teachers in the building.

Such reports provide an opportunity for reading teachers to summarize their instructional efforts and to comment on the overall behavior of the child. Classroom teachers appreciate the form because of its brevity and because it tells them what type of instruction their students have been receiving. In short, reports

Figure 10-1 Remedial Reading Bimonthly Report

Name _____

Instructional Date _____

Instructional Efforts:

   Word Attack _____

   _____

   _____

   Comprehension _____

   _____

   _____

   General Behavior _____

   _____

such as these do much to insure that classroom and reading teachers work toward the same objectives. Under such an arrangement, students with reading problems are apt to make quick progress.

Parental Reports

Today, the courts of the country have guaranteed parents access to their children's school records. This is as it should be. Parents need to know how their children perform in school. At one time, the only report available to parents was the report card. Unfortunately, report cards are usually so vague that they provide little guidance for parents who are concerned that their child is receiving the best possible instruction, instruction in line with diagnosed needs.

We have seen report cards so nondescriptive that teachers are hard-pressed to describe the meaning of the subsections. On the other hand, there are report cards so inclusive that they boggle the minds of both teachers and par-

Figure 10-2   An Example of a Chapter I Report Card

SUNNYTOWN SCHOOL DEPARTMENT

E.S.E.A.

CHAPTER I

Name _____   Date _____

School _____   Teacher _____

Note to Parents:

This school year your child has been selected to receive small group instruction to expand his/her background in decoding, comprehension, listening, and writing. This instruction is provided in addition to the child's regular classroom instruction in reading.

Please sign and return this report to the regular classroom teacher with the report card. Thank you.

The Remedial Reading Program is designed to supplement your child's classroom reading activities. Since Remedial Reading instruction is based on *reading level* rather than *grade level*, please be aware that there may be a difference between this report and the reading mark on your child's report card.

Reading Level _____

	Making Satisfactory Progress		Needs More Help	
	2nd Qtr	4th Qtr	2nd Qtr	4th Qtr
Decoding:				
1. Sight Words				
2. Phonics				
3. Structural Analysis				
Comprehension:				
1. Main Idea				
2. Details				
3. Sequence				
4. Following Directions				
5. Drawing Conclusions				
Listening:				
1. Following Teacher's Directions				
2. Recalls Information				
Writing:				
1. Sentence Structure				
2. Capitalization, Punctuation, etc.				

	Excellent		Good		Fair	
	2nd Qtr	4th Qtr	2nd Qtr	4th Qtr	2nd Qtr	4th Qtr
Observations:						
1. Motivation to Read						
2. Concentration and Attention						
3. Independent Work Habits						
4. Attitude Toward Reading Program						

Comments:

Second Quarter _____

_____

_____

Fourth Quarter _____

_____

_____

Parent Signature _____

ents. At one extreme are found relatively meaningless categories such as "Attacks New Words" or "Oral Reading." On these types of report cards, students frequently receive a letter grade for their efforts (for example, H = honors, N = needs help, or U = unsatisfactory). The other extreme are elaborate checklists which were sent home with "mastered" or "not mastered" columns checked after each skill. Parents were forced to wade through educational jargon only a doctor in linguistics could understand. Can you imagine a layperson trying to understand what "knows schwa sound in an unaccented syllable" means? Or how many parents understand terms such as *dipthongs* or *digraphs?* Report cards using such terms are too detailed and hence incomprehensible to those outside of the educational establishment.

We hope that a compromise can be reached whereby enough information is provided to assure parents that teachers are doing their best; but at the same time educators need to be sensitive to parents' limited understanding of educational jargon. One report that is used satisfactorily with parents of Chapter I students is shown in Figure 10-2 on pages 267 and 268.

This report, issued in addition to the regular school report card, attempts to provide some information from a "language arts perspective," since the areas of reading, listening, and writing provide the focal point. The report also provides opportunities for teachers to comment on behavioral aspects of learning.

A relatively simple system such as this frequently helps parents appreciate the fact that the reading teacher is trying to bridge the gap between school and home.

Referral Agencies

Occasionally, reading teachers may be asked to supply information to outside agencies regarding a child's reading progress. Typically, these requests come from pediatricians, vision specialists, child development centers at local hospitals or universities, social agencies, or mental health clinics. As a legal precaution, it's advisable to have the referral agency's request in writing and to make certain that the parents' consent has been given before releasing any reports.

GENERAL SUGGESTIONS FOR WRITING REPORTS

Up to this point, we have identified individuals who may read school reports and have described the two types of papers that reading specialists may be asked to prepare. To help polish your writing ability, we now offer ten suggestions to improve the quality of your individualized educational plans and case studies.

Use a Model

To begin, it's important to understand that there is no one best way to prepare a diagnostic report. Each reading teacher probably has his or her own particular format. Yet most of these reports share common characteristics. Each, for example, will include the child's name, sex, grade, and school. Parental information and home background will generally be included. The names of specific tests and scores received on each test will certainly be an important part of a report. Sometimes personality factors may be included. Every report should also include a summary of the findings. Finally, and most important, recommendations for dealing with the problem should be presented. Since the majority of reports include most of these components, it makes sense to devise a model you can follow to save precious hours later on.

From experience, we have found that reading teachers need three or four different models to work from, depending on the nature of the report they are asked to write. There may be instances, however, when none of the models is suitable, although even in unusual circumstances teachers may be able to combine two or more of the models or, omit a section of one model. The point is, following a model will ease the pain of writing any type of diagnostic report.

Earlier in this chapter we presented a form which reading teachers could use to convey information between themselves and classroom teachers. In a sense, these bimonthly notices could be considered a type of report. Even though it is relatively brief, it provides a structured outline from which to work.

Reading specialists are sometimes asked by a classroom teacher or the school principal to prepare a special report. Parents occasionally hire reading teachers to do independent evaluations of their child's reading ability, too. In each of these instances, the reading teacher will probably need to select three or four tests which can be administered within a one- or two-hour time limit. Since the tests chosen may vary from situation to situation, it is difficult to prescribe a specific model or report to follow. However, a brief description of the test(s) in a

Figure 10-3 An Example Paragraph from a Written Report

The Reading Miscue Inventory. The Reading Miscue Inventory (RMI) is an in-depth analysis of a child's oral reading. Unlike conventional informal reading inventories, the RMI analyzes nine types of reading miscues (errors). These miscues include

1. Dialect.
2. Intonation.
3. Graphic similarity.
4. Sound similarity.
5. Grammatical function.
6. Correction.
7. Grammatical acceptability.
8. Semantic acceptability.
9. Meaning change.

Once the child's oral reading has been tape-recorded and analyzed, comprehension is checked. Through this procedure, it is possible to determine if a child's miscues actually affect his or her comprehension. On the basis of this test. . . .

Gates-MacGinitie Reading Survey.   This silent reading test mesures two factors of reading: vocabulary and comprehension.   (Child's name)   was administered Primary   (Level of test) , Form 1, of this norm-referenced test. The test measures the child's *general* reading ability as compared to other children at his/her grade level.   (Child's name)   's scores on this test were

	Grade Equivalent	Percentile Ranking	Standard Score
Vocabulary	_____	_____	_____
Comprehension	_____	_____	_____

Figure 10-4   A Sentence Completion Paragraph from a Written Report

somewhat standardized paragraph may help. Let's suppose, for example, that you were asked by a teacher to evaluate a second-grader's reading ability. One of the instruments you might select is the Reading Miscue Inventory (Goodman and Burke, 1972). If you have a brief description of the test already prepared, such as that in Figure 10-3, your job is considerably easier. Once the test is administered and scored all you need to do is complete the paragraph supplying a summary of your findings.

An even easier way to report the results of testing is illustrated in Figure 10-4. Here the examiner merely needs to fill in the blanks to complete the report. You should, however, elaborate on the meaning of these scores later in the report.

It should be obvious that working from an established format can save reading teachers a great deal of time, but the final report should not appear to come from an assembly line. Although working from a model may ease teachers' writing tasks it doesn't free them from the responsibility of being a compassionate individual who is able to perceive the students' individual characteristics and traits. The teachers' job is to convey these individual idiosyncracies to the readers of the report. To do this effectively requires melding the relatively straightforward reporting of data with the personality traits of the examinee. The knack of doing so comes only with time and practice.

Avoid Educational Jargon

Educators, because they frequently communicate with the public, need to be especially sensitive to the fact that the language of the profession may not be always understood by the lay reader—especially when teachers are required to provide a written report to a parent or outside agency. We're not implying that educational jargon is implicitly bad and should be avoided. Each profession has its own language "shorthand" which expedites communication. But put yourself in the place of a parent who isn't exposed to the technical language of education on a daily basis. Terms such as *auditory memory, auditory reception, central processing dysfunction, code-emphasis approach, criterion-referenced test, dyslexia, hyperkinesis, learning style, multisensory approach, VAKT approach,* and *visual memory* aren't apt to be known by those outside of the profession. Indeed, some of these terms are so nebulous that they even confuse educators. Pity the poor parent who receives a report filled with these terms.

Teachers need to be especially cautious in their choice of terms when writing reports. Instead of using phrases such as *auditory reception* or *visual memory,* use *listening ability* or *ability to remember letters or shapes from memory.* By doing so, there is less chance for misunderstanding.

Write in the Appropriate Person

As a rule of thumb, it is a good idea to write diagnostic reports in the third person. If teachers, for example, believe students need instruction in beginning consonant sounds, they might indicate so in their report with a recommendation such as this:

> On the basis of testing done in the diagnostic learning center, the clinician recommends that Jamie receives instruction in phonics at a very basic level. Since he knows only a few beginning consonant sounds, this might be an appropriate place to initiate instruction. Starting at this level would also provide him with successful experiences, something he needs badly.

There are many times, however, when writing in the third person appears stuffy, forced, and downright artificial. If teachers have worked with a student for an extended period of time and perhaps have met the parents or guardian several times, they may choose to write in a more casual (but still professional) manner. Here's how that style might appear in a written report:

> Jamie has made considerable progress in the reading program. Since we have spent considerable time working on beginning consonant sounds, it might be appropriate if his classroom teacher built on what he already knows. Practice and many successful experiences should help Jamie become a more independent reader.

Here, the same information is conveyed, albeit in a slightly different way, without resorting to the phrase *the clinician.* The tone of the passage, however, is still professional. Here's an excerpt from a report that illustrates what teachers should avoid.

> I think Jamie has been a very good student. He's learned his beginning consonant sounds but I think he could still benefit from lots of practice. Starting at an easy level would give him something I think he badly needs—practice.

This style tends to project the writer into the forefront rather than the student. Notice, too, that each sentence contains the word *I.*

To summarize, sometimes teachers may want to write in the third person; other times they need not. If a reading teacher is unsure which style sounds best for a particular situation, the school principal could be consulted. If in doubt, it's probably better to err on the more formal side. Once teachers become confident and experienced, however, they soon realize that just as we vary our language patterns to conform to differing social situations, so can we vary our style of writing. As a writer of reports, make sure you choose the style that is most appropriate for a given situation.

Identify Specific Tests and Scores

Frequently, we overlook the fact that the identifying data in a report may be used as benchmarks to determine how well a student is learning. For this reason, teachers should specify which tests were given. Since some tests are available in multiple forms, it's also necessary to identify which form of the instrument was administered. Finally, it is important to know the dates tests were given so that if desired, growth profiles may be plotted.

A rule of thumb to follow when reporting test data is to include all pertinent information identifying the test, especially if more than one test has been developed and/or published by the same author or company. As an example, suppose the Gates-MacGinitie Reading Survey was administered in your district. These tests are available in numerous levels and forms. If teachers were to write something like "John's performance on the Gates' showed him reading at a 2.4 level," they would be leaving more questions unanswered than answered. Which Gates test? Which level of test? What form of the test was used? When was the test administered? What does 2.4 indicate? A vocabulary score perhaps? Or maybe it was a comprehension subtest score? Unless teachers are careful to report complete data, others won't understand fully what is being said. If scores are worth reporting, make sure they are reported accurately and the tests are clearly identified.

Include Only Pertinent Information

Individuals writing plans or case studies for the first time frequently use a style so terse that little more than test scores is reported. This is understandable because tests are relatively easy to administer and quick to score. Furthermore, the results can be reported in a straightforward manner. The astute reading teacher, however, synthesizes these test data, detecting trends among the scores, and provides an analysis of what these scores or profiles may mean.

Another sign of an amateur writer are reports that are exceedingly long. These documents seem to drag on and on, much like a soap opera. Being articulate and fluent are commendable features, but good writers know how to condense their thoughts into a minimal number of words.

A common characteristic of well-written reports is that they include only information useful for educational decision making. Just as a good athlete carries no additional weight, so does the well-written report exclude excess verbiage.

Stress the Positive

Most children, even those with severe reading problems, have many positive personal attributes. Some are happy, outgoing individuals, whereas others are shy and withdrawn. Many have interesting hobbies and out-of-school activities. Some are extremely verbal and articulate. Others have overcompensated for their reading problem by superior performances in other academic disciplines—math, for example. Our point is that we frequently look only at the deficits students with reading problems exhibit. Yet there are many positive features that can be stressed when writing reports on these students. Wouldn't you appreciate receiving some positive information about your son or daughter?

Frequently, the report writer will inadvertently make statements that have negative connotations. This insensitivity may result in later confrontations with parents. Here are a few examples of statements which appeared in first drafts of case study reports and, we felt, had possible negative connotations. We have also provided the rewritten revisions to underscore how subtle phrasing changes can affect a report.

DRAFT

At the beginning of the reading clinic he demonstrated a very genuine interest in attending classes; however, his lack of attendance at school showed otherwise.

REVISION

At the beginning of the reading clinic, he was interested in attending; however as the clinic progressed, Richard was frequently absent.

In the draft, the writer has made an evaluative statement which may be offensive to the parent or guardian. In the revision, however, the writer has simply described an existing condition without imposing a value judgment.

Here is another example of how an idea can be conveyed in a positive manner.

DRAFT

If he feels he can do something, he will; if he does not, he won't make the effort to try.

REVISION

Andrew will attempt a task only if he feels he can be successful.

In this example, the draft implies that Andrew is not motivated. The revision, though, is more explicit in pointing out that Andrew is apprehensive when attempting a task because he feels he may fail to perform in a satisfactory manner.

DRAFT

It appears that Tammie has had some beneficial experiences, but not as much as others her age. As a result, due to the nature of the test, this clinician feels that her potential is somewhat depressed.

REVISION

Although it appears as if Tammie has had many beneficial experiences, perhaps others her age have experienced more. For this reason, her potential may actually be greater than indicated by the testing done during the clinic.

Here is a case where the writer's revision changed the emphasis from what appears to be a deficiency to a need for more experiences. The revision evokes a more positive connotation and, hence, is preferred over the draft.

To conclude, here are two actual sentences which we encountered in reports. How would you revise these sentences?

DRAFT

Mary appears to have a very poor attitude toward school.

YOUR REVISION

_____

_____

_____

And finally:

DRAFT

Dan appears to be a nonverbal boy.

YOUR REVISION

_____

_____

_____

Use the Report to Educate the Reader

As we mentioned earlier, reading evaluations can be read by two groups of individuals—educators and the lay public. In the first group, we could include classroom teachers, principals, guidance counselors, school psychologists, speech and hearing specialists, and special education teachers. In the latter group, there are parents, vision and hearing specialists, social workers, physicians, and psychiatrists.

Earlier, we stated that some terms you may use will be unfamiliar to many of those outside the field of education. These individuals probably won't know the difference between a digraph and a diphthong or a blend and a schwa. Neither will they know the difference between an independent reading level and an instructional level. Report writers, then, need to write so that their reports will be understood by those outside the profession.

One especially good technique teachers can use is to give a brief explanation of the test when reporting their findings. If you are reporting the results of

Gray Oral Reading Test.   This is an oral test consisting of a series of graded passages. Students read short passages and then are asked comprehension questions. Three levels of reading are measured: independent or recreational, instructional, and frustration.

Roger's independent level is at the first-grade level. This is the level at which he should read for pleasure and enjoyment.

His instructional level is at the second-grade level. This is where Roger should be receiving instruction in school.

Roger's frustration level is at the third-grade level. He should not be asked to read materials at this level either at home or at school.

Figure 10-5   A Paragraph from a Report Written to Educate the Reader

an oral reading test, for example, you might follow the example provided in Figure 10-5.

You can see that the one-sentence explanations in paragraphs two through four help the reader comprehend the meaning of these levels.

Although most classroom teachers would have little difficulty understanding the content of the example just cited, they might be unfamiliar with some of the tests reading teachers frequently use. Suppose, for instance, that a vision screening was administered to all pupils. The reading specialist may want to acquaint the reader with the fact that this screening is more than the typical school visual screening. Figure 10-6 illustrates how a short statement can subtly educate the readers by informing them that it's important to test a child's vision at near-point as well as far-point.

Match Recommendations with Findings

It is crucial that reading teachers have either objective or subjective data to support their recommendations. If, for example, a student was recommended to receive focused instruction on phonic skills, there should be test results to document this underlying weakness. We know of instances, however, where almost every child tested received the same remedial recommendations regardless of what the diagnostic tests revealed. This is clearly unprofessional and unethical.

A final important point to remember when writing recommendations is that they should be included in the recommendations section of the report and not interspersed with the findings.

Figure 10-6   A Paragraph from a Report Written to Educate Teachers

Kenneth was given the Keystone Telebinocular Vision Survey. This test measures a child's vision at both far-point (twenty feet) as well as near-point (eighteen inches), the distance at which the child reads. On the basis of this test . . . .

Figure 10-7 A Remediation Plan Form

Student: _____   Student: _____

Date: _____   Date: _____

Objective: *Objective:*

Activity: *Activity:*

Objective: *Objective:*

Activity: *Activity:*

Objective: *Objective:*

Activity: *Activity:*

Reaction:

Include a Summary of Strengths and Weaknesses

Well-written evaluations always include a summary of the examiner's findings. This summary can be organized in one of two ways. One way is to organize your thoughts in a paragraph format. In this manner, each strength—or weakness—can be discussed in a separate paragraph. This format tends to read smoothly and yet conveys the important diagnostic information that your readers will need.

Another way to present a summary is to use separate subheadings entitled "Strengths" and "Weaknesses." Then, under each subheading, teachers can itemize their summary by using numerals or arabic numbers. One possible dilemma is that it is frequently difficult to include an important piece of information under either of the subheadings. Furthermore, a strategy which may be repeatedly used by the student—say phonics—may be both a strength and a weakness. The child who has learned an exhaustive list of phonic generalizations, for example, may be considered to have good decoding skills (and hence, this would be considered a strength); but if this is the only technique the child can use to decode an unfamiliar word, it might be considered a weakness.

Once teachers have had an opportunity to work with a student over a period of time, it's much easier to write a summary of strengths and weaknesses. One valuable technique is to keep a log or remediation plan. By keeping a plan book and reacting to successes and failures, teachers become more perceptive and prescriptive in their teaching. It also helps them formulate their recommendations, which might later be included in a written report. A form we've used with success is offered for your consideration (Figure 10-7). Generally, we've found that teachers need to have two or three activities planned for each hour they work with problem readers.

Notice that we've included three areas for teachers to identify their objective(s) and activities. After the lessons, there's a place for them to add their introspective comments, a spot for their "successes" or "flops" to be recorded. Although this form is designed to be used with individual students, teachers can adapt it for small groups.

Figure 10-8, on pages 279–283, shows a few sample pages from an actual teacher's remediation plan. It should help to illustrate what we are talking about.

Conclude with a Prognosis

A question parents usually ask once their child has been tested is "What are the chances of my child becoming a better reader?" For this reason, it's usually a good idea to conclude a diagnostic report by providing a prognosis. It's also a chance for teachers to put in their final words about the child. Here's an example of how one of us concluded a report on a second-grade girl whose parents wanted her placed in a special education classroom. (A placement, by the way, which everyone on the evaluation team opposed.)

> Heidi's best chances for becoming a better reader are probably in a regular elementary school classroom. She needs good developmental reading instruction more than special out-of-the classroom instruction. As long as her instruction is focused on her needs, she will continue to

Figure 10-8 Examples of Completed Remediation Plan Forms

Student: <u>Joseph</u>   Student: _____

Date: <u>7/14/83 (Friday)</u>   Date: _____

Objective: to teach sight words from Johnson word list and LEA stories.

Objective: to give reading practice.

Activity: make a game of seeing how many words he knows.

Activity: reread LEA stories and look at books while I work with Kenny.

Objective: continue to teach blending of phonic elements—work on final and medial sounds.

Objective: to encourage him to read.

Activity: have Joseph blend the words as I write them; ex. rag, rug, rut, rat, ran, run, bun, but, bug, bag. . . .

Activity: read directions for constructing a flashlight which I printed on a card.

Objective: to reinforce vowel sounds ā and ă.

Objective:

Activity: auditory discrimination of ā and ă (use pictures). Blend and decode ā + ă words, then sentences.

Activity:

Reaction: Joseph is tiring of blending words.

He was delighted with the flashlight—is going to get Grandfather to make a switch.

Figure 10-8 Continued

Student: <u>Joseph</u>   Student: _____

Date: <u>7/17/83 (Monday)</u>   Date: _____

Objective: to teach sight words   *Objective:*
  and comprehension.

Activity: have him arrange word   *Activity:*
  cards in sentences on flannel
  board (LEA).

Objective: to test for sight words.   *Objective:* strengthen phonic skills

Activity: give Johnson list #100   *Activity:*   review ai and a-e
  on. He has learned the words he   words—if attention warrants.
  missed from 1 to 99.   Help him discover silent e rule.

Objective: *Objective:*

Activity: *Activity:*

Reaction: Seems pleased to have   Gave Gates-MacGintie Reading
  learned 1st 100 words of   Test because Kenny was not
  Johnson list. Now working on   here. He enjoyed it!
  next 50.

Figure 10-8 Continued

Student: <u>Joseph</u>   Student: _____

Date: <u>7/18/83 (Tuesday)</u>   Date: _____

Objective: to teach sight voc.   *Objective:* to test comprehension.

Activity: use 3rd day LEA   *Activity:* give WISC Design Comp.
activities—emphasis on sight   Level B.4.
voc., compound words.

Objective: to teach sight words.   *Objective:* teach sight voc.

Activity: use word cards from   *Activity:* make up sentences to go
Johnson list for game.   with my pictures.

Objective: learn child's IQ.   *Objective:*

Activity: give Peabody Picture   *Activity:*
Voc. Test.

Reaction: Joseph altered his   Liked to make up sentences to go
progress chart to his liking to   with pictures. Insisted on writing
keep track of his progress   sentences himself.
learning words.

Figure 10-8 Continued

Student: <u>Joseph</u> Student: _____

Date: <u>7/19/83 (Wednesday)</u> Date: _____

Objective: to test comprehension. *Objective:* teach more sight words.

Activity: give Wisc. Design Level B.1. *Activity:* write LEA story— electromagnet stimulus.

Objective: to spark interest in reading. *Objective:* teach comprehension.

Activity: give him written directions and equipment for making an electromagnet. *Activity:* try a cloze passage from his old experience story.

Objective: teach sight voc. *Objective:*

Activity: review words from Johnson list. *Activity:*

Reaction: did not like comprehension test. Did well with cloze procedure.

Figure 10-8 Continued

Student: <u>Joseph</u>   Student: _____

Date: <u>7/20/83 (Thursday)</u>   Date: _____

Objective: to test comprehension.   *Objective:* teach more sight words.

Activity: WISC Design Level B.2.   *Activity:* make up sentences to go with picture stimulus.

Objective: to spark an interest in reading.   *Objective:* strengthen phonetic skills

Activity: make a toy from activity book. Read directions from book.   *Activity:* review ai and a-e words and sentences. Apply silent e rule.

Objective: work on comprehension.   *Objective:* to spark interest in reading.

Activity: rearrange sentence strips from experience story.   *Activity:* read to Joseph and Kenny. Perhaps Joseph will read a line or two.

Reaction: rearranging sentence strips was a challenge. Resisted reading directions printed in activity book (they were easy and he had immediate help with unknown words).   Joseph would *not* read a line or two. I did all the reading. He did not even listen. *Hated* phonics lesson.

progress in reading in her classroom. Heidi's parents and teachers, by working together closely, can do much to help her become a good reader and certainly read at grade level.

INDIVIDUALIZED EDUCATIONAL PLANS

Individualized educational plans (IEPs) are tailor-made instructional outlines for students who are having trouble learning in school. Currently, IEPs are written for students who are failing in one or more academic areas. To help you better understand IEPs, allow us to describe how they are used in today's school districts.

An Overview

Historically, good teachers have always provided instruction attuned to the needs of their students. To ensure that all students with handicaps received this focused instruction, however, in November 1975, the U.S. Congress passed Public Law 94-142. This law, commonly called the Education for All Handicapped Children Act, formalized the procedures that state departments of education and local educational agencies must follow when planning educational programs for handicapped students. Unless districts follow established procedures, they are ineligible to receive federal support.

Public Law 94-142 requires the state departments of education to have a formal plan outlining how local school districts shall provide appropriate services for all handicapped students. Monitoring the local educational agency by the state departments of education insures that districts within its jurisdiction comply with the act.

Some Specifics

There are some important concepts that reading teachers should be familiar with since in many cases they are asked to attend IEP staffing team meetings.

Under the law all handicapped students are entitled to a free and appropriate public education. Within thirty days of determining that a student needs special services, a meeting must be held to develop an appropriate individualized educational plan. Before this meeting, any number of individuals may be involved in testing the referred student. Here is a partial list of those who may be called on to assist in the evaluation:

1. Previous teachers.
2. Reading teacher.
3. Learning disabilities teacher.
4. Audiologist.
5. Counselor.
6. Speech and language specialist.
7. Nurse.

8. Physician.
9. Psychiatrist.
10. Psychologist.
11. Anyone else who may be involved in evaluating the progress of a child once he or she is included in the program.

This list doesn't even include the school principal and the director of special education, two individuals who are usually at every IEP meeting. It isn't necessary for everyone who assisted in the student evaluation to attend the meeting when the IEP is drawn up. Generally, the principal, the special education director (or a designee), a member of the evaluation team, the child's classroom teacher, and the child's parents are those who initially meet.

Since one of the provisions of P.L. 94-142 stipulates that the student be placed in a "least restrictive environment" (that is, to the maximum extent, be placed with nonhandicapped students), the IEP meeting is devoted to (1) examining the completed evaluation, (2) discussing possible modifications in the student's educational program, and (3) completing the written IEP.

Each IEP must provide the following data:

1. A record of the student's present level of educational performance.
2. A statement of annual goals as well as short-term objectives.
3. A statement describing the services to be provided.
4. A statement of the projected dates of services and an indication of their duration.
5. A statement describing the evaluative procedures to be used in determining whether the short-term objectives have been reached.

A student may be referred for special services in any number of ways. One of the most frequent sources of referral is the classroom teacher. Other professionals such as a speech teacher or a reading teacher may also refer a student for further assessment. Frequently, preschool screening programs alert parents to the fact that their child may need services upon entering school. These are all legitimate ways to request referral for further testing.

Presently, there are no standardized guidelines specifying the IEP format. Some state departments of education have felt that local school districts should be permitted to devise their own IEP forms. Other states have generated guidelines for completing IEPs and have supplied forms which all districts within the state are expected to use.

Where We Are

Our position is that there is an intrinsic value in a close examination of the unique educational needs of children—especially those with reading problems. Yet, we have a certain uneasiness about what we are seeing as an outcome of P.L. 94-142. To put it straightforwardly, we think the theory and intent of the process behind IEP are well intended. It is the execution of the plan that troubles us the most. Marver and David (1978) said it well after interviewing over 200 participants in fifteen districts who were involved in the IEP process. By attending numerous IEP meetings and reading more than 150 IEPs they concluded that

1. The services available often determine where a child is placed.
2. The record keeping is difficult and at times inaccurate.
3. Parents attending the IEP meetings sometimes fail to understand the technical educational jargon used.
4. Some of the professionals are insensitive to the feelings of parents.
5. Parents frequently fail to question the opinions of the "experts."
6. Teachers frequently are afraid that the IEP objectives will force them to be accountable.
7. The IEPs tend to be written in very general terms.
8. Teachers frequently feel inundated by the paperwork involved in preparing an IEP.
9. The people responsible for selecting diagnostic tests are frequently not thoroughly trained in psychometric techniques.
10. There are sometimes professional jealousies which interfere with the design of appropriate IEPs.
11. The quality of IEPs varies tremendously.
12. There is sometimes no relationship between the assessment data and the specified goals and objectives.

Although these shortcomings were all linked with attempts to write IEPs, they are by no means unique to just those documents. Many attempts to provide more focused instruction have encountered these same problems. Because there is such an interest in putting our intentions in a written form, though, the limitations of some of our educational practices have become increasingly obvious.

It is clear that if IEPs are to have a significant impact on the learning of students with reading problems, major refinements must be made. Unless, for example, the plans are comprehensive, clearly written, and sufficiently detailed, they will be of limited value in guiding educators toward more focused instruction. Furthermore, unless valid and reliable tests are chosen to measure reading performance, the data collected on each student will be suspect. Only when these conditions are met and when there is a close working relationship among the professionals involved will IEPs be what they were meant to be.

CASE STUDIES

Case studies, the most detailed reports reading teachers are asked to write, generally include the following information:

1. Referral data (child's name, age, birthdate, sex, parents' names, address, and telephone number).
2. Physical and developmental data (health history and preschool developmental history).

3. Environmental data (home life, parents' and siblings' interaction with the child, playmates, and so on).

4. Emotional and personality data (attitudes toward school and home, recreational activities, emotional adjustment and personality characteristics).

5. Educational data (progress in school, schools attended and dates, interviews with teachers, previous remedial instruction).

6. Results of testing (visual and auditory screenings, tests measuring intellectual level of functioning, specific reading tests, spelling tests).

7. A summary of testing and interpretation of test results.

8. Recommendations for home and school.

In some instances, other professionals may assist the reading teacher in testing students. Speech therapists, school nurses, and school psychologists are usually asked to diagnose students in their area of specialty. In some instances, though, reading teachers may not have the luxury of having these professionals at their disposal. In this case, the reading teachers may be responsible for administering tests outside their area.

The purpose of conducting a case study is to have an in-depth evaluation of a student's reading and learning problem. Because of the time needed to interview and test students, however, preparing a case study is usually a major, lengthy undertaking.

Guidelines for Writing Case Studies

To help teachers improve their writing of case study reports, we will provide examples of forms they may want to use, or modify, to help them collect the information they will need.

REFERRAL DATA   Students may be referred for help in a number of different ways. In a school, teachers or parents will solicit the reading teacher's help and a student population is readily available. If a specialist is attempting to establish a private reading clinic or if you are a student working at a college or university clinic, students need to be recruited. Regardless of how the population is obtained, it's important to get accurate referral data:

1. Child's name.
2. Child's date of birth.
3. Grade level.
4. Parents' name.
5. Parents' address.
6. Parents' telephone number.

BACKGROUND INFORMATION   Once a student has been considered for inclusion in a program, try to meet with the parents or guardians of the child. Usually, they can supply important physical and developmental data about the student. Here is a model of a letter used to invite parents and guardians to a personal conference (see Figure 10-9).

Dear Parent:

In an effort to learn more about your child, we are requesting that you attend a short conference with your child's reading teacher on Monday, July 9. During this meeting you will be given an opportunity to share any information that will make the teacher's job more effective. In addition, the teacher will have a few brief questions for you. Hopefully, the conference will not last more than thirty minutes.

We sincerely hope you will be able to attend and we look forward to meeting you.

Sincerely,

Robert T. Rude, Ph.D.

Your child's teacher is _____

Conference Time: _____

_____

Please return with your child

Parent's Name _____   Reading Teacher _____

Child's Name _____   Conference Time _____

I will be able to attend at this time _____

Please schedule a different time for me _____

Figure 10-9   A Letter Requesting a Parent Conference

Once the parent and the reading teacher have an opportunity to meet, it is the teacher's responsibility to collect all pertinent data about the child. Frequently, some of the information that may bear heavily on the case is sensitive or even confidential. Parents who are undergoing a divorce, for example, may be reluctant to offer freely information related to the breakup. A rule of thumb when interviewing parents is to be sensitive to their feelings and respect their privacy. If you sense any reluctance on their part to offer information during the conference, proceed cautiously and respect their rights.

Frequently, it is a good idea not to ask sensitive questions until toward the end of the conference. This provides ample time for the parent to offer information without your needing to pry.

To assist in the collection of information about students, note the Parental Interview Form (Figure 10-10). We prefer to conduct the interview in a casual fashion, referring to the form only to guide our questioning or to jot down responses. It's not a good idea to ask questions in rapid-fire sequence. Individuals object to being grilled, and besides, it isn't polite.

In addition to talking with the parents, it's also important to collect information about the child's home life. Occasionally you'll find a discrepancy between reports from the child and from the parent. In our reading clinics, for example, we usually work with the students for a few days before we meet and talk with parents. To break the ice with the student during these meetings, we usually ask questions taken from the Individual Interview Schedule described in Chapter 5. While the children are drawing, coloring, playing with clay, or playing a game, we simply ask them to tell us about themselves. The items on the forms provide cues for the teacher if a child is reluctant to offer information.

In addition to the areas we've covered already, reading teachers will probably want to have visual and auditory screening tests conducted on their students before writing the case study report.

VISUAL SCREENING   It is important to examine a child's vision at far-point and near-point. A number of tests are available which are easy to administer and require no highly specialized training. Some of them have been discussed in detail in Chapter 4, "Correlates of Reading Disability." If a visual problem is detected, a good procedure is to alert the parents, who can then arrange an appointment with a qualified specialist for a more in-depth examination.

AUDITORY SCREENING   It is also important to check a student's ability to hear clearly and accurately. Again, in Chapter 4, instruments that can be used to diagnose any hearing abnormality are identified. Students falling below acceptable standards should be examined by a certified audiologist.

INTELLECTUAL ABILITY   When writing a case study report include intellectual ability since it enables a reading teacher to determine whether the student is working up to capacity. Usually school psychologists are qualified to administer either a WISC-R or a Stanford-Binet. Two other frequently administered tests given by reading teachers are the Peabody Picture Vocabulary Test and the Slosson Intelligence Test.

GENERAL READING ABILITY   It is also necessary to determine the student's overall and specific reading ability. This first area can be measured by administering norm-referenced reading tests, informal reading inventories, or miscue inventories. Each of these instruments attempts to determine the competence of a student in connected discourse.

Figure 10-10 Parental Interview Form

Student's Name _____

Age _____ _____   Date of Birth _____
     years   months

Father's age _____   Mother's age _____

Father's nationality _____   Mother's nationality _____

Father's education _____   Mother's education _____

Father's occupation _____   Mother's occupation _____

Parents are: 1.   Living together.
                   2.   Separated.
                   3.   Divorced.
                   4.   Deceased: father/mother.

Other children in the family:

	Name	Age	Grade in school
M/F	_____	____	_____
M/F	_____	____	_____
M/F	_____	____	_____
M/F	_____	____	_____
M/F	_____	____	_____
M/F	_____	____	_____
M/F	_____	____	_____

School(s) attended by child:

_____

_____

_____

_____

_____

Has the child repeated any grades? If so, which ones?

_____

_____

Has the child ever been out of school for more than a week at a time? If so, explain.

_____

_____

What language(s) is spoken in the home?

_____

Health history of the child (e.g., prolonged illness, health problems, accidents, etc.)

_____

_____

_____

_____

_____

Was the child a full-term baby? _____

Were there any complications during the pregnancy or during the birth?

_____

At what age did the child begin to talk? _____

At what age did the child begin to walk? _____

Was there any change in handedness as the child grew up?

_____

Does the child have any special interests? Describe.

_____

_____

What vocational aspirations does the child have?

_____

_____

_____

What does the child do in his/her free time?

_____

_____

_____

How would you describe the child's emotional attitude?

_____

Has the child received any special tutoring?

_____

What newspapers or books are available in the home?

_____

What time does the child go to bed at night?

_____

What time does the child get up in the morning?

_____

What do the parents perceive the child's problem to be?

_____

_____

_____

_____

Norm-referenced tests allow teachers to compare a student's performance with other students of the same grade. Occasionally, these tests and their grade equivalent, percentile ranking, and standard scores are already available from school records. If this is the case, and if the test was given recently, it is unnecessary to retest the child.

Informal reading inventories permit teachers to assess the various levels at which the student reads. There are many inventories available as part of basal reading programs or commercially produced. We suggest selecting one which meets the standards we have discussed in Chapter 11.

A number of miscue inventories have appeared on the market in recent years. Essentially, they are little more than IRIs which have modified scoring criteria similar to those used in the original Reading Miscue Inventory. Some prefer to use the RMI because of its in-depth explanation of miscues. Others tend to avoid it for this very reason. Regardless of a teacher's decision, we feel it is important to be able to interpret orally read passages utilizing psycholinguistic insights. In Chapter 5, we have offered one possible way to interpret these reading miscues.

SPECIFIC READING ABILITY   Specific reading ability is usually interpreted to mean performance on criterion-referenced reading tests. Since the reading teacher will want to give the reader of the case study report some idea of which specific skills the student has learned, the report should specify performance on a test of word recognition and sight vocabulary. The child's decoding ability or phonic and structural analysis skills should also be stated. Some examiners also choose to administer criterion-referenced comprehension tests. (Some authorities have argued that comprehension cannot be subdivided into specific skills and measured with criterion-referenced tests. If you are theoretically in agreement with this position, you may choose to report comprehension ability only in general terms.) All these test findings can be appropriately classified under the specific category.

SUMMARY OF TESTING RESULTS   This section of the case study report is where test data are reviewed and synthesized into discernible trends. Administering and scoring tests are relatively easy. Summarizing the test results based on the response patterns calls for astute perception. Teachers should be careful that their written summary is clear and logical.

RECOMMENDATIONS   This is perhaps the most difficult and challenging section to prepare in a case study report. Unless teachers have experience with reading disabled students, it is difficult to know what techniques and materials will prove effective in overcoming their reading handicaps. Even after years of experience, veteran reading teachers still are challenged when it comes to making useful and reasonable recommendations.

A Case Study Report

Now that the topics to be covered in a report have been proposed, here is a format teachers might consider using (Figure 10-11). We have also included an actual case study of an elementary school student (Figure 10-12).

Figure 10-11 Reading Case Study Report Form

I. Referral data

Name: _____ Date: _____

Age: _____ Birthdate: _____ Sex: _____

School: _____

School Address (in full): _____

Parents' names   Occupations

  Father: _____   _____

  Mother: _____   _____

Parents' address: _____ Phone: _____

II. Physical and developmental data
  A. Preschool developmental history:
  B. Health history:

III. Environmental data
  A. Home:
  B. Parents:
  C. Siblings:
  D. Friends:
  E. Miscellaneous:

IV. Emotional and personality data
  A. Attitude toward home:
  B. Attitude toward school:
  C. Recreation:
  D. Emotional adjustment:
  E. Personality characteristics:

V. Educational data
  A. School progress:
  B. Schools attended and dates:
  C. Attendance:

VI. Results of testing
  A. Visual screening:
    _____ was administered the Keystone Tele-
    binocular Vision Survey. This test measures a child's vision at
    both far-point as well as near-point, the distance at which the
    child reads. On the basis of this test . . .

B.   Auditory discrimination:
     The Beltone Audiometer was used to determine if _____ _____ has the ability to hear sounds of differing intensity and pitch. On the basis of this testing it appears as if _____ _____ has . . .

     The Wepman Test of Auditory Discrimination was administered in an attempt to discern whether _____ has the ability to auditorally discriminate between matching and different pairs of words. The results of this screening indicate that . . .

C.   Intellectual ability:
     Form _____ of the Peabody Picture Vocabulary Test was given in an effort to determine _____'s reading expectancy. On the basis of this test, _____ would be categorized as a _____ learner. Using the Bond-Tinker Reading Expectancy Formula, his/her expected reading level is _____.

D.   General reading ability:
     1.   *Gates-MacGinitie Reading Survey.* This silent reading test measures two (three) factors of reading: vocabulary and comprehension. _____ was administered Primary _____, Form I, of this norm-referenced test. The test measures the child's *general* reading ability as compared to other children at his/her grade level. _____ _____'s scores on this test were:

	Grade Equivalent	Percentile Ranking	Standard Score
Speed and Accuracy (if applicable)	_____	_____	_____
Vocabulary	_____	_____	_____
Comprehension	_____	_____	_____

     2a. *Gray Oral Reading Test.* This is an oral test consisting of a series of graded passages. Three levels of reading are measured: independent or recreational, instructional, and frustration.
          _____'s independent level is _____. This is the level at which he/she should read for pleasure and enjoyment.
          His/her instructional level is at the _____ grade level. This is where _____ should be receiving instruction at school.
          _____'s frustration level was at the _____ grade level. The child should not be asked to read materials at this level either at home or at school.

2b. *The Reading Miscue Inventory.* The Reading Miscue Inventory (RMI) is an in-depth analysis of a child's oral reading. Unlike conventional informal reading inventories, the RMI analyzes nine types of reading miscues (errors). These miscues include

(1) Dialect.
(2) Intonation.
(3) Graphic similarity.
(4) Sound similarity.
(5) Grammatical function.
(6) Correction.
(7) Grammatical acceptability.
(8) Semantic acceptability.
(9) Meaning change.

Once the child's oral reading has been tape-recorded and analyzed, comprehension is checked. Through this procedure, it is possible to determine if a child's miscues actually affect his/her comprehension. On the basis of this test . . .

E. Specific reading ability:

1. *Decoding assessment.* This test is used to determine what decoding skills a child possesses. These are the skills a child needs to unlock an unfamiliar word. On the basis of this test, _____'s profile follows:

    Phonic skills:
    Beginning consonants—mastered or not mastered.
    Consonant blends—mastered or not mastered.
    Structural analysis skills:
    Compound words—mastered or not mastered.

2. *Comprehension assessment.* This test determines whether the child comprehends what he/she reads. On the basis of this test and on my informal observation of his/her reading it appears that . . .

3. *Basic sight vocabulary.* The words on this test [insert test name here] comprise many of the service words a child must have in his/her reading vocabulary. _____ knew _____ percent of these words.

VII. Summary of Testing Results:

VIII. Recommendations:

A. Home:
   1.
   2.
   3.

B. School:
   1.
   2.
   3.

Submitted by _____

Figure 10-12 Reading Case Study Report

I. Referral data

Name: ___George Thames___ Date: ___July 26, 1983___

Age: __8.3__ Birthdate: ___4-3-75___ Sex: __Male__

School: __Black Elementary School__

School Address (in full): ___162 Lafayette Drive, Providence, R.I. 02908___

Parents' names   Occupations

  Father: ___John Thames___   ___Executive___

  Mother: ___Patricia Thames___   ___College Student/Housewife___

Parents' address: ___1616 Ellis St., Providence, R.I. 02906___ Phone: ___277-4423___

II. Background Information

George was a full-term baby with no complications during birth. Furthermore, Mrs. Thames did not experience any complications during the pregnancy. All of his milestones were at an appropriate age. George is left-handed; however, there were no changes in handedness as he grew up.

This child has not had any health problems, major accidents, or prolonged illnesses. His mother has expressed that enuresis occurs except when his three brothers are not at home. George's pediatrician feels that this is not abnormal for an eight-year-old.

George now lives with his mother and stepfather. He has three stepbrothers—Paul, age fourteen; Jim, age ten; and Hank, age eight. Mrs. Thames said that George often imitates his brother Paul, he dislikes Jim, and he is often in intellectual competition with Hank. Nevertheless, he far exceeds Hank in sports.

The home appears to be a happy one where the parents make special provisions to have books and magazines available. They also take trips. George often speaks enthusiastically about activities with his family such as going to the movies or plays, jogging with his parents, or going camping.

Mrs. Thames is very concerned about George's academic progress, especially his ability to read. She often uses positive reinforcement by giving him twenty-five cents daily for proper behavior and doing a good job at school.

George is a socially well-adjusted boy who enjoys playing with his friends on a one-to-basis. In his free time his interests are his club house, skateboard, sports (soccer, baseball), and toys such as Legos and G.I. Joe. He does not read in his free time, even though he expressed an interest in science fiction, sports stories, and comic books.

George appears to enjoy school and said that he mostly likes the teachers, art, and the activity room. He seems to have enjoyed the reading clinic, although on two occasions he had altercations with two of the students.

Throughout the clinic, George appeared to be a well-adjusted boy who was cooperative and anxious to succeed. He seemed to be overly competitive in reading-related games in an attempt to prove his abilities. For example, he often attempted to alter the rules of a game or create situations in which there was no chance for the other student to win.

George also manifested sensitive qualities toward anything which concerned an emotional response in the categories of his brothers. For example, on The Individual Interview Schedule he made the following responses. I don't like *when my brother hits me*. My brother *is bad*.

George is an effervescent, verbal boy who is very anxious to please. He is highly motivated when praised and progress charts are used as reinforcements. Highly competitive, he functions best in small groups where he can be reassured that he is doing a good job. Learning is further fostered when he receives one-to-one attention and when extraneous visual and auditory stimuli are kept at a minimum.

George attended the Dean Day Preschool and the Black Elementary School in kindergarten, first grade, and second grade. He had uninterrupted school attendance except on occasions when the family went on vacations.

III. Results of testing
   A. Visual screening:
      George was administered the Keystone Telebinocular Vision Survey. This test measures a child's vision at both far-point as well as near-point, the distance at which the child reads. On the basis of this test, it appears that this child has no difficulty with visual acuity.
   B. Auditory discrimination:
      The Wepman Test of Auditory Discrimination was administered in an attempt to discern whether George has the ability to discriminate between matching and different pairs of words. The results of this screening indicate that he has no deficiencies in this area.
   C. Intellectual ability:
      Form B of the Peabody Picture Vocabulary Test was given in an effort to determine George's reading expectancy. On the basis of this test, he would be categorized as a rapid learner. He received a reading expectancy grade of 3.5, using the Bond-Tinker Reading Expectancy Formula.

D. General reading ability:
1. *Gates-MacGinitie Reading Survey.* This silent reading test measures two (three) factors of reading: vocabulary and comprehension. George was administered Primary B, Form I, of this norm-referenced test. The test measures the child's general reading ability as compared to other children at his/her grade level. George's scores on this test were:

	Grade Equivalent	Percentile Ranking	Standard Score
Vocabulary	2.5	34	46
Comprehension	2.2	18	41

2a. *Gray Oral Reading Test.* This is an oral test consisting of a series of graded passages. Three levels of reading are measured: independent or recreational, instructional, and frustration.

George's independent level is first or beginning second grade. This is the level at which he should read for pleasure and enjoyment.

His instructional level is at the second half of the second grade. This is where he should be receiving instruction at school.

His frustration level was at the third grade. The child should not be asked to read materials at this level either at home or at school.

2b. *The Reading Miscue Inventory.* The Reading Miscue Inventory (RMI) is an in-depth analysis of a child's oral reading. Unlike conventional informal reading inventories, the RMI analyzes nine types of reading miscues (errors). These miscues include
(1) Dialect.
(2) Intonation.
(3) Graphic similarity.
(4) Sound similarity.
(5) Grammatical function.
(6) Correction.
(7) Grammatical acceptability.
(8) Semantic acceptability.
(9) Meaning change.
Once the child's oral reading has been tape-recorded and analyzed, comprehension is checked. Through this procedure, it is possible to determine if a child's miscues actually affect his comprehension. George was admin-

istered the second grade level of the test. On the basis of this test the miscues indicated the following percentages:

(1) Dialect—zero percent miscues.
(2) Intonation—zero percent miscues.
(3) Graphic similarity—68 percent miscues.
(4) Sound similarity—48 percent miscues.
(5) Grammatical function—52 percent miscues.
(6) Comprehension loss—40 percent affected by miscues.
(7) Grammatical relationships—40 percent indicated weaknesses.
(8) Retelling of the story—52 percent total comprehension.

These scores indicate that George makes moderately effective use of reading strategies to help him comprehend the passage.

E. Specific reading ability:
1. *Wisconsin Test of Reading Skill Development: Word Attack.*

These tests are used to determine what decoding skills a child possesses. These are the skills a child needs to unlock an unfamiliar word. On the basis of these tests, George's profile follows:

a. *Phonic skills—mastered*
(1) Letters and numbers (visual discrimination).
(2) Words and phrases (visual discrimination).
(3) Initial consonant sounds.
(4) Beginning consonant sounds.
(5) Ending consonants.
(6) Consonant blends—bl, cl, fl, gl, pl, sl, br, cr, dr, fr, gr, pr, tr.
(7) Consonant blends—st, sk, sn, sw, sp.

b. *Structural analysis skills—mastered*
(1) Compound words.

c. *Phonic skills—fair mastery*
(1) Consonant digraphs—ch, sh, st.
(2) Long vowel sounds.
(3) Consonant digraphs—wh, nk, sh, th.

d. *Phonic skills—not mastered*
(1) Short vowel sounds.
(2) Consonants and their variant sounds—hard and soft c and g.
(3) Consonant digraphs—ch, nk, sh, ng, th, wh.
(4) Consonant blends—three letters.
(5) Silent letters.
(6) Ar, er, ir, ur, or, al, aw.
(7) Two vowels separated, silent e.
(8) Final vowel.

e. *Structural analysis skills—not mastered*
(1) Syllabication.

2. *Wisconsin Test of Reading Skill Development: Comprehension.* Unlike the Gates-MacGinitie Reading Survey, these tests break general comprehension down into its component parts. For his age, George's profile is as follows:
   a. *Comprehension—Mastered*—When the exercises are read to him.
      (1) Main idea: Picture topics or paragraph topics.
      (2) Sequence: First or last event from a set of pictures.
      (3) Detail in sentences.
   b. *Comprehension—Not Mastered*—When he reads the exercises.
      (1) Main idea: Paragraph topics.
      (2) Sequence: Events which occur before and after.
      (3) Locating details in a passage.
      (4) Affixes: Prefixes and suffixes.
      (5) Context clues.
3. *Dolch 220 Basic Sight Vocabulary.* These 220 words comprise about 50 percent of the running words a child encounters in his reading. George knew 80 percent of these words. This should be about equal to reading at the second-grade level.

IV. Summary of Testing Results:

George's reading difficulty is not due to deficiencies in visual acuity or auditory discrimination. According to the Gates-MacGinitie Reading Survey and the Gray Oral Reading Test, he is reading at about a beginning second-year level. There is a discrepancy of about one year when one compares these test scores to this child's expected reading grade level of 3.5 indicated by the Peabody Picture Vocabulary Test and the Bond and Tinker Reading Expectancy Formula.

In investigating George's strengths and weaknesses in essential reading skills such as comprehension, phonic analysis, structural analysis, and sight vocabulary, we see no one outstanding strength or weakness.

During the summer reading clinic it appeared that George's reading problems were manifested by the lack of interest in reading, and therefore, a general failure to read more at leisure or take an active interest in reading activities at school.

V. Recommendations:

The following home and school recommendations are suggested in an attempt to focus on George's reading problem. We hope that by following those suggestions, George's reading ability will improve.

A. Home:
   1. George needs to read high-interest books which are written at his independent reading level. The community li-

brarian should be able to prescribe some books written at a first or second-grade level.

2. George's parents might be able to afford books written at his reading level. A list of some good series and titles is included at the end of this report.

3. George needs to have a quiet place where he can read silently each evening. A minimum of fifteen minutes practice each evening would be good for George.

4. George might enjoy keeping a chart or file of the books he reads. This would be a visual representation of his accomplishments and could encourage his future reading of books and/or magazines.

5. George needs to have a good model to emulate. If Mr. and Mrs. Thomas could read each evening, George might see the value that could be derived by reading for enjoyment.

6. Since George loves to receive praise, his parents should compliment him whenever he reads. Perhaps a special word of encouragement could be given whenever he finishes a book.

7. Practice is the best way to become a good reader. George could spend a few minutes reading to his folks each evening. Remember, his books should be written at a first- or second-grade level. It is better to practice reading books that seem too easy rather than too difficult.

8. It is important for children to think about what they are reading. One way to do this is to have George predict what he thinks will happen next in a story.

9. When George comes to a word he doesn't know, have him read to the end of the sentence to see if he can discover the word from the context. Then have him use skills he knows to unlock the unknown word. Last, you supply the word.

10. George enjoys playing commercially available board games which require some reading. Two good games are Scrabble for Juniors and Scribbage. Any game which requires easy reading should prove beneficial.

11. George has developed a strategy for avoiding reading. He continually verbalizes about topics unrelated to reading. By doing this, he is avoiding what he most needs—practice in reading. Mr. and Mrs. Thames need to be aware of this avoidance technique and should not let George use it.

B. School

1. A language-experience approach was utilized this summer with George. This proved most successful in interesting George in reading and providing practice in his reading skills. The words from each language-experience

story were recorded on file cards and placed in his file box. These words were then practiced daily to ensure mastery.

2. Review the words on the Johnson Basic Sight Vocabulary. An attached list of these words is provided.

3. Review the following skills.
   a. Short and long vowels.
   b. Hard and soft c and g.
   c. Final consonant blends—nt, st.
   d. Vowel digraphs—ow, ee, oa, ay, ai, ea.
   e. Vowel diphthongs—oy, oi, ou, ow.
   f. Syllabication.
   g. Root words and endings.
   h. Main idea, sequencing events, details, making inferences, and critical judgment.

4. George needs to have expectations spelled out before each day's lesson. To help him reach these expectations, he needs structure and guidance. The use of a "contract" system is one way which will work with George. It will allow him to know where he is and where he is going. Once he has completed certain requirements he should be rewarded, for example, allowing him to go to the activity room.

5. Keep a chart of all successful experiences and make George well aware of his progress. The use of stickers as a reward system are most effective on charts for keeping track of the number of books read or the number of new words learned.

6. Utilize a directed reading thinking activity lesson (DRTA), as suggested by Russell G. Stauffer in *Directing the Reading-Thinking Process* (New York: Harper & Row, 1975). This will permit George to advance in critical reading skills through inquiry, processing information, and validating answers.

7. Send a progress checklist home weekly.

8. George is an active boy who needs to work in an atmosphere where he is expected to complete his assignments. He needs a firm—but fair—teacher. His teacher should make George aware of her expectations and then follow through to see that he completes his assignments.

George has the ability to do good work and to become a very good reader, *if* his instruction is appropriate and he does his assignments. George's parents can foster the idea that he must follow directions and complete his assignments. The prognosis for George is good *if* the school and his parents work together cooperatively.

Submitted by <u>Francis Allen</u>
<u>Reading Specialist</u>

BOOKS AND MAGAZINES

Series Books

Sailor Jack Books. Selma Wassermann and Jack Wassermann. Chicago: Benefic Press.

Space-Age Books. Hazel W. Carson. Chicago: Benefic Press.

Tom Logan Series. Edna Walker Chandler. Chicago: Benefic Press.

Read to Read. New York: MacMillan.

Aviation Readers. New York: MacMillan.

I Can Read Books. New York: Harper & Row.

The Moonbeam Series. Selma and Jack Wassermann. Chicago: Benefic Press.

The Magic Bridge Readers. Miriam E. Mason. Englewood Cliffs, New Jersey: Prentice-Hall.

Magazines and Newspapers

Child Life, 1100 Waterway Boulevard, Indianapolis, Indiana 466702.

Children's Digest, Parents Magazine Enterprises, Inc., Bergenfield, New Jersey 07621.

Highlights for Children, Highlights for Children, Inc., 2300 West Fifth Avenue, Columbus, Ohio 43216.

News Ranger, Scholastic Magazines, Inc., 50 West 44th Street, New York, New York 10036.

Scholastic News Trails, Scholastic News Trails, 902 Sylvan Avenue, Englewood Cliffs, New Jersey 07632.

Specific Book Titles

Ten Apples Up on Top. Theo LeSieg. New York: Random House, 1961.

Peter and the Rocket Ship. Hazel W. Corson. Chicago: Benefic Press, 1955.

Science Book of Flying. Rocco V. Feravolo. Champaign, Ill.: Garrard, 1960.

Animal Riddles. Bennet Cerf. New York: Random House, 1964.

Olaf Reads. Joan Lexau. New York: Dial Press, 1961.

Here Comes the Strikeout. Leonard Kessler. New York: Harper & Row, 1965.

Kick, Pass and Run. Leonard Kessler. New York: Harper & Row, 1966.

Publishers

Garrard Publishing Co., 1607 North Market Street, Champaign, Illinois 61820

Benefic Press, 10300 West Roosevelt Road, Westchester, Illinois 60153

Bowmar Publishing Co., 622 Rodier Drive, Glendale, California 91201

Childrens Press, 1224 West Van Buren Street, Chicago, Illinois 60607

MacMillan Publishing Co., Inc., 866 Third Avenue, New York, New York 10022

SUMMARY

This chapter has covered the topics of writing IEPs and case studies. We have explained how written reports are used by individuals both inside and outside of the educational community.

Ten guidelines were presented to help teachers do a better job when writing reports. These guidelines, when used with the suggested formats for reporting data, should ease the writing task and produce professional-looking reports.

We have also discussed two variations of reports. The purposes of each have been explained and actual samples were provided for your inspection. With practice, your writing of reports should become easier and less time-consuming so that you can get on with the job of helping students.

RELATED ACTIVITIES

1. Using the general suggestions for writing reports that were presented in this chapter, ask a reading teacher if you may review several case studies. Make notes on how you might use these reports to help you write your own case study reports. Also think how you might edit the reports to improve their overall quality.
2. Ask a school principal if you might examine some IEPs drawn up in his or her school. Ask the principal how IEPs are used in the building. Talk to several teachers to determine their attitudes toward IEPs.
3. Review three to five reading diagnosis books to determine how their authors suggest case study reports should be written. Pay special attention to the suggested formats. Make a list of the common features found in all the reports; then make a list on how the reports differ. Using these data, construct your own case study report and subject it to a peer review.
4. Practice administering several reading tests and writing a case study report from these data. Submit your report to your professor for a review.

RELATED READINGS

CALFEE, ROBERT C., AND PRISCILLA A. DRUM, EDS. *Teaching Reading in Compensatory Classes.* Newark, Del.: International Reading Association, 1979.

SPACHE, GEORGE, KEN MCILROY, AND PAUL C. BERG. *Case Studies in Reading Disability.* Boston: Allyn & Bacon, 1981.

STRUNK, WILLIAM, JR., AND E. B. WHITE. *The Elements of Style.* New York: Macmillan, 1959.

TURNBULL, ANN P., BONNIE B. STRICKLAND, AND JOHN C. BRANTLEY. *Developing and Implementing Individualized Education Programs.* Columbus, Ohio: Chas. C Merrill, 1978.

WILSON, ROBERT M. *Diagnostic and Remedial Reading for Classroom and Clinic,* 4th ed. Columbus, Ohio: Chas. C Merrill, 1981.

REFERENCES

GOODMAN, YETTA, AND CAROLYN BURKE. *Reading Miscue Inventory.* New York: MacMillan, 1972.

GORDON, THOMAS. *Parent Effectiveness Training.* New York: P. H. Wyden, 1970.

MARVER, JAMES D., AND JANE L. DAVID. *Three*

States' Experiences with Individualized Education Program (IEP) Requirements Similar to P.L. 94-142. Research Report EPRC 23. Menlo Park, Calif.: SRI International, Educational Policy Research Center, 1978.

MASLOW, ABRAHAM H. *Toward a Psychology of Being.* New York: D. Van Nostrand, 1962.

ROGERS, CARL. *On Becoming a Person.* Boston: Houghton-Mifflin, 1961.

11

EVALUATION OF READING TESTS AND PROGRAMS

Upon completion of this chapter, you will be able to

1. State the need and purposes for evaluating reading programs.
2. Match commonly used testing and evaluation terms with their appropriate meanings.
3. Explain the characteristics of norm- and criterion-referenced tests and state when each should be used.
4. Decide when it is appropriate to use formative and summative evaluation techniques.

One of our daughters recently wrote a note to her grandparents after receiving her nine-week report card. In the letter she said, "I like getting good grades. It makes me feel good." We think most teachers feel positive and rewarded by doing a good job with their students, too. They enjoy working with students who are interested in learning and who do well on assignments and tests. Most people, regardless of age, need and seek feedback on their behavior. We receive feedback from students in the form of smiles, approving nods, outbursts, and sullenness. Why is it, then, that so often we think of feedback from testing and evaluation as intrusions into our teaching day? Perhaps we have failed to see the true values—and limitations—that accompany testing and assessment. We hope that this chapter will demonstrate that testing and evaluation can, and should, play an important part in a school reading program.

Before we get to the central issues, allow us to clarify one point. There is an important difference between the terms *testing* and *evaluation*. *Testing* connotes paper-and-pencil assessments that provide objective (albeit, not always accurate) data about students' performances. *Evaluation,* on the other hand, implies a much broader-based approach. Although paper-and-pencil tests may be used in an evaluation, other important facets are also included. Evaluations of a student, for instance, may consist of teachers' observations, samples of daily work, and performance on selected tasks. Thus, paper-and-pencil tests are only a part of a comprehensive evaluation profile. With this in mind, let us now turn to more specific means and reasons for measuring students' performances.

THE PURPOSE AND NEED
FOR EVALUATION

The concept of evaluation can be traced back more than 4,000 years (Popham, 1980) to when civil service examinations were used in China to identify individuals who could best meet selected job specifications. In this country, evaluation has played a role in education for approximately half a century. Today, evaluation—and especially the testing industry—is big business. In fact, almost everyone in education becomes involved in testing controversies sooner or later. The need for hard data is so pervasive that MacGinitie (1973) was led to summarize the state of testing by saying

> Some people make money by producing and selling tests. Some people make money by writing about what's wrong with tests. Some people like tests because they feel tests help them in evaluating the work of the schools. Some people like tests because they feel tests help them in guiding individual development. Some people dislike tests because some testing is a large commercial enterprise. Some people dislike tests because they feel tests sometimes damage a person's evaluation of himself. Some people like tests because they believe tests tell them *more* than the tests really do. Some people dislike tests because they believe tests tell them *less* than the tests really do. Some people have been told by tests that they aren't as bright as they think they are. Other people have been told by tests that they are at least *almost* as bright as they think they are (p. 13)—

(Reprinted with permission of the author and the International Reading Association)

If this is an accurate appraisal of testing in America—and we believe it is—why should we bother to evaluate students' reading ability? There are many answers to this question, but most of them are related to one central theme. Testing and evaluation can assist us in the decision-making process as we attempt to improve instruction for school children.

Evaluation, especially paper-and-pencil tests, can provide objective and reliable information. When children make suitable progress during our contact with them, these data are perceived as rewarding and motivating. The data can also indicate if reading growth has not occurred, which is an indication that adjustments need to be made. In both instances, information gathered from testing permits us to make professional judgments about the appropriateness of our educational efforts, and hence, increases our accountability to ourselves, our students, and the community at large.

We believe there are other valid reasons for evaluating students' reading ability:

1. Testing (tempered with professional judgment) permits us to determine objectively who should be included in special reading programs (such as Chapter I, learning disabilities, or gifted).

2. Testing provides a means for evaluating individual progress on either a short- or long-term basis.

3. Testing gives insights into students' reading strengths and weaknesses (for example, the word recognition tests and IRIs discussed in Chapter 5).

4. Testing allows us to assess the strengths and weaknesses of a national, state, district, school, or classroom reading program (more about this later).

5. Testing lets administrators determine if school committees and the taxpayers are receiving what they are paying for.

6. Testing permits us to evaluate new curricula, new materials, or other experimental variables.

7. Testing, especially in programs that utilize skills management systems, enables the monitoring of pupils' progress.

8. Testing allows us to make better informed decisions, which can have long-range consequences on students, teachers, parents, and the community.

To put testing in perspective, we will describe how it is used to improve reading programs. First, we will examine testing from a national perspective. Then we will show you how evaluation helps educators at numerous other levels until we finally reach the level that you are probably most concerned with: the classroom. Keep in mind that tests are used at each of these levels to improve our delivery of reading instruction to students.

The National Assessment
of Educational Progress

The National Assessment of Educational Progress (NAEP) is an evaluation of the reading status of persons nine, thirteen, seventeen, and twenty-six to thirty-five years old in the United States. Federally funded, the NAEP assessments are conducted every five years and are designed to detect trends in the reading ability of the American populace. Because it samples and tests individuals throughout the nation, comparisons among geographical regions as well as ethnic groups can be made.

Since sampling procedures are used, it is difficult to arrive at any specific conclusion about a state, district, or school reading program. Instead, broad generalizations about a region's reading ability are the best that can be extrapolated from the data. The reading ability of individuals in the Northeast, for example, can be compared to those in the Southwest, West, and Central United States. Comparisons are also possible by sex, race, parents' education, and community type. Although classroom teachers may find such comparisons mundane and of little interest, policy makers at the national level can use these data when deciding how to allocate funds based on need.

The goal of the first NAEP, done in 1971, was to collect baseline data which would permit later comparisons. The second NAEP was carried out in 1975 and allowed educators to evaluate what was happening to reading ability in the United States. The findings revealed, for example, that whereas nine-year-olds improved overall, thirteen-year-olds declined in ability. Nine-year-old blacks showed a large improvement in all skills (Venezky, 1977).

There have been major changes in the objectives and test items since the 1975 evaluation. These are most evident in the area of reading comprehension (NAEP, 1980). The 1979–80 objectives were categorized into four major areas:

1. Values reading and literature.
2. Comprehends written works.
3. Responds to written works.
4. Applies study skills in reading.

Although the NAEP has been criticized for providing data that are too general and take too long to collect (Venezky, 1977), it does tell us what percentage of the population can perform a given task as required by a series of test items.

To summarize, the NAEP gives educators a valuable profile of reading ability in the United States. To help states improve their respective programs, on the other hand, it comes up short. To achieve this goal, we need to go to the next level of testing: evaluation at a statewide level.

Statewide Evaluation of Reading

Although the NAEP provides insights from a national perspective, most officials in state departments of education are more concerned with the status of reading ability within their own states. Thus, many states have mandated yearly statewide testing programs. A state, for example, may decide to test all fourth-, eighth-, and eleventh-graders enrolled in public and private schools. Or this same population may be sampled and only a portion of each group tested. Whatever plan is chosen, the objectives are usually the same: to compare reading achievement among districts or within the state over a period of years.

In the case of district comparisons, individuals within departments of education can determine what factors influence reading scores within their state. Why, for example, should two allegedly similar districts produce dissimilar test score averages?

Yearly statewide testing programs also permit officials to monitor trends in reading performance over a period of years. This analysis may lead to special projects or to an overall effort to improve scores in a specific area (for example, study skills).

Statewide testing, like the NAEP, however, fails to provide substantive data for describing the reading performance of individual students. To obtain this information, we must move to the next level of testing: district-wide assessment.

District-Wide Assessment

For many classroom and reading teachers, this level of assessment is the first to have a direct bearing on their instructional programs. Most school districts test students on a yearly basis to help administrators evaluate district-wide goals and to spot weaknesses within the instructional program. This level of assessment relies heavily, if not exclusively, on standardized tests that have been normed on large samples of students.

Many districts avail themselves of automated test-scoring services available from major test-publishing companies. Thus local testing norms are established, which when used with the nationally derived norms, permit a thorough, school-by-school analysis of the district's students. Some companies also provide analyses of individual items on each test.

Since later in this chapter we will devote considerable space to discussing the specific steps in evaluating programs, let us move on to the next level of testing: school-wide assessment.

School-Wide Assessment

School-wide assessment is usually related directly to the district-wide testing program, if one exists, because an individual school's scores are easily obtained from the district's data. In some communities, though, there is no coordinated testing program, and each school is free to select a test of its own choosing. Thus, a variety of instruments may be used in any one school or among the combined schools within the district. Such situations make it difficult to monitor the progress of students or groups as they move through the grades. And because individual tests have been normed on different populations, it is difficult to compare scores from two or more instruments.

One major difference between school-wide assessment and other programs we have discussed is that for the first time, a more comprehensive evaluation of the reading program is possible, and thus, its direct impact can be determined. Informal tests, samples of students' work, IRI scores, and the like, as well as criterion-referenced test results, can all be scrutinized.

Tests should measure what you have been trying to teach.
(Peter P. Tobia)

As you have probably surmised, the nearer the testing and evaluation process gets to the classroom, the more types of data are available to assess the program's effectiveness—which leads us to our next and final level of evaluation.

Classroom Assessment

This level of assessment has special meaning to a teacher, whether a classroom reading teacher or one who has a case load of severely disabled readers. In both instances, your personal effectiveness will, in part, be determined by your students' performance. Although you will want to use many procedures to determine whether your efforts have succeeded or been in vain, paper-and-pencil tests will probably provide at least one objective measure of performance. The majority of your testing will no doubt be less formal than the other tests we've described, however. You will probably administer IRIs and teacher-made tests to determine reading levels. You might rely on criterion-referenced tests to determine what specific skills your pupils need. One thing is certain: your main reason for testing will be to gain diagnostic insights about your students. Keep in mind, however, that the administrators who are ultimately responsible for the program will occasionally require you to give standardized, norm-referenced tests. Although you may question their wisdom—as will your students—you should remember that they have an obligation to their constituents (that is, taxpayers) to be accountable for the overall educational program.

Conclusion

We have tried to demonstrate that testing and evaluation are designed to help individuals make intelligent, objective decisions about reading programs. The intent of testing depends largely on the organization that administers the tests. And each organization may have a unique purpose, depending on its domain.

Testing should be thought of as only a part of an evaluation program. The closer the testing program moves toward the classroom, the greater the opportunity for using more informal techniques of measurement.

Viewed in one light, testing can be perceived as a valuable contribution to the improvement of instruction. At the other extreme, it can be seen as threatening and needless. Our belief is that in a proper context, testing can be the first step in improving instruction.

THE TERMINOLOGY OF TESTING AND EVALUATION

Many teachers are opposed to testing because they have not been involved in the selection process. As a consequence, the instruments used to determine reading growth sometimes fail to reflect teachers' objectives for instruction. Simply put, the tests don't measure what teachers teach.

Another possible reason for antitesting sentiment is that testing and its related terminology are sometimes mystifying and threatening. To overcome this fear, we have included some of the terminology that you will encounter when selecting and using tests, especially in reading. If you are already using tests in your classroom, this is an opportunity to compare them with tests we can recommend; and if you are now reviewing or selecting tests, you will become more aware of what factors make a test "good."

Validity

Any book on educational measurement will quickly inform you that validity means "Does the test measure what it purports to measure?" In actuality, however, questions of validity are more complex than this and, hence, usually defy a simple "yes" or "no" answer. Since there are a number of different kinds of validity, it's good to be acquainted with each. Here are some of the more frequently mentioned types.

FACE VALIDITY   If a test looks like it measures what it intends to measure, it probably has high face validity. In other words, "on the face of it" the test items must be judged to measure what they are designed to assess.

A word of warning: you cannot determine face validity by simply reading the test's title. Names of tests are sometimes misleading. Take time to look at individual items before drawing any conclusions about face validity.

CONSTRUCT VALIDITY   In Chapter 3 we discussed the role of reading theory and its impact on instructional decision making. Implicitly, a reading test must be designed with a theory of reading in mind. If, for instance, you believe the reading act to be a subset of discrete reading skills, you would probably select a test with many short subtests assessing such areas as phonics and structural analysis. If, on the other hand, you believe reading to be a more holistic process such as that described by psycholinguistics, your tests might include items measuring general comprehension rather than discrete subskills.

Construct validity, then, is directly related to the theoretical belief teachers have about the reading process. The closer the test parallels an individual's belief about the reading process, the greater its construct validity. Obviously, reviewers might feel a test lacks construct validity if it does not reflect their biases about the act of reading, and thus the degree to which they feel a reading test has construct validity may vary.

CONTENT VALIDITY   Content validity is the degree to which a test measures the content that is taught. In one sense, the test might be thought of as sampling the content of instruction. If 50 percent of the reading instruction focuses on word identification and 50 percent on comprehension, half the items on the test(s) should measure word identification and half should measure comprehension. An instrument on which half the items measured word identification and the remaining items measured map reading and reference skills would have questionable validity in this case. Like construct validity, content validity may be perceived differently by different reviewers.

Also, like the other forms of validity, content validity is best determined by examining each test item. Teachers may want to take the test, too. In this way, they can determine the appropriateness of the test items and at the same time become familiar with the administration procedures.

CONCURRENT VALIDITY   Concurrent validity is the degree to which a test is related to another test. The relationship is usually expressed with a correlation coefficient, $+1.0$ being a perfect positive correlation (the tests measure the exact same attributes) and -1.0 being a perfect negative correlation (the tests do not measure the same attributes). In practical terms, most similar tests probably correlate in the area of $+.20$ to $+.90$; that is, they range from a low positive correlation to a high positive correlation.

If teachers developed their own reading tests, they could check its concurrent validity by administering it along with a recognized reading test. By computing and comparing the correlation coefficient between the test scores, they could establish the concurrent validity of their instrument. A high correlation coefficient would indicate that the test taps some of the same abilities as the recognized test. A low correlation would mean that the two instruments measure different factors.

PREDICTIVE VALIDITY   As you might have guessed, predictive validity is the ability of an instrument to predict performance or success in another area. Tests of reading readiness, for example, have been designed to identify students ready for reading instruction as well as to predict how well they will perform once they have received formal instruction.

The predictive ability of any instrument always contains a degree of error. Factors such as student motivation and appropriateness of instruction are just two variables that can affect the predictive ability of the test—and there are others. Thus, it is important to understand that tests that purport to measure predictive qualities must be used with caution.

Reliability

Not only must reading tests be valid, but also they must be of sufficient quality so that the examiner can have confidence that the scores are, indeed, true representations of the students' abilities and are not based on chance. This is where test reliabilities enter the picture.

There are many factors that can influence the reliability of an instrument. Kavale (1979) has identified some of them:

1. The length of the test.
2. The homogeneity of the items.
3. The difficulty of the items.
4. The homogeneity of the norming sample.

Generally, longer tests are more reliable than shorter ones. A criterion-referenced test, for example, should have a *minimum* of four items to measure *each objective* (Morris and Fitz-Gibbon, 1978). Tests composed of similar types of items will be more reliable than those consisting of unlike items, other things being equal. Tests with a large proportion of items that are too easy or too difficult will be less reliable than tests with items that have a mid-range of difficulty. And a norming group that has a wide range of ability will produce a test of greater reliability than a norming group that is homogeneous.

Test reliabilities are stated as reliability coefficients and are expressed in a decimal format much like concurrent validity. Although reliability is a relative concept, some arbitrary standards do exist. Acceptable reliability levels are generally considered to be +.80 or higher. The higher the reliability level, the more confidence teachers can have in the accuracy of the score. There are three important kinds of reliability: test-retest, alternate form, and split-half.

TEST-RETEST RELIABILITY   Test-retest reliability is perhaps the simplest form. It is the degree to which a test would produce the same score if given a second time to the same individual or group. If a wide discrepancy exists between the two scores, the test-retest reliability should be questioned. This type of reliability is extremely important in selecting diagnostic instruments. According to Arter and Jenkins (1979) the test-retest reliabilities of most diagnostic tests are unacceptable because each test contains a degree of error. If the error is substantial, there is a good probability that the student's score is not a "true score." Hence, students could achieve scores classifying them as having disabilities when taking a test for the first time, but upon retesting, they could be ineligible for inclusion in a reading program. Only tests with reliabilities in the +.80 to +.90 range should be considered for diagnosis. Tests with low test-retest reliabilities should not be used in making important educational decisions about disabled readers. Instruments for which no test-retest reliability data exist should be used with caution.

ALTERNATE FORM RELIABILITY   Alternate form reliability has sometimes been called *parallel form reliability* or *equivalent form reliability*. It refers to the degree of commonality between two tests and is important if teachers plan to select two instruments to measure reading progress. For example, if teachers wanted to measure the impact of a new program on the reading ability of their students, they would probably choose two tests from the same publisher to measure the students' pretest to posttest gain. They would probably choose the alternate forms of the same instrument to measure "before program" and "after program" differences (that is, gain scores). If the two tests were not of equal difficulty, teachers could not be confident that any gain (or loss) was the result of the instructional program. The "change score" may simply reflect the lack of precision of the two instruments.

SPLIT-HALF RELIABILITY   Frequently, the reliability of a test is determined by comparing odd- and even-numbered test items. It is possible to calculate the reliability of an instrument in a relatively short time by using a common statistical technique. This statistic, called the Spearman-Brown formula, yields a correlation coefficient that permits an objective comparison of tests. If the test is to be used for individual diagnosis, reliabilities in the area of .90 are preferred. Survey tests can have slightly lower reliabilities (.75 to .85) and still be acceptable because they are used to make decisions about groups, not individuals.

Standard Error of Measurement

The score a student receives on a test is, at best, only an approximation of the individual's true score. In actuality, the true score may be slightly higher or lower. Thus, an individual's test score should be considered only as a gross indication of the true score since the actual score may vary within a predetermined range. This range is called the *standard error of measurement* and is a function of the reliability of the test as well as the standard deviation of the score(s). Although this information may appear esoteric and uninteresting to those not interested in measurement techniques, the implication for teachers is apparent. Scores students receive on tests are not exact representations of their abilities and should therefore be interpreted with caution. On a 100-item test with a standard error of 4.0, for example, a student who received a score of 76 might fall anywhere between the true score range of 72 and 80. The less reliable the test, the greater the standard error of measurement and the less confidence a teacher can place in the accuracy of a student's score.

Passage Dependency

The term *passage dependency* is frequently used when discussing the measurement of reading comprehension. It refers to the degree to which the student can answer a question without ever having read the paragraph on which it was based. It has been argued that *reading* comprehension is measured only if a passage must be read before the accompanying comprehension question(s) can be answered.

Tuinman (1973–74) and Allington *et al.* (1977) have demonstrated that many of the popular norm-referenced and diagnostic reading tests lack passage dependency. By using grammatical clues, knowing answers from prior learning, eliminating irrelevant distractors, and using clues obtained in other questions, children are able to answer up to one-fourth of the comprehension questions frequently asked.

Since passage dependency is usually not discussed in a test's administration or technical manual, it is up to the teachers to make sure that tests with a high level of passage dependency are used. Otherwise, they are more apt to be measuring *general* comprehension than *reading* comprehension.

THE USE
OF EVALUATION INSTRUMENTS

The selection of reading tests should be dependent on a teacher's need for data when planning instruction. Assuming that individuals can identify tests with high validity or reliability, they are now ready to choose tests that they can use in their reading program. (In actuality, this choice may not be solely theirs. School-, district-, or state-mandated testing may be something they have little control over.)

The tests that are reviewed will probably be one of two varieties: norm-referenced or criterion-referenced. Since each is intended for a different purpose, we need to look at the characteristics of both in more detail.

Norm-Referenced Tests

Norm-referenced tests, sometimes called survey tests, are designed to rank students according to ability. The test items are written to produce a wide variance among the examinees. Furthermore, only *general* reading ability, not specific skills, is measured. Typically, norm-referenced tests measure such facets as speed of reading, word meaning or vocabulary, and paragraph meaning or comprehension.

Popular norm-referenced reading tests which are frequently used in schools include the Iowa Tests of Basic Skills (1971), the Stanford Achievement Test: Reading Test (1973), the Gates-MacGinitie Reading Tests (1978), the Comprehensive Test of Basic Skills (1968), the Metropolitan Achievement Tests: Reading (1978), and the California Achievement Test (1963). There are many other norm-referenced reading tests also used, but these are some of the most popular and, hence, most frequently encountered by reading teachers.

Most widely used and respected norm-referenced reading tests have been meticulously developed and include only items that are capable of discriminating among learners. A broad cross-section of subjects are tested to develop the norming tables. Usually, norm-referenced reading tests have been thoroughly field-tested.

Standardized test scores are reported in a number of ways.

RAW SCORES   Raw scores reflect the number of correct responses a subject makes on a given test or subtest. By themselves, raw scores don't mean much. A raw score of 10, for example, doesn't tell you whether there were ten or forty items on the complete battery. In the former case, a score of 10 would be something to celebrate; in the latter, it would not. To summarize, raw scores are meaningless unless we know the total number of items on the test.

GRADE EQUIVALENT   Grade equivalent scores are the most revered, most misunderstood, and most misused of all test scores. They are an artifact that have little meaning for a number of reasons.

First, grade-level scores cannot be equated with a graded-reading-text level. Grade-level scores are only the average scores at that grade level for all subjects on which the test was standardized (Schwartz, 1977). Students at different grade levels could be administered different levels of the same test (for example, Stanford Achievement Test) and achieve the same grade equivalent score. In actuality, however, their reading levels may vary considerably.

A second danger in using grade equivalent scores is that the scale on which the scores are derived is not an interval scale but an ordinal scale. This means that an increase (or decrease) in raw score will not yield equal grade equivalent scores over the range of the norming table. An increase of one raw score point in the middle of the scale, for example, may not result in any grade equivalent score change. This same one point change at either end of the scale, however, might result in as much as .7 of a grade-level change.

The practice of averaging grade-level scores is not recommended. For that matter, since there are many more meaningful ways to report test scores, grade equivalent scores should be used carefully and only when necessary.

PERCENTILE RANK   Percentile rank scores indicate the percentage of students who scored below the testee on the given test. A percentile score of 65, for instance, indicates that 65 percent of the individuals on whom the test was normed scored below the student whose scores you are examining. Like all test scores, percentile ranks are only approximations of a student's true test score since factors such as guessing and other testing variables can affect the scores. Percentile ranks, therefore, should be perceived as only one of a possible number of scores within a band of scores. (The error of measurement in all tests require that we keep this in mind.)

As with other scores that are based on a norming group, percentile ranks should be intercepted in light of the group on which the instrument was normed (Massad, 1972). In other words, if the composition of the norming group were to change, there is a high probability that the norming tables would be altered.

A final point to remember when interpreting percentile rank scores is that like grade equivalent scores, they are also based on an ordinal and not an interval scale. Thus, scores that are extremely high or low are less apt to reflect true ability than are scores near the middle of the scale.

STANINE SCORES   The stanine score indicates how far a student's score deviates from the mean of the norm group. *Stanine* is derived from the words *standard* and *nine*. A stanine score of 5 is the midpoint for the distribution of scores. The highest stanine score possible is 9, the lowest is 1. Unlike the other scores we have discussed, the stanine score is computed by determining the mean and the standard deviation scores for a group. The standard deviation for stanine scores is two. Thus, a stanine score of 7 would be one standard deviation above the mean.

As educators, we are often quick to discuss grade equivalent or percentile scores and reluctant to use stanine scores. This is unfortunate, for stanine scores are computed on a more substantive basis and allow teachers to compare an individual's scores from two or more tests.

NORMAL CURVE EQUIVALENT   A normal curve equivalent (NCE) is a standard score that has been transformed to match the percentile distribution at values of 1, 50, and 99. The NCE mean is 50, and the standard deviation equals

21.06. The NCE scale is an equal-interval scale unlike the percentile score scale. That is, an equal distance exists between any two adjacent scores on the scale. Although NCEs resemble stanine scores (both are equal-interval scales), NCEs are more sensitive to changes in scores. There are eleven NCEs for every stanine.

Normal curve equivalent scores can be quickly determined by examining a test administrator's manual. Once the student's percentile score is computed, a conversion table in the manual usually allows the teacher to interpret percentile scores in NCEs.

One way NCEs are used is to see if there has been significant reading growth between two testing periods. By computing their group's average NCE in the fall and again in the spring, teachers could see if their program was responsible for a change in scores. If the average NCE was greater in the spring, for example, they could conclude that their program had a positive effect on reading achievement (all other things being equal). Thus, the difference between the two NCE scores is a measure of a project's impact. Generally, an increase of seven NCEs between two testing periods is considered a significant gain.

Before we move on, allow us to make a few final points about norm-referenced instruments. First, a norm-referenced test (or any test for that matter) should be selected with a specific purpose in mind. Perhaps the administrators of a district want to monitor the yearly performance of students. Or maybe students need to be selected for an intervention program. Standardized, norm-referenced reading tests probably best serve these functions.

Second, if teachers are going to compare their students with those on which the test was normed (that is, use the norming tables), they should select only instruments that included students like theirs in the norming sample. The more unique their group is from the norming sample, the less confidence they should have in the test scores. Factors such as age, race, sex, educational level, socioeconomic class, and geographical location of the groups should be considered.

Criterion-Referenced Tests

Criterion-referenced tests differ from norm-referenced tests—although outwardly they may resemble each other—in the nature of their items and the use to which the test is put.

Earlier, we mentioned that developers of norm-referenced tests try to obtain items that maximize differences in students' performance. In other words, the items are written at a level that is maximally discriminating. Items included in criterion-referenced tests, on the other hand, are written to measure skills or abilities explicated by earlier identified objectives. Thus, students who know the skill should correctly answer the item when taking the test. Those not possessing the skill should fail.

The notion of criterion-referenced testing is not new. At one time, these types of instruments were called *mastery tests*. In reality, any test on which a passing score is needed might be thought of as a criterion-referenced test.

The past decade has brought a renewed interest in this kind of testing, partly because of the work conducted at the Instructional Objectives Exchange at the University of California—Los Angeles, and the Wisconsin Research and

Development Center for Individualized Schooling. Both university-affiliated organizations were instrumental in developing criterion-referenced reading tests that could relate to the commercial reading programs used in classrooms. The success of these two efforts soon led to a growing number of publishing companies developing and including criterion-referenced tests with their reading programs. Presently, both program-independent as well as program-embedded tests are available from a number of sources. Some of the former are these:

> Wisconsin Tests of Reading Skill Development: Word Attack, Comprehension, Study Skills (Otto and Askov, 1973).
>
> IOX Objective-Based Tests—Reading: Word Attack and Comprehension (1973).
>
> The Cooper-McGuire Diagnostic Word-Analysis Test (Cooper and McGuire, 1971).
>
> The Croft Inservice Program: Reading Comprehension Skills (McGuire and Bumpus, 1971).
>
> Prescriptive Reading Inventory (1974).

The program-imbedded tests from publishers of basal readers are usually purchased separately from other materials but are closely correlated with the readers and workbooks. Teachers should check with the salesperson who sells the basal readers to see if criterion-referenced tests are available for their particular program.

Developing valid and reliable criterion-referenced tests (or any tests, for that matter) is difficult and requires expertise frequently found only at institutions of higher learning and within test-development companies. It is easier and considerably less expensive to purchase already existing criterion-referenced tests than it is to develop them oneself.

Before teachers select criterion-referenced tests there are a few things they should keep in mind. First, they should select only enough tests to measure the important objectives. In our experience, this is one of the most important, yet overlooked, aspects of test selection.

Second, they should examine each test to see that it has acceptable construct validity. In other words, does the test reflect their beliefs about the reading process? Since most criterion-referenced tests have not been validated or have been subjected to inappropriate validation procedures, this step may prove frustrating (Sheehan and Marcus, 1977).

Third, they should try to use tests that have test-retest and split-half reliabilities in the area of $+.75$ (Morris and Fitz-Gibbon, 1978). Hayward (1968) suggests even higher reliabilities. Since teachers will be making instructional decisions based on these test scores, they want to be sure that the scores are not primarily a function of chance but instead reflect the students' knowledge of the skills being assessed.

Finally, teachers should try to determine the subtest intercorrelations among the tests in the battery. Unless a low to moderate correlation coefficient (for example $<+.65$) exists between tests, there is a danger that they may be measuring the same factor. Since criterion-referenced reading tests are designed to measure discrete skills, it is important that the tests selected do indeed perform this function. High correlations among subtests indicate that the same ability(ies) are being measured. By squaring the correlation, teachers can determine what percent of the variance is shared by the two subtests. A subtest correlation of +.82, for example, indicates that 67 percent of the factor being measured is shared by the two instruments ($.82 \times .82 = .67$). Since a differential diagnosis is based on the assumption that discrete abilities exist and can be measured, it's important to choose tests that measure these independent factors.

Selecting a Reading Test

By now, teachers should have an idea of what factors influence the quality of tests. We have discussed the various kinds of validity and reliability. We've also touched on the meaning of error of measurement and passage dependency. Norm- and criterion-referenced reading tests were also described. Now teachers are ready to select a reading test to use with their students.

The first question to be answered when selecting a test is "What is the purpose of the testing?" If teachers intend to judge the overall reading ability of their class, they probably need a norm-referenced test. If they want to check the specific skills of their students, on the other hand, they should use a criterion-referenced test. Once they have determined their purpose, they are ready to choose a test.

After teachers have located a test for potential use, they should double-check to see that it is of the appropriate difficulty for the age and grade level they teach. A quick perusal of the subtests and items may reveal that it is too difficult or too easy. The test should be of sufficient length to provide the information teachers are looking for but not so long that students tire or give up prematurely.

It's also important to determine whether the test can be administered to a group or must be individually administered. Occasionally, criterion-referenced tests of word identification must be given individually unless encoding (spelling) ability rather than decoding (reading) is measured. This format allows the tests to be given to groups. Individuals must weigh the trade-offs when such compromises are made. (The format could raise questions about construct validity of the instrument.)

The content the test measures is of obvious importance. The abilities that are assessed should be an integral part of the instructional program. Some of these areas include word identification, comprehension, and study skills. A good rule of thumb teachers should follow is to test only what they teach.

Teachers should make sure the tests possess adequate validity and reliability. Unless high-quality tests are used, teachers will not have faith in the scores their students receive, and they will have wasted valuable time and energy. We cannot overemphasize the importance of choosing tests with appropriate psychometric properties. In addition to the validity and reliability scores, teachers must be sure the tests have a low standard error of measurement, and if comprehension is assessed, adequate passage dependency.

If teachers are considering giving the test more than once during the year, they might find out whether alternate forms of the test are available. If they are, different forms could be used whenever it was necessary to test. Or if frequent repeated testing is required, alternate forms might be used during the year.

Since time is a precious commodity to teachers, they should inspect each test to see how long it takes to administer and score it. Sometimes, machine-scoring is available from the publishing company. (Usually for an additional fee we might add.) Nevertheless, if teachers are responsible for a large number of students, machine-scoring could save them considerable time.

Most tests include an administrator's manual, and some even provide a technical manual. Information describing the development of the test, descriptions of the norming group, and other specifics relating to the instrument are frequently found in one of these two publications. The administrator's manual is necessary for giving the test; the technical manual covers technical aspects of design and development.

Finally, teachers need to determine whether the test is appropriate for classroom use. Some instruments are excessively long or must be individually administered, and thus their use is prohibitive. Special teachers of reading, however, might find that these same tests can be used in remedial settings where small groups are the norm rather than the exception.

To help teachers select tests that are appropriate for their particular situation, we have provided a Reading Test Review Form (see Figure 11-1). Since reading objectives vary from district to district, and even from school to school, it is important to select tests that measure these unique objectives. This form will help systemize the selection process.

In addition to forming their own opinion about individual tests, we recommend that teachers read what others have to say. One of the best sources is *Reading: Tests and Reviews I and II* (Buros, 1968, 1975). Figure 11-2 is an excerpt from this publication and should indicate what to expect from a review. This particular one is of the Classroom Reading Inventory but virtually all important reading tests have been reviewed at one time or another.

EVALUATION OF PROGRAMS

Most of us engage in program evaluation without realizing it. We make informal judgments about our students' reading ability. We "shift gears" and change the pace of instruction; we regroup students for instruction; and we administer norm-referenced reading tests.

In this section, we will make a case for a more formalized or systematic approach to evaluation. By choice, our treatment will be light-handed. Classroom and reading teachers shouldn't be expected to become evaluation experts. After all, their primary responsibility is to teach reading. But they should at least be acquainted with some basic evaluation principles.

The Need for Evaluation

As employees of an agency (school committee or board) we, as teachers, have an obligation to provide services to our clients—children. How effective we are in providing this service can be determined in a number of ways. Administra-

Figure 11.1 Reading Test Review Form

Name of Test Reviewed: _____

Author(s): _____

Publisher: _____

Date of Publication: _____

1. What is the intended purpose of the test?
2. What age level is the test designed for?
3. What grade level is the test designed for?
4. Is the test individually or group administered?
5. Is there a subtest to measure sight vocabulary?
6. Is there a subtest to measure phonic analysis skills? (If yes, what skills are assessed?)
7. Is there a subtest to measure structural analysis skills? (If yes, what skills are assessed?)
8. Is there a subtest designed to measure comprehension skills? (If yes, what specific abilities are measured?)
9. Does the test have the following types of validity:
    a. Face validity?
    b. Construct validity?
    c. Content validity?
    d. Concurrent validity?
    e. Predictive validity?
10. Does the test have the following types of reliability:
    a. Test-retest reliability?
    b. Alternate form reliability?
    c. Split-half reliability?
11. Does the test have an acceptable standard error of measurement?
12. Do the reading selections have adequate passage dependency?
13. Are there alternate forms of the test?
14. Approximately how long does it take to administer the test?
15. Approximately how long does it take to score the test?
16. Is machine-scoring available?
17. Is information provided on how the test was developed or field-tested? (If so, include a short description.)
18. What is the cost of the following materials?
    a. Test booklet.
    b. Administrators manual.
    c. Answer sheets.
    d. Technical manual.
    e. Score service (if machine-scored).
19. Is this test appropriate for a classroom teacher's use? Why or why not?
20. Is this test appropriate for a reading teacher's or learning disabilities teacher's use? Why or why not?
21. Additional comments:

Figure 11-2 Sample Page from Buros' Reading Tests and Reviews II   Reprinted from Reading: Tests and Reviews II by Oscar Krisen Buros by permission of University of Nebraska Press. Copyright 1975 by Oscar Krisen Buros; copyright © 1979 University of Nebraska.

For a review by Thomas E. Culliton, Jr., see 6:820.

[715]

★**Classroom Reading Inventory.**   Grades 2–8; 1965–69; CRI; 6 scores: word recognition, independent reading level, instructional reading level, frustration level, hearing capacity level, spelling; individual in part; Forms A, B, ('69, 14 pages); manual ('69, 13 pages plus test materials; perforated pages permit test materials to be removed from the manual); record sheets and teacher's worksheets ('69, 10–12 pages) must be reproduced locally; no data on reliability; no norms; $1.95 per manual, postage extra; (12) minutes for individual parts, administration time for spelling not reported; Nicholas J. Silvaroli; Wm. C. Brown Co. Publishers.*

Read Teach 22(8):757 My '69. Donald L. Cleland.   Silvaroli has provided an answer to the ubiquitous question: "Where can the teacher find a compact volume which includes appropriately graded reading materials, wordlists, and suggested techniques for ascertaining the instructional needs and levels of students in their classrooms?" The Classroom Reading Inventory (CRI) is designed for the elementary classroom teacher who has not had prior experience with either individual or group diagnostic measures. More specifically, this diagnostic tool may be used with children in grades two through eight and will yield, according to the author, information concerning a child's *hearing-capacity, frustration, instructional,* and *independent* reading levels. Part I (the graded wordlists) and Part II (graded oral paragraphs) are designed to be administered individually, while Part III (spelling survey) may be administered to a group. After the teacher has gained some facility in administering the CRI, she should be able to administer the tests, excluding the spelling survey, to a child in approximately fifteen minutes. According to the author, the testing can be done at the teacher's desk while the other children are engaged in quiet seatwork activity. The booklet is economically priced, with the added feature that permission is granted by the publisher to reproduce the *Inventory Record*, Pp. 17 through 26. While some may question the validity of such concepts as *hearing-capacity, frustration, instructional,* and *independent* reading levels and their practicality in a learning situation, yet those who are convinced of their feasibility in a total reading program will find the CRI a most valuable adjunct, when judiciously used, to their repertoire of teaching skills.

[716]

★**The Denver Public Schools Reading Inventory.**   Grades 1–8; 1965–68; 3 scores (instructional level, independent level, capacity level) and ratings of areas of both strength and weakness; based upon the *Sheldon Basic Reading Series*; individual; inventory ('68, 31 pages, entitled *Let's Read Together*); manual ('68, 26 pages); scoring booklet ('64, 14 pages, entitled *Reading Inventory*); no data on reliability; no norms; 60¢ per inventory; 15¢ per scoring booklet; 40¢ per manual; $1.15 per specimen set; postpaid; [30–40] minutes; Department of Instructional Services, Denver Public Schools.*

[717]
Diagnostic Reading Scales. Grades 1–8 and retarded readers in grades 9–12; 1963; DRS; 10 or 11 scores: word recognition, instructional level (oral reading), independent level (silent reading), rate of silent reading (optional), potential level (auditory comprehension), and 6 phonics scores (consonant sounds, vowel sounds, consonant blends, common syllables, blends, letter sounds); individual; 1 form (28 pages); record booklet (29 pages); manual (27 pages); no data on reliability of rate of silent reading and phonics scores; $1.10 per test; $9.60 per 35 record booklets and manual; 50¢ per manual; postage extra; $1.90 per specimen set, postpaid; [20–30] minutes; George D. Spache; CTB/McGraw-Hill.*

REFERENCES

1. GLASER, NICHOLAS ADAM. *A Comparison of Specific Reading Skills of Advanced and Retarded Readers of Fifth Grade Reading Achievement.* Doctor's thesis, University of Oregon (Eugene, Ore.), 1964. (*DA* 25:5785)
2. ATTEA, MARY. *A Comparison of Three Diagnostic Reading Tests.* Doctor's thesis, State University of New York (Buffalo, N.Y.), 1966. (*DA* 27:1530A)
3. TRELA, THADDEUS M. "What Do Diagnostic Reading Tests Diagnose?" *El Engl* 43:370–2 Ap '66.*
4. DAHLKE, ANITA B. *The Use of WISC Scores to Predict Reading Improvement After Remedial Tutoring.* Doctor's thesis, University of Florida (Gainesville, Fla.), 1968. (*DAI* 30:165A)
5. RAINWATER, HAROLD G. "Reading Problem Indicators Among Children with Reading Problems," *Psychol* 5:81–3 N '68.*
6. MANN, GLORIA T. "Reversal Reading Errors in Children Trained in Dual Directionality." *Read Teach* 22(7):646–8 Ap '69.*
7. BOTEL, MORTON; BRADLEY, JOHN; AND KASHUBA, MICHAEL. "The Validity of Informal Reading Testing," pp. 85–103. In *Reading Difficulties: Diagnosis, Correction, and Remediation.* Edited by William K. Durr. Newark, Del.: International Reading Association, 1970. Pp. vii, 276.*

REBECCA C. BARR, *Director, The Reading Clinic, The University of Chicago, Chicago, Illinois.*

The scales present a systematic approach to the diagnosis of reading skills at the elementary school level and, for retarded readers, at the secondary level. The tests determine Instructional, Independent, and Potential Reading Levels and specify patterns of reading skill development (word attack and analysis and sight recognition). The instrument is beautifully conceived but standardization leaves much to be desired.

The battery consists of three word recognition lists, two reading passages at each of 11 levels ranging from first to eighth grade in difficulty, and six supplementary phonics tests.

---

tors make formal and informal observations of our teaching. Students, through subtle—and sometimes not so subtle—means, provide feedback concerning our performance. Their parents may compliment us. We interact with other teachers in ways that allow us to take stock of our performance. And we use observations and tests to determine whether our students are learning the content, concepts, and attitudes we are trying to impart. Wherever we turn, we are forced to make judgments about our performance.

Reporting our accomplishments is nonthreatening; it is those occasional shortcomings that we most fear. Yet as professionals, we must accept the fact that we cannot always be successful. We should also understand that through evaluation, we can identify and overcome our shortcomings.

Evaluation of reading programs can help us carry out a number of responsibilities. For one thing, it helps answer the question, "How effective is the present reading program?" Second, it can pinpoint areas within the program that we are not fulfilling. Third, it can help us select and order instructional resources. Fourth, it can help us group students for instruction. Students with common skill shortcomings, for example, might be grouped together for focused instruction. Finally, assessment provides a means of collecting data for reporting a program's effectiveness.

McAndrews (1979) has identified a number of important components that should be included in an evaluation report: (1) a listing and description of tests used, (2) a statement describing pupils' expectations, (3) results of the evaluation, (4) conclusions, and (5) strengths and weaknesses of the existing program. A report with these ingredients has a number of potential audiences, among which are

1. Students.
2. Parents of students (PTAs, Parent Advisory Councils).
3. Citizen groups.
4. Mass media.
5. Teachers.
6. School administrators (superintendents, curriculum directors, Chapter I directors, reading coordinators).
7. State educational associations.
8. National education associations.
9. Federal educational agencies.
10. Professional associations (International Reading Association, Association for Childhood Education International).

One last point concerning the need for evaluation must be made. Perhaps we may reject the notion of evaluation solely on the basis of our own self-interest. Other groups may have a stake in assessment and may be overlooked if we are not careful. Parents, for instance, may view evaluation and reporting as important ingredients in the school reading program, whereas we as teachers may feel less strongly about the need for feedback to parents (Cassidy, 1977). It is for this reason that we should consider the needs others might have for assessment data before we decide to forego evaluation.

Formative Evaluation

According to Popham (1975), the term *formative evaluation* refers to any type of assessment that supplies data which can lead to program modification. In Chapter 5, "Diagnosing Word Identification," and Chapter 7, "Diagnosing Comprehension," we gave numerous examples of instruments that could be used to determine students' reading strengths and weaknesses. The results obtained from these tests help teachers adjust instruction for their students. By definition, then, teachers may have unknowingly been conducting a formative evaluation of their program. However, we now want to offer a slightly different perspective. Instead of the student being the focal point, we shall now focus on the reading program and how formative evaluation plays an important part in developing and maintaining effective instruction.

Frequently, we think of formative evaluation as being synonymous with testing, perhaps because we have more confidence in paper-and-pencil tests than we do in our informal judgments. Yet there are many opportunities throughout the school day to evaluate reading progress. Casual observations, checklists, anecdotal records, informal written assignments, and assigned projects are examples of how we collect data to use in decision making.

With the renewed interest in criterion-referenced tests, there are more formal instruments from which to choose. The increased emphasis being given to the field of learning disabilities has produced a plethora of instruments that purport to measure factors which inhibit reading progress. Our advice, however, is to review these tests critically before including them as part of your formative evaluation procedures. Arter and Jenkins (1979) identified several assumptions on which these instruments were based:

1. The ability must exist and be able to be measured.
2. The test must be reliable.
3. The test must be valid.
4. A prescription must be able to be generated from the test.
5. Remediation of the weak ability must improve achievement.

Unless instruments meet these assumptions, they probably should not be used in planning your instructional program.

When conducting formative evaluations of their programs, teachers should continually ask themselves, "How well have my students attained my specific program's objectives?" Tests should be selected and observations made with this question in mind. Although criterion-referenced reading tests and informal observations will frequently help teachers evaluate their program, they should remember, too, that simply recording test scores and anecdotal information does not mean that students will be able to apply the skill while reading. Thus, formative evaluation should not occur outside of actual reading. To put it more succinctly, to conduct formative evaluation has no meaning unless the skills students learn are used when they read.

Summative Evaluation

Summative evaluations are assessments of completed educational programs. Sometimes, they are conducted by individuals or teams hired from outside of the school district. Many federally funded school reading programs, for example, explicitly state in the guidelines that such independent evaluations must be conducted. In some instances, summative evaluations can be designed and executed by individuals within the district. The effectiveness of an innovative middle-school reading program, for example, might be evaluated by a team consisting of an assistant superintendent, the reading consultant, and a handful of teachers. In both of these examples, though, the evaluations concern the program's overall effectiveness and measure the completed program.

Unlike formative evaluations, which rely primarily on criterion-referenced tests and other informal measures, summative evaluations *usually* involve standardized, norm-referenced reading tests. Criterion-referenced instruments can be used to assess a program's effectiveness, however. Students' increased recognition of sight words between September and May, for instance, could be reported in a summative evaluation even though most sight word tests would be considered criterion-referenced.

Earlier we mentioned the necessity of selecting tests to measure a program's objectives. The importance of identifying these objectives cannot be emphasized enough, especially in a summative evaluation. The tests teachers administer should reflect both the content they teach and the emphasis they place on the content. If 25 percent of their time is spent teaching word identification, they should select an instrument with approximately one-fourth of its items designed to assess that skill. It makes little sense to spend time assessing skills that haven't been taught or to choose a test that doesn't accurately represent what was covered.

SUMMARY

Testing and evaluating pupils' reading ability can help teachers and administrators plan instruction. In this chapter we have explained how evaluation of reading occurs at a host of levels: national, state, district, school, and classroom. The purpose for evaluation will to a large degree determine the tests that are used as well as the assessment procedures that are followed. At one extreme, testing provides a glimpse of the state of reading in the country. At the other extreme, it permits teachers to focus their instruction on the needs of their students.

In order to select the most appropriate instruments for testing, teachers must be knowledgeable about what makes a "good" reading test. Thus, five common types of validity and three types of reliability were explained. Two additional factors were also discussed: standard error of measurement and passage dependency.

Two types of instruments are commonly used to assess reading ability. The first are norm-referenced reading tests, whose scores are typically reported as raw scores, grade equivalents, percentile ranks, stanines, or normal curve equivalents. We also described how the renewed interest in criterion-referenced tests is affecting instruction. Criterion-referenced tests provide data about specific skill development, and hence, allow teachers to adjust instruction frequently.

The procedures teachers might follow when selecting a test were also described, and a form was provided to help them objectively choose a test.

Finally, we attempted to explain why both formative and summative evaluation should be an integral part of the reading program.

Testing and evaluation have sometimes been thought to be an intrusion into teachers' professional lives. In this chapter we have tried to show that much of what we are recommending is already done in schools. In this decade, we will continue to witness increased efforts to make teachers and administrators more accountable for their actions. We think that by becoming knowledgeable about testing and evaluation, teachers are less apt to become anxious about this trend.

RELATED ACTIVITIES

1. Compare and contrast the construct and content validity of two well-known reading tests. Explain how the tests are similar as well as different. Be prepared to discuss the author's assumptions about the nature of reading.
2. Examine the technical manual of a popular reading test. If alternate forms of the test are available, check the alternate-form reliability of the instrument. Explain why caution should be exercised if both forms of the test are used. Be able to state the implications for teaching.
3. Examine three or more popular informal reading inventories. Check the comprehension questions to determine how many are passage dependent. To check your conclusions, ask a group of students the questions before they read the paragraph selections. See what percentage of questions can be answered before the selection is read.
4. Design a one-page handout that could be given to classroom teachers. The focus of the paper should be on the interpretation of norm-referenced reading test scores. Include warnings to be exercised when interpreting raw scores, grade equivalent scores, and percentile ranks.
5. Form a committee and establish a set of standards for selecting a reading test. Devise a point system whereby some factors are weighted more heavily than others. Then select five or more tests to review. Order the tests in the way you would choose to use them.
6. Draw up a chart illustrating the difference between norm-referenced and criterion-referenced reading tests. Describe when it would be appropriate to use each type of test. Check with three or more reading teachers to see if they use both types of tests. If they do, try to surmise if they are using them correctly.

RELATED READINGS

ARTER, JUDITH A., AND JOSEPH R. JENKINS. "Differential Diagnosis—Prescriptive Teaching: A Critical Appraisal." *Review of Educational Research*, 49, no. 4 (1979), 517–55.

BAUMANN, JAMES F., AND JENNIFER A. STEVENSON. "Understanding Standardized Reading Achievement Test Scores." *The Reading Teacher*, 35, no. 6 (Mar. 1982), 648–54.

————. "Using Scores from Standardized Reading Achievement Tests." *The Reading Teacher*, 35, no. 5 (Feb. 1982), 528–32.

EBEL, ROBERT. *Essentials of Educational Measurement*, 3rd ed. Englewood Cliffs, N.J.: Prentice-Hall, 1979.

FARR, ROGER. *Measurement and Evaluation of Reading.* New York: Harcourt Brace Jovanovich, Inc., 1970.

POPHAM, W. JAMES. *Educational Evaluation.* Englewood Cliffs, N.J.: Prentice-Hall, 1975.

SCHREINER, ROBERT, ED. *Reading Tests and Teachers: A Practical Guide.* Newark, Del.: International Reading Association, 1979.

REFERENCES

ALLINGTON, RICHARD L., LAURA CHODOS, JANE DOMARACKI, AND SHARON GRUEX. "Passage Dependency: Four Diagnostic Oral Reading Tests." *The Reading Teacher*, 30, no. 4 (Jan. 1977), 369–75.

ARTER, JUDITH A., AND JOSEPH R. JENKINS.

"Differential Diagnosis—Prescriptive Teaching: A Critical Appraisal." *Review of Educational Research*, 49, no. 4 (1979), 517–55.

BUROS, OSCAR K., ED. *Reading: Tests and Reviews I and II*. Highland Park, N.J.: Gryphon Press, 1968, 1975.

California Achievement Test. Monterey, Calif.: CTB/McGraw-Hill, 1963.

CASSIDY, JACK. "Reporting Pupil Progress in Reading—Parent vs. Teachers." *The Reading Teacher*, 31, no. 3 (Dec. 1977), 249–96.

Comprehensive Test of Basic Skills. Monterey, Calif.: CTB/McGraw-Hill, 1968.

COOPER, J. LOUIS, AND MARION L. MCGUIRE. *The Cooper-McGuire Diagnostic Word-Analysis Test*. New London, Conn.: Croft Educational Services, 1971.

Gates-MacGinitie Reading Tests. Boston: Houghton-Mifflin, 1978.

HAYWARD, PRISCILLA. "Evaluating Diagnostic Reading Tests." *The Reading Teacher*, 21, no. 6 (Mar. 1968), 523–28.

Iowa Tests of Basic Skills. Boston: Houghton-Mifflin, 1971.

IOX Objectives-Based Tests-Reading: Word Attack and Comprehension. Los Angeles: Instructional Objectives Exchange, 1973.

KAVALE, KENNETH. "Selecting and Evaluating Reading Tests." In *Reading Tests and Teachers: A Practical Guide*, pp. 9–34. Robert Schreiner, ed. Newark, Del.: International Reading Association, 1979.

MCANDREWS, J. BRIGGS. "Measuring Performance: An Assistant Superintendent's Perspective (Or We Mean Business)." Mimeo, 1979.

MACGINITIE, WALTER H. "Testing Reading Achievement in Urban Schools." *The Reading Teacher*, 27, no. 1 (Oct. 1973), 13–21.

MCGUIRE, MARION L., AND MARGUERITE J. BUMPUS. *The Croft Inservice Program: Reading Comprehension Skills*. New London, Conn.: Croft Educational Services, 1971.

MASSAD, CAROLYN EMRICK. "Interpreting and Using Test Norms." *The Reading Teacher*, 26, no. 3 (Dec. 1972), 286–92.

Metropolitan Achievement Tests: Reading. New York: The Psychological Corporation, 1978.

MORRIS, LYNN L., AND CAROL TAYLOR FITZ-GIBBON. *How to Measure Achievement*. Beverly Hills, Calif.: Sage Publications, 1978.

NATIONAL ASSESSMENT OF EDUCATIONAL PROGRESS. *Reading and Literature Objectives: 1979–1980 Assessment*. No. 11-RL-10. Denver, Col.: Education Commission of the States, 1980.

OTTO, WAYNE, AND EUNICE ASKOV. *The Wisconsin Design for Reading Skill Development*. Minneapolis, Minn.: National Computer Systems, 1973.

POPHAM, W. JAMES. *Educational Evaluation*. Englewood Cliffs, N.J.: Prentice-Hall, 1975.

———. "Educational Measurement for the Improvement of Instruction." *Phi Delta Kappan*, 61, no. 8 (1980), 531–34.

Prescriptive Reading Inventory. Monterey Park, Calif.: CTB/McGraw-Hill, 1974.

SCHWARTZ, JUDY I. "Standardizing a Reading Test." *The Reading Teacher*, 30, no. 4 (Jan. 1977), 364–68.

SHEEHAN, DANIEL S., AND MARY MARCUS. "Validating Criterion-Referenced Reading Tests." *Journal of Reading Behavior*, 9 no. 2 (1977), 129–35.

Stanford Achievement Test: Reading Tests. New York: Harcourt Brace Jovanovich, Inc., 1973.

TUINMAN, J. JAPP. "Determining the Passage Dependency of Comprehension Questions in 5 Major Tests." *Reading Research Quarterly*, 9, no. 2 (1973–74), 206–23.

VENEZKY, RICHARD L. "NAEP—Should We Kill the Messenger Who Brings Bad News." *The Reading Teacher*, 30, no. 7 (Apr. 1977), 750–55.

12

GETTING IT ALL TOGETHER

After reading this chapter you should be able to
1. Describe the various roles of a school reading specialist.
2. Defend the selection of students for inclusion into a school reading program.
3. State important considerations when scheduling students for instruction.
4. Describe the organization and operation of a typical reading center.

THE ROLE OF THE READING SPECIALIST

One of the confusing issues within the educational profession is the role of a reading specialist. Frequently, the duties of individuals who work with problem readers overlap, and hence, a reading specialist in one school district may have similiar responsibilities to a remedial reading teacher in another district. In a similar vein, it may be impossible to differentiate between a reading supervisor and a reading coordinator. So rather than attempt to define arbitrarily the work of these individuals (and invariably be "wrong" in some peoples' minds), we advise when considering the position of a reading specialist to ask for a job description.

Working with Students

Reading teachers are usually asked to work with students with moderate to severe reading problems. Sometimes, people who perform only this function are labeled remedial reading teachers. Working with students who have failed in reading—and probably in other academic areas—is not as easy as it may sound. The teacher must be sensitive to students' feelings and must be able to establish rapport easily and quickly. Furthermore, the teacher must be able to diagnose the problems without subjecting the reader to needless testing. Then the teacher must be able to prescribe appropriate materials to motivate these students, even though they may be reluctant to attack unknown words or dislike reading for pleasure.

Reading teachers are also expected to be good organizers and managers. Sometimes they need to plan lessons for individual students, whereas on other occasions they may call small groups together for specific kinds of instruction. Sometimes they may teach a lesson to an entire group of students.

Part of their responsibility is to keep accurate, up-to-date records of students' performances. Thus they need to manage their record keeping in such a way that they can prescribe instruction and materials quickly and efficiently once they have surveyed pupils' records.

Working with Teachers

Working with teachers is perhaps one of the most demanding jobs reading specialists face, primarily because each teacher has a different expectation of the reading specialist's role. And since each teacher's personality is so unique, the specialist must be skillful in establishing good interpersonal relationships.

The exact type of services reading teachers supply to classroom teachers will depend largely on the type of program they will be working in as well as their job description. In many instances, reading teachers are expected to divide their services between teaching students with reading problems and serving as a resource teacher for classroom teachers. In a survey of reading specialists, Bean (1979) found that teachers perceived the three most highly valued roles of a reading specialist to be (1) providing in-service education, (2) developing materials for teachers, and (3) conferring with teachers.

In addition, reading specialists are frequently called on to fulfill other obligations to teachers. They may, for example, be asked to diagnose students

The reading specialist can help teachers be more effective by selecting materials consistent with program goals.   (Peter P. Tobia)

and to suggest commercial materials for the teachers' use. Frequently, teaching a demonstration lesson for a particular teacher will help win the confidence and support of the school's staff. Demonstrating how to give a quick and easy-to-administer diagnostic test will also help establish close working relationships between teachers and the specialist. Another responsibility reading specialists sometimes assume is to provide written bulletins describing a new test or set of materials which might be useful to classroom teachers.

Occasionally, some teachers may not actively seek out the services of the reading teacher. By doing so, they may feel they are admitting inadequacy. A perceptive reading teacher is able to recognize these individuals and offer help in a nonthreatening way. Simply keeping alert to conversation in the teachers' lounge will often help determine which teachers could benefit from some special help. By volunteering to teach a lesson or assist in testing some reluctant readers, the specialist may be taking the first step in helping some classroom teachers improve their teaching.

It should be clear by now that a good portion of the reading specialist's time will be spent working with other teachers. Knowledge of reading and ability to translate that knowledge to teachers in a nonthreatening fashion will to a large degree determine the reading teacher's effectiveness. Experience as a classroom teacher sometimes helps reading teachers win the confidence of their coworkers. But even more important is their ability to empathize with their colleagues and to treat them fairly, recognizing that they possess individual strengths and weaknesses, just like students.

Working with School Administrators

Reading specialists, regardless of their job descriptions, spend a portion of their time working with school administrators. The first-line administrator most reading teachers are accountable to is the school principal. Even if most of the specialists' time is devoted to instructing students with reading problems, they still need to work out student referral and admission procedures with the principal. And if a portion of the specialists' time will be devoted to working with teachers, it is important to understand the principal's expectations of their role.

The more responsibility specialists have for observing teachers and monitoring the overall reading program, the more closely they will need to work with the administrators in the district. Usually, the less contact reading teachers have with students, the more contact they have with principals, directors of instruction, assistant superintendents, and superintendents.

Much of the reading specialist's work with administrators will center on such tasks as serving on individualized educational planning committees, planning in-service meetings, planning a reading program's goals, or stating its objectives. The specialist might also serve on textbook selection committees or help select and interpret reading tests.

Those hired as a reading consultant or supervisor should expect to be treated more like an administrator than a teacher. In this role, they would probably make frequent observations in teachers' classrooms and report their findings to the principal. They might also suggest new grouping practices for teachers to use. In some cases, they might even have a number of reading specialists working under them. In this type of situation, they are usually responsible for other reading teachers' performance, which must be reported to a designated administrator. The reading consultant might also have partial or total responsibility for evaluating the district's reading program. In large school districts, there would probably be an evaluation unit composed of administrators with whom the consultant would work. In smaller districts, evaluation of the reading program might be their sole responsibility.

The districts' administrators may turn to the reading specialist, as a person knowledgeable in the field of reading, for advice concerning program modification. The consultant might also be asked to keep them posted on the latest research in the field of reading. In each of these instances, the consultant is assuming the responsibility for coordinating district curriculum. Thus, the major goal is to improve the quality of instruction within the district.

Working with Parents

An important function of the reading specialist is to enlist the support of parents in an effort to prevent and remediate reading difficulties. Accordingly, some of the reading teacher's activities should be centered around working with parents who have preschool or primary-age children. Another tack needs to be taken with those parents of children who are having trouble learning to read.

Of these two groups of parents, the reading specialist is apt to find the first group more eager and receptive to help. One beneficial activity is a social hour or workshop describing things parents may do to help their children learn to read. Some topics useful to cover at these workshops include the following:

1. Displaying and explaining selected reading-related games.
2. Describing magazines and books for young children.
3. Fostering self-concept through reading.
4. Selecting and monitoring children's television viewing.
3. Creating a conducive study environment for young learners.
6. Do's and don'ts when reading with children.
7. Fostering language development and reading.

Parents of children who are having difficulty present a different population and, hence, may need to be dealt with differently. Sometimes the biggest hurdle is simply to get these parents to attend parent-teacher conferences, open houses, or parent advisory committee meetings, particularly when both parents must work to support a household. Also, sometimes these parents simply aren't interested in what's happening at school. Reading specialists will need to use all their creative talents to invite, coerce, and convince these parents to attend meetings. If they are unable to meet during the regular school hours, the specialist may want to call them on the telephone to learn more about their child and to offer ideas on how the teachers and the parents might work together cooperatively to overcome a reading problem. In a few instances, it is even beneficial to visit the child's home—providing an invitation is offered. Our point is this: don't expect parents always to be eager to visit their child's school. If reading teachers truly want to enlist a parent's support, they may have to extend themselves more than they might expect.

We have found that a nonthreatening, low-keyed workshop format is usually successful when dealing with parents of reading-disabled children. Since many of these parents suffer guilt feelings about their child's reading problems, one of the reading specialist's first jobs is to reassure parents that there are many causes of such problems. Schools and teachers, for example, frequently must bear some of the responsibility. Large classes, outdated teaching methods, and inadequate grouping procedures are three common reasons for reading failure. Faulty vision, hearing losses, and frequent absences also contribute to reading difficulties. Parents need to know that they aren't always the sole cause of a child's inability to read. Once this sensitive point is broached, parents are usually more receptive to working with teachers and administrators. From this point on, the reading specialist can devote time demonstrating how parents can help their child. Parental frustration and anxiety can be quickly laid to rest once guidance and direction are given.

Parents of disabled readers sometimes need to be shown the importance of reading and listening to their children. Guidance can be offered on how to assist children when they encounter unfamiliar words. They can be shown how to help select books written at easy-to-read levels. They might also keep a list of topics that interest their children and show it to the reading teacher or the regular classroom teacher.

These are only a few ways that reading teachers and parents might work together. Although students may progress in reading without parental support, cooperation between the school and home will expedite the child's progress.

Working with Other Professionals

Teachers of reading have many opportunities to work with other professionals both within and outside the educational field. The size and composition of a community and school district will, in part, determine the type of professionals reading specialists will encounter. Some of those frequently met are described here.

LEARNING DISABILITIES SPECIALIST As we have already mentioned, passage of Public Law 94-142 has resulted in an increased number of learning disabilities teachers in our schools. We feel this is a positive step in attempting to alleviate the reading problems of school-age children.

Since most learning disabilities teachers are graduates of special education training programs and most reading teachers are graduates of reading education programs, a philosophical conflict may arise regarding the identification of learning disabled children. The former have traditionally perceived the nonreaders's problem to be related to cerebral dysfunctioning, whereas reading teachers usually regard it as an educational, psychological, sociological, or physiological problem, or a combination of any of these.

Fortunately, both types of teacher have begun to understand that the primary reason for their existence is to help students who can't read. Furthermore, their training has become more and more similar. Learning disabilities teachers are enrolling in an increased number of university reading courses, and conversely, reading teachers have begun to attend special education courses. We believe this is a healthy trend which should result in better qualified teachers of reading—whatever their titles might be.

In our experience, one of the major hurdles these two professional groups need to overcome in working with disabled readers is a clarification of terminology. Unless there is a clear understanding by both parties of such terms as *auditory closure, VAKT approach,* and *visual memory,* confusion and lack of communication will continue to exist. Esoteric terminology will only foster distrust and impede a coordinated, unified attack on a student's reading problem.

Another perplexing problem centers on who should provide instruction to whom. Presently, both learning disabilities teachers and reading teachers

Figure 12-1 A Comparison of Reading and Learning Disability Personnel From "Is There a Difference between Learning Disability and Reading Personnel" by Russell E. Burgett and Roger W. Dodge, *Journal of Reading,* April 1976, p. 542. Reprinted with permission of the authors and the International Reading Association.

POSITION RESPONSIBILITIES	TOTAL RESPONSES 41	X^2	LEVEL OF SIGNIFICANCE (0.5)
1. Apprise staff of new educational developments	38	4.99	N.S.
2. Provide inservice training for teachers.	39	1.58	N.S.
3. Encourage and stimulate teachers to use a variety of teaching strategies.	39	1.16	N.S.
4. Provide technical aid to classroom teachers.	39	8.23	.01(L)
5. Help teachers plan and provide instruction in the classroom.	41	.77	N.S.
6. Suggest and demonstrate the use of instructional material.	40	3.34	N.S.
7. Implement techniques by providing small group instruction, demonstration, teaching, and/or assistance.	40	3.99	N.S.
8. Provide assistance to new and experienced teachers with instruction for children with special problems.	40	10.84	.004(L)
9. Observe classroom pupil behavior.	41	4.63	N.S.
10. Construct informal inventories, assessments, or tests.	41	2.03	N.S.
11. Assist personnel in the selection of appropriate screening devices.	40	2.98	N.S.
12. Supervise the administration of screening devices.	40	.93	N.S.
13. Assist teachers in the diagnosis of pupil learning problems.	41	.60	N.S.
14. Provide guidance in interpreting intelligence tests, motor test, etc.	40	4.32	N.S.
15. Assist with the interpretation of the results of standardized, criterion-referenced, and informal screening devices.	41	.60	N.S.
16. Provide guidance in identifying candidates for special classes.	40	8.11	.017(L)
17. Guide the preparation of record forms.	40	3.93	N.S.
18. Supervise the inventory of books, supplies, and equipment.	40	.92	N.S.
19. Promote the creation of activities, games, and devices for classroom use.	39	.07	N.S.
20. Stimulate and guide analysis and selection of instructional materials.	39	.15	N.S.

21.	Determine the difficulty of learning materials.	40	.46	N.S.
22.	Provide lists of resource material.	40	.26	N.S.
23.	Act as a resource to teachers and/or provide leadership in developing curriculum units.	41	3.38	N.S.
24.	Provide guidelines and assistance for evaluating student progress in remediation.	40	1.65	N.S.
25.	Select and suggest techniques for appraising instruction.	39	3.84	N.S.
26.	Provide guidance in writing case studies of problem learners.	39	1.94	N.S.
27.	Assist teachers with parent conferences.	40	7.03	.02(L)(R)
28.	Attend and participate in local, C.E.S.A., regional, state, and national meetings.	39	1.46	N.S.
29.	Evaluate published research for its relevance to school district needs.	39	.43	N.S.
30.	Develop with teachers and administrators, general goals and objectives.	39	.27	N.S.
31.	Determine the philosophy of the district in specialized areas.	38	3.7	N.S.
32.	Inform administrators and teachers of problems within the district.	39	2.0	N.S.
33.	Make pupil referrals to other agencies.	40	1.29	N.S.
34.	In cooperation with other specialists recommend treatment for children with complex disabilities involving learning.	41	6.94	.03(L)
35.	Acquaint board members with educational goals and needs for financial support in areas.	40	.78	N.S.
36.	Inform public of program needs.	41	.92	N.S.
37.	Write proposals for local and federal funding.	40	5.26	N.S.
38.	Implement educational experimentation.	40	.75	N.S.
39.	Evaluate, appraise, and write reports concerning the status of a program.	40	2.31	N.S.

(R) Reading Personnel
(L) Learning Disabilities Personnel

provide essentially the same services in a school district. Burgett and Dodge (1976) found that over 85 percent of the role responsibilities of the two groups were similar (see Figure 12-1). The only significant differences were that learning disabilities teachers generally supplied more technical assistance to classroom teachers who had learning disabled students in their classrooms and they frequently sat in on parent-teacher conferences.

As the training programs of these two disciplines continue to overlap, we expect to see less distinction between them. In the future, training programs for both will probably be distinguished by their similarities, not their differences.

SPEECH AND HEARING SPECIALIST   Good teachers of reading understand the relationship between language and reading. Occasionally, however, questions arise concerning speech development or hearing ability that are beyond the expertise of the reading teacher. It is good to know that a speech and hearing specialist can answer such questions as well as help plan instructional programs for those students who need them.

All students who receive special assistance in reading should be screened early in the school year for hearing losses. Speech and hearing specialists are specially trained to diagnose descrepancies in hearing acuity and discrimination, and this information can help eliminate fruitless instruction in phonics or other listening skills.

Another advantage of working closely with the speech and hearing specialist is that instruction can be correlated for students who receive help in both disciplines, reducing the time the student must spend with specialists. Furthermore, correlated instruction demonstrates to the student that a unified attempt is being made to overcome the specific disability.

SCHOOL PSYCHOLOGIST   Today, most school districts employ either a full-time or part-time school psychologist. Since they are frequently responsible for coordinating IEP staffing sessions, reading teachers are apt to have numerous contacts with them. Furthermore, because of the psychologists' qualifications to administer, score, and interpret intelligence and projective tests, reading teachers may want them to assess some reading disabled students.

School psychologists frequently observe students in and out of the remedial classroom. By comparing students' performance in the reading room with that in the regular classroom, they can see if transfer of learning is taking place. Behavioral performance can also be monitored. For students exhibiting disruptive behavior, the school psychologist can help plan a program of behavior modification. A reinforcement schedule may result in increased attention to the task and hence more rapid progress. Conferring with the psychologist should help the reading specialist when planning, modifying, or eliminating a reinforcement schedule.

Cooperation with the psychologist and the child's parents may sometimes be necessary to overcome a reading disability. A trauma within the family, such as a death, divorce, accident, or severe illness, may have such a devastating effect on a child that only a well-planned, united effort can help maintain academic performance.

SCHOOL LIBRARIAN   Since many of the students who have reading problems come from homes where reading is held in low esteem, a major obstacle is to convince students that reading can be an enjoyable, worthwhile endeavor. No one has the potential to help more in this undertaking than the school librarian.

Effective librarians are those individuals who not only value high-quality literature but also are sympathetic to the problems and needs of reluctant readers. Forcing a Newbery Award winner on nonreaders will not convince them that reading is a pleasant undertaking. But helping to select a highly interesting limited vocabulary trade book is apt to demonstrate to the reader that reading books may not be an unconquerable task after all.

Working closely with the school librarian in the annual selection and ordering of library books is another important job many reading specialists undertake. Helping the librarian will insure that books appropriate for students with limited reading ability will be procured. Ideally, a portion of each school's budget should be set aside especially for these types of materials. Then when reluctant readers are taken to the library, all teachers will have confidence that an adequate selection of books will be awaiting even the poorest reader.

GUIDANCE COUNSELOR   Guidance counselors, or adjustment counselors as they are sometimes called, can also play a key role in helping a student overcome reading disabilities. One of the primary duties of the counselor is to improve the learning climate, which may be done in a variety of ways.

Many guidance counselors prefer to conduct a thorough case study of referred children, and thus to assess teachers', specialists', and parents' attitudes about the student. In each instance, the counselor would want to know if specific pressures on the child might be causing the academic difficulties. Individual or small group counseling sessions might be used to gain a further understanding of the problem. The child may be asked to respond to questionnaires or checklists or to take part in role playing.

Regardless of the techniques used, the major responsibility of the counselor is to seek solutions to the student's difficulty. Through cooperation with the reading teacher, other school personnel, and the child's parents or guardians, a plan of action can be discussed, agreed upon, and implemented. Coordinated efforts such as these can go far in reducing behavioral problems frequently associated with reading disabilities.

INSTRUCTIONAL AND CLERICAL AIDE   A frequently overlooked person in the reading program is the instructional and clerical aide, who may or may not hold a teaching certificate. If reading teachers have never worked with aides before, they should be aware of two important points. First, they shouldn't assume that the aides have been trained to work with disabled readers. The reading specialist may have to do some on-the-job training before aides can be used effectively in the reading program.

Second, the competence of aides varies widely, and reading teachers should adjust responsibilities to abilities. Some aides function well in instructional settings, whereas others are best suited for clerical duties. Regardless of assignment, however, aides need to be especially sensitive to the unique problems of by disabled readers. We can recall one case in which an aide was chastising a group of students for being "lazy" and "stupid." Obviously, such behavior cannot be tolerated. Fortunately, however, most aides do an outstanding job working with teachers and students.

If a reading specialist is fortunate enough to have an aide there are numerous duties they can perform:

1.   Keep up-to-date cumulative folders.

2. Prepare instructional materials.
3. Score tests.
4. Set up materials for instructional groups.
5. Monitor individual students.
6. Listen to children read orally.
7. Type notices for meetings.
8. Make telephone calls for conference appointments.
9. Administer nontechnical tests.
10. Type book and material orders.
11. Type reports sent to teachers or parents.
12. Update records on a computer terminal.

It should be obvious that aides can greatly reduce the workload of a reading teacher as well as contribute to the quality of instruction.

PHYSICIAN   The physician is an example of someone outside the educational community whom the reading teacher may occasionally encounter. The doctor can play an important part in a child's educational program if a physical (and sometimes an emotional or psychological) factor is affecting an ability to learn. Although physicians are usually called on only in severe or extended illness, there may be times when the reading specialist will be asked to work closely with them. We can recall several instances where reading teachers were asked to monitor the behavior of students who were taking prescription medicine. Each day the teachers reported the behavioral patterns of the children to help the doctor determine whether the medication was producing the desired effects. Since the teachers were unaware of the frequency or the dosage of medication, the doctor had an unbiased observer assessing the behavior of the child. This close working relationship quickly resulted in improved performance and, fortunately, a rapid reduction in the dosage of the medication. Shortly thereafter, it was eliminated altogether.

VISION SPECIALIST   Ophthalmologists (who are technically physicians) and optometrists also have reason to work closely with reading teachers. Abnormal vision sometimes requires visual training or corrective lenses. If either of these prescriptions is necessary, the vision specialist may expect the student's teachers and parents to monitor or assist in the treatment.

Parents whose child is receiving treatment for strabismus may be asked to work on strengthening muscles which control the eye. Occasionally, these students may be required to wear a patch over one eye during the treatment period. The reading teacher may be asked to see that the patch is worn during school hours as prescribed.

If a student wears corrective lenses either the parents or the vision specialist may ask the reading specialist to see if the glasses are worn during school hours. Since some students object to wearing glasses, the specialist may have to insist that they be worn during reading instruction. Cooperation of parents and professionals will demonstrate to the child that everyone means business when it comes to rectifying the visual anomaly.

OTHER SPECIALISTS   There may be occasion for the reading teacher to work with other professionals, too, including social workers, neurologists, neuropsychologists, and psychiatrists. Obviously, each of them can play an important role in diagnosing and correcting a student's reading problem, but since they are only infrequently called on to help, their specific functions will not be discussed here.

SELECTING STUDENTS
FOR THE READING PROGRAM

Selecting students for a school reading program may turn out to be a more formidable task than it might first appear. In some districts, the reading teachers have free reign to enroll whomever they feel could benefit from extra help. In other districts, however, federal, state, or local guidelines explicitly specify who can—and cannot—be included.

A first step in selecting students is to survey the standardized test scores of students within a particular building. If the scores are ranked from highest to lowest, a general list of eligible candidates will emerge. In some districts, reading teachers are required to include only those subjects who score lowest at their particular grade level. If, for example, a case load was to include a maximum of thirty students, the specialists may be required to instruct the five lowest scoring pupils at each grade level, grades one to six. Practices such as this, however, run contrary to what we know about objective test validity and reliability. Since test scores are only samplings of student behaviors at one point in time, there is usually some degree of error in each score. By using only test scores, teachers may be overlooking students who could benefit from instruction yet who scored above some arbitrary cutoff point. Also, this procedure denies teachers the opportunity to exercise professional judgment. In a very real sense, the responsibility of the teacher is stripped away and replaced by the arbitrary test score.

We prefer to see a combination of methods used for selecting students. Classroom teachers, using standardized tests as well as informal methods, frequently can identify the problem readers in their classes. After initial identification, more in-depth testing to determine specific needs can be done by the reading teacher.

At this point, reading teachers may need to establish some guidelines. Our advice is to include primarily those students who have the capacity to learn at an average or above-average rate. This can be determined by using a reading expectancy formula (discussed in detail in Chapter 2) or an informal reading inventory and measuring the discrepancy between the instructional level and the listening level.

The admission guidelines should remain flexible enough to allow the acceptance or rejection of students who may deviate from the established admissions criteria. There may be instances, for example, when the reading teacher will be asked to include a student who has a negative attitude about reading but reads very well. The child may be exhibiting negative behavior in the classroom and may need special counseling in the reading teacher's room. If the student responds to an adapted program, reading trade books, for example, the specialist can not only improve the child's attitude toward reading but also relieve the classroom teacher of a disruptive student.

Reading teachers should be aware of the danger of filling their programs with slow learners. Students with limited capacity who are working up to their ability should receive their reading instruction in the classroom. The reading teacher's students should be those who have a good chance of returning to the classroom once their problem is overcome. Slow learners are apt to make no greater progress with remedial help outside the classroom than they are in the classroom. Furthermore, the additional time these students demand from the specialist is time that could be spent working with classroom teachers and administrators to prevent reading problems from occurring in the first place. Ideally, the reading teacher's job should be to help students overcome their reading difficulty and return to the regular classroom as rapidly as possible, not to teach reading to the school's population of slow learners.

It may be of interest to examine a typical student population in a compensatory reading program. After studying such programs across the country, Calfee and Drum (1979) concluded that the typical program included twenty-eight students. Pupils from poorer families were more highly represented than their proportionate distribution in the school population. Frequently, they were from ethnic minority backgrounds. Instruction in small groups of three to ten students was common, although occasionally there was a one-to-one teacher-pupil ratio. The typical student received instruction once a day, five days a week, for between sixteen and thirty minutes. Finally, once a primary student was included in the program, he or she tended to remain there throughout the elementary grades.

SCHEDULING STUDENTS

Scheduling students should be easier than selecting them. To be sure, there will always be problems to overcome, but scheduling pupils is more of a juggling feat than an intellectual task.

One of the first questions reading teachers need to consider is how many times per week they will schedule each student. A related question concerns the length of each instructional session. Our advice is to meet with each student every day if possible and keep instructional sessions limited to sixty minutes at most.

In reality, there are a number of things teachers must remember when scheduling students into their programs. First, they must consider grade levels. As a rule of thumb, it's a good idea not to mix students from three different grades. Instead, try to keep the grade-level spread to no more than two grades.

The chronological age of the students will also influence the length of the instructional sessions. Younger students usually have shorter attention spans, so a thirty- to- forty-five-minute session is the maximum time a primary-age child will be able to attend. Intermediate, junior high school, and senior high school students can usually be scheduled for forty-five to sixty minutes without serious consequences. As a rule of thumb, it's much better to meet more often in shorter sessions than vice versa, particularly at the primary-grade level.

A third factor to be considered is the overall school schedule. With today's schedules, arranging to meet with students may seem a Herculean task. Since most compensatory instruction usually occurs outside the regular classroom, reading teachers need to work around each teacher's classroom schedule. Art and music teachers' schedules also need to be considered, as do recesses, lunch periods, and an occasional field trip.

If it is possible, we prefer to see students receive help during the regularly scheduled reading period. Obviously, this is not always possible. In some instances, for example, a reading program's guidelines explicitly state that supplemental help in reading cannot supplant regular classroom reading instruction. In other instances, a reading teacher's only choice is to schedule students after they have received their classroom reading instruction. When faced with this situation, we prefer to see students miss social studies before any other subject. Many science programs require less reading than they once did, so disabled readers can frequently take part in experiments and demonstrations without being penalized by their limited reading ability. Since mathematics instruction is so sequential in nature, it probably is not a good idea to remove students from this class. Because art, music, and physical education classes are usually enjoyed by most students, disabled readers should be allowed to attend these sessions. Sometimes, however, reading teachers have no choice but to provide instruction during a much enjoyed subject. In these cases, our advice is to have a face-to-face talk with the student and explain the dilemma. Most students are understanding and will give their all if they are informed and dealt with in a matter-of-fact fashion. The creative reading teacher might even be able to turn such a situation into a special "treat" for the student. Special "prizes" or privileges during the reading period help a child overcome the sadness of missing a favorite subject.

Many reading authorities recommend that a student's special reading instruction take place within the classroom. With this arrangement the reading teacher comes to the student rather than vice versa. Teaching disabled readers in the classroom certainly has merit, since it allows the students to see the correlation between the developmental reading program and the remedial program. Making a special effort to talk to the classroom teacher will also show the students that the two of you are working together toward a common goal. However, many classroom teachers are threatened by and don't want another teacher in their classroom. A further problem is that it is sometimes physically impossible to transport reading materials from classroom to classroom. Thus, it is not surprising to learn that three out of four pupils who receive special help in reading are pulled out of their classrooms for instruction (Calfee and Drum, 1979). When an opportunity presents itself for instructing students in their regular classrooms, however, we suggest reading specialists take advantage of the situation.

ORGANIZING YOUR READING CENTER

Good teachers of reading are more important than the materials they use. This was clearly demonstrated in the mid-1960s when the U.S. Office of Education supported the implementation and evaluation of twenty-seven separate first-grade reading projects. When the performance of pupils was compared after the projects, it was implied that the teacher had more effect on achievement than did the curriculum or materials. Since that time, researchers and practitioners have generally considered the search for more and better materials to be an elusive dream. Instead, both groups have sought to identify the characteristics of a teacher or program which may have a significant impact on students' reading achievement. Since we have addressed the importance of the teacher in detail throughout this book, however, we now want to turn our attention more toward specific steps teachers might take to organize their instructional programs.

The Teacher's Role in Programming

Teachers affect instructional programming in two ways: first, in the physical manipulation of materials such as desks, books, and audiovisual material; second, and perhaps more important, by the atmosphere which surrounds instruction. Since we feel the latter is of primary importance, allow us to discuss our perceptions with you.

Reading teachers should know that their behavior in dealing with pupils is apt to be communicated to them at an intuitive level. Furthermore a teacher's behavior occurs in regular patterns, patterns that are predictable. This is important to keep in mind since the relationships and impressions reading specialists establish with their students early in the school year are apt to remain relatively stable. If, for example, students perceive a teacher to be well organized, compassionate, and goal-oriented, they are more apt to be respectful than if the teacher is perceived as poorly organized, calloused, and directionless. To put it another way, students are astute observers of human behavior and usually respond accordingly. It is also important to understand that a teacher's expectations of students will frequently be reflected in their performance. If the specialists believe that their students are capable of learning and they plan appropriate instruction for them, they usually will learn. If, on the other hand, teachers have little hope that their students will learn to read, the students will probably perform accordingly. This self-fulfilling prophecy can be a powerful force in helping disabled readers.

In our minds, good teachers of reading identify their goals and plan appropriate instruction. They teach diagnostically, using both objective and subjective data in the decision-making process. They encourage risk-taking when their students encounter unknown words. They are open to multiple interpretation of teacher- or pupil-generated questions. They value reading as a process and encourage students to read for pleasure. All of these factors set the tone of instruction—the instructional milieu. Although difficult to quantify, experienced classroom observers can quickly identify whether a classroom meets this description. There is an "air of learning" in such classrooms.

A more tangible factor identified with good reading programs is the room or area in which the reading teacher works. One of us vividly recalls the teaching conditions experienced as a beginning remedial reading teacher, in which a small room was shared with the school nurse. The room held one large desk, four student desks, and two cots. You can imagine the difficulty encountered trying to teach dipththongs to a small group of students while in the background two sick children rested on the adjoining beds. Boiler rooms, closets, and hallways were sometimes the first teaching stations of many reading specialists during the early 1960s.

Fortunately, today's reading teacher faces a brighter prospect. Rooms need seldom be shared with other professionals, audiovisual materials are readily available, and excellent educational materials are at hand. Briefly, here is what we would consider to be an appropriate environment for the teaching of reading.

1. The room should be relatively free of noise. Carpeting or rugs, acoustical ceiling tiles, and drapes should be used to lower noise levels.
2. The room should be well lighted. Windows or lights should provide adequate illumination throughout the room. Shades should be available to reduce glare. If individual carrels are used for work, each should have a separate light.
3. There should be provisions for group as well as individual instruction. A large rectangular or semicircular table is handy for working with groups; carrels or desks can be used for individual assignments.
4. Bookshelves should be available to display high-interest low-vocabulary books. Some books should be displayed with their covers facing outward.
5. Adequate shelving is needed to store games, kits, teacher-made materials, and records. Student dioramas and projects can also be displayed on the shelves.
6. Instructional hardware should be readily accessible to the teacher and students. A primary-type typewriter, overhead projector, projector screen, cassette tape recorder, phonograph player, and Language Master should be available. In the future, more and more reading teachers will probably have access to microcomputers in which to store test data or to serve as instructional devices.
7. Movable or permanent chalkboards and bulletin boards should be distributed throughout the room for students to write on and display their work.
8. A sufficient number of file cabinets must be available to store test data, cumulative folders, reports, and copies of correspondence.

Testing Materials

Although we have already covered the important points of testing in Chapter 11, "Evaluation of Reading Tests and Programs," some general suggestions reading teachers should consider when organizing their programs should help avoid some common frustrations.

First, teachers should order tests well before they expect to use them. Ordering six months to a year in advance is not out of line. Since suppliers of standardized tests frequently deplete their supplies and must wait for new printings, teachers won't be caught shorthanded if they plan ahead.

Second, teachers should institute a systematic filing system so tests are organized by title and form. Administrator's manuals and technical manuals also should be filed separately, allowing a quick inventory of supplies when it's time to order new tests. A filing system also permits the specialist quickly to supply a test to a classroom teacher in need.

Finally, in addition to a "core" of frequently used tests, the reading specialist should try to build a file of instruments that may be of use to classroom teachers. Most companies sell specimen sets which will permit an individual to become familiar with the contents before ordering a complete set of, say, thirty-five tests and an administrator's manual. The reading teacher should keep abreast of new developments in the field of measurement.

Monitoring and Reporting Students' Performance

There is increasing evidence that a reading teacher's managerial skills are an important ingredient in promoting students' independence and responsibility. One facet of management is the close monitoring of pupils' reading development. Although norm-referenced tests play a part in assessment and monitoring, they frequently are insensitive to measuring growth over short periods of time (for example, three- to nine-week intervals). This same criticism applies to informal reading inventories. Thus, the reading teacher needs to rely on data collected from criterion-referenced tests, attitudinal scales, work samples, performance tests, and behavioral observations to monitor most pupils' performance.

When monitoring students' growth in reading, teachers should keep the reading process in perspective. We have seen teachers who have become so enamored with monitoring skill development that they spend most of their time administering, scoring, and recording test results. Little time is left for actually instructing the students. Reading should not become fractionated into what some people have dubbed "atomistic parts." The purpose of monitoring progress is to help teachers better focus their instruction.

The primary aim of reporting a pupil's performance is to inform both classroom teachers and parents that progress is being made in overcoming the reading disability. Since we have already discussed how reading teachers might report progress to classroom teachers (Chapter 10), our aim now is to discuss what parents expect.

Because most schools require parent-teacher conferences, the reading teacher needs to plan for them adequately. During these visits, the reading teacher should be prepared to discuss the students' test results as well as comment on their attitude and behavior. If a cumulative file folder is kept for each student, tests, assignments, and other anecdotal information can be easily retrieved and discussed during these meetings. These objective pieces of data will more than satisfy most parents and will go far in demonstrating that all school personnel are making every effort to help their child.

Instruction

Obviously, focused instruction is the key to learning. Although remedial reading instruction resembles developmental reading instruction in many ways, a major difference is that reduced pupil-teacher ratio allows the reading teacher to prescribe and monitor instruction more closely.

Ideally, the efforts of both remedial and developmental reading teachers closely parallel one another. One way to help coordinate their efforts is to identify their goals through the use of specific objectives. By establishing bi-monthly or monthly objectives for their students, both teachers can work to-gether to overcome the students' difficulties. And since some students receive help from the learning disabilities teacher as well as the reading teacher, every-one can keep abreast of these instructional efforts.

When planning instruction it's important to remember that a teacher's ultimate goal is to have students able to read connected discourse. Too often we become more concerned with performance on ditto pages, workbooks, and games, and in the process, lose sight of reading books, magazines, and other materials that the child faces outside of school. To keep our plans in perspective, Harker (1976) proposes that we plan lessons at four distinct levels. First, students need lessons which expand their experiential background, concepts of reading, and vocabulary. This is the readiness stage. Second, there is the skill develop-ment phase. Lessons at this level are the ones most teachers are most familiar with. They entail the skill lessons prescribed on ditto sheets, workbook pages, and teacher-directed board work. Most instruction that occurs in today's schools is at this level. A third level involves skill application. As the name implies, these lessons attempt to utilize the learned behavior in settings outside of the skill development level, in high-interest trade books and magazines, for example. Finally, there is skill extension. Lessons at this level stress the utilization of the skill in content area reading.

Another fact to keep in mind when planning instruction is the amount of time students will be expected to work. This is commonly known as *time on task*. Simply put, the more time students spend on tasks, the greater the oppor-tunity they have of learning the behavior. In a study of beginning teachers, it was learned that 33 percent of the reading lesson was devoted to decoding tasks, and only 10 percent was spent on comprehension skills (O'Donnell, 1978). Durkin (1978–79) found that teachers spent almost no time teaching comprehension skills to elementary school students. Instead, most of their time was spent assign-ing and scoring worksheets or workbook pages. This can hardly be considered "teaching." One wonders why teachers frequently complain about the com-prehension ability of their students! If time is not spent teaching these skills, students are bound to suffer when comprehension is assessed. Reading teachers should remember that students will usually learn only what they are taught. Teachers need to use a variety of interesting materials and closely monitor the students' work habits. Remedial readers need to be encouraged to attend to the task.

Materials

Anyone who has attended a local, regional, or national reading associa-tion convention can vouch for the fact that materials for disabled readers exist in bountiful proportions. Usually, the major frustration facing reading teachers is to select materials of high quality. Although a plethora of audiovisual materials, supplementary readers, games, and kits exist, it is frequently difficult to deter-mine their real worth until they are actually used.

Another concern we have is the attempt to teach reading by using differ-ent alphabets or derivations from normally accepted print. We believe reading

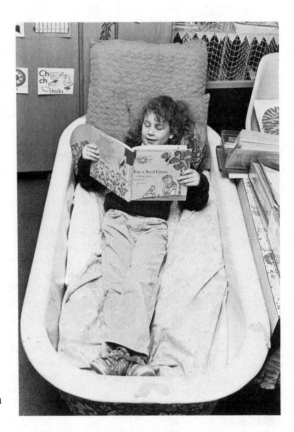

This student knows how to relax with a good book.   (Peter P. Tobia)

should be taught in the traditional, native orthography. That is the orthography (letters) that you are reading now. First, augmented alphabets, the coloring or shading of letters to represent sounds, rebus (picture) systems, and the like force an artificial "crutch" into the system which often impedes rather than fosters reading progress.

Second, children learn to read by reading. Thus the primary reading method should involve the reading of connected discourse. The material can be generated from students' own language (individual or group language-experience stories) or language that is as similar to theirs as possible and written at their independent or instructional level. A rich variety of these materials should be made available so that each student can freely select something of interest.

Games and worksheets should be used, providing they teach decoding (reading) and not only encoding (spelling). Furthermore, the skill or ability should be taught in contextual settings. Sight words, for example, should be taught in phrases or sentences—which permits the phonological, syntactic, and semantic cueing systems to interact concurrently, just as they would during the reading of books or magazines. Games and worksheets, contrary to what many teachers believe, do not teach. Only teachers (and some computerized learning machines) teach. Good teachers, in our minds, know how to interact intelligently with students to get them to think. Games and worksheets are unlikely to "teach" because they lack this interactive component, and thus, are better used to evaluate the application of learned skills.

Finally, and most important, reading teachers should use every means at their disposal to show students the value and joy that can be derived from reading. One way is to provide time for recreational reading within the school day, which will implicitly indicate to students that reading is important. If authors or poets reside nearby, they might be invited to visit the school and read their works to the class. Another idea that works well is to have students design posters of interesting books they have read. Showing these posters to other students can spark interest and enthusiasm. Designing bookmarks is a similar idea which children enjoy. Each bookmark can depict a favorite book or story. If teachers in the school participate in a free book distribution program such as that sponsored by Reading is Fundamental (RIF), disabled readers can become involved. The RIF program is a dollar-for-dollar matching of local and federal funds used to buy inexpensive paperback books. Periodically throughout the year, book displays are set up at the school and children are free to select a book they would like to keep. A minimum of three books are selected during the school year. The reading teacher might choose to be the program coordinator and let students help display and "sell" the books. One teacher we know enlists her disabled readers to run a "swap shop" where RIF books are exchanged once they are read. This "shop" is open for business on Friday afternoons.

Organizing an instructional program is a difficult, time-consuming task, but one that can make a consistent difference in students' attitudes and achievements. The ideas, thoughts, beliefs, and suggestions we have offered here will, we hope, help teachers plan and implement an effective instructional program.

SUMMARY

In this chapter, we have tried to leave you with the final information you will need to fulfill your role as a special teacher of reading.

We have provided practical information describing how teachers might select and schedule students for their reading program. Finally, we have provided tips on how to organize a reading center.

Soon you will be on your own. In these chapters we have tried to point out what we consider to be important ideas and suggestions for reading teachers. As we have stated many times throughout this book, the key to good teaching is the teacher. Now that you know what to do, it is up to you to see that it gets done. We wish you success.

RELATED ACTIVITIES

1. Interview four reading teachers to determine their roles. Ask for their specific suggestions for working with students, teachers, administrators, and parents. Ask them to describe any particular problems they see year after year, as well as their program's best features.
2. Visit a learning disabilities teacher and a reading teacher who work in the same school. Try to determine the similarities and differences in their jobs. Observe them working with students and compare how their instructional strategies vary.

3. Interview a Chapter I and a non-Chapter I reading teacher. Ask how students are selected for the program. Compare and contrast the two procedures. What teacher might have more flexibility in selecting a case load? Explain why.

4. Talk to teachers at various grade levels to see if any of their students receive special help in reading. Determine whether instruction takes place within the classroom or in a special location. Determine whether teachers prefer in-class or outside instruction for their students.

5. Using grid paper, draw the floor plan of three or more reading rooms that you have visited. Determine how the plan might be changed to improve the instructional setting. Make a list of materials that each teacher uses in his or her program. Affix the list to the floor plan.

RELATED READINGS

BAGFORD, JACK. "Evaluating Teachers on Reading Instruction." *The Reading Teacher,* 34, no. 4 (Jan. 1981), 400–404.

CALFEE, ROBERT C., AND PRISCILLA A. DRUM, EDS. *Teaching Reading in Compensatory Classes.* Newark, Del.: International Reading Association, 1979.

DURKIN, DOLORES. "What Classroom Observations Reveal About Reading Comprehension Instruction." *Reading Research Quarterly,* 14, no. 4 (1978–79), 481–533.

GUTHRIE, JOHN T. "Research Views: Effective Teaching Practices." *The Reading Teacher,* 35, no. 6 (Mar. 1982), 766–68.

———. "Research Views: Teacher Effectiveness: The Quest for Refinement." *The Reading Teacher,* 35, no. 5 (Feb. 1982), 636–38.

———. "Research Views: Teacher-Student Interaction." *The Reading Teacher,* 33, no. 3 (Dec. 1979), 372–74.

HARRIS, ALBERT J. "What Is New in Remedial Reading?" *The Reading Teacher,* 34, no. 4 (Jan. 1981), 405–10.

OTTO, WAYNE, NATHANIEL A. PETERS, AND CHARLES W. PETERS. *Reading Problems: A Multidisciplinary Perspective.* Reading, Mass.: Addison-Wesley, 1977.

SPIEGEL, DIXIE LEE. "Desirable Teaching Behaviors for Effective Instruction in Reading." *The Reading Teacher,* 34, no. 3 (Dec. 1980), 324–30.

REFERENCES

BEAN, RITA. "Role of the Reading Specialist: A Multifaceted Dilemma." *The Reading Teacher,* 32, no. 4 (Jan. 1979), 409–13.

BURGETT, RUSSELL E., AND R. W. DODGE. "Is There a Difference Between Learning Disability and Reading Personnel?" *Journal of Reading,* 19, no. 7 (Apr. 1976), 540–44.

CALFEE, ROBERT C., AND PRISCILLA A. DRUM, EDS. *Teaching Reading in Compensatory Classes.* Newark, Del.: International Reading Association, 1979.

DURKIN, DOLORES. "What Classroom Observations Reveal About Reading Comprehension Instruction." *Reading Research Quarterly,* 14, no. 4 (1978–79), 481–533.

HARKER, JOHN. "Lesson Planning for Remedial Reading," *The Reading Teacher,* 29, no. 6 (March 1976), 568–71.

O'DONNELL, HOLLY. "Instructional Time as Related to Reading Achievement." *The Reading Teacher,* 32, no. 2 (Nov. 1978), 246–51.

NAME INDEX

SUBJECT INDEX